Beginning ASP.NET Databases using VB.NET

D0851649

Jesudas Chinnathampi (Das)

Fabio Claudio Ferrachiati

James Greenwood

John Kauffman

Brian Matsik

Eric N. Mintz

Jan D. Narkiewicz

Kent Tegels

John West

Donald Xie

Wrox Press Ltd. ®

Beginning ASP.NET Databases using VB.NET

Published by Wrox Press Ltd,
Arden House, 1102 Warwick Road, Acocks Green,
Birmingham, B27 6BH, UK
Printed in the USA
ISBN 1-86100-619-5

Trademark Acknowledgements

Wrox has endeavored to adhere to trademark conventions for all companies and products mentioned in this book, such as the appropriate use of capitalization. Wrox cannot however guarantee the accuracy of this information.

Credits

Authors
Jesudas Chinnathampi (Das)
Fabio Claudio Ferrachiati
James Greenwood
John Kauffman
Brian Matsik
Eric N. Mintz
Jan D. Narkiewicz
Kent Tegels
John West
Donald Xie

Additional Material
Matt Butler
Dave Sussman

Commisioning Editor
Craig Berry

Lead Technical Editors
Jon Hill
David Mercer

Technical Editors
Catherine Alexander
Helen Callaghan
Alastair Ewins
Ian Nutt
Douglas Paterson
Rob Shaw

Managing Editor
Louay Fatoohi

Author Agent
Cilmara Lion

Project Manager
Christianne Bailey

Technical Reviewers
Richard Conway
Damien Foggon
Mark Horner
Eric Mintz
Osiris Navarro Reglero
Adil Rehan
David Schultz
Brian Sherwin

Production Coordinator
Abbie Forletta

Proof Reader
Dev Lunsford
Chris Smith

Cover
Natalie O'Donnell

Index
Martin Brooks

About the Authors

Jesudas Chinnathampi (Das)

Jesudas Chinnathampi, also known as Das, has been working with Active Server Pages since 1998. Currently he is working with Silicomm Corporation, http://silicomm.com. Das is also a member of the ASPElite, a select group of developers who help to manage the discussions at ASPFriends.com. Das has been working with ASP .NET since the first Beta.

Das also writes article// for ASPAlliance, http://aspalliance.com, the number one ASP.NET developer community. You can read the articles written by Das at http://aspalliance.com/das.

Das has a Masters Degree in Computer Application. During leisure time, he enjoys driving, playing chess and watching games (Cricket, Basketball, Shuttle Badminton). You can reach Das at das@aspalliance.com.

Fabio Claudio Ferracchiati

Fabio Claudio Ferracchiati is a software developer and technical writer. In the early years of his ten-year career he worked with classical languages and old Microsoft tools like Visual Basic and Visual C++. After five years he decided to dedicate his attention to the Internet and related technologies. In 1998 he started a parallel career writing technical articles for Italian and international magazines. He works in Rome for CPI Progetti Spa (http://www.cpiprogetti.it) where he develops Internet/intranet solutions using Microsoft technologies. Fabio would like to thank the Wrox people who have given him the chance to write on this book, and especially Alastair for his kindness and consideration.

To Danila: What are three years of love? Perhaps a long time for some; perhaps little time for others. To me, they have been so intense that they have seemed like an eternity. You have become part of me. You are the air that I breathe.

Three years of pure love.

Happy anniversary.

I love you.

James Greenwood

James Greenwood is a technical architect and author based in West Yorkshire, England. He spends his days (and most of his nights) designing and implementing .NET solutions from government knowledge-management systems to mobile integration platforms, all the while waxing lyrical on the latest Microsoft technologies. His professional interests include research into distributed interfaces, the automation of application development, and human-machine convergence. When prised away from the keyboard, James can be found out and about, indulging in his other great loves – British sports cars and Egyptology. You can reach him at jsg@altervisitor.com.

John Kauffman

John Kauffman was born in Philadelphia, the son of a chemist and a nurse. John's family of six shared daily brain teasers and annual camping forays that covered most of the 50 United States. After jobs weeding strawberry patches, bussing tables, running spotlights for rock and roll concerts, touring North America with a drum and bugle corps, prematurely leaving three colleges, stuffing voles for a mammologist, packing boxes of rat poison, tarring roofs, delivering drapes in New York City, laboring in a candy factory, teaching canoeing, driving a forklift, studying tiger beetles in the Chihuahua desert, managing a picture framing factory, coaching a youth yacht racing team, and volunteering as a human guinea pig for medical research, John (to the great relief of all around him) earned a pair of degrees in the sciences from The Pennsylvania State University and appeared to settle down. He then conducted research for Hershey Foods in the genetics of the cacao tree and the molecular biology of chocolate production. Subsequently he moved to the Rockefeller University where he identified, cloned and sequenced DNA regions which control the day and night biochemical cycles of plants.

But science didn't hold a candle to a woman he met in 1985 and married. Since then he has followed Liz in her career as a diplomat across four continents. They moved to Tanzania in 1986 and John began work with computers and business management in an assistance program for subsistence-level farmers. In 1990 they moved to Taiwan and then mainland China where John provided software training services to multi-national corporations and the diplomatic community in Beijing, Hong Kong, Shanghai, and Sichuan. During the graduation banquet for one course he was honored by his students with a special entree of snake bile, frog skin, and turtle meats.

John and Liz performed their most significant genetics experiments in 1988 and 1990 with the production of their children Sylvia and John. Growing up in Africa and China, the kids are doing well hashing through another generation's worth of brain teasers and camping trips.

John continues to teach, write, and program in Asia and North America, primarily in the areas of ASP, ASP.NET, Access, SQL and Visual Basic.

This book is dedicated to Sylvia and John. Nothing else in my life makes me as proud as seeing you mature into fine young people. Keep up your good work in academics, fight hard on the field of play, and continue to improve your music. Never forget that each of the people around you has feelings that deserve your respect – "No boasting when you win, no gloating when you lose." Be leaders by being the hardest workers and offering the hand of magnanimity. And above all, avoid what is expedient and do what you know is right. Thanks for being a part of our family.

Brian Matsik

Brian Matsik is the President and Senior Consultant at OOCS in Charlotte, NC and is currently a Microsoft Certified Solution Developer and Microsoft Certified Trainer. His experience with Visual Basic, VBScript, and VBA goes back to the DOS days and VB 2.0. Brian currently specializes in ASP, SQL Server, ADO, and VB COM. When he is not coding, training, or writing he is either in his scuba gear or in the garage trying to turn perfectly good oak into perfectly good kindling. Brian can be reached at brianmat@oocs.com.

Eric N. Mintz

Eric Mintz is a software analyst with over 20 years' experience in a variety of technical and leadership positions. His ceaseless enthusiasm and curiosity have contributed to wide-ranging expertise, particularly in the areas of computer/human-interaction, data and object modeling, SQL, and Visual Basic. Currently, Eric is CEO of American Webware, Inc. in Atlanta where he resides with his wife and her three cats who all think he works way too hard. When he does have spare time, Eric likes to play jazz guitar and trumpet or go fly-fishing. Eric holds a BSEE, earned at the University of Houston, TX.

Jan D. Narkiewicz

Jan D. Narkiewicz is Chief Technical Officer at Software Pronto, Inc (jann@softwarepronto.com). In his spare time Jan is Academic Coordinator for the Windows curriculum at U.C. Berkeley Extension, teaches at U.C. Santa Cruz Extension and writes for *ASP Today*.

Kent Tegels

Kent Tegels is a system developer and engineer working for HDR, Inc., a leading Engineering, Architecture and Consulting Firm. He is a Microsoft Certified Professional, plus Site Builder, System Engineer (plus Internet), and Database Administrator.

John West

John West is a Principal Consultant at Intellinet, based out of Atlanta, Georgia. He specializes in leading Microsoft .NET application development efforts. When not working, he usually spends his time reading, hanging out with friends from church, and trying to learn to wakeboard.

Donald Xie

Donald Xie has 14 years experience in enterprise application development for various types of businesses. He is a co-author of *Professional CDO Programming* and a contributing author for a number of books. Donald currently works as a consulting system architect for the Department of Training in Western Australia, Australia. You can contact Donald at donald@iinet.net.au.

Solution
BM
References
System
System.Data
System.Drawing
System.Web
System.XML
AssemblyInfo.vb
Assembly
BM.vsdisco
Global.asax
Styles.css
Web.config
WebForm1.aspx

WebForm1.aspx* | WebForm1.aspx.

WebForm1.aspx*

Table of Contents

Table of Contents

Table of Contents

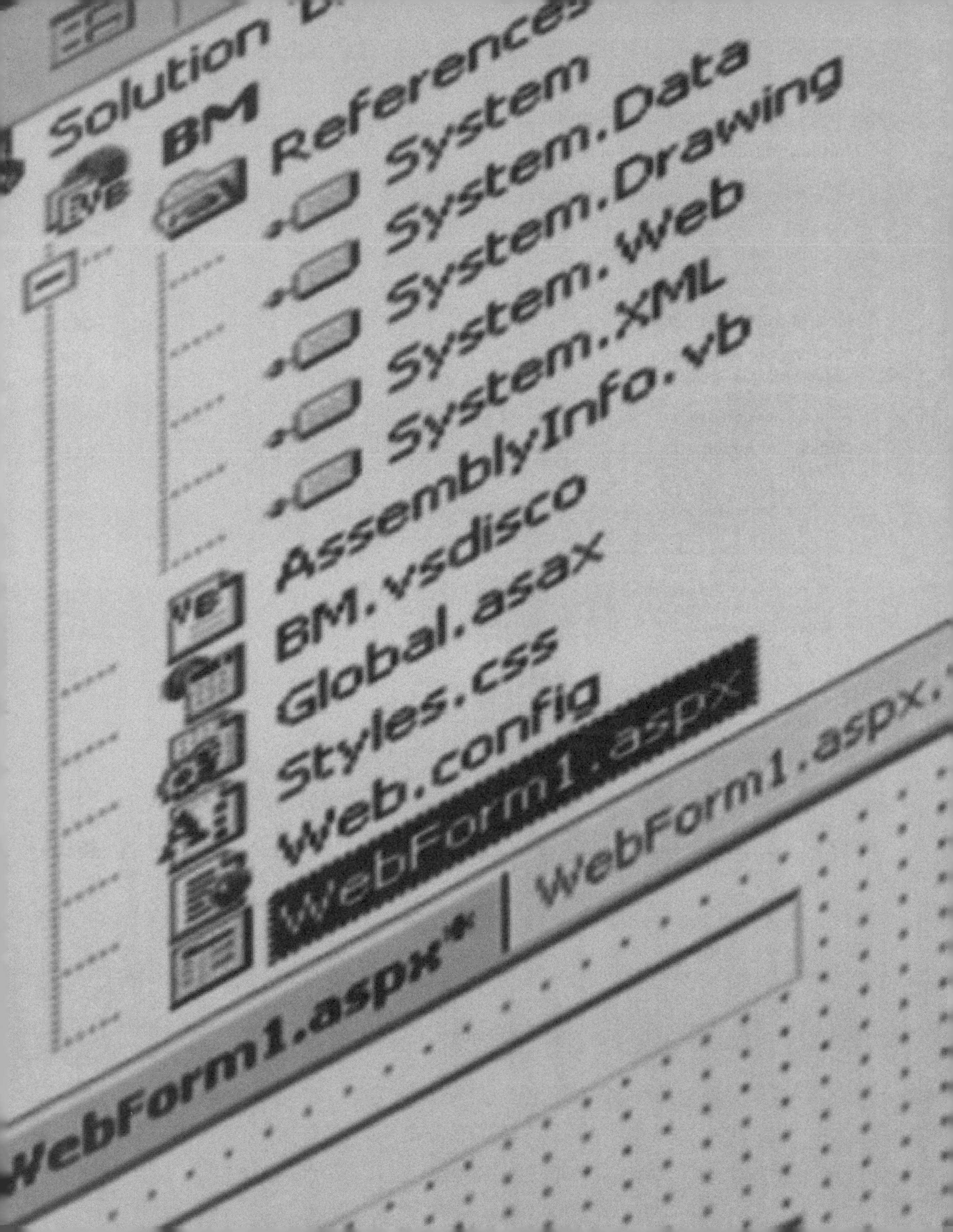

Solution '...'

BM

References

System

System.Data

System.Drawing

System.Web

System.XML

AssemblyInfo.vb

BM.vsdisco

Global.asax

Styles.css

Web.config

WebForm1.aspx

WebForm1.aspx* | WebForm1.aspx.

Introduction

One of the most important requirements for any web site is to accurately and safely transmit and store information. This information could be in any form, from the credit card details stored by a credit company, to the results of a straw poll on a marketing site. Whatever you use ASP.NET web pages for, you'll find that sooner or later you're going to need to access, read from, write to, and generally master operations involving a database.

Luckily for us, working with databases from a web application is much simpler than it used to be. The .NET Framework has revolutionized the way in which we can develop sophisticated web sites. ASP.NET has made enormous improvements to the ways in which we can develop complex and interactive web sites, and ADO.NET – which provides powerful and flexible data processing functionality – has radically changed the ways that we can retrieve, process, and store data from within a web application.

In this book, we're going to explain how to can create data-enabled ASP.NET applications. Written with hands-on learning in mind, it is packed with code examples that demonstrate important fundamental principles. Requiring some basic knowledge of ASP.NET and Visual Basic .NET, but assuming no prior experience of working with databases, the authors will guide you through the processes involved in connecting ASP.NET pages to a database, and investigate the various ways of reading, processing, and updating data. They'll then explore all the major issues involved in data-heavy ASP.NET programming, including some more advanced topics such as using stored procedures and components. The book concludes with a case study that puts everything in the preceding chapters into context.

What Does This Book Cover?

Chapter 1 begins by looking at the general notion of creating data-driven web sites. More specifically, we talk about the relationship between web sites and data, introducing ADO.NET in the process. Later in the chapter, we look at setting up our development environment for the rest of the book, and discuss some of the stumbling blocks that you may encounter.

It seems like a strange question, but what exactly *is* a database? In Chapter 2 we examine different types of databases, how they are designed, and how we can use them to store and retrieve information. We then move on to present an overview of the SQL language, and draw a quick comparison between Microsoft's database solutions.

Having taken our first look at databases, we need to learn how to connect to them from our ASP.NET code. Chapter 3 begins by building on the overview of ADO.NET that was presented in Chapter 1, clarifying the important terms that you need to know. We then move on to create and test a connection to the sample Northwind database that we'll be using throughout the book. This chapter contains numerous examples that demonstrate how to connect to diverse data sources such as Access, SQL Server, Excel, and XML, enabling us to be confident in whatever environment we have to develop in.

Packed with examples, Chapter 4 looks at reading and displaying data using data reader objects. We start with a discussion of the theory of handling data in ASP.NET and ADO.NET that introduces command objects. After that, we go on to look at how we can use data readers to obtain data, and then bind that data to different controls like radio buttons, check boxes, and most importantly, the `DataGrid`.

Chapter 5 talks about an important ADO.NET object called `DataSet`, which is used to store and retrieve data of any complexity on the server. Once the initial theory is dealt with, we use plenty of examples to demonstrate different ways to use a dataset.

Of course, we don't always just read other people's data, so Chapter 6 explains how to create our own records in existing databases. Topics covered in this chapter include ASP.NET's validation controls, and using command and DataSet objects to perform record insertions.

Following on from the previous chapter, Chapter 7 demonstrates how to modify and delete records. We look at how to edit data using the `DataGrid` and `DataView` controls, and at how to update and delete records from a dataset object

Next in line is Chapter 8, which looks at stored procedures. In it, we explain what they are, what they can be used for, and some of their advantages and disadvantages. After demonstrating how to create stored procedures with Visual Basic .NET, this chapter shows how to invoke them from your ASP.NET code, and how to supply them with parameters to perform certain tasks.

Chapter 9 is a mine of information regarding some of the more advanced topics that can crop up when you're creating commercial-quality data-driven ASP.NET applications. The four subjects that we introduce and explain here are error handling, code structure, scalability and concurrency, and security.

Approaching the end of the book, Chapter 10 introduces components, explaining why they can be valuable before discussing how to create them. The code samples in this chapter center around the creation of a class library that includes numerous methods for accessing a database.

Since one of the goals of any programmer should be to write the best code possible, Chapter 11 is devoted to performance issues. We look at connection pooling and performance counters, and produce some metrics on the relative performance of dataset and data reader objects in different situations. We also highlight the importance of porting old ADO code to new ADO.NET as soon as you can.

We finish with a case study in Chapter 12. This builds on all the subjects that have been presented in the book, and presents a complete, real-world application that uses multiple ASPX pages, ASP.NET web server controls, VB.NET components, and stored procedures.

Who Is This Book For?

This book is for people who:

- ❑ Have some experience of Visual Basic .NET and ASP.NET
- ❑ Have some familiarity with the .NET Framework and related technologies
- ❑ Want to learn how to use ASP.NET to create data-enabled web applications

However, you need to know nothing about databases in order to understand this book – although, of course, a little prior knowledge never goes amiss.

What You Need to Use This Book

To run the examples in this book, you need to have a PC running the following:

- ❑ Microsoft Windows NT, Windows 2000, or Windows XP
- ❑ The .NET Framework
- ❑ A version of Visual Studio .NET that includes, as a minimum, the Standard Edition of Visual Basic .NET

In addition, some of the examples use Microsoft Access and Microsoft SQL Server, but there is *no* requirement for you to own either. All of the important examples use the MSDE as their database engine, and this ships with all versions of Microsoft Visual Studio .NET.

Conventions

We've used a number of different styles of text and layout in this book to help differentiate between different kinds of information. Here are examples of the styles we use, and an explanation of what they mean.

Code has several styles. If it's a word that we're talking about in the text – for example, when discussing a For...Next loop – it's in `this font`. If it's a block of code that can be typed as a program and run, then it's also in a gray box:

```
<?xml version 1.0?>
```

Sometimes, you'll see code in a mixture of styles, like this:

```
<?xml version 1.0?>
<Invoice>
    <part>
        <name>Widget</name>
        <price>$10.00</price>
    </part>
</invoice>
```

In these cases, the code with a white background represents either something that we're already familiar with, or something that's not important in the current discussion. The line highlighted in gray is either a new addition to the code since we last looked at it, or the focus of the current discussion.

Advice, hints, and background information come in this style.

> **Important pieces of information come in boxes like this.**

Bullets appear indented, with each new bullet marked as follows:

❑ **Important Words** are in a bold font

❑ Words that appear on the screen, or in menus like Open or Close, are in a similar font to the one you would see on a Windows desktop

❑ Keys that you press on the keyboard, like *Ctrl* and *Enter*, are in italics

Customer Support

We always value hearing from our readers, and we want to know what you think about this book: what you liked, what you didn't like, and what you think we can do better next time. You can send us your comments either by returning the reply card in the back of the book, or by e-mail to feedback@wrox.com. Please be sure to mention the book's title in your message.

How to Download the Sample Code for the Book

When you visit the Wrox web site at www.wrox.com, simply locate this book through our Search facility or by using one of the title lists. Click on Download in the Code column, or on Download Code on the book's detail page.

The files that are available for download from our site have been archived using WinZip. When you've saved the attachments to a folder on your hard drive, you need to extract the files using a decompression program such as WinZip or PKUnzip. When you extract the files, the code will be extracted into chapter folders. When you start the extraction process, ensure that your software is set up to use folder names.

Errata

We've made every effort to make sure that there are no errors in this book. However, no one is perfect, and mistakes do occur. If you find an error, like a spelling mistake or a faulty piece of code, we would be very grateful for feedback. By sending in errata, you may save another reader hours of frustration, and you will be helping us to provide even higher quality information. Simply e-mail the information to support@wrox.com; your information will be checked and (if correct) posted to the errata page for that title and used in any subsequent editions of the book.

To find existing errata messages on the web site, click on the Book Errata link, which is below the cover graphic on the book's detail page.

E-mail Support

If you wish to query a problem in the book with an expert who knows the book in detail, e-mail support@wrox.com with the title of the book and the last four numbers of the ISBN in the subject field of the e-mail. A typical e-mail should include the following things:

- ❑ The **title of the book**, the **last four digits of the ISBN (6195)**, and the **page number** of the problem in the Subject field

- ❑ Your **name**, **contact information**, and the **problem** in the body of the message

We *won't* send you junk mail. We need the details to save your time and ours. When you send an e-mail message, it will go through the following chain of support:

- ❑ Customer Support – Your message is delivered to our customer support staff, who are the first people to read it. They have files on most frequently asked questions, and will answer general queries about the book or the web site immediately.

- ❑ Editorial – Deeper queries are forwarded to the technical editor responsible for that book. They have experience with the programming language or particular product, and are able to answer detailed technical questions on the subject.

- ❑ The Authors – Finally, in the unlikely event that the editor cannot answer your problem, they will forward the question to the author. We do try to protect our authors from distractions, but we're quite happy to forward specific requests to them. All Wrox authors help with the support on their books; they will e-mail the customer and the editor with their response, and again all readers should benefit.

The Wrox support process can only offer support to issues that are directly pertinent to the content of our published title. Support for questions that fall outside the scope of normal book support is provided via the community lists of our http://p2p.wrox.com forum.

p2p.wrox.com

For author and peer discussion, join the P2P mailing lists. Our unique system provides **programmer to programmer**™ contact on mailing lists, forums, and newsgroups, all in addition to our one-to-one e-mail support system. If you post a query to P2P, you can be confident that the many Wrox authors and other industry experts who are present on our mailing lists are examining it. At p2p.wrox.com, you will find a number of different lists that will help you not only while you read this book, but also as you develop your own applications. Particularly appropriate to this book are the aspx_beginners and the vb_dotnet lists.

To subscribe to a mailing list, follow these steps:

1. Go to http://p2p.wrox.com.

2. Choose the appropriate category from the left menu bar.

3. Click on the mailing list you wish to join.

4. Follow the instructions to subscribe, and fill in your e-mail address and password.

5. Reply to the confirmation e-mail you receive.

6. Use the subscription manager to join more lists and set your e-mail preferences.

Why This System Offers the Best Support

You can choose to join the mailing lists, or you can receive them as a weekly digest. If you don't have the time or facility to receive the mailing list, then you can search our online archives. Junk and spam mails are deleted, and your own e-mail address is protected by the Lyris system. Queries about joining or leaving lists, and any other general queries about lists, should be sent to listsupport@p2p.wrox.com.

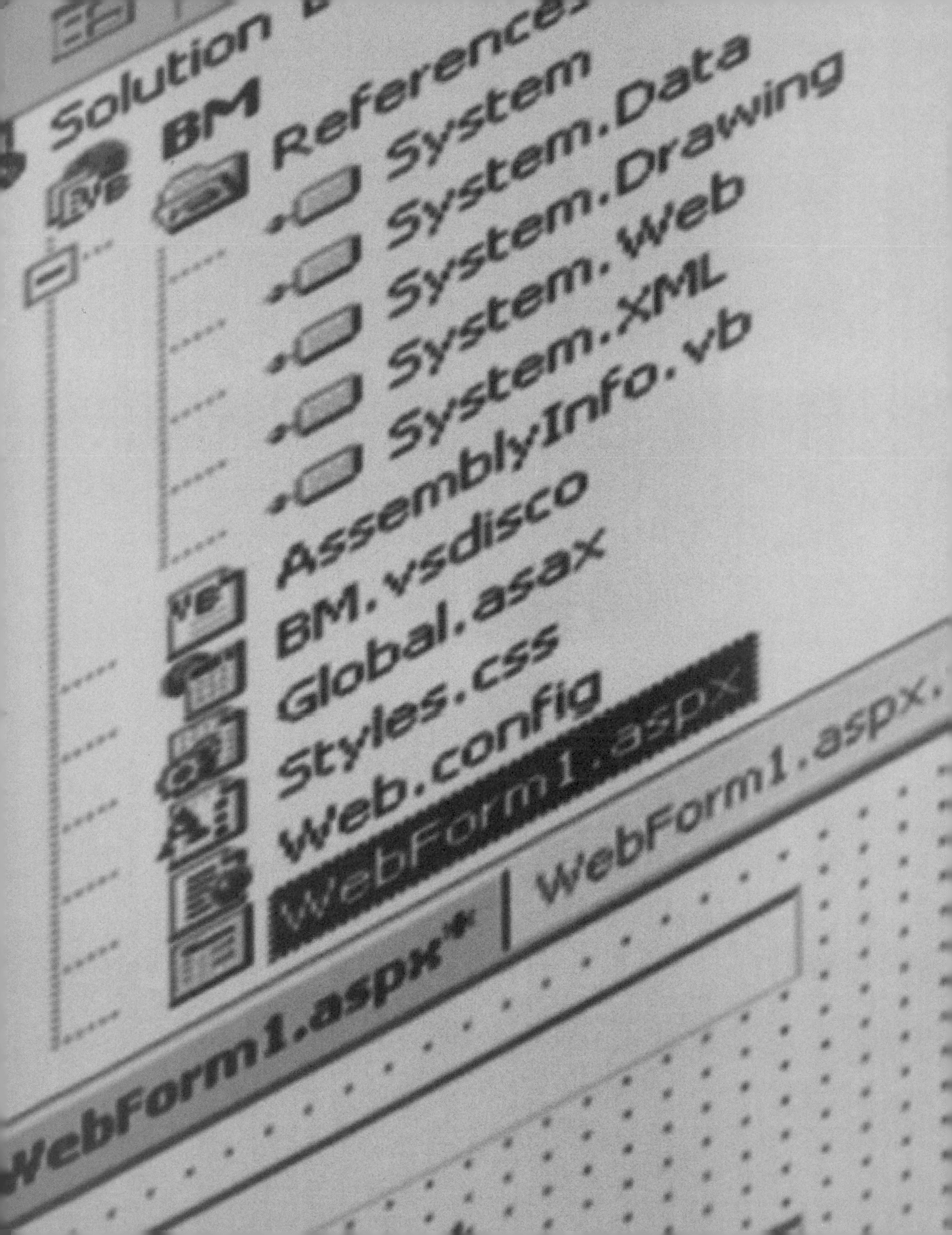

Solution Explorer

BM

References
- System
- System.Data
- System.Drawing
- System.Web
- System.XML
- AssemblyInfo.vb
- BM.vsdisco
- Global.asax
- Styles.css
- Web.config
- WebForm1.aspx

WebForm1.aspx* | WebForm1.aspx

WebForm1.aspx*

Displaying Data on the Web

When the Web first appeared, people had to find a metaphor for how information should be presented on it. If you took a sample of web sites from that period, the content largely was based around what you'd find in traditional media such as books, magazines, and newspapers. This led to the Web serving the same purpose as those other formats: it provided a snapshot of information as it stood at the time the pages were created. Of course, there was nothing wrong with that, but it placed restrictions on what the Web could reasonably be used for.

Over time, the technologies powering the Web have matured, and it has changed from only being able to provide static *sites*, to providing dynamic *applications* as well. These applications invite their users to make choices about the information they're interested in, providing a customized user experience that can be modified in real time.

The key to these applications is the data they contain. Regardless of what it is – it could be a product catalogue, or a set of customer details, or a document repository – it's the data that makes them dynamic. In the past, providing data over the Web has been a harder task than providing it through traditional desktop applications, due both to the development tools and functionality available, and the nature of the Web itself, where users are far removed from the applications and data. Over time, and in particular (from our point of view) with the introduction of Microsoft's .NET Framework, this situation has been improved. Web application developers are now on a more equal footing with their desktop-developing counterparts.

In this first chapter, we'll provide a broad introduction to the topic of data-driven web sites, and how they are implemented in ASP.NET. It starts with a discussion of the advantages and disadvantages of data-driven sites, and then moves on to examine the sources that such data can come from. After that, we'll look at the .NET Framework's data access strategy of choice – ADO.NET – including its architecture, its classes, and how it fits into the structure of data-driven applications. We'll finish by covering the installation of a database server that we'll use throughout this book.

> **A data-driven web application is a web site that displays dynamic data. The user experience changes to reflect the information held in a data store.**

Pros and Cons of Data-Driven Web Sites

Some of the advantages of having a data-driven system are immediately apparent, but there are others that are less tangible and not so readily evident. Naturally enough, there are also reasons why you might *not* want to attach a web site to a database. In this section, we'll examine the benefits and the drawbacks of creating a web site that's based around a data source.

Advantages

There are many secondary benefits of making a web site data-driven, such as the ability to reuse portions of functionality in other projects, and being able to share common pieces of information across systems – these tend to kick in when you start to work on your second or your third web application. Here, we're going to look at some of the advantages that can start to accrue as soon as you make the decision to create a data-driven site:

❑ *Quality and timeliness of content.* The most immediate advantages to making a site data-driven are the speed with which new information can be presented on the Web, and the controls that can be put in place to guarantee the quality of this information. Rather than having to get a web designer to create a page containing the information, and then get it uploaded again every time a price changes or a new product is added, a tool can be created that enables the instant publishing of new or updated information simply by modifying the database. This is one of the key benefits of the Web over traditional media – the ability to view information in real time, rather seeing than a snapshot of old data. By enforcing rules on who can add and amend data, how it is checked, and whether it is approved, data can be verified prior to being published in a much more rigorous manner, ensuring that the user only sees accurate details.

❑ *Functionality.* The other main benefit of storing all of the data required for a site in a database is that of improved functionality in terms of the actions that the user can perform on the system. Rather than producing 'catalogues', which (like this book) just have an index and a contents table as a means of searching, forms can be created that allow the user to specify what is being looked for, and have the system scour the database for that information. A great example of this is a search engine. Without a database, such a site would present only a manual categorization of other web sites, with a huge structure of pages that you could (try to) navigate between.

❑ *Maintenance.* With the data for a site stored in a separate location from the presentation code, there is no longer a need to maintain static links in HTML files between related sections of a site, forcing you to reapply formatting and menu structures to hundreds of pages each time the site is redesigned. In a data-driven system, web pages are typically **templates** that act for entire classes of pages, rather than having one page for each piece of information.

As an example of this, you could imagine the on-screen appearance of a page that displays the details of a product for sale. Rather than this being a separate HTML page, in a data-driven system there would be *one* page containing fields and tables that could be populated with data regarding *any* product. This means that there is far less to do each time a redesign is implemented. Similarly, as the relationship between different pieces of information can be stored in the database (rather than hard-coded in the pages), links to related products and other information can be generated on the fly.

Disadvantages

Although there are many advantages to making a web site data-driven, some of them come at a price, and a data-driven site is not always the right solution to your problem. There are several hurdles that must be overcome in order to provide a richer experience to the end user, and it's important that you consider them before taking the plunge:

❑ *Development.* A large number of web sites that are now data-driven started out being static, and there are still many static sites being created to this day. The nature of the content you want to present is not always suited to a data-driven site, and the creation of a data-driven system requires extra time and skills, resulting in a product that is more complex, and (inevitably) more prone to errors. These costs have to be weighed up against the advantages that such a system provides.

❑ *Performance.* The performance of data-driven web sites is an issue that crops up regularly. If a site is entirely static, then there are no constraints on the way the system is organized, or on how it can expand to cater for higher volumes of users. The simplest way to increase performance is to buy a faster processor and more memory. When that stops being viable, multiple versions of the site can be created, and users redirected to whichever one is under least load. This can continue in a linear fashion, with the same increase in performance each time a new web server is added.

With a data-driven site, this is not the case, because the entire system is dependent upon one resource: the database. If it's not carefully designed, the database can create a bottleneck in the system, whereby the rest of the application is held up while it waits for information to be retrieved. Removing this bottleneck is a difficult problem to solve – having multiple synchronized databases is one of the few real solutions, but it can prove very expensive, and the overheads involved in this synchronization are significant.

❑ *Cost.* In addition to the technical considerations mentioned above, there are also associated commercial issues. For a relatively static site, the time required to create a database and write the code to access it may be longer than it would take just to edit some HTML pages. Also, enterprise-class database systems are themselves expensive. Considering Microsoft's data storage solutions alone, it's well known that producing a solution using SQL Server (Microsoft's enterprise-level database server) provides many benefits over Access (its desktop database), such as higher performance and better support for industry standards, but comes with a price tag to match.

Data Sources

So: you've already considered some or all of the issues in the above lists, and you're still with us, which means that it's reasonable to assume you want to write a data-driven web application. The first question that needs to be answered, then, is where the information that will eventually end up on the user's screen is going to come from. Depending on factors such as the type of data, what operations are to be performed on the data, and the amount of use that is going to be made of the system, there are a multitude of options available. This section describes the reasons for and against using three of the most common data source types, along with an overview of the other types available.

Databases

When you start thinking about data sources, the most obvious one that springs to mind is the database, which will generally provide the most reliable, scaleable, and secure option for data storage. When you're dealing with large amounts of data, databases also offer the best performance. However, the very fact that other solutions exist is a sure indication that in some circumstances, they're not the best choice.

In general, databases are designed to store large amounts of data in a manner that allows arbitrary quantities of data to be retrieved in arbitrary order. For small collections of data, such as a set of contact details, the time and other costs involved in creating and accessing a database might outweigh the benefits that databases provide.

We'll have much more to say about the structure of databases in the next chapter, but as a quick example, wanting to store some information about a company employee in a database might move us to create a table called `Employee` that can contain the same pieces of data about a number of employees. Such information could include their `EmployeeID` (number), `LastName`, `FirstName`, `BirthDate`, and `Country`:

Throughout this chapter, comparisons and demonstrations will be made of how data can be stored and represented. For consistency, the same example is used throughout: that of storing details about the employees in an organization.

One thing to note when we display a database diagram, compared to the diagrams of other data sources, is that it's based on a *model* of the information being stored, rather than examples of the data. The way in which databases *actually* hold information is largely hidden from the outside world, leaving us to depict concepts rather than actual data items.

Text Files

At the opposite end of the scale from using databases to store information for a web site is the use of text files. Although text files can store information in almost any conceivable format, they are generally used for storing a set of data, one item on each line. If we were to capture the employee information detailed above, we could store the `LastName`, `FirstName`, `BirthDate`, and `Country` of two employees in a text file as follows:

```
Smith, John, 05-04-1979, UK
Bloggs, Joe, 29-09-1981, US
```

For simple information such as this, a text file provides an easy way of reading and writing data. If the data to be stored has more structure, however, it becomes far more time consuming. For example, it could be the case that each of these employees has placed an order for some office supplies. Rather than adding all of that information to the text file as well, it would be better to hold it separately, and then define relationships between the two sets of data.

When the data starts to gain 'structure' in this manner, a method of giving the file itself some structure must be found, and a way of retrieving it and representing it in memory must also implemented. One way of doing this is through the use of XML.

XML

In some ways, XML documents can be thought of as a stepping-stone between text files and databases; they store data using text files, but use a hierarchical and relational format that is both extensible and self-describing, providing a number of the benefits of a database system. Before we go any further in explaining the use of XML as a data source, a sample fragment of an XML document is shown below:

```
<company>
  <employees>
    <employee LastName="Smith" FirstName="John"
              BirthDate="05-04-1979" Country="UK" />
    <employee LastName="Bloggs" FirstName="Joe"
              BirthDate ="29-09-1981" Country="US" />
  </employees>
</company>
```

As you can see, the same information is being stored as in the text file, but there's also an indication of the nature of that information. You know that `29-09-1981` is the `BirthDate` of `Joe Bloggs`, because the data says so. Another benefit of XML is that it can contain multiple types of information in one document; a fragment like the one below could be inserted after `<employees>`:

```
<orders>
  <order ID="1">
    <product>Staples</product>
    <product>Pencils</product>
  </order>
  <order ID="2">
    <product>Biros</product>
    <product>Erasers</product>
  <order>
</orders>
```

Using the comprehensive functionality that's built into the XML-handling support provided by the .NET Framework (and other platforms), retrieving and manipulating the orders separately from the employees can be accomplished quite easily. This makes it possible to specify an order from the list for each employee by storing the ID of each order as part of the employee's details:

```
<employee LastName="Smith" FirstName="John"
          BirthDate="05-04-79" Country="UK" Order="2" />
```

XML is a powerful way of representing information, but in some circumstances performance can be a problem: updating and retrieving data from XML can be a time-consuming process. This is rarely an issue when a few users are accessing a small amount of data, but if there's a lot of data (or a lot of users) it can sometimes become one.

Other Sources

Between them, the three options enumerated above cover the main categories of data store, but there are many others that either fall between these, or follow a completely different paradigm. Most of the types that we haven't covered, though, are domain-specific – that is, that they've been developed to suit a specific task. On the Windows platform, typical examples of these include:

❑ *Microsoft Exchange Server* – the data store containing e-mail, calendar, and contact information

❑ *Active Directory* – the information that's stored by Windows-based servers regarding the users on the system, their permissions, etc.

❑ *Spreadsheets* – applications such as Excel store their data in a tabular format, a grid containing values that are used in tasks such as financial calculations.

In summary, although this book is focusing on databases (and uses them in the majority of its examples), it is important to remember that databases are not the only kind of data store, and that other mechanisms for storing data can often achieve the same goal more efficiently.

Retrieving Data from a Database

Regardless of the data store involved, there are three steps to using it that will be common to almost every web application you write. You need to 'connect' to the data source; you need to read the data (and possibly convert it or otherwise perform operations upon it); and you need to display the results. Before we begin to delve into the way that .NET deals with handling data, we'll elaborate on these three topics in a more general way, as a quick heads-up on how data-driven sites function.

The diagram below lays out the three steps mentioned above, and places them in context with the code that you'll need to write, and the data store itself.

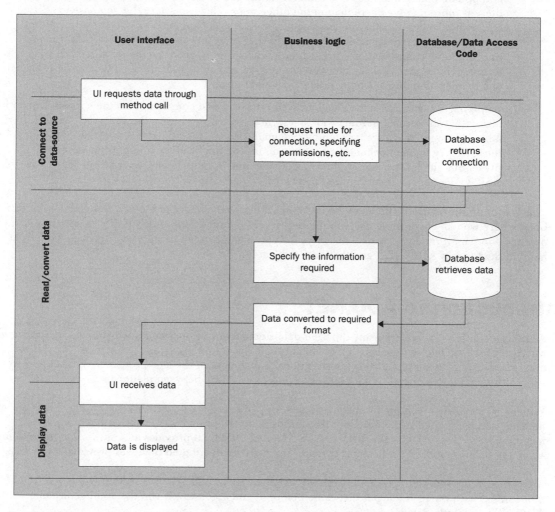

Reading it from left to right, this diagram shows that there are three clearly separated aspects to the system: the application that requests the data, the code that communicates with the database and operates on the data, and the database itself. The details of this three-part structure and how it can be used to best effect are given later on in this chapter; for now, we'll continue on our top-to-bottom route.

❑ *Connecting to the data source.* Before we can issue any commands to the database or retrieve any data from it, we must create a **connection** to it. This provides a conduit through which we can send and retrieve data. To establish a connection, we need to specify such things as the type of database we are opening, where it is located, and any necessary security permissions. Once this has been done, and the connection has been opened, we can start to send instructions to the database.

❑ *Reading/converting the data.* Through the connection, we can tell the database to add, delete, and update records, to return information to us, and so on. As you can see from the diagram, there is more involved here than in the other steps. This is because the database expects commands to be in a different language from that of the application, and the application expects data to be returned in a different format from that stored in the database. Once information has *been* sent or retrieved, however, the connection to the database can usually be terminated. In special cases, an open connection is maintained, allowing data to be returned and displayed a little at a time, rather than all at once.

❑ *Displaying the data.* Once the data has been retrieved and converted into the correct format, it is usually transformed in some way to a format that's viewable by the user, such as an HTML table. Although there are far more *operations* during the reading and converting of the data, these largely happen behind the scenes, and in web applications it's often the case that presenting the information well takes the most time to implement. As we'll see later, however, ASP.NET offers us some help in this regard.

That's a lot of information, and lot of the things we'll be talking about in the first few chapters of this book where we will cover these issues more slowly, and in much greater depth. It also sounds like a lot of work – in fact, it *is* a lot of work – but mercifully we don't have to do all of it ourselves. Help is at hand in the form of ADO.NET, and that's our subject for the next section.

Introduction to ADO.NET

As described above, there are many different data stores that can provide information to an application. Microsoft realized a long time ago that having a single programming interface for accessing these diverse stores makes sense – it allows applications to make use of the latest versions of database servers with minimal changes to code, and it makes for interoperability between platforms.

With every new Microsoft platform comes a new way of accessing data stores. In the .NET Framework, the technology is called ADO.NET, but that builds upon the previous data-access functionality of technologies such as ADO, OLE DB, RDO, DAO, and ODBC. It provides an appropriate method for accessing data in modern applications that are more widely distributed than was previously the case.

After describing underlying technologies such as OLE DB and ODBC, this section will place ADO.NET into context with the technologies that came before it, and go on to explain the architecture of ADO.NET in a little detail.

A History of Data Access on the Windows Platform

As soon as you start to think about accessing data on the Windows platform, you find yourself confronted with a list of abbreviations rather like the one in the second paragraph above. Here, we'll try to untangle the letters, and help you to understand how all of these technologies fit together – which, by and large, they do.

In the recent past, most applications communicated with data stores through the software objects provided by ADO, which made use of the lower-level technologies OLE DB and ODBC. In order for this to happen, ADO (and its replacement, ADO.NET) rely on a database conforming to an underlying set of standards. A significant difference between old and new is that ADO.NET has a less demanding, more flexible set of rules, allowing for a greater variety of data sources.

To allow applications to make connections to their databases, database vendors have to implement some common sets of functionality (interfaces) that have been devised for this purpose. One such interface is the highly successful **ODBC**, which is still supported by the vast majority of databases you'll come across. Another technology, **OLE DB**, was designed as the successor to ODBC, and was the cornerstone of Microsoft's Universal Data Access strategy. It too has become highly successful, and has gained broad support.

The diagram below shows a simplified version of how the various pre-.NET data access technologies connect to databases – and even in this diagram you can see that it was all getting a bit complicated! As well as ADO, OLE DB, and ODBC, technologies like RDO and DAO were getting involved too:

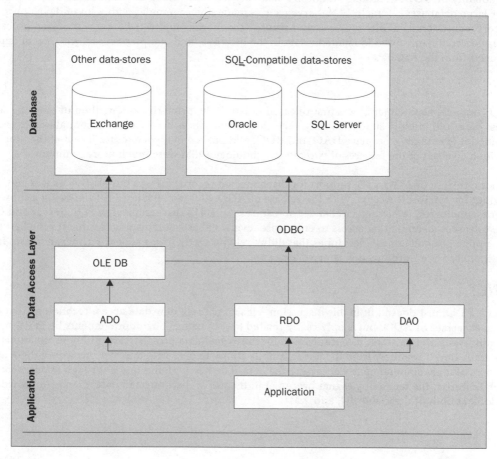

DAO

Let's start to put some meat on these bones. DAO (Data Access Objects) was Microsoft's first attempt at providing programmers with an object-oriented way of manipulating databases. It was invented for Access v1.0, and updated in later versions of Access and Visual Basic up to Access 97 and Visual Basic v5.0. Many of the original DAO commands have been retained through the years for backwards compatibility, meaning that the syntax required for performing operations can be quite ugly at times.

One of the biggest drawbacks of DAO is that it assumes data sources to be present on the local machine. While it can deal with ODBC connections to database servers such as Oracle and FoxPro, there are some things that make sense with remote data sources that cannot be achieved.

RDO

RDO (Remote Data Objects) is another object-oriented data access interface to ODBC. The methods and objects that it contains are similar in style to DAO, but they expose much more of the low-level functionality of ODBC. Although it doesn't deal very well with databases such as Access, its support for other large databases – Oracle, SQL Server, etc. – made it very popular with a lot of developers. This support focuses on its ability to access and manage the more complicated aspects of stored procedures (compiled commands used to maintain data in the database) and complex record sets (sets of data retrieved from the database).

ADO

ADO (ActiveX Data Objects) was first released in late 1996, primarily as a method of allowing ASP to access data, and initially supported only very basic client-server data-access functionality. Microsoft intended it eventually to replace DAO and RDO, and pushed everyone to use it, but at the time it only provided a subset of the features of two other technologies that were much more popular.

With the release of ADO v1.5, support for disconnected record sets was introduced, as was an OLE DB provider for Microsoft Access. With the release of ADO v2.0 in 1998, it went from being a subset of other technologies, to having a richer set of features. OLE DB drivers for both SQL Server and Oracle were released, meaning that access to enterprise-level database systems was feasible for the first time, and support for native providers (ones that didn't rely on ODBC) was added. Further increases in functionality were introduced in later versions up to v2.7.

ADO.NET

ADO.NET almost doesn't fit in this discussion – it's an entirely new data access technology that builds on the successes of ADO, but is only really related to it in name. The improvements lie in its support for different types of data store, its optimization for individual data providers, its utility in situations where the data is stored remotely from the client, and its ability to deal with applications where there are large numbers of users simultaneously accessing the data. The key to doing this is through features that separate it from the technologies that preceded it: the use of disconnected data, managed providers (we will look at both of these shortly), and XML.

ADO.NET Architecture

You now know that ADO.NET draws on a long history of data access. Almost inevitably, this means that there is quite a lot to learn. Thankfully, Microsoft has put a great deal of thought into its new data access technology, making it more logical and structured than previous attempts, while still providing a wealth of features.

> *ADO.NET is made up of a collection of objects, some of which are entirely new, and others of which have evolved from ADO. The main difference between these and their predecessors is that there is now generally only one way to accomplish a task – ADO was a little infamous for providing several means to exactly the same end!*

The next few pages are concerned with taking a look at the main ADO.NET objects, and how they cooperate to provide data manipulation. Laid out below is a diagram of the five main object types that you'll be dealing with when you use ADO.NET:

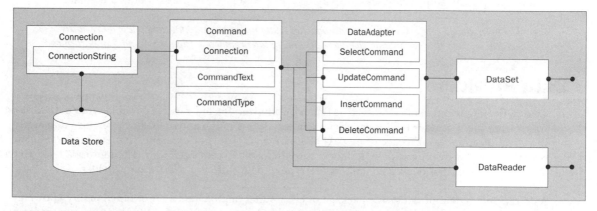

If we work our way back from the database, taking the objects one by one, we can see how these objects work together, and what functions they perform:

- ❑ The **connection** object is the route through which all instructions to (and results from) the data store are sent. The user can specify which database to connect to, what authentication to use, and so on.

- ❑ The **command** object contains the instructions that specify what information should be sent to (or retrieved from) the database. It also contains a link to the connection that it's going to use.

- ❑ The **data reader** object provides a way of 'getting at' the information that's been retrieved by the command object. The information is provided on a read-only basis – so it can't be edited – and only one item of data is read at a time. Data readers provide an efficient (if inflexible) way of processing large amounts of data; they are sometimes described as providing **connected** access, since the connection with the database must remain open for as long as the data reader is in use.

- ❑ The **data adapter** object *represents* a set of commands and a database connection, providing an alternative method of retrieving data. It provides support for the data to be updated as well as just read, so in some ways it can be seen as a big brother to the data reader. Even so, the data adapter does not allow for direct editing of the data source; rather, it fills a dataset with a copy of information from the data source, and can then be used to write any changes to the data back to the database.

- ❑ The **dataset** can be thought of as a local copy of a portion of the data store. In this copy, rows of data can be read, added, edited, and deleted. Because the data is cached locally, it can be read in a random manner, as opposed to the forward-only manner of the data reader. When the required changes have been made to the data, they can be sent back to the data store through the data adapter. Until this point, the dataset is **disconnected** from the data store.

Looking to the far right of the diagram, you can see two unattached lines – this is where the 'front end' of your application connects to the ADO.NET architecture. The data that is returned here can be used in any way the developer chooses – displaying it to a web page, writing it out to a file, etc.

The twin concepts of "connected" and "disconnected" data are important ones, and while we've barely touched on them here, we'll be developing these ideas in later chapters – Chapters 4 and 5 in particular.

Data Providers

One of the key features of ADO.NET is that it's optimized for the various possible types of data store. Apart from the dataset, which is generic, the other objects in the above list have versions that are specifically geared towards accessing data of a particular type. For example, there are separate data reader classes for dealing with SQL Server and Microsoft Access databases. The umbrella term given to the 'set' of classes that deals with a particular type of data store is a **.NET data provider**.

As discussed, a data provider is a package of classes that implements a set of functionality allowing access to a specific type of data store. While there's a base set of functionality that a data provider must supply in order to be called as such, a particular data provider can have any number of extra properties and methods that are unique to the type of data store that is being accessed. This is very different from ADO, where there was a single set of classes that was used for accessing dissimilar data sources.

Where do Data Providers Fit in the Scheme of Things?

At this point, you're probably starting to think that you're getting a feel for the basic architecture of .NET, and that you can see why data providers allow for more types of data store to be accessed, but you don't know how the two relate to each other. Earlier on, we had a diagram of the technologies that were involved in data access before the introduction of ADO.NET. The following diagram shows how this changes – and how it gets simpler – under ADO.NET.

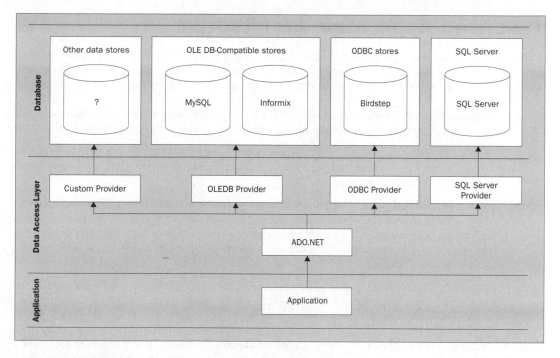

Standard Providers

Microsoft ships the .NET Framework with two data providers as standard: the SQL Server .NET data provider, and the OLE DB .NET data provider. The first of these provides a means of connecting to a SQL Server v7.0 (or later) database, and the classes that it comprises can be found in the `System.Data.SqlClient` namespace. The second allows access to any of the multitude of OLE DB-compatible data stores that are on the market, and implements similar functionality to the `SqlClient` provider; it resides in the `System.Data.OleDb` namespace.

A third data provider, which supports ODBC, is available but not installed by default; at the time of writing, it could be downloaded from http://msdn.microsoft.com/downloads/default.asp?URL=/downloads/sample.asp?url=/MSDN-FILES/027/001/668/msdncompositedoc.xml. Once installed, the classes for this provider can be found in the `Microsoft.Data.Odbc` namespace. Further data providers are under development, including one for Oracle that's in beta at the time of writing. This is also available for download from Microsoft's web site.

Data-driven Application Architecture

Although it's an important part of the puzzle, simply getting hold of a database and knowing the commands for retrieving and maintaining the data it contains does not guarantee the creation of an application that can achieve the goals of modern software development. In no particular order, these are:

❑ *Maintainability.* The ability to add and amend functionality to an application continually, without incurring large costs from having to revisit and re-implement existing portions of code.

❑ *Performance.* The application's ability to carry out its functionality responsively from the start, so users don't have to wait for lengthy periods for processing to complete, and resources on the machine are used responsibly.

❑ *Scalability.* The ability for an application to be extended in order to maintain performance when large numbers of users are accessing it simultaneously. Obviously, the more users there are, the more resources will be needed; scalability is the study of how rapidly the need for resources grows in relation to the increase in users, whether this need can be satisfied, and if so how this can be done.

❑ *Reusability.* The ultimate goal of software development; the ability to take functionality that has already been implemented and drop it into other projects and systems, removing the need for (re)development.

There have been many attempts to provide solutions to these problems, first through the introduction of proceduralization and modularization – the splitting of code into functions and separate files – and then through object-oriented techniques that hide the implementation from the user. Microsoft has produced guidelines on how applications developed on its platform should achieve the goals laid out above.

> *You can learn more about this subject in* VB.NET Design Patterns Applied *(ISBN 1-86100-698-5), also from Wrox Press.*

Earlier in the chapter, when we were talking about *Retrieving Data from a Database*, we briefly mentioned a "three-part structure" for web applications that deal with data access. In fact, this was a preview of the architecture that Microsoft (and many others) recommends. More formally, it's known as an **n-tier** architecture, which basically means that each application has code 'layers' that each communicate only with the layers around them. This section describes one of the most common approaches: the 3-tier model, which consists of the following:

❑ *Data tier.* Contains the database and stored procedures, and data access code.

❑ *Business tier.* Contains the business logic – methods that define the unique functionality of this system, and abstract these workings away from other tiers. This is sometimes referred to as the "middle tier".

❑ *Presentation tier.* Provides a user interface and control of process flow to the application, along with validation of user input.

> While it could be argued that all applications make use of n-tier architectures, it has become commonplace to use the term to mean an application that has multiple tiers (where 'n' is greater than two) that abstract implementation details from each other.

Data Tier, Business Tier, and Presentation Tier

The 3-tier model has become the most popular due mainly to its simplicity. It's also the basis for all other models, which tend to break down the three tiers still further. The diagram below should help you to visualize the three tiers before we move on to their description. One thing you might want to keep in mind is that in ADO.NET, datasets are regularly passed between tiers, which means that the business and presentation tiers know more about the structure of the database than they would in a 'pure' model.

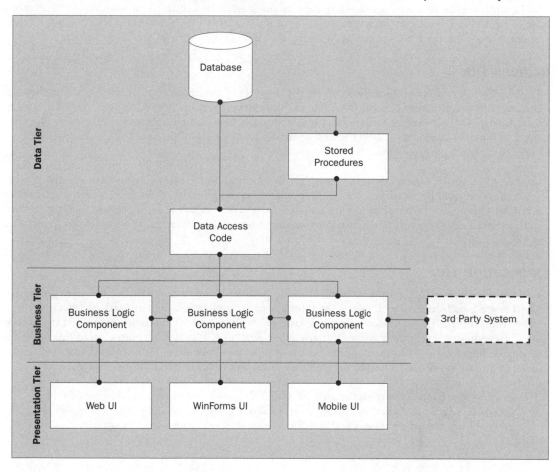

Data Tier

The data tier consists mainly of the table definitions, relationships, and data items that constitute the database itself, along with any pieces of code used for retrieving information from the database in its natural format. In SQL Server, these would be SQL statements that are usually kept in stored procedures.

One of the hardest issues to address is where the data tier ends, and where the business tier begins. This problem arises because it's quite easy to implement a lot of the functionality of the business logic (business tier) in the database code (as stored procedures). Where the line should be drawn is largely dependent upon the requirements of the application; whether rapid portability to other database server products is a key concern, or whether high performance is preferable. If the former is more important, then putting the majority of the functionality in the business tier is a preferable solution, and vice versa.

In the diagram above, there is a separate item called "data access code". This may simply represent the use of ADO.NET, or it may be a separate layer of functionality that hides ADO.NET from the other layers, preventing them from needing to know what type of data store(s) are being accessed.

Business Tier

The business tier of the application is where the majority of the application-specific functionality resides. Usually, this functionality consists of calling multiple atomic actions (`Read`, `Write`, `Delete` commands, etc.) in order to insulate the presentation tier from the complexities of the rules that the application must conform to. This tier also generally contains any links necessary to the methods exposed by third-party systems.

Contrary to popular object-oriented principles, any components created for the business tier of web applications should be **stateless** – that is, they should make use of functions and procedures that take in multiple parameters, rather than having properties that allow values to be set before making method calls. In .NET, the business tier is often implemented using class libraries, as we'll discuss in more detail in Chapter 10.

Presentation Tier

The presentation tier of the application is the only portion of the system that the end user gets to see, whether it's a collection of web pages, the interface to an application such as Outlook, or even a command prompt. This tier functions by making use of the functionality exposed to it via the business tier – it can never access the database (or any other portion of the data tier) directly. In this way, it is kept from being exposed to many of the details of how the application has been implemented, and can focus on providing the most usable presentation of the information and options possible.

> *As stated above, the nature of data access with ADO.NET is such that on occasion, these guidelines are not strictly adhered to. Indeed, we'll make use of this fact to abbreviate some of our early examples. But as we progress through this book, you'll find this architecture cropping up again and again.*

Presenting Data with Controls

Since we just talked about presentation, it makes sense to take a moment here to discuss an important new feature of ASP.NET. One of the biggest hurdles to overcome in the past has been finding a common way of presenting the information that is being returned from the business tier. In a nutshell, this problem has arisen from the differences between the stateless world of web applications, and the world of client-server applications, where large amounts of data can be kept at the client.

Quite simply, data that was suited to one interface was often not suited to the other, due to the different mechanisms that were available for presenting it. Attempts were made to bridge this gap using ActiveX controls that could be created in languages such as Visual Basic, but these were specific to Windows machines running Internet Explorer, removing a lot of the benefit of having HTML-based applications.

Thankfully, this problem has been greatly lessened in .NET by the introduction of ASP.NET **web server controls**. These behave like ActiveX controls when you're developing code, but by the time the user sees them in their browser, they've been converted into standard HTML elements. The main advantage in doing this is that it brings development for all platforms into line (even minority platforms such as WAP applications, through the use of mobile controls). A single source of data can be used to populate all of the different control types, which include such things as drop-down lists, check box lists, and the data grid, which is a highly versatile kind of table.

This book contains examples of working with all of the most important web server controls, starting with the first exercises in Chapter 3.

Data Binding to Controls

The key to allowing a single source of data to provide all controls with exactly what they need is **data binding**. This is a technique where, when given a data source in the correct format, the control itself decides what pieces of information are useful to it, and which are irrelevant.

Due to the highly structured nature of the .NET Framework, many different data sources can be used for data binding, as long as they implement the right interfaces. As well as datasets, standard data structures such as arrays and hash tables also fit the bill. The same types of objects that can be used to add items to a drop-down list control can also be used to populate a data grid, or any other web server control.

If similar end-user functionality was to be implemented in classic ASP, the developer would generally have to loop through a set of data, making calls to `Response.Write()`, and creating lines of HTML with `<option>` tags interspersed throughout. From this alone, you should start to get an idea of just how much the use of web server controls allows the developer to forget about the actual target language (HTML) they're developing for, and concentrate on what it is that they are trying to present to the user. The ASP.NET web server controls can even adjust themselves to support different browsers, so the need for developers to consider what platform the application will run on is also greatly reduced.

> **As the internal workings of the controls that .NET provides are hidden from the developer, support is not only guaranteed for current browsers, but also can be implemented for future ones without requiring changes to the applications that use them. This will largely remove the need for browser and version testing, traditionally an expensive part of the development cycle.**

Custom Controls

While the controls that come built into .NET provide us with a great deal of functionality, and cater for most situations, there are always circumstances where we require something unique. After all, if applications were all the same, then there would be none left to write by now! When we find ourselves in this situation, .NET doesn't leave us in the lurch. We can create our own controls that support all of the features of the built-in ones, and more. We don't even have to write these controls from scratch, because custom controls can be created:

❑ By deriving a new one from an existing control, and adding the required functionality

❑ By composing a new custom control using two or more existing controls

❑ By creating a control from scratch, making use of base controls such as `Tables` and `Input` elements

Although it's not a subject we'll be pursuing further in this book – we've got enough on our plate as it is! – this aspect of ASP.NET web server controls is yet another reason to be enthusiastic about the wealth of options available for data access under ASP.NET.

The Microsoft SQL Server Desktop Engine

As our final act in this chapter, we need to do something that will set us up for the rest of the book. During the course of the discussion so far, we've mentioned the names of a number of different databases, but it can't have escaped your attention that if we're going to demonstrate anything useful in the chapters to come, we need to set up a database of our own.

Our choice is to use the Microsoft SQL Server Desktop Engine (MSDE), which is a specialized version of SQL Server 2000. In this section, we'll explain what it is, why we've chosen to use it, and – most important of all – how you can get hold of it and install it.

A Smaller SQL Server

The first thing to say about MSDE is that it's entirely compatible with SQL Server, which is truly an enterprise-class database server. This means that the things you learn while using MSDE will stand you in good stead when you come to use SQL Server itself – it behaves in exactly the same way. From our perspective here, though, the immediate benefits of MSDE are:

❑ It's freely distributable

❑ It's currently sitting on your Visual Basic .NET discs, just waiting for you to install it

What this means is that as well as providing the perfect system for us to learn and experiment with, a complete web application can initially be produced and distributed without incurring any costs for the database server. If the system expands at a later date, it can be ported to the commercial distribution of SQL Server with next to no effort. The only features cut down from the full version of SQL Server are that the MSDE is optimized for (but not limited to) up to five connections at a time, that the maximum database size is limited to 2GB, and that some enterprise features are absent.

Throughout this book, the code samples and text will assume that MSDE is being used as the data provider, with the Northwind database (which is included with it) acting as the data source. To ensure that the code in the book will all function correctly, the next section details the installation of MSDE.

> **All of the features that MSDE supports are also supported by SQL Server. The converse is not true, however; some of the richer functionality of SQL Server is not present in MSDE. However, none of this functionality is required for any of the code in this book to operate correctly.**

Obtaining and Installing MSDE

When Visual Basic .NET (or any of the various Visual Studio .NET products) is installed, an item called Microsoft .NET Framework SDK is added to your Start | Programs menu. Beneath this is an item called Samples and QuickStart Tutorials; if you select it, this is what you'll see:

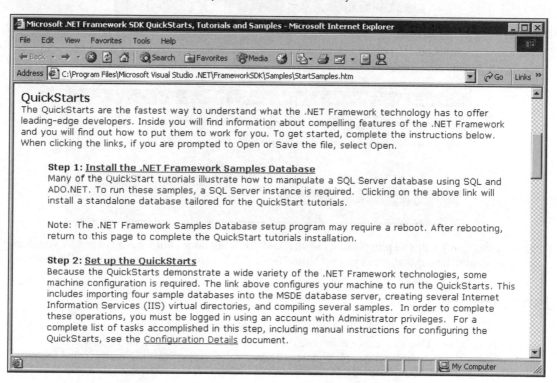

This page is self-explanatory: clicking on the first link will install the MSDE engine; clicking on the second will cause the sample databases – including Northwind, which we'll be using throughout this book – to be created.

This page will only appear once, so if you (or someone else) have been here before, you won't see it. Don't worry: you'll find the instmsde.exe *and* configsamples.exe *files that these links invoke beneath the* FrameworkSDK\Samples *folder of your Visual Studio installation.*

Ensure that you're logged on as a user with Administrator privileges on the current machine, and click on the first link (or run the executable). The following dialog will appear:

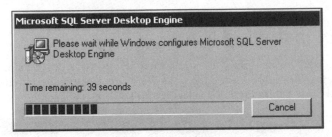

When this has finished, there's no need to restart your machine. You can go straight on to the next step, which will produce another dialog:

Once again, wait for this step to finish its work... and you're all done. But what exactly *have* you done? The best way to understand that is to open up Visual Basic .NET, ready for the quick tour in the next section.

Using MSDE

Once it has been successfully installed on the local machine, you need to make sure that the MSDE service has started. This procedure differs slightly from platform to platform, but the instruction here, for Windows 2000, should tell you all you need to know. From the Start Menu, open the Control Panel, and go to Administrative Tools | Services:

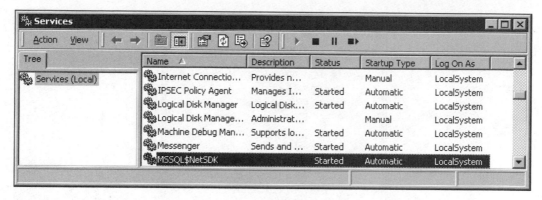

The service called MSSQL$NetSDK *is* MSDE. Make sure that the Status and Startup Type are set to Started and Automatic, as they are here, and you can rest assured that from now, when Windows is running, MSDE will be running too. Close this window, head into Visual Studio, and choose the View | Server Explorer menu item. Right-click on the Data Connections item at the top of the Server Explorer window, choose Add Connection from the context menu, and you'll see the following:

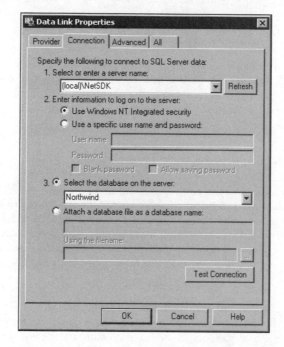

On choosing the appropriate settings in this dialog, the Server Explorer allows you to browse SQL Server databases, examining their content and performing some simple operations. To view the Northwind database that we just installed, you should make your dialog match the screenshot above. When you return to the Server Explorer, you'll be rewarded with a view of the database:

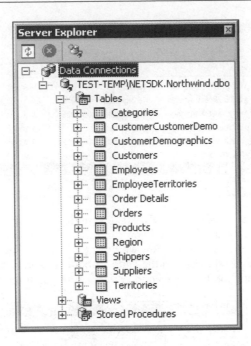

Having made it this far, you can be sure that the MSDE database is ready for action, and with that our work in this chapter is done. It's been quite a fast ride, but we've covered a lot of ground in the hope that it will look familiar when you see it again in the chapters ahead. That slower, more careful journey begins in the next chapter.

Summary

In this chapter, we have discussed the advantages and disadvantages of creating data-driven sites, showing that although they can provide a wealth of functionality, there are problems associated with their creation. This was followed by an introduction to data sources, and how they are handled using ADO.NET. The architecture of an application that involves data access was then covered, showing why the separation of data and presentation can provide many benefits to developers. Finally, details about MSDE – the database server we'll use in examples throughout this book – were given, and the product was installed.

Now that the background to the creation of data-driven web sites in .NET has been dealt with, we can move on to finding out the details of each of the technologies, and putting them to use. In the next chapter, we'll look at some of the theory involved in creating databases, along with a quick introduction to the SQL language, and a tour of the Northwind database. In Chapter 3, our brief description of connecting to databases will be expanded to cover the finer points, along with other topics such as the storing of connection strings. Following this, Chapters 4 and 5 are concerned with data readers and datasets, with Chapters 6 and 7 covering the adding, modification, and deletion of records. The rest of the book then makes use of this knowledge of ADO.NET, discussing the creation of components, applications, and stored procedures, and looking at performance issues. We finish with a case study, which pulls all this knowledge together in a practical application.

Solution b...
BM References
System
System.Data
System.Drawing
System.Web
System.XML
AssemblyInfo.vb
BM.vsdisco
Global.asax
Styles.css
Web.config
WebForm1.aspx
WebForm1.aspx

WebForm1.aspx* | WebForm1.aspx.

Relational Databases

If you're already familiar with database theory, you may just want to skim this chapter. But if you're new to databases, or you feel that you need a bit of a refresher, this chapter is intended to provide you with enough theory to prepare you for those that follow. In it, we'll become familiar with the key concepts and common terms that you will run across throughout your career as a database developer and user. Relax, become familiar with the ideas, and don't get caught up on any one issue if it doesn't make sense to you right away. You can always refer back to this chapter later as a reference.

We'll begin with a discussion of a few key database concepts, such as tables, rows, and fields. Then, we'll explore the key differences between relational and non-relational databases. After that, we'll provide an introduction to SQL, to database design, and to normalization. We'll conclude with a brief comparison between SQL Server and Microsoft Access. By the end, you'll know enough to smooth your passage through the next few chapters, and you'll have a base upon which the rest of the book will build.

Database Terms and Concepts

The term 'database' has many interpretations, the simplest of which is 'a collection of persistent data'. By this definition, a hard drive is a database, since it is certainly a repository of data. But to software developers, a database is much more than ad hoc data on a hard drive. The definition we will use here is more specific, and more useful to software developers who use database management systems (DBMSs) for application development.

> **A database is a collection of persistent data that is stored in tables.**
> **A table is a collection of rows.**
> **A row is a collection of fields.**
> **A field is a repository for a value.**

Even this definition is not particularly narrow – these criteria are met, for example, by properly formatted comma-separated value files (`.csv` files), and by spreadsheets. Consider this example of the former:

```
Herbert Hoover, Ex-President
Marcus Welbey, M.D.
Gandalf, The Grey
Jabba, The Hutt
Attila, The Hun
```

This whole file represents a single table in a database that contains information about people. Each row in this file represents a row in the table, and contains information about one person. Each row contains two fields: the first is the person's name, and the second is the person's title. And finally, the fields have values – for example, the first field of the first row has the value `Herbert Hoover`.

However, although 'databases' such as this one have their place (and we looked this subject in the previous chapter), this book will concentrate for the most part on the kinds of database that are managed by DBMSs, of which well-known products such as SQL Server and Microsoft Access are but two examples. Such systems are responsible for managing the details of storing and retrieving physical data in the form of a database, and making that data available to the developer.

In this chapter, as in the rest of the book, we'll be basing our experiments on and around the sample Northwind database that not only comes with the MSDE we've already installed, but also is available for MS Access and MS SQL Server version 7.0 and later. Northwind is a fictitious company that buys products from suppliers and sells and ships them to its customers. The Northwind database, like our `.csv` example above, contains tables, one of which is named `Customers`. This table, like all of the others in the Northwind database, contains rows and fields.

Try It Out – Our First Look at Northwind

In this chapter, we're going to use Microsoft Access as our tool for analyzing the Northwind database. If you don't have Access installed, that's not a problem – we'll be illustrating the discussion with screenshots that show exactly what's going on. The Access version of the Northwind database ships with the product, or you can download it from the Microsoft web site (http://office.microsoft.com).

1. Assuming that you have Microsoft Access on your computer, locate the `Northwind.mdb` file in the `Program Files\Microsoft Office\Office\Samples` folder, and double-click on it to open it in with Access. If you get a dialog asking you to convert the database, accept the option – you'll need it later on.

2. Choose the Tools | Relationships... menu item to display the relationship diagram for the Northwind database:

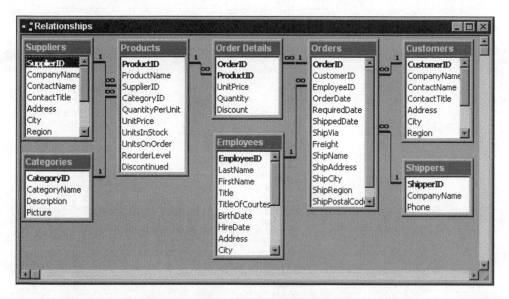

3. This diagram includes all of the tables in the Northwind database, but for now, let's take a closer look at the Customers table that we can see in the above screenshot:

From the diagram above, you can see the fields in each of the tables – but didn't we just say that a table is a collection of rows, not a collection of fields? The thing is, when we're designing a table in a database, or just looking at the tables in a relationship diagram, we are only interested in the fields that make up each row that the table contains. Every table in the Northwind database has rows, every row contains the fields that appear in the relationship diagram, and every field in each row has a value (see below).

35

4. Later in this chapter, we'll discuss how to view and modify the data (that is, the rows and values) in a table. For now, you can just return to the main Database window, ensure that Tables is selected in the Objects list, and then double-click on the Customers table to see the rows of data it contains:

Customer ID	Company Name	Contact Name	Contact Title	Address
ALFKI	Alfreds Futterkiste	Maria Anders	Sales Representative	Obere Str. 57
ANATR	Ana Trujillo Emparedados y helados	Ana Trujillo	Owner	Avda. de la Constitución 2222
ANTON	Antonio Moreno Taquería	Antonio Moreno	Owner	Mataderos 2312
AROUT	Around the Horn	Thomas Hardy	Sales Representative	120 Hanover Sq.
BERGS	Berglunds snabbköp	Christina Berglund	Order Administrator	Berguvsvägen 8
BLAUS	Blauer See Delikatessen	Hanna Moos	Sales Representative	Forsterstr. 57
BLONP	Blondel père et fils	Frédérique Citeaux	Marketing Manager	24, place Kléber
BOLID	Bólido Comidas preparadas	Martín Sommer	Owner	C/ Araquil, 67
BONAP	Bon app'	Laurence Lebihan	Owner	12, rue des Bouchers
BOTTM	Bottom-Dollar Markets	Elizabeth Lincoln	Accounting Manager	23 Tsawassen Blvd.
BSBEV	B's Beverages	Victoria Ashworth	Sales Representative	Fauntleroy Circus
CACTU	Cactus Comidas para llevar	Patricio Simpson	Sales Agent	Cerrito 333
CENTC	Centro comercial Moctezuma	Francisco Chang	Marketing Manager	Sierras de Granada 9993
CHOPS	Chop-suey Chinese	Yang Wang	Owner	Hauptstr. 29
COMMI	Comércio Mineiro	Pedro Afonso	Sales Associate	Av. dos Lusíadas, 23
CONSH	Consolidated Holdings	Elizabeth Brown	Sales Representative	Berkeley Gardens
DRACD	Drachenblut Delikatessen	Sven Ottlieb	Order Administrator	Walserweg 21
DUMON	Du monde entier	Janine Labrune	Owner	67, rue des Cinquante Otages
EASTC	Eastern Connection	Ann Devon	Sales Agent	35 King George
ERNSH	Ernst Handel	Roland Mendel	Sales Manager	Kirchgasse 6

Record: 1 of 91

Data and Entities

The basic purpose of a database is to provide a construct in which we can model entities. **Entities** are **models** of the physical things or concepts that we will deal with in our applications. When we speak of **modeling**, we refer to the way we represent only those elements of an object that we are interested in storing.

For example, a model airplane represents only certain elements of a real airplane, such as its appearance. In most other ways, it differs significantly from the real airplane: for example, the material is different (plastic vs. metal), so if you were interested in modeling the stress on the wings of a real airplane during flight, the plastic model would be a poor model indeed. In this case, strips of the material used in wing construction – even if they don't look like the airplane – might serve as a much better model.

When we speak of entities, we refer to people, places, things or concepts that we want to store information about. Let's imagine that we're designing a database that would keep track of people, their addresses, and their phone numbers. In this example, the people, addresses, and phone numbers are the entities.

Moving on, each of these entities is a collection of attributes. An **attribute** is simply a descriptive piece of information that describes an entity. For example, the 'person' entity might have attributes such as 'first name' and 'last name', while the 'address' entity would have 'city' and 'country' (among others). A set of one or more attributes is called a **tuple**.

> An entity is a person, a place, a thing, or a concept.
> An attribute is a characteristic of an entity. In other words, it is a piece of data that describes the entity.
> A tuple is a set of differentiating attributes. That is, a tuple is the set of attributes that make one entity different from another.

In data modeling terms, then, a person is represented by the tuple that is the collection of attributes such as 'first name', 'last name', 'address', 'phone number', and so on. Notice that an entity can also be an attribute of another entity. In this case, 'address' is an entity that has attributes like 'ZIP code' and 'country', but 'person' is an entity that has 'address' as one of its attributes.

It is no coincidence that there is a very strong correlation between the terms we've defined in this section, and those we mentioned in the previous section.; you will see terms like 'fields' and 'attributes' used almost interchangeably in much of the literature. As is so often the case, the jargon is more confusing than the basic concepts it seeks to explain, so it's important to understand how these concepts relate to one another. One set of terms, like 'field', refers to the data in a database. The other set of terms, like 'attribute', refers to design concepts.

Relational Databases

Practically speaking, we tend to think of a **relational database** as a database in which there can exist relationships, or logical links, between tables. These links associate rows in one table with rows in another table, by matching values in one or more fields from the first table to one or more fields in the second table. In the Northwind database, the `Shippers` and `Orders` tables are related by the fields `ShipperID` and `ShipVia`, as we can see in the figure below:

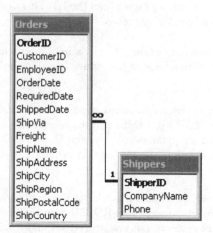

For each row in the `Orders` table (that is, for each customer order), there is a row in the `Shippers` table where the value in the `ShipperID` field is equal to the value in the `ShipVia` field of the `Orders` table. Let's examine this in more detail with an example.

Try It Out – Linking the Shippers and Orders Tables

We're going to take a look at a row in the Orders table, along with its related row in the Shippers table.

1. Back in Access, double-click on the **Orders** and **Shippers** tables to open up views of the data in both:

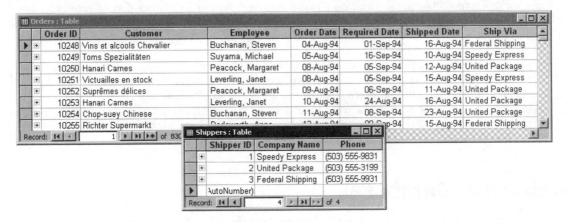

2. If we look at the Shippers table, we see that there are a total of three rows. In each row, the ShipperID field has a value that's unique to that row – 1, 2, and 3 in this case. Back in the Orders table, the ShipVia field is logically linked to the ShipperID field, so the RDBMS will only allow values in former that exist in the latter. (As a courtesy, Access is automatically displaying the 'friendlier' name, rather than the ID. This does not change the fact that ShipVia field holds numerical values.)

3. If you try to change the value of the ShipVia field in any of the rows, Access won't allow you to give it anything other than one of the values found in the ShipperID field of the Shippers table.

Relational DBMSs (RDBMSs) are by far the most popular form of DBMS in today's software industry. The quality, ubiquity, and stability of RDBMSs and the relational model contribute to making relational databases the de facto standard for database developers. Database theory has come a long way since the days of 'flat-file data', but you shouldn't be misled into believing that relational is always good, and non-relational is always bad.

Since Dr E.F. Codd first formally proposed the relational model in 1970, database research has continued to develop and expand. Newer, post-RDBMS non-relational databases, including object-oriented database management systems, have appeared and have gained considerable popularity. Object-oriented databases are designed to work well with object-oriented programming languages such as Java and C++. They extend the languages with transparently persistent objects (vs. simple data), concurrency control, data recovery, associative queries, and other database capabilities.

Examples of some of the more popular relational databases are Sybase Adaptive Server, Microsoft FoxPro, Microsoft Access, Microsoft SQL Server, Oracle, Informix, Teradata, IBM DB2, MySQL, and GNU SQL Server. Examples of object-oriented databases are Object Design's Objectstore, Objectivity/DB, Versant enJin, Gemstone, O2 Technology, Mjølner, Poet Software, and Ontos.

Before we continue our journey into the realm of relational database theory, we need to be acquainted with SQL (Structured Query Language), the de facto standard programming language for communicating with and manipulating relational databases – or at least, enough to be able to talk about the theory. Once we are familiar with relational database theory, we will have the background for a more in-depth look at SQL.

Brief Introduction to SQL

SQL is a declarative language, as distinct from procedural languages such as C, C++, C#, Visual Basic, and Java. In programs written in a procedural language, the programmer describes a sequence of steps that execution should follow (that is, a procedure). In SQL, programmers describe sets of data and the actions to be applied to those sets. It is up to the RDBMS to determine how and in what order to construct the set, and how to process each member of the set. In fact, the SQL developer has little (if any) control over *how* the RDBMS accomplishes its task.

Consider this example, which uses a procedural language to display rows from the Orders table that were shipped by Speedy Express. For now, we'll just use pseudo-code:

```
Begin Function
  For each row in the Shippers table
  Loop
    If Shippers.CompanyName = 'Speedy Express' Then
      X = ShipperID
      Exit the loop
    End If
  End Loop
  For each row in the Orders Table
  Loop
    If Orders.ShipVia = X Then
      Display all fields for this row
    End If
  End Loop
End Function
```

By contrast, here's what the pseudo-code for a declarative language might look like:

```
Begin Function
  Show all fields for the set of rows in Orders where the following is true:
  The value in Orders.ShipVia = the value in Shippers.ShipperID
    and Shippers.CompanyName = 'Speedy Express'
End Function
```

In the declarative code, we declared two sets of rows:

❑ The set of rows in `Shippers` where `CompanyName` has the value `'Speedy Express'`. This set contains only one row, since there is only one row in the `Shippers` table for which `CompanyName = 'Speedy Express'`. The value of `ShipperID` in this one-row set is 1.

❑ The set of rows in `Orders` in which `ShipVia` equals the value of `ShipperID` in the one-row set from the `Shippers` table. Since `ShipVia` must equal one of the values for `ShipperID` in the set of `Shippers` rows, we effectively limit this set to rows from the `Orders` table in which `ShipVia` is 1.

In the procedural language, we explicitly looped through all of the rows in both tables, and displayed each of the rows that met our test criteria one by one. In the declarative language, the DBMS was responsible for those details. Later in this chapter, we'll examine SQL in enough detail that we can use the SQL language for our examples, instead of pseudo-code.

Until now, we've been talking about database theory, and we've have been referring to the "rows" in a table. When we're talking about rows in a programming context, we sometimes use the term "rows", but more frequently we use the term "records" to mean the same thing. A set of rows is then a set of records, or a record set.

> **Rows *are* records.**
> **A set of rows (or records) is a record set.**

Codd's Twelve Rules

In theory, a relational database is more than just data organized into related tables. Before we continue our investigations of the SQL language, let's examine this concept in more detail. The relational database model is based firmly in the mathematical theory of relational algebra and calculus. Dr E.F. Codd proposed the original concept for the model in a 1970 paper entitled *A Relational Model of Data for Large Shared Data Banks*. Later, Dr Codd clarified his model in a two-part article in *Computer World* (14th and 21st October, 1985). He defined twelve rules (**Codd's Rules**) that a DBMS must meet to be considered a relational database management system (RDBMS). We will now examine each of these rules.

Note that many database products are considered "relational" even if they do not strictly adhere to all twelve of these rules.

1. Data is presented in tables.
This rule has already been covered in detail in the sections above.

2. Data is logically accessible.
We don't reference a row by its position in the table. Instead, we must specify a particular row in a table based on the values contained in its fields. In the `Shippers` table of the Northwind database, we wouldn't try to refer to the second record; rather, we'd refer to the record with a `ShipperID` of 2.

3. Nulls are treated uniformly as unknown.
When its value is not known, a field may be 'empty'. That empty field is said to have a null value, which is quite different from a zero-length string or a zero integer; these are known to be "blank" or zero respectively. Any calculation that includes a null value will yield NULL. This means that $1 + 1 + \text{NULL} = \text{NULL}$, and $(100 > \text{NULL}) = \text{NULL}$ (not TRUE or FALSE).

> Developers who are new to database development often find that their calculations return a null value when they are expecting data. The reason for this is that at least one of the fields in the calculation contains a null value.

4. The DBMS is self-describing.
RDBMSs contain crucial, self-describing information called **metadata**; this is data that a database keeps about itself (such as the relationship between the Orders table and the Shippers table that we saw earlier). This metadata is stored in special tables called **system tables** or **system catalogs**. You can see these tables in Microsoft Access by selecting the Tables tab to view all of the tables in the Northwind database. Next, click Tools | Options from the menu and select the View tab on the Options dialog box. Check System objects, and click OK. You should now see a number of additional tables whose names begin with MSys (see screenshot below). All Access databases have the same system tables, but the data in these tables will vary to describe the particular database.

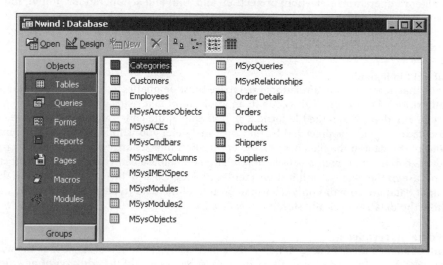

5. A single language is used to communicate with the DBMS.
SQL is the *de facto* standard database language. We will discuss some SQL basics in this chapter, while subsequent chapters will use and explain it at length.

6. The DBMS provides alternatives for viewing data.
Views act rather like virtual tables and provide an alternative way of looking at data from one or more tables. In Microsoft Access jargon, views are called **queries**. You can see the queries in the Northwind database by clicking on the Queries tab (see screenshot below). Note that these queries are *not* tables, but are simply an alternative view of the data.

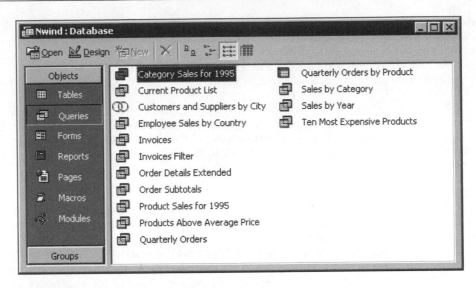

7. The DBMS supports set-based or relational operations.

Rows are treated as sets for data manipulation operations. A relational database must support basic relational algebra operations (selection, projection, and join) and set operations (union, intersection, division, and difference). Set operations and relational algebra are used to operate on 'relations' (tables) to produce other relations. A database that supports only row-at-a-time (navigational) operations does not meet this requirement, and is not considered relational.

8. Physical data independence.

Applications that access data in a relational database must be unaffected by changes in the way the data is physically stored. For example, the code in an application that reads and writes data in a file-based database typically depends on the file format. (For example, the code references a 'phone number' field that is ten characters wide, is preceded by the 'zip code' field, and is followed by the 'fax number' field). If the layout of the data in the file changes, the application must change accordingly. By contrast, the physical storage and access methods used in a relational database can change without affecting the application's use of the data – it still just sees tables (the logical structure). An application that uses data in a relational database contains only a basic definition of the data (type and length), and does not need to know how the data is physically stored or accessed.

9. Logical data independence.

Logical independence means that changes to the relationships among tables (such as the addition of new tables to the database, the ordering of fields in an existing table, and the addition of new fields to an existing table) can occur without impairing the function of an application using the database. The database's schema (its structure of tables and relationships) can change without you having to recreate the database or the applications that use it.

10. Data integrity is a function of the DBMS.

For a DBMS to be relational, it must have the ability to regulate data integrity internally – as an internal function of the DBMS – rather than in an application program. Data integrity means that when we define fields in two or more tables as being related, the RDBMS guarantees that the values of those fields in each pair of rows always match, regardless of the operations that the application performs. Examples of data that lacks integrity are orphaned rows and duplicate rows.

11. The DBMS supports distributed operations.

Data in a relational database can be stored centrally, or it can be distributed. Users can join data from tables from different databases on the same server, or on different servers (distributed queries), or from other RDBMSs (heterogeneous queries).

12. Data integrity cannot be subverted.

There cannot be other paths into a database that subvert the integrity of the data it contains. In other words, you can't get in through the 'back door' and change the data. The RDBMS must protect data from being modified by machine language intervention.

All together, Codd's rules provide us with a precise definition of relational database management systems, how they behave, and how we can interact with them. We have looked a bit beyond the rules in an attempt to identify the most powerful features of the relational model, so that we can learn to take full advantage of them in our database design and database programming.

An SQL Primer

Having looked at Codd's Rules that define what a relational database *is*, we can return to our discussion of SQL, which effectively defines what we can *do* with a relational database.

In fact, the name "Structured Query Language" is a bit of a misnomer, since a query means a *request* for data. While SQL's syntax includes statements like SELECT, which certainly is about requesting data, it also includes statements like INSERT (to insert new rows into a table), UPDATE (to modify existing rows in a table), and DELETE (to delete rows from a table). In fact, SQL is composed of two main parts:

❑ **DML**, or **Data Manipulation Language**, which is composed of SELECT, INSERT, UPDATE, and DELETE statements

❑ **DDL**, or **Data Definition Language**, which includes statements like CREATE, DROP, and ALTER to create, destroy, and modify database objects (like tables and views), and statements like GRANT to grant and revoke user permissions for database objects

We use the DML component of SQL to manipulate data, and the DDL component of SQL to design our databases. In this section, and for the overwhelming majority of this book, our focus will be aimed at working with data, so we will examine DML in a little detail.

SELECT Statements

Let us begin our journey into SQL with the SELECT statement, which is the one we use to retrieve data. The SELECT statement has three basic clauses:

❑ The SELECT clause itself, which contains the list of fields to retrieve

❑ The FROM clause, which specifies the tables from which we will retrieve data

❑ The WHERE clause, which limits the rows to retrieve, based on the values of certain fields

Try It Out – SELECT Statements

Let's write our first SQL query in MS Access. As a preliminary to this example, choose the Insert | Query menu item, and select Design View in the dialog box that appears. Then, choose View | SQL View, and you'll be presented with something like this:

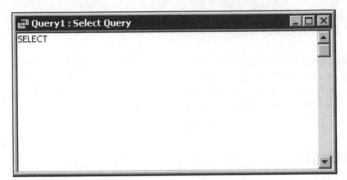

1. In a SELECT statement, only the SELECT clause is mandatory, but in a real-world program you'll rarely see a query without a FROM clause, and probably a WHERE clause too. Let's look at an example of a very basic, yet meaningful query:

```
SELECT
   ShipperID,
   CompanyName,
   Phone
FROM
   Shippers
```

2. Type this query into the Query1 box, noticing as you do so that the SELECT clause contains the fields we want to retrieve, separated by commas. The FROM clause specifies that we want to retrieve these fields from Shippers table. Since we don't have a WHERE clause to limit the rows, we expect *all* of the rows to be retrieved from the Shippers table. Choose Query | Run, and this is what you'll see:

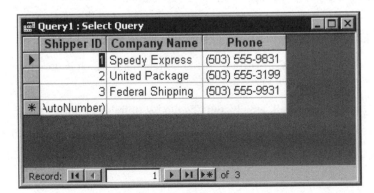

3. We can limit both the rows and the fields that our query returns by modifying the SELECT clause to include only those fields we want back, and by including a WHERE clause to limit only those rows we want back. Since the ShipperID of Speedy Express is 1, changing the query to the following just returns that company name:

```
SELECT
  CompanyName
FROM
  Shippers
WHERE ShipperID = 1
```

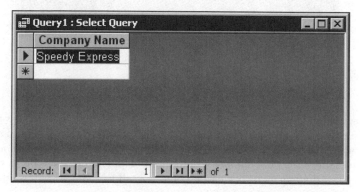

4. While we haven't yet begun to exploit the power of a relational database, we now have a sample of very simple syntax from which we can build. Suppose the Northwind sales reps have been getting complaints that orders shipped to Caracas, Venezuela have frequently arrived damaged. They would like to know which shipper(s) has been shipping to that region. This is a perfect opportunity to expand our FROM clause to include the Orders table as well, since that contains the "ship to" data, as well as the ShipVia field that links the shipment to the shipper via the ShipperID field in the Shippers table. We can exploit this relationship by typing in the following query:

```
SELECT
  Shippers.CompanyName,
  Shippers.Phone
FROM Orders INNER JOIN Shippers
  ON Orders.ShipVia = Shippers.ShipperID
WHERE Orders.ShipCity = 'Caracas'
AND Orders.ShipCountry = 'Venezuela'
```

5. On running this query, we learn that Federal Shipping is the only shipper that has ever shipped to Caracas, Venezuela, and we can call them to complain:

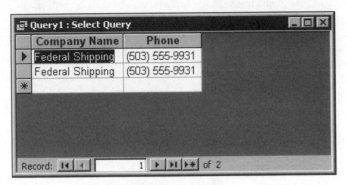

How It Works

This SELECT query is a little trickier than the ones we've looked at so far, and as such it merits some further explanation. The first change comes in the SELECT clause, where to specify the fields we want to retrieve we've used the syntax *<table name>*. *<field name>*, instead of just *<field name>*. That's because this query references more than one table – if both tables happened to have fields with the same name, Access would have returned an error because it could not tell which field you wanted.

> *In this case, there was no ambiguity, because the Orders table does not have fields called Phone or CompanyName. However, we still prefer the <table name>. <field name> syntax, because it's clearer to the readers of our code.*

With the above in mind, the new features of the WHERE clause are quite easy to explain: we've used the *<table name>*. *<field name>* syntax because our query contains more than one table, and we've also added the AND keyword, which allows us to place an extra condition on the rows retrieved.

That leaves the FROM clause, which has a new feature that's particularly relevant to this chapter on relational databases. However, before we can talk about what that INNER JOIN part means – and how it seems to be able to let us select Shippers fields from the Orders table – we need to take a closer look at some of the features of the Shippers table.

The first thing to observe is that the ShipperID field of the Shippers table is a **unique index**. This guarantees that a value in this field won't occur in the table more than once. A ramification of this is that you can identify a single row in a table through the value of a unique index. Now, in a relational database, a field in one table that has been designated as a **foreign key** can be related (or linked) to a unique index in a second table that's been designated as **primary key** – and this forms the basis for the kinds of relationship between tables that we saw in the diagrams earlier in this chapter.

An RDBMS will honor a private key-foreign key relationship by not allowing values in the foreign key that do not exist in the primary key. For example, the Shippers table has only three rows: one row has ShipperID = 1, another has ShipperID = 2, and the other has ShipperID = 3. Now, since ShipVia in the Orders table is the foreign key to the ShipperID primary key, the only values allowed for ShipVia are 1, 2, and 3. If a row in Orders has a ShipVia field equal to 1, then it corresponds to the row in Shippers where ShipperID = 1, and so on. The RDBMS would return an error if we attempted to place in the foreign key field a value not found in the primary key field.

Getting back to our query, the FROM clause exploits the private key-foreign key relationship by **joining** the two tables Orders and Shippers using the INNER JOIN syntax. This INNER JOIN syntax is the way we 'join' each record in Orders with its corresponding record in the Shippers table to form a new record. The new record contains all of the data from Orders *and* all of the corresponding records from Shippers. The SELECT clause can then return fields from *either* of the two tables, and the WHERE clause can filter the rows returned by the query, based on values from either table.

The selected rows from the Shippers table are limited by the results of the INNER JOIN. We can decompose the example to see how the join works:

```
SELECT ShipVia
FROM Orders
WHERE ShipCity = 'Caracas'
AND ShipCountry = 'Venezuela'
```

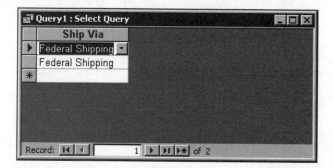

Using the same criteria in the WHERE clause as we did previously, we SELECT records from Orders WHERE ShipCity = 'Caracas' AND ShipCountry = 'Venezuela', but this time we return the ShipVia values from the Orders table. We still get the same two records back from Orders, as we would expect, but this time we examine the values of ShipVia for those records, and we see that the value is 3 in both. Or at least, we would, were it not for the fact that Access is being 'helpful' again by assuming that we'd rather see the company name.

In general, you can add as many tables as you need to a SQL query, depending on the data you want to retrieve. In the chapters to come, you'll have ample opportunity to practice writing SELECT statements, as well as learning to use them in your Visual Basic and ASP.NET applications.

INSERT, UPDATE, and DELETE Statements

We have used the SELECT statement to cover quite a bit of difficult ground. We've looked at primary and foreign keys, at what they mean for relationships, and how you can exploit them with joins. INSERT, UPDATE, and DELETE queries use those same basic concepts to allow us to modify data.

Try It Out – INSERT Statements

1. Let's begin by inserting a new row into the Shippers table of the Northwind database. Type the following code into the **Query1** window, and run it:

```
INSERT INTO Shippers
(CompanyName, Phone)
VALUES ('Wrox Deliveries', '(504) 666-6836')
```

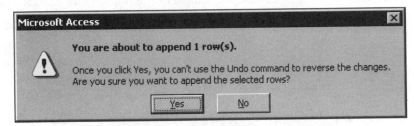

2. As you can see from the above screenshot, we have appended one row. We can examine our new row by typing in the following query. Don't worry about the format for now; we will explain it shortly in the *How It Works* section.

```
SELECT
   *
FROM
   Shippers
```

3. On running this new query, we find our new row in the query results:

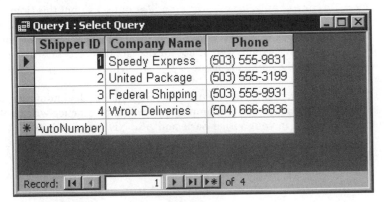

How It Works

In an INSERT query, the INSERT clause contains the keywords INSERT INTO (where INTO is optional) and the list of fields that will receive values. The VALUES clause contains the values that will get placed into the fields; the field values should be in the same order as the field list.

Once the new row has been inserted, we examine it with the following syntax:

```
SELECT
   *
FROM
   Shippers
```

The obvious thing to notice here is that in the SELECT clause, there's an asterisk in place of the field names you'd expect to see. An asterisk in the SELECT clause is a shorthand way to retrieve all of the fields for a particular row. This can be useful when you want to examine data quickly, or while you are developing your queries. Generally speaking, however, you should not use this syntax in your applications, as it provides no control over the order in which fields are retrieved.

> **Avoid the SELECT * syntax in applications; use the SELECT field1, field2, ... syntax instead.**

Notice that we didn't provide a value for the ShipperID field, and yet it has a new value – 4, in this case. This is because the designers of the Northwind database designated ShipperID as an **identity field** (Microsoft Access calls this an "AutoNumber" field). An identity field is a numeric field that automatically receives a new, unique value whenever a new row is added to its table. If you attempt to assign you own value to an identity field, you get an error.

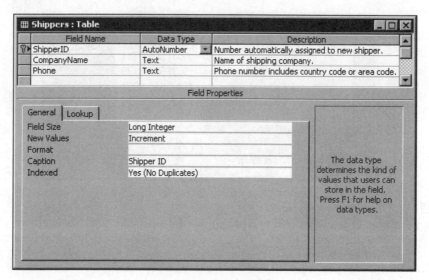

Try It Out – UPDATE Statements

1. Let's now change the value of the phone number in the row we just added by using an UPDATE statement. Type the following into the **Query1** window (you may need to use a different value for the `ShipperID`), and run the query.

```
UPDATE Shippers
SET Phone = '(503) 555-6836'
WHERE ShipperID = 4
```

2. As you see from the screenshot below, we have again altered one row.

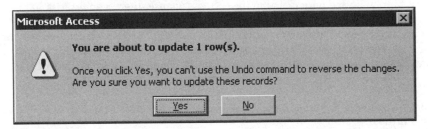

3. Our row now has the new phone number:

```
SELECT
     *
FROM
    Shippers
```

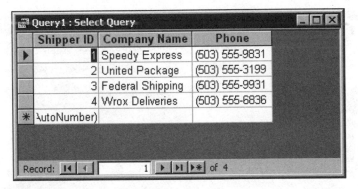

How It Works

This UPDATE statement looks straightforward and, for the most part, it is. The UPDATE clause includes the name of the table we want to update. The SET clause contains the field(s) and their new values (if you want to update multiple fields at the same time, separate each 'field = value' pair by a comma). Again we see the WHERE clause, just like in our other examples. Here, it ensures that we only affect the row that we just added, with `ShipperID = 4`.

> Be careful with **UPDATE** (and **DELETE**) statements! If you forget to add the **WHERE** clause in a **SELECT** statement, the query returns more rows than you wanted. But if you forget to add the **WHERE** clause in an **UPDATE** or **DELETE** statement, the statement will modify or delete every row in the whole table!

Try It Out – DELETE Statements

1. Finally, we can use the DELETE statement to delete our new row from the Shippers table:

```
DELETE FROM Shippers
WHERE ShipperID = 4
```

2. As you see in the screenshot below, we have again affected one row.

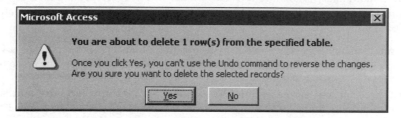

Once again, the basic DELETE syntax is simple, but don't forget the WHERE clause! If you leave out the WHERE clause, you will delete every row in the table!

Normalization

Now that we've taken a look at primary keys and foreign keys, and (briefly) at selecting, inserting, updating, and deleting the information in a database, we can have a little look at one final aspect of using and designing relational databases. **Normalization** is a term that's often bandied about, but tends to be poorly understood. In this section, we'll try to make things a little clearer.

For an explanation of exactly what database normalization *is*, we can return to our friend Dr Codd, who outlined the first three rules of normalization in his 1972 paper, *Further Normalization of the Data Base Relational Model*. Since his work, other rules have been added to the list, but we won't discuss them here – this is not a book about database theory, and to go further would take us beyond the scope of what it necessary for us to cover.

Normalization has several purposes. One of these is to prevent the possibility of redundant data that can become out of sync (such as when a field in one record with a particular value gets updated, but other duplicate instances of the data fail to get updated). Another is to prepare for unforeseen scalability issues. Thinking about the Customers table of the Northwind database, what if a later requirement were to mandate that we should store more than one shipping address per client? That would precipitate a change to the database itself, to all related SQL code, and possibly to the code of applications that use it too.

More succinctly stated, the purpose of normalization is to reduce the chances for anomalies to occur in a database during the processes of inserting, deleting, and updating data.

❑ An **insertion anomaly** is a failure to place a value into all the places in the database where it should be stored. In a properly normalized database, a single value needs to be inserted into only one place in the database; in an inadequately normalized database, data may need to be inserted into more than one place. There is a risk that one or more insertions will get overlooked.

❑ A **deletion anomaly** is a failure to remove data. In a properly normalized database, obsolete data needs to be deleted from only one place in the database; in an inadequately normalized database, obsolete data may need to be deleted from several places.

❑ An **update anomaly** is very similar to an insertion anomaly. It occurs when a value is stored in multiple places in the database, and our UPDATE fails to update one or more of those values.

When the first three rules of normalization (the so-called first, second, and third normal forms) are adhered to, these three potential problems are dealt with. Through normalization, we ensure that our database will:

❑ Serve current as well as unforeseeable future needs

❑ Have as little redundancy as possible

❑ Accommodate multiple values for types of data that require them

❑ Permit efficient updates of the data in the database

❑ Avoid the danger of losing data unknowingly

First Normal Form (1NF)

> **Formal definition: A relation is in first normal form (1NF) if and only if all underlying simple domains contain only atomic values.**

To put the formal definition of the first normal form in more practical terms, 1NF really has two parts. The first is that any value in a field should be atomic (indivisible). An example of a table that is *not* in 1NF is:

```
ID            Supplier_Products                                      Price
----------    ---------------------------------------------------   -------
1             Lenox Serving Platter                                  156.95
2             Mikasa Serving Platter                                 93.95
3             Noritake Serving Platter                               206.95
```

This violates the principle of atomic data because the values in the `Supplier_Products` field contain two distinct data elements: the supplier, and the product they supply. One step we could take to fix this problem would be:

```
ID            ServingPlatter  LenuxPrice MikasaPrice NoritakePrice
----------    --------------- ---------- ----------- -------------
1             Serving Platter 156.95     93.95       206.95
```

But this 'solution' violates the second part of 1NF, which demands that an atomic value should not be spread across various fields. In this case, the price is an atomic value, but we've spread it across `LenuxPrice`, `MikasaPrice`, and `NoritakePrice`. Let's make one last attempt to reach 1NF in this example:

Products

```
ID            Name
----------    ----------------
1             Serving Platter
```

Suppliers

```
ID            ProductID   Name             Price
----------    ----------- ---------------- -------
1             1           Lenux            156.95
2             1           Mikasa           93.95
3             1           Noritake         206.95
```

By creating separate `Products` and `Suppliers` tables, we now have a `Price` field with atomic data: the price.

Second Normal Form (2NF)

> **Formal definition: A relation is in second normal form (2NF) if and only if it is in 1NF, and every non-key attribute is fully dependent on the primary key.**

The first part of this rule says that for a database to be in 2NF, it must first fulfill all the criteria of a 1NF database. In fact, all of the rules are cumulative – each rule depends on the criteria of all previous rules being met.

If we examine our `Products` table above, we see that it meets 2NF. The key is `ID`, so the only non-key attribute is `Name`. `Name` is fully dependent on the `ID` field, which identifies a unique product.

If we look at the `Suppliers` table, however, we find that it does *not* meet 2NF. Again, `Name` is fully dependent on the `ID`, since the latter is the key field that identifies a unique supplier. However, the non-key `ProductID` and `Price` fields *don't* completely depend on `ID` – not all of Lenux's products cost $156.95, for example. We need to add a third table to reach 2NF and retain all of the data and the relationships between them:

```
Products

ID            Name
----------- ----------------
1             Serving Platter
```

```
Suppliers

ID            Name
----------- ----------------
1             Lenux
2             Mikasa
3             Noritake
```

```
Products_Suppliers

ProductID   SupplierID   Price
----------- ----------- -------
1             1           156.95
1             2           93.95
1             3           206.95
```

Here, the `Products` table remains the same – `Products.Name` still depends entirely on `Products.ID`, so it's still in 2NF. `Suppliers` is also now in 2NF, since it has a key field (`ID`) and a non-key field (`Name`) that's completely dependent on it. `Products_Suppliers` has a **compound key** made up of `ProductID` and `SupplierID`. The only non-key field is `Price`, and `Price` is completely dependent on the key.

Third Normal Form (3NF)

> **Formal definition: A relation is in third normal form (3NF) if and only if it is in 2NF and every non-key attribute is non-transitively dependent on the primary key.**

Let's now add the supplier's phone number to our example, as follows:

```
Products_Suppliers

ProductID    SupplierID   Price    SupplierPhone
-----------  -----------  -------  -------------
1            1            156.95   301-3344
1            2            93.95    302-4455
1            3            206.95   303-5566
```

Does this table still meet 1NF? Certainly – all fields are atomic. Does it meet 2NF? Yes – Price and SupplierPhone depend on the key. Does it meet 3NF? As you may have already guessed, it does not. SupplierPhone depends on the key, but only partially so. That is, it depends on the SupplierID part of the key, but not the ProductID part. This type of dependency is said to be **transitive**. The solution should be fairly obvious: we need to move the SupplierPhone from the Products_Suppliers table to the Suppliers table. If this sounds too easy, it really is. Once you understand these three normal forms, it becomes quite easy to spot non-normalized tables, and then to do something about them.

> If a table is in 2NF and its key is simple (rather than compound), it is automatically in 3NF as well. You only have to worry about 3NF for tables with compound keys.

SQL Server vs. Access

For our final act in this chapter (and therefore just prior to putting some of the things we've looked at into practice in real ASP.NET applications), we're going to have a quick look at Microsoft's two RDBMS products, with a view to helping you decide which to use in your production applications. As you know, we're going to be using MSDE as we work through the examples in this book, but commercial applications tend to require commercial solutions.

Microsoft Access can be a good database choice when you need a relatively small-footprint, relatively inexpensive database that resides on the client. However, performance begins to breaks down for large databases, and for many simultaneous users. Using Access as a server-side database for even small databases will yield poor performance, since Access does not have a server component. That is, the client application *always* has to read the entire table from the file server (that is, the computer on which the Access database resides), even if the SELECT is requesting a single record.

Microsoft SQL Server is much more expensive, and may be subject to license fees per user. It has a larger footprint than Access, but it will virtually always reside on a server. It performs well for medium-sized databases, and it has a server component that is designed to operate very efficiently over a network. It also supports stored procedures (see Chapter 8) that can perform significantly better than Access's queries, since the stored procedure execution plan is optimized on the fly. SQL Server has a much richer and more robust security model than Access. Finally, SQL Server allows richer maintenance operations, since it keeps a transaction log that can be used to recover a corrupt database without loss of data.

MSDE

As we described in the previous chapter, to a large extent MSDE *is* SQL Server, but without client tools like the Query Analyzer and the Enterprise Manager. Without the aid of these tools, routine database maintenance becomes more difficult – but not prohibitively so, as you'll soon see.

Summary

In this chapter, we've scratched the surface of an enormous subject. We have reviewed theory ranging from Codd's rules to database design and normalization. We have introduced SQL, the lingua franca of RDBMSs, and have compared SQL Server and Access, two of the most common RDBMSs for Windows. The chapters that follow will cover SQL in greater depth, but our emphasis will turn away from database design, and toward database programming. The focus shifts from theory to practice as you get hands-on experience and learn techniques to apply the theory to real-world problems.

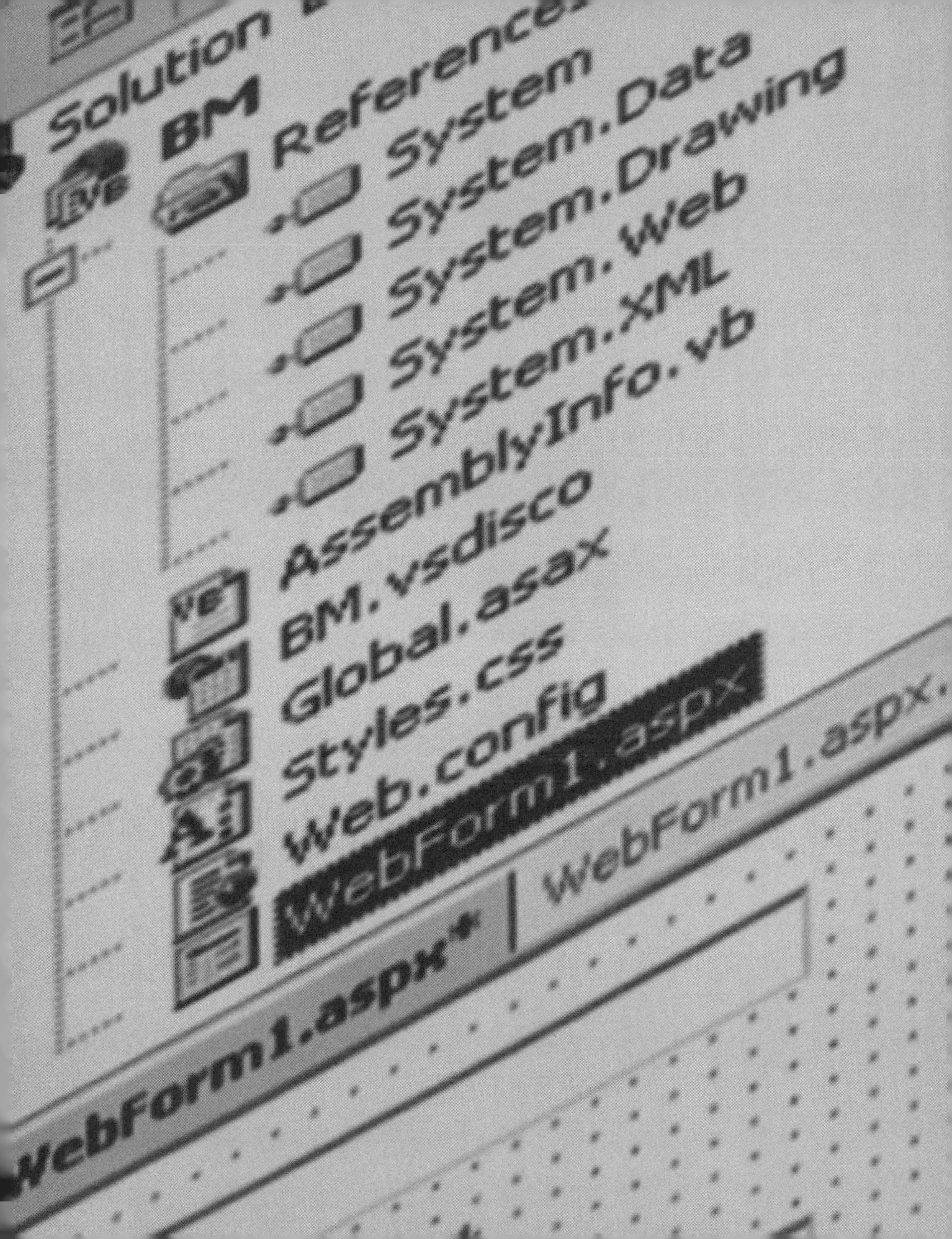

Solution
BM
Live
References
System
System.Data
System.Drawing
System.Web
System.XML
AssemblyInfo.vb
BM.vsdisco
Global.asax
Styles.css
Web.config
WebForm1.aspx

WebForm1.aspx* | WebForm1.aspx

WebForm1.aspx*

Connecting to a Data Source

As we discussed in Chapter 1, all of the interactions between ASP.NET and data that you'll see in this book will start with an ADO.NET **connection**. The connection establishes what data source the page will use, the security details necessary to authorize access to the data, and the data provider that will handle the translations between the data source and the ADO.NET objects. However, the syntax you use to create the connection, and the options available to you, vary considerably with different sources of data.

You know that in ASP.NET, getting data from a database to the web page that your users will see in their browsers requires a number of ADO.NET objects: connections, datasets, data readers, data adapters, and so on. In order to provide useful demonstrations, we'll be using quite a few of these different objects in this chapter, but our focus is on the first item in that list – the others will have their time in the sun a little later on. Our aim here is to understand ADO.NET connection objects, and in order to do so we'll look at the following topics:

- ❑ The basics of ADO.NET connections
- ❑ Connecting to Microsoft SQL Server data
- ❑ Connecting to an MS Access database
- ❑ Connecting to an MS Excel spreadsheet
- ❑ Connecting to an XML data file
- ❑ Getting schema information about a data store
- ❑ Some common mistakes

What is a Connection?

An ADO.NET connection provides a conduit for communication between the data consumer (say, the ASP.NET code that you write, executed on IIS) and the source from which you need to retrieve data. This conduit, though, does more than just relay information – it can also perform *translation* of the data as it moves from the store to the ASP.NET page.

> *The word "connection" can be used in many ways, but in this chapter (and in this book in general) we mean a data connection between Internet Information Server (IIS) and a data store. We are not discussing the HTTP connection between the web browser and IIS.*

In a superficial way, we can think of the connection as a layer between the data and the page that's eventually displayed on the user's screen. More specifically, it is the layer between the provider that interacts directly with the data source, and the ADO.NET objects that use the data (for example, the `DataSet` object). These objects (with help from command objects, `DataTables`, and others) then pass information to ASP.NET controls for display.

Like so much else in the .NET Framework, an ADO.NET connection is presented to the programmer as an object. In fact, there are a number of different connection objects; which one you find yourself using will depend upon the data source you're dealing with. Once you've created a connection object, however, the range of operations that you can perform with it is for the most part independent of the data source. The following diagram shows where the connection object fits in the layers of communication that exist between a data source and an ASP.NET page:

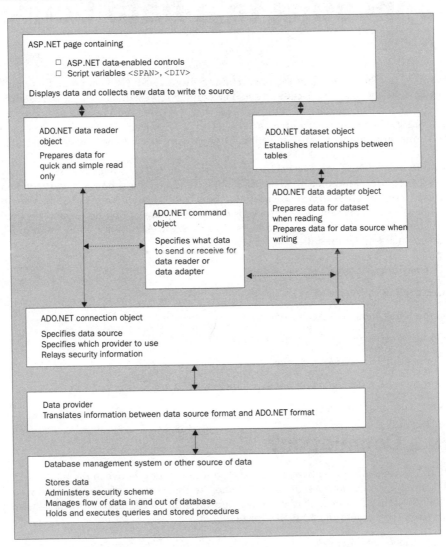

As this discussion develops, it's important to keep in mind two things that a connection object *doesn't* do. First, a connection object *doesn't* specify what data (what fields and what records) to get from a specified source – as we'll see later, this is done by a command object, working in conjunction with a data reader or data adapter object. Second, the connection object *doesn't* directly cause the data store to perform reading or writing on the data. The connection simply starts a data session that's supported by ADO.NET at the data consumer end, and by the database engine (or some other data source) at the data provider end.

> *The word "session" is used in two different contexts, and it is important to distinguish them properly. While you may be familiar with the term as it refers to a visitor's interaction with the pages of a web site, a session may also be understood in the context of establishing a connection with a source of data. A data session is created between the web server and the data source when a connection is established, and exists for the duration of that connection.*

Differences between ADO and ADO.NET Connections

If you've had any dealings with 'classic' versions of ADO (ADO 2.0, ADO 2.1, and so on), you may be wondering about the differences between ADO.NET and ADO. With regard to connection objects, there are five basic changes:

❑ Classic ADO connections were usually used to fill a `Recordset` object. In ADO.NET, the role of `Recordset` is taken by `DataSet`, while data reader objects replace the old read-only, forward-only semantics that the `Recordset` object embodied.

❑ DSNs and UDLs have gone away. In ADO.NET, we simply specify the data provider and the location of the data as properties of the connection object. (Although this *could* be done with the old connection object, it was not the most common technique.)

❑ In classic ADO, OLE DB providers and ODBC drivers were used. Now, the preferred way of accessing data is with the .NET data providers, which we'll discuss below.

❑ In ADO.NET, we cannot execute an SQL statement directly from a connection object. At a minimum, we must use a command object too.

❑ Classic ADO enables a connection to persist in an open state. In almost all cases, ADO.NET works with disconnected data.

If you haven't dealt with ADO before, don't worry: in ADO.NET, many of the complexities alluded to above have been ironed out. In the pages to come, we'll be covering all that you need to know in order to use ADO.NET with confidence.

Database Connections Available in ADO.NET

As mentioned briefly above, one of the most important advances from classic ADO to ADO.NET is the creation of **.NET data providers**. When you install the .NET Framework, two such providers come along with it: the OLE DB .NET data provider, and the SQL Server .NET data provider. A third – the ODBC .NET data provider – may be downloaded from Microsoft (http://www.microsoft.com/downloads; search for 'ODBC .NET data provider'). It's likely that other specialized .NET data providers will become available in the future, not necessarily from Microsoft.

The SQL Server .NET data provider is highly optimized for connections to just one type of data source: Microsoft SQL Server 7, or higher. It isn't even able to talk to other SQL-language RDBMSs (such as Oracle, or IBM's DB2). The SQL Server .NET data provider connects to the RDBMS at the level of the Tabular Data Stream (TDS), and thus completely avoids the OLE DB layer. If you're using Microsoft SQL Server, as we'll spend most of our time doing in this book, then the SQL Server data provider is by far your best choice.

> *TDS is an internal data transfer protocol for Microsoft SQL Server that can be exposed to allow communication between different operating systems, using a variety of different network transport technologies.*

For almost all other data sources, we can use the OLE DB .NET data provider. This works with any OLE DB-compliant data source, including SQL Server, but in that particular case it's slower than the SQL Server .NET data provider we just mentioned. The OLE DB .NET data provider's versatility is such that it can be used with non-relational data such as Excel spreadsheets, right up to enterprise-strength relational systems such as Oracle and IBM's DB2.

Our third alternative here – the ODBC .NET data provider – has two uses. First, we can employ it to connect to data at the ODBC level – this is 'lower down' than OLE DB, and thus slightly faster. Second, there are some old data stores for which only an ODBC service is available, such as Borland's Paradox. Unless your situation *requires* ODBC, however, it's better to work with the supplied OLE DB .NET data provider.

> **In fact, there's a fourth kind of 'connection', which takes place when we work with data in XML format. However, since XML data resides in files without a data management system, we don't actually use a connection object. Instead, a `DataSet` can be used to read the XML file directly. We'll investigate how to do this later in the chapter.**

Connection Syntax

Having covered the necessary groundwork, we can at last begin to look at using Visual Basic .NET to write ASP.NET pages that use ADO.NET objects to access data stores. To understand this process properly, it's useful to break the discussion into two parts: *creating* the connection, and *using* the connection. Each of these parts has three steps, and if you keep these in mind, you'll find that you're able to write the necessary code almost immediately.

First up, creating a connection to a data store requires the instantiation of a connection object. Code for doing this is characterized by three features:

❑ The namespaces containing the appropriate ADO.NET classes must be imported

❑ A string variable to hold some information necessary for making the connection is created and filled

❑ The connection object is instantiated

Then, once a connection object has been created, the code that makes use of the connection tends to look like this:

❑ The connection is opened

❑ Using the connection, data is read from or written to the data store, or a SQL statement is executed

❑ The connection is closed

Returning to the start of that list, you won't be surprised to discover that the ADO.NET classes, like all of the classes in the .NET Framework class library, are organized into namespaces. A few moments ago, we saw that ADO.NET provides three ways to access data: the SQL Server .NET data provider, the OLE DB .NET data provider, and the ODBC .NET data provider. Accordingly, there are three namespaces, as follows:

❑ `System.Data.SqlClient` contains the classes that comprise the SQL Server .NET data provider

❑ `System.Data.OleDb` contains the classes that comprise the OLE DB .NET data provider

❑ `System.Data.ODBC` contains the classes that comprise the ODBC .NET data provider (note that, as already mentioned, this provider must be downloaded and installed separately)

In addition to these, we'll almost always find ourselves making use of the `System.Data` namespace, which contains a large number of classes and other entities that form the 'backbone' of ADO.NET. The classes in this namespace are not specific to a particular data provider.

> In ADO.NET, the word "provider" has been overloaded. In this section, we've been talking about .NET data providers, which are entirely synonymous with the namespaces that implement them – **System.Data.OleDb** *is* the OLE DB .NET data provider. The other kind of provider is the one that appears in the architecture diagrams, and will appear in our connection strings. These providers handle the specific task of translating data from its format in the data source, to the format in which it's manipulated by ADO.NET.

Connections using the SQL Server .NET Data Provider

As we discussed above, the SQL Server .NET data provider offers a specialized service by virtue of its internal code for communicating with the Tabular Data Stream. On the surface, however, to the ADO.NET programmer, it's almost exactly the same as the OLE DB .NET data provider (and, for that matter, the ODBC .NET data provider). This means that once we understand how to use one data provider, we will be all set to use the other two.

> *There are many databases that support SQL communications (Oracle, IBM DB2, mySQL, etc.), but the SQL Server .NET data provider is only for Microsoft SQL Server version 7 and above. For the others – including earlier versions of SQL Server – you must use the OLE DB .NET data provider.*

If you compare the following diagram with the generic one we looked at earlier, you'll see that we've included the names of the specialized SQL Server classes (plus `DataSet` and `DataTable`, which are used for all data source types), but removed any specific reference to a provider layer – the .NET data provider communicates with the TDS, and no translation is necessary.

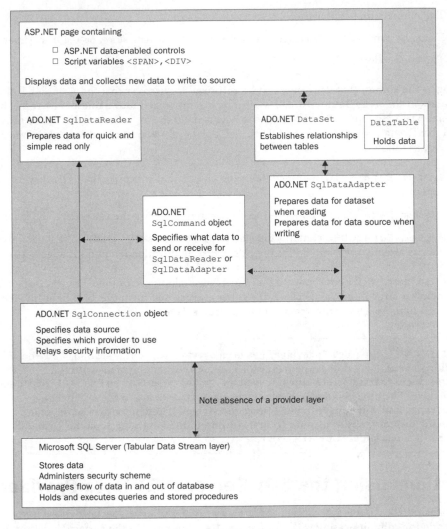

In the remainder of this section, we'll translate this diagram into ASP.NET code that retrieves data from the MSDE Northwind database we set up in Chapter 1. Later in the book, we'll look at the help for writing data-driven web sites that's provided by the Visual Studio environment, but for now we'll just use a text editor, so that you can see exactly what's going on.

SQL Connection Syntax

Earlier in the chapter, we talked about the three programmatic steps necessary to create an ADO.NET connection object. In summary, these were:

❑ Import the appropriate namespaces

❑ Create and fill a connection string

❑ Instantiate the connection object

Starting at the top of that list, writing an ASP.NET page that connects to a SQL Server database requires classes from two .NET Framework namespaces: the high-level, more general System.Data (which we'll use in every example we consider), and the task-specific System.Data.SqlClient. In other words, every SQL Server-accessing ASPX file you ever write will start like this:

```
<%@ Import namespace="System.Data" %>
<%@ Import namespace="System.Data.SqlClient" %>
```

Next, in order to create a connection object, we need first to specify a connection string. When it comes to creating a connection object for a SQL Server database (and therefore for an MSDE database), we need to provide at least three pieces of information:

❑   The name of the server that holds our database

❑   The name of the database that we want to use

❑   Whether the connection to the database we're using is secure

These requirements result in the creation of a connection string that looks something like this, where the items in italics will be replaced with specific values in actual code:

```
Dim strConnection As String = "server=MyServer; database=MyDatabase; " & _
                              "integrated security=<true | false>;"
```

Finally, once we have the connection string, we can create the connection object. For SQL Server, this object will be an instance of the System.Data.SqlClient.SqlConnection class, and its creation is as easy as this:

```
Dim objConnection As New SqlConnection(strConnection)
```

Once created, using a SqlConnection object is a matter of opening it, performing operations on it, and closing it. While that's not our focus in this chapter, it would be hard to prove that everything's working properly without doing *something* with the data to which we've gained access, so we'll do precisely that in the following example.

> **Be careful not to confuse the connection *string* and the connection *object*. The connection string (usually named strConnection or strConn) is a simple variable that holds information that will be used by the object. The connection object (usually named objConnection or objConn) is the actual object that will be used on the rest of the page to work with the data.**

Try It Out – Creating a Connection to a SQL Server Database

We set up MSDE and the Northwind database in Chapter 1, but there's a little extra work that we should do before assembling our first data-driven ASP.NET page. To keep the examples we write in this book away from any other code, it makes sense to place them in a virtual directory, and that's where we'll begin this part of the story.

1. While the code in this book was being tested, we set up a virtual directory called BegASPNETdb, mapped to a file system directory called C:\BegASPNETdb\webroot. To do the same, go to Start | Settings | Control Panel | Administrative Tools | Personal Web Manager, and enter the following in the Add Directory dialog:

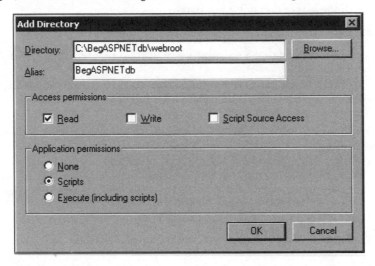

2. In the webroot folder, create a text file called web.config, and fill it with *exactly* the following:

```xml
<?xml version="1.0" encoding="utf-8" ?>
<configuration>
  <system.web>
    <customErrors mode="Off" />
    <compilation debug="true"/>
  </system.web>
</configuration>
```

The presence of this file will ensure that if and when anything goes wrong with one of our ASPX files, we'll get a useful, descriptive error message.

3. Create a subfolder called C:\BegASPNETdb\webroot\ch03, and place a new text file called SQLServer_connection.aspx inside it.

4. Add the following code (or download it from www.wrox.com).

```
<%@ Import namespace="System.Data" %>
<%@ Import namespace="System.Data.SqlClient" %>

<html>
  <head>
    <title>Beginning ASP.NET Databases Chapter 3</title>
  </head>

  <body>
    <h4>First Example: Listing data from the Employees table</h4>
    <asp:DataGrid id="dgNameList"
                  runat="server"
                  GridLines="None"
                  BackColor="LightBlue"
                  CellPadding="5"
                  CellSpacing="5"
                  BorderWidth="2"
                  BorderColor="Black"
                  ToolTip="Includes only those employees who are at HQ" />
  </body>
</html>

<script language="VB" runat="server">
Sub Page_Load(Source As Object, E As EventArgs)
  Dim strConnection As String = "server=(local)\NetSDK; database=Northwind; " & _
                                "integrated security=true;"
  Dim objConnection As New SqlConnection(strConnection)

  Dim strSQL As String = "SELECT FirstName, LastName, Country " & _
                         "FROM Employees"
  Dim objCommand As New SqlCommand(strSQL, objConnection)

  objConnection.Open()
  dgNameList.DataSource = objCommand.ExecuteReader()
  dgNameList.DataBind()
  objConnection.Close()
End Sub
</script>
```

5. Everything is now in place for you to browse to http://localhost/BegASPNETdb/ch03/ SQLServer_connection.aspx, where you should see the screen overleaf.

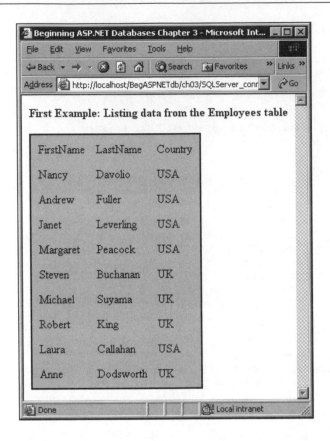

How It Works

After the opening lines of code that import the namespaces we've already talked about, the rest of the ASPX file breaks into two rather obvious halves. The section contained in <html>...</html> tags is familiar-looking HTML, but a point of interest is the <asp:DataGrid> element:

```
<asp:DataGrid id="dgNameList"
              runat="server"
              GridLines="None"
              BackColor="LightBlue"
              CellPadding="5"
              CellSpacing="5"
              BorderWidth="2"
              BorderColor="Black"
              ToolTip="Includes only those employees who are at HQ" />
```

The <asp:DataGrid> element instructs ASP.NET to use a DataGrid **web server control** in the course of generating the HTML page that's eventually displayed to the client – we can populate it with data, and it will display that data in the form of an HTML <table>. Most of the attributes of the <asp:DataGrid> element just describe how the table should look on the screen (in this case, you can see that we've requested a light blue background, a black border, and so on), but rather more interesting is the id attribute, the purpose of which we will see in a moment.

The DataGrid *web server control is just one of more than twenty available to you. We'll say little more about this one here, but you'll see more and more as we proceed, and they're well described in the MSDN documentation (.NET Framework | Reference | ASP.NET Syntax | Web Server Controls).*

With the above in mind, we can study the Page_Load() event handler that occupies the second half of the ASPX file. This begins in a way that should be familiar, but after that – in order to get something that's worth displaying – we have to perform a couple of operations that will be new to you.

```
<script language="VB" runat="server">
Sub Page_Load(Source As Object, E As EventArgs)
  Dim strConnection As String = "server=(local)\NetSDK; database=Northwind; " & _
                                "integrated security=true;"
  Dim objConnection As New SqlConnection(strConnection)
```

The first two lines of this implementation just add some specifics to the generalized discussion of connection strings that you've already seen. We set the server to (local)\NetSDK (the MSDE instance that we set up in Chapter 1), the database to Northwind, and integrated security to true (again, this matches the "use Windows NT integrated security" option that we saw in Chapter 1).

It's also possible to specify a user name and a password to access a SQL Server or MSDE database. For more information on this subject, consult the online documentation for the SqlConnection *object's constructor.*

```
  Dim strSQL As String = "SELECT FirstName, LastName, Country " & _
                         "FROM Employees"
  Dim objCommand As New SqlCommand(strSQL, objConnection)
```

The next two lines of code create a **command object** that will soon be used to extract information from the Northwind database. We'll have much more to say on the subject of command objects in the next chapter, but you can already begin to see how they work. When we instantiate it, we pass the SqlCommand constructor a string containing the SQL query we want to execute, and the connection to the database we want to operate on. Once we have it, we can go through the steps that we talked about earlier: open, use, and then close the connection.

> It's important to close a connection explicitly. ADO.NET *will* automatically close a connection when it is not being used, but only after a period of time has passed. For best performance, *always* include an explicit call to the connection object's Close() method as soon as you've finished using the connection.

```
  objConnection.Open()
  dgNameList.DataSource = objCommand.ExecuteReader()
  dgNameList.DataBind()
  objConnection.Close()
End Sub
</script>
```

In general, 'using' the database will involve data reader objects, dataset objects, and data adapter objects, all of which will be discussed in detail in Chapters 4 and 5. In this case, however, we've short-circuited the process into just two lines of code, making use of the fact that programmatically, the data grid control behaves like an object of class `System.Web.UI.WebControls.DataGrid`. The first line specifies that the source of data for the data grid named `dgNameList` (as defined by the `id` attribute in our HTML section) will be the results that come from invoking the `ExecuteReader()` method of our `SqlCommand` object. The second **binds** the data: it deals with the process of reading the data and putting it into the grid.

As you've already seen, the result of this relatively straightforward ASP.NET code is an HTML page containing the names and locations of nine people, extracted from the Northwind database.

Connecting to MS Access using the OLE DB .NET Data Provider

As you know, we'll be using MSDE databases for the majority of this book. However, since one of ADO.NET's selling points is that it provides near-uniform access to diverse data sources, it makes sense here to look at some alternatives, starting with an MS Access database.

Microsoft Access is a great database engine for cutting your teeth on, and its use is widespread, but in truth it was never designed to support more then ten or twenty simultaneous users – degradation in performance occurs when there are more than this. Nevertheless, it's highly likely that you'll be asked to interact with an Access database at some point in your programming career, and it's possible that you'll find an application for one yourself. Either way, you'll need to know how to do it.

To make a connection to a database that was created with MS Access, you don't need to have Access installed on your machine, and the code we'll use is really very similar to the code you've already seen. The difference is that we'll be using the OLE DB .NET data provider (which includes the `OleDbConnection` object), and assembling a connection string that specifies the MDB file created by Access, and the OLE DB-compliant JET provider.

> *JET is the name of the data engine used by Access. In the above configuration, information flows from the Access database, through the JET engine, and then through ADO.NET's OLE DB JET provider.*

The diagram below displays the relationship of ADO.NET objects as they apply to using an Access file as a data source. Notice that we use specific OLE DB objects, except for the `DataSet` and `DataTable` objects, which are generic.

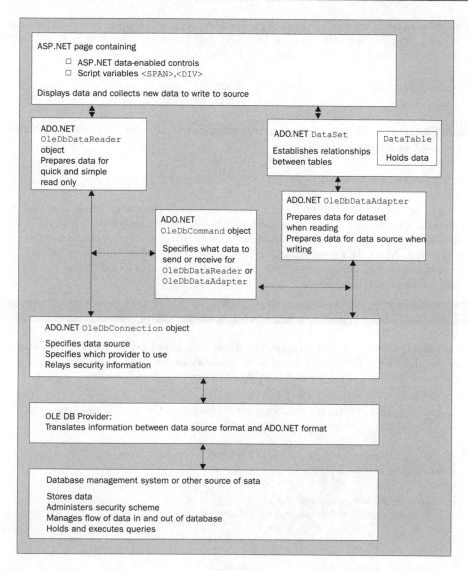

Access Connection Syntax

Despite the choice of a different data source, creating a connection to an Access database involves the same three steps as before: import the appropriate namespaces; create the connection string; instantiate the connection object. When we connect to Access, we use the OLE DB .NET data provider, so we must import the System.Data.OleDb namespace alongside the System.Data namespace.

```
<%@ Import namespace="System.Data" %>
<%@ Import namespace="System.Data.OleDb" %>
```

The connection string is the part of the process that exhibits most changes from what we had with SQL Server. When you're dealing with the OLE DB .NET data provider, it must contain at least two pieces of information: the type of provider we're going to use, and the name of the Access file:

```
Dim strConnection As String = "Provider=MyProvider; " & _
                              "data source=MyDataSource;"
```

Apart from the fact that it belongs to a different class, however, creating the connection object involves exactly the same operation we used before:

```
Dim objConnection As New OleDbConnection(strConnection)
```

A key thing to be aware of here is that when you connect to an Access database, you must specify the file in which the data is stored. With enterprise-capable database management systems (Oracle, Microsoft SQL Server, IBM DB2, etc.), you don't need to worry about how the information in the database is stored. ADO.NET connections to these latter kinds of data stores can switch between different databases within the one connection. If we want to connect to a different Access database, we must create a new connection object.

Try It Out – Connecting to an Access Database

In this example, we'll make a connection to the Access version of the Northwind database using the syntax we just described. For variety – and to make the example a little more interesting – we'll also display the results of a slightly different query from the one we used last time.

1. Locate the `nwind.mdb` file that we were looking at in Chapter 2, and copy it to `C:\BegASPNETdb\datastores\nwind.mdb`.

2. In the `ch03` folder, create a new text file named `Access_connection.aspx`, enter the following code into it, and save it.

```
<%@ Import namespace="System.Data" %>
<%@ Import namespace="System.Data.OleDb" %>

<html>
  <head>
    <title>Connecting to an Access Database</title>
  </head>

  <body>
    <H3>Connecting to an Access Database</H3>
    <asp:DataGrid id="dgSuppliers" runat="server" />
  </body>
</html>

<script language="VB" runat="server">
Sub Page_Load(Source As Object, E As EventArgs)
  Dim strConnection As String = "Provider=Microsoft.Jet.OleDb.4.0;" & _
                      "data source=C:\BegASPNETdb\datastores\nwind.mdb;"
```

```
   Dim objConnection As New OleDbConnection(strConnection)

   Dim strSQL As String = "SELECT SupplierID, CompanyName " & _
                      "FROM Suppliers"
   Dim objCommand As New OleDbCommand(strSQL, objConnection)

   objConnection.Open()
   dgSuppliers.DataSource = objCommand.ExecuteReader()
   dgSuppliers.DataBind()
   objConnection.Close()
End Sub
</script>
```

3. Viewing the above page in your browser by navigating to http://localhost/BegASPNETdb/
ch03/Access_connection.aspx should yield the following:

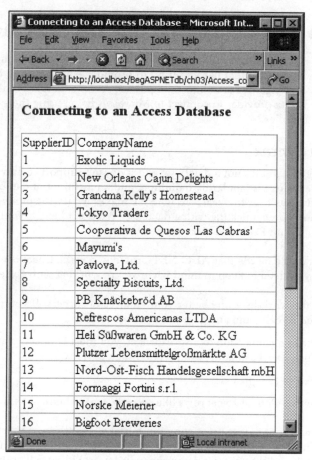

How It Works

We've been at pains to point out that ADO.NET does a good job of hiding the differences between connections to different data stores, so that once you've created them, one connection object is very much like another. Hopefully, the similarity between this example and our previous one has helped to convince you that this is a good thing. Aside from the use of different classes (OleDbCommand and OleDbConnection, rather than their Sql varieties), the only change of note was to the connection string:

```
Dim strConnection As String = "Provider=Microsoft.Jet.OleDb.4.0;" & _
                    "data source=C:\BegASPNETdb\datastores\nwind.mdb;"
```

Here, instead of identifying a host data server and the name of a database on that host, we're specifying a data file and a provider that will translate the contents of that file into something that's usable by ADO.NET. Although the objects involved are different, we find that we're able to call the same methods as we used in the SQL Server example.

Connecting to Excel Using the OLE DB .NET Data Provider

The versatility of the System.Data.OleDb.OleDbConnection object is such that it can act as a conduit for data from any source that has an OLE DB provider – and because the OLE DB standards have been around for so long, they are almost ubiquitous. As an example of this functionality, we can use the OLE DB .NET data provider to connect to Microsoft Excel using the syntax that you're familiar with from our earlier samples.

Excel Connection Syntax

A spreadsheet stores data, but it's not a database, and it doesn't support relational data structures. On the other hand, a spreadsheet is tabular by definition, and an awful lot of database-style information has been stored in spreadsheets over the years. ADO.NET makes it easy to connect to and use Excel data just as though you were communicating with a database. We don't have to fool around with cell addresses; we just work with fields and records.

Of course, regardless of the facade that ADO.NET provides, a spreadsheet is not a database, and there are some points that you need to keep in mind when you're working with Excel data:

❑ The cleaner the worksheet, the better your chances of success. If you can, try to eliminate any notes attached to cells, and any gaps in rows and columns.

❑ When you make a connection to a spreadsheet, you must connect to an Excel **named range**. You cannot use Excel cell addressing syntax, such as A1:C3.

❑ You must use the JET provider.

❑ SQL statements will treat Excel rows like records, and columns like fields.

To reiterate the second point in that list, a common mistake is to try to connect to an Excel spreadsheet that does not have a named range. You *cannot*, as you might have thought, connect to an entire worksheet or workbook and then extract data from cells by providing cell addresses. In case you haven't done it before, creating a named range is a three-part process:

- ❑ Select the cells that you wish to include in the range

- ❑ Choose Insert | Name | Define

- ❑ Type the name that you want to give to the range

If you need to, you can select every cell in the worksheet to be part of your named range. You can even select a set of cells that run in the Z dimension, back through several sheets of one workbook. Whatever range you define, though, when you make a connection to an Excel spreadsheet, you have to use a special extended property of the JET provider, specified by adding an attribute to the connection string. You can see this on the last line of the following excerpt:

```
Dim strConnection As String = "Provider=Microsoft.Jet.OleDb.4.0;" & _
                              "Data Source=MySource;" & _
                              "Extended Properties=Excel 8.0;"
```

With such a connection in place, we can write a SQL statement that treats the Excel columns as data fields, and Excel rows as data records:

```
Dim strSQL As String = "SELECT MyColumn1, MyColumn2 FROM MyRangeName"
```

As you can see, the format of this query is identical to those we've been using for 'real' databases. Once the connection is in place, the fact that we're communicating with an underlying Excel spreadsheet is obscured.

Try It Out – Connecting to an Excel Spreadsheet

Let's see how the above theory works in practice. We'll create an Excel workbook, read some data from it, and then display it in an ASP.NET-generated web page using ADO.NET.

1. Create an Excel workbook named C:\BegASPNETdb\datastores\inventory.xls, and fill in the first few cells as follows:

	A	B	C	D
1	ItemNo	Description	Source	Note
2	1001	CPU	Dell	Pentium 4
3	1002	Monitor	NEC	17 inch
4	1003	Keyboard	MicroTex	PS2 plug

2. Using the technique described above, give the range A1:D4 the name "Items", and check that when you select A1:D4, the name "Items" appears in the box at left end of the formula bar. Close the workbook (you do not have to close Excel).

3. In the folder for this chapter, create an ASP.NET page called Excel_connection.aspx, and add (or download) the following code:

```
<%@ Import namespace="System.Data" %>
<%@ Import namespace="System.Data.OleDb" %>
```

```
<html>
  <head>
    <title>Reading from an Excel Workbook</title>
  </head>

  <body>
    <H3>Reading from an Excel Workbook</H3>
    <asp:DataGrid id="dgInventory" runat="server" />
  </body>
</html>

<script language="VB" runat="server">
Sub Page_Load(Source As Object, E As EventArgs)
  Dim strConnection As String = "Provider=Microsoft.Jet.OleDb.4.0;" & _
                "data source=C:\BegASPNETdb\datastores\inventory.xls;" & _
                "Extended Properties=Excel 8.0;"
  Dim objConnection As New OleDbConnection(strConnection)

  Dim strSQL As String = "SELECT * FROM Items"
  Dim objCommand As New OleDbCommand(strSQL, objConnection)

  objConnection.Open()
  dgInventory.DataSource = objCommand.ExecuteReader()
  dgInventory.DataBind()
  objConnection.Close()
End Sub
</script>
```

4. Then, navigate to the new page in your web browser, and you should see something like this:

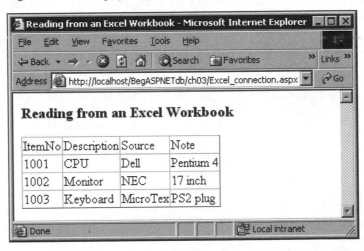

5. To prove that SQL commands really do work as though we're communicating directly with a database, we can try a few variations. Make the following change to the SQL statement to see how to select only certain fields (Excel columns).

```
Dim strSQL As String = "SELECT Description FROM Items"
```

This modification should yield the following in the browser:

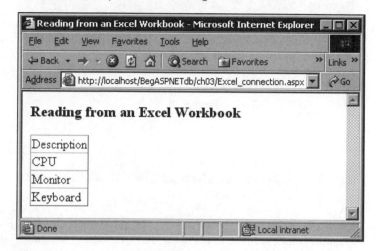

6. Another variation is this next query, which selects a single record from the database (or, if you like, a single row from the table):

```
Dim strSQL As String = "SELECT * FROM Items WHERE ItemNo=1002"
```

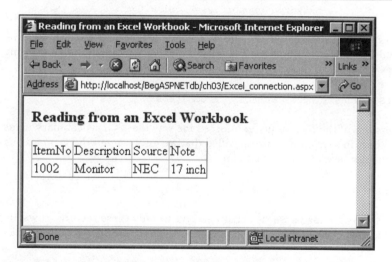

7. And finally, we can try the following, which proves that it's possible to select on the basis of text fields as well as numeric ones:

```
Dim strSQL As String = "SELECT * FROM Items WHERE Source='Dell'"
```

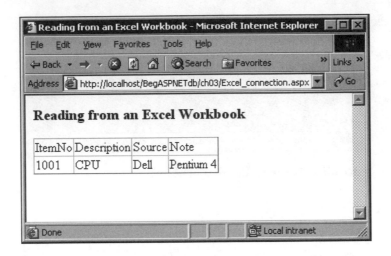

How It Works

It's worth reiterating that setting up properly in Excel is critical before you can connect to it with ADO.NET: you *must* name ranges in order to make the data available. That done, you can use the JET provider to connect to Excel, *provided that* you include the `extended properties` attribute in the connection string, as we did here:

```
Dim strConnection As String = "Provider=Microsoft.Jet.OleDb.4.0;" & _
                "data source=C:\BegASPNETdb\datastores\inventory.xls;" & _
                "extended properties=Excel 8.0;"
```

With the connection established, we wrote SQL statements that treat Excel rows as records, and Excel columns as fields. In the first instance, we indicated that we wanted all the fields using the asterisk, and ensured that we'd get all the records by leaving off a WHERE clause.

```
Dim strSQL As String = "SELECT * FROM Items"
```

In the other versions of the file, we just reinforced the way that SQL vocabulary maps to Excel terminology. When, in version two, we specified that we only wanted the Description field, we only got the Excel column headed Description.

```
Dim strSQL As String = "SELECT Description FROM Items"
```

In our third version, we added a WHERE clause to give us only those records (rows) in which the value for ItemNo was 1002. (Since this is a numeric value, we do not need quotation marks around it.)

```
Dim strSQL As String = "SELECT * FROM Items WHERE ItemNo=1002"
```

Lastly, in our fourth version, we saw that if we're searching for rows matching a text value, we must encapsulate the string in single quotes.

```
Dim strSQL As String = "SELECT * FROM Items WHERE Source='Dell'"
```

Practicalities of Connections to Excel

Although it's easy to connect to Excel for the purposes of a demonstration, the task can become very difficult in the real world. An organization's data may be stored in scores or even hundreds of Excel workbooks, scattered over various parts of a network. They will probably not be on your IIS or data servers, and may not be on any type of server at all.

Keep in mind that if you're called upon to access many workbooks that do not have named ranges, you could be in for a lot of preparation work – naming ranges is easy, *as long as you have permission to alter the original workbook*. It's likely that the sheets you're given will already have named ranges, in which case you should either use existing ranges (and risk the author making changes), or give your new ranges names that will not interfere with existing ones (you could start your range names with w_ for Web, for example).

ADO.NET will not open an Excel workbook that's already opened in write mode by some other application. This is cumbersome during development, when you might want to be keeping an eye on the worksheet's named ranges while writing your ADO.NET code. It can also a problem after deployment if the workbook that's the source of data for your ASP.NET page is also in use by other employees as part of their work.

More About Connection Objects

Having examined how to make connections using the SQL Server and OLE DB .NET providers, it's worth taking just a little time here to look more closely at the connection objects we've been working with. First of all, it's interesting to discover exactly how the strings that we've been passing as arguments to the SqlConnection and OleDbConnection object constructors cause changes in the objects' behavior. In fact, on being passed to the constructor, the connection strings are immediately assigned to a property called ConnectionString, as the following alternative syntax demonstrates explicitly:

```
Dim objConnection As New SqlConnection()

objConnection.ConnectionString = "server=(local)\NetSDK; " & _
                                 "database=Northwind; integrated security=true;"
```

Regardless of how you set the ConnectionString property, the attributes in that string are then used not only used to make the connection, but also to fill further, read-only properties of the connection object when the connection is opened. Continuing the above example, on execution of objConnection.Open(), objConnection.DataSource will be set to (local)\NetSDK, while objConnection.Database will be set to Northwind.

Additional Connection Object Properties

At this point, you've seen the most important attributes that can be placed in a connection string (server, database, and integrated security above; provider, data source and extended properties in earlier examples), but there are numerous others that you can read about in the MSDN documentation. In this section, we'll take a look at two that work exclusively with SQL Server databases: connection timeout and packet size.

By default, the size of the packets of data that the database will send to ADO.NET is 8,192 bytes, which is sometimes rather more than you need. Imagine a connection that will only be used to request the results of a query that yields a simple True or False value, or one person's name and membership number – this data would take up very little space, and using a smaller packet size would likely increase performance. We can make the packet size as low as 512 bytes, like this:

```
Dim strConnection As String = "server=(local)\NetSDK; database=Northwind; " & _
                              "integrated security=true; packet size=512;"
```

Like the server and database connection string attributes, packet size has an associated connection object property – PacketSize – that will be set to 512 as a result of this statement.

Another default setting is that ADO.NET will wait 15 seconds for a connection to open. That time must be adequate to find the server, get a confirmation that the database exists, confirm security permissions, and establish the communication pathway. If these tasks are *not* complete in 15 seconds, then the attempt will time out and an error will be generated. This is plenty for most installations – imagine the problems we would face if it were not enough! – but in the rare event that it's not (perhaps because we need to connect over a Wide Area Network (WAN) to a SQL Server in another location), we can increase it using the following syntax:

```
Dim strConnection As String = "server=(local)\NetSDK; database=Northwind; " & _
                              "integrated security=true; connection timeout=30;"
```

Specifying a timeout value in the connection string like this will result in a change in the value of the read-only SqlConnection.ConnectionTimeout property.

Additional Connection Object Methods

Unlike the majority of connection object properties, ConnectionString is *not* read-only. However, if you do decide to make changes to the connection string, they won't take effect until you've closed and reopened the connection – a potentially time-consuming process. A partial fix for this problem – at least for SQL Server database users – is provided by the SqlConnection.ChangeDatabase() method, which allows us to switch to a different database on the same server without closing the connection. In use, it looks something like this:

```
Dim strConnection As String = "server=(local)\NetSDK; database=Northwind; " & _
                              "integrated security=true;"
Dim objConnection As New SqlConnection(strConnection)

Dim strSQL As String = "SELECT * FROM Employees"
Dim objCommand As New SqlCommand(strSQL, objConnection)
```

```
objConnection.Open()

' Perform some operation on the current (Northwind) database

objConnection.ChangeDataBase("Master")

' Perform some operation on the Master database

objConnection.Close()
```

The OleDbConnection and SqlConnection objects have just a few more methods that you can read about in the MSDN documentation. Among the most important is BeginTransaction(), which we'll be looking at in Chapter 9.

Connecting to XML Sources

As you know, SQL is a standard language used by almost every platform to communicate between data providers and data consumers – the fact that ADO.NET aims to allow SQL queries to be run against as many different data sources as possible is testament to that. On the other hand, XML is becoming the universal *format* for data transfer – more and more organizations are using it because it's expressive, it's easy to read (it's just text, after all), and it's easy to manipulate or transform for different tasks. It's also the format in which data is transferred between entities in the .NET architecture.

Given all of the above, it's hardly surprising that the ADO.NET objects also provide ways to read from and write to XML files with some ease. We'll take a look at reading XML data in this chapter, and at writing it in Chapter 5, when we discuss datasets in detail.

> *More thorough explorations of SQL and XML may be found in* Beginning SQL Programming *(ISBN 1-861001-80-0), and* Beginning XML *(ISBN 1-861003-41-2) respectively, also from Wrox Press.*

Extracting data from an XML file using ADO.NET is fairly straightforward, and involves just three steps. First, we need to identify the location on disk of the XML file. Second, we need to create a System.Data.DataSet object and use its powerful ReadXml() method to fill the dataset from the XML file. Third, we have to designate the dataset as the source of data for a DataGrid control, and bind.

Depending on whether and how you've worked with XML before, you may have written code for parsing through XML files that involved loops inside other loops. With ADO.NET, there's no need: the DataSet object takes care of that for us. All of the operations that we'll perform on datasets in Chapter 5 apply to DataSet objects that could have been filled from an XML file as easily as they could have been filled from a relational database. It's another example of how ADO.NET insulates us from having to learn different techniques (other than connection strings) for different data sources.

The following diagram shows ADO.NET objects interacting with an XML file. The DataSet can use its ReadXml() method to retrieve information without the need for a data adapter, or a command or connection object. Since the DataSet object is universal, there are no separate OleDb... or Sql... versions, and no provider (of either variety) is at work.

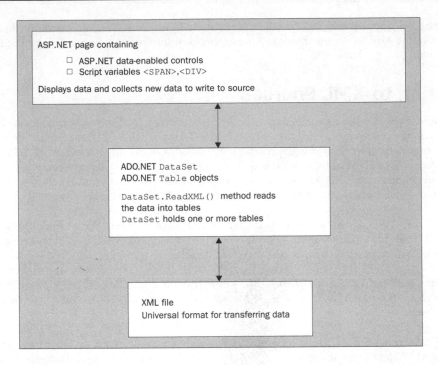

XML Connection Syntax

Without connection strings and connection objects, the process of getting data from an XML file becomes – for the ADO.NET programmer, at least – a remarkably straightforward one. As described above, the first step in the retrieval code is to identify the name and location of the XML file, like this:

```
Dim strXMLFile As String = "MyDrive:MyPath\MyFile.xml"
```

Secondly, we create a `DataSet` object, and use its `ReadXml()` method to read the contents of the XML file into the dataset. We'll discuss the `DataSet` class in more detail in the next chapter, but for now you can consider it to be like a table (or rather, a set of tables) of data that's held in the memory of your Internet Information Server, disconnected from its source.

```
Dim objDataSet As New DataSet()
objDataSet.ReadXml(strXMLFile)
```

Conceptually, the third step is no different from our studies of displaying Access and SQL data: we set the source for the data grid, and then perform the bind, as follows:

```
dgNameList.DataSource = objDataSet.Tables(0).DefaultView
dgNameList.DataBind()
```

The expression on the right-hand side of the assignment statement simply identifies the default representation of the data contained in the first table of the dataset, which is where the contents of the XML file will have been placed.

Try It Out – Reading Data from an XML File

As ever, the process of reading XML data using ADO.NET is best demonstrated through an example. In this one, we'll write a few short XML files, and see what happens when we read data from each of them.

1. Create a simple XML file named `Server_inventory.xml`. You can either type it in or download it from **www.wrox.com**, but you should save it in the `C:\BegASPNETdb\datastores` folder that we created earlier.

```xml
<?xml version="1.0" standalone="yes"?>
<ServerFarm>
  <Server>
    <ServerID>11</ServerID>
    <CPU>P3</CPU>
    <RAM>256</RAM>
  </Server>
  <Server>
    <ServerID>22</ServerID>
    <CPU>P4</CPU>
    <RAM>512</RAM>
  </Server>
</ServerFarm>
```

2. Next, create a text file called `XML_connection.aspx` in the `ch03` folder, and fill it with the following code:

```aspx
<%@ Import namespace="System.Data" %>

<html>
  <head>
    <title>Read XML file</title>
  </head>
  <body>
    <H2>Read XML file</H2>
      <asp:Label id="lblXMLFileName" runat="server" /><BR/><BR/>
      <asp:DataGrid id="dgServers" runat="server" />
  </body>
</html>

<script language="VB" runat="server">
Sub Page_Load(Source As Object, E As EventArgs)
  Dim strXMLFile As String = "C:\BegASPNETdb\datastores\" & _
                             "Server_inventory.xml"
  lblXMLFileName.Text = strXMLFile

  Dim objDataSet As New DataSet()
  objDataSet.ReadXml(strXMLFile)

  dgServers.DataSource = objDataSet.Tables(0).DefaultView
  dgServers.DataBind()
```

```
End Sub
</script>
```

3. When you browse to this new page, you should see the name and contents of the XML file presented neatly:

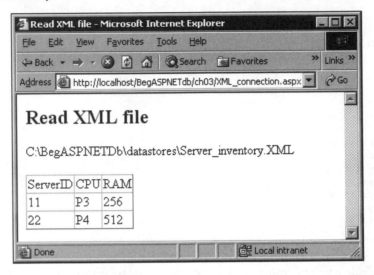

Because we've used neither SQL Server nor Access here, we only had to import one namespace at the top of this file: the generic `System.Data`. Other than that, this part of the exercise should have held few surprises, and we can go on to look at another example with some confidence.

4. Let's see what happens with a potentially more problematic XML file: one whose elements include attributes. Save the `Server_inventory.xml` file with a new name (say, `Server_inventory_2.xml`), and within the new file change the `ServerID` element into an attribute, reorganizing the data as follows:

```
<?xml version="1.0" standalone="yes"?>
<ServerFarm>
  <Server ServerID="33">
    <CPU>P3</CPU>
    <RAM>256</RAM>
  </Server>
  <Server ServerID="44">
    <CPU>P4</CPU>
    <RAM>512</RAM>
  </Server>
</ServerFarm>
```

5. Make the small change to the ASPX file that will allow you to read the new XML file (`Server_inventory.xml` should become `Server_inventory_2.xml`), and load it into your browser. This is what you should see:

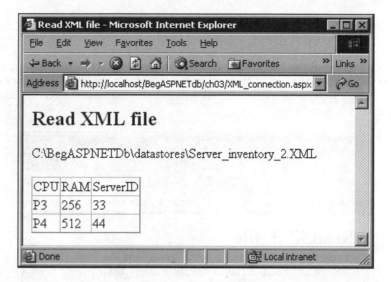

The two obvious results of our change here are that while the format of the DataGrid remains the same (implying that the ReadXml() method can deal with attributes as easily as it can deal with elements), the ServerID column moves to the right-hand end of the table (implying that elements are processed before attributes).

Limitations of Connections to XML Data

Before we leave this section, it's worth mentioning that the DataSet.ReadXml() method can run into difficulties when the XML file in question contains more than one 'level' of items (not counting the root as a level). There's no problem if we have a <Car> tag, and within that we have tags for <Model> and <Color> – but if we were to have a <ColorList>, and then many instances of <Color>, we would have issues. For example, consider the following XML file (named Multiple_levels.xml in the downloads).

```xml
<?xml version="1.0" standalone="yes"?>
<CarList>
  <Car>
    <ModelName>AlphaFast</ModelName>
    <Doors>2</Doors>
    <ColorList>
      <Color>Argent</Color>
      <Color>Blue</Color>
      <Color>Chrome</Color>
    </ColorList>
  </Car>
  <Car>
    <ModelName>BetaQuick</ModelName>
    <Doors>3</Doors>
    <ColorList>
      <Color>Deep Red</Color>
      <Color>Emerald</Color>
      <Color>Flying Yellow</Color>
    </ColorList>
```

```
    </Car>
  </CarList>
```

The *logical* output here would be for the DataSet to format the DataGrid with a grid of <Color> items within the <ColorList> cell of each row – but this would rapidly descend into a rather untidy browser view. Instead, ADO.NET and ASP.NET will merely condense the second-level tags into a new column called Car_Id, as below:

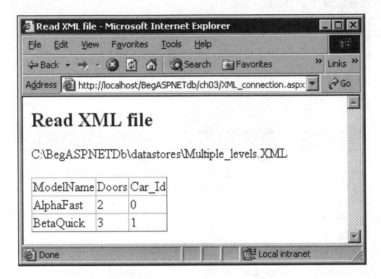

We'll have more to say about connecting to and manipulating data sources in Chapter 5, when we cover the DataSet object in more detail.

Getting Schema Information (OLE DB)

Earlier in the chapter, we talked about some of the methods exposed by ADO.NET connection objects, but we deliberately weren't exhaustive. In this section, we'll take a look at a method that's supported only by the OleDbConnection class, but which can be enormously useful – especially when you're working with a data source whose precise structure you don't know.

If you always have good documentation about all of the data sources that you ever use, then not only will you be incredibly lucky, but also you'll never need to read this section. More likely, however, is that there will be inadequate (if any) documentation, and the guy who knows about the database will have left the company, using his stock-option wealth for a year's windsurfing in Bali. Fortunately, we can use an ADO.NET connection to dig up quite a bit of information about the **schema**, or structure, of the database being connected to.

> **Just to reiterate, this technique is for OLE DB providers only. If you're connected to a SQL Server database (or some other enterprise DBMS), you can use standard SQL procedures for gathering schema information.**

To get hold of this information, the syntax for connecting to the database is the same as we've studied so far, and we use DataSet and DataTable objects rather as we did with our XML connections. The difference comes when we fill these data containers with the results of a connection object method called GetOleDbSchemaTable(), which reads the *structure* of the connected database. To see how this works, we can start by looking at the syntax for getting a list of the tables in a given database. Let's say that we've set up a connection with the following lines of code:

```
Dim strConnection As String = "provider=Microsoft.Jet.OLEDB.4.0;" & _
                    "data source=C:\BegASPNETdb\datastores\nwind.mdb"
Dim objConnection As New OleDbConnection(strConnection)
```

Given that, the next step is not to instantiate a command object, but to create a DataSet and a DataTable object:

```
Dim dsSchema As DataSet = New DataSet()
Dim dtSchema As DataTable
```

Then, we open the connection and employ GetOleDbSchemaTable() to read the schema information into the DataTable object. Note the italicized *SchemaInformation* below; here we can substitute the specific type of information we want to extract, such as "Tables":

```
objConnection.Open()
dtSchema = objConnection.GetOleDbSchemaTable( _
                    OleDbSchemaGuid.SchemaInformation, Nothing)
```

Finally, we add the table to our DataSet, and use that as the source of information for a DataGrid:

```
dsSchema.Tables.Add(dtSchema)
dgSchema.DataSource = dsSchema
dgSchema.DataBind()
objConnection.Close()
```

The OleDbSchemaGuid class has static members that specify almost three dozen different kinds of information that can be extracted from the database; the most frequently used of these include:

❑ Tables

❑ Columns

❑ Views

❑ Indexes

❑ Procedures

❑ Foreign_Keys

❑ Primary_Keys

❑ Table_Constraints

❑ Check_Constraints

Additional information may be found in sections of the ADO.NET Programmer's Reference *(ISBN 1-86100-5-58-X), or in the MSDN documentation.*

Try It Out – Discovering Schema Information

Let's imagine for now that the only thing we know about the Northwind database is that it exists in C:\BegASPNETdb\datastores, and that there is no password. Our goal is to find out the names of tables, and the columns within those tables.

1. Create a new page in the Ch03 folder named Schema.aspx and type (or download) the following code:

```
<%@ Import namespace="System.Data" %>
<%@ Import namespace="System.Data.Oledb" %>

<html>
  <head>
    <title> Discovering Schema Information</title>
  </head>
  <body>
    <h3>Discovering Schema Information</h3>
    <asp:DataGrid id="dgSchema" runat="server" />
  </body>
</html>

<script language="VB" runat="server">
Sub Page_Load(Source As Object, E As EventArgs)
  Dim strConnection As String = "provider=Microsoft.Jet.OLEDB.4.0;" & _
                     "data source=C:\BegASPNETdb\datastores\nwind.mdb"
  Dim objConnection As New OleDbConnection(strConnection)

  Dim dsSchema As DataSet = New DataSet()
  Dim dtSchema As DataTable

  objConnection.Open()
  dtSchema = objConnection.GetOleDbSchemaTable( _
                     OleDbSchemaGuid.Tables, Nothing)

  dsSchema.Tables.Add(dtSchema)
  dgSchema.DataSource = dsSchema
  dgSchema.DataBind()
  objConnection.Close()
End Sub
</script>
```

2. Load up the page, and check the output for the tables that we've been working with. (Note that the tables whose names begin with MSys are for the internal use of Access, and are normally hidden from our view.)

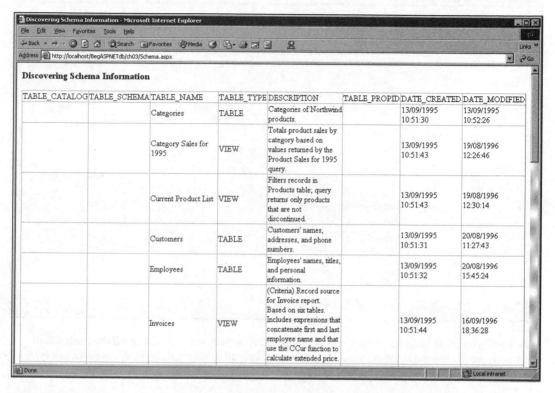

3. If you want to explore the columns instead of the tables, it's easy – just change one part of one line:

```
dtSchema = objConnection.GetOleDbSchemaTable( _
                OleDbSchemaGuid.Columns, Nothing)
```

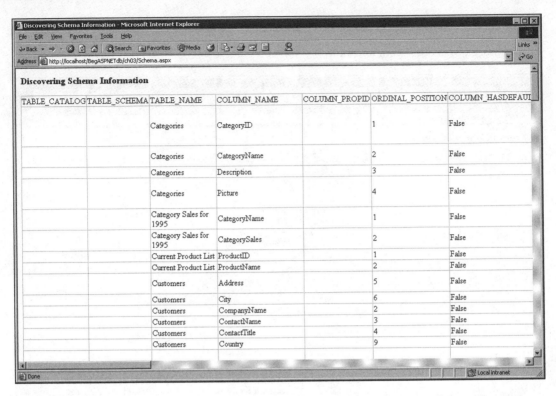

When you view this last page, there will be some delay – Access is searching *all* the tables, and eventually sends information on some 150 columns, spread across a dozen tables. Fortunately, we get the rows sorted by table name, so that all the columns of one table are adjacent to one another.

How It Works

The technique for getting schema information is not difficult, even though we're not entirely familiar with the `DataSet` and `DataTable` classes. Having created the connection as normal, our first task is to create an instance of each:

```
Dim dsSchema As DataSet = New DataSet()
Dim dtSchema As DataTable
```

Then, we execute a method of the connection object to get the schema (the first parameter specifies the information set we want: tables, columns, foreign keys, etc.). That information is fed directly into our table object.

```
objConnection.Open()
dtSchema = objConnection.GetOleDbSchemaTable( _
                    OleDbSchemaGuid.Tables, Nothing)
```

Because a `DataTable` object cannot serve directly as the data source for a `DataGrid`, we must add our table to a `DataSet` object:

```
dsSchema.Tables.Add(dtSchema)
```

The rest we are familiar with: just set and bind the dataset as the data source for the `DataGrid`.

```
dgSchema.DataSource = dsSchema
dgSchema.DataBind()
objConnection.Close()
```

Of course, once you've used this technique to extract the schema, you still have a job ahead of you to put all of the data into context – but at least you have the pieces of the puzzle. I find that extracting schema information can be useful even with databases I know, in order to verify the exact spelling of a column or a procedure.

A Better Connection String

Before we leave this chapter behind, we can take a step that will make things a great deal easier as we proceed. The trouble with specifying connection strings as we've been doing it so far is that if we were ever to change the location of our data sources, we'd have to change every ASPX file as a result. A more durable alternative is to define all our connection strings in a single location, and then to refer to them from our ASPX code. That location is the `web.config` file, and we can see how the technique works with the help of a quick demonstration.

Try It Out – Connection Strings and Application Settings

For this example, we're going to go back to the first ASPX file we wrote in this chapter, and improve it a little. First, though, we need to add some lines to `web.config`.

1. Open up your `webroot\web.config` file, and make the following changes:

```
<?xml version="1.0" encoding="utf-8" ?>
<configuration>
 <system.web>
  <customErrors mode="Off" />
  <compilation debug="true"/>
 </system.web>
 <appSettings>
  <add key="NWind"
    value="server=(local)\NetSDK; database=Northwind; integrated security=true;"/>
 </appSettings>
</configuration>
```

2. Then, having set up this key-value pair, you can refer to it from the ASPX file (copied and named `SQLServer_connection_2.aspx`) like this:

```
<script language="VB" runat="server">
Sub Page_Load(Source As Object, E As EventArgs)
   Dim strConnection As String = ConfigurationSettings.AppSettings("NWind")
   Dim objConnection As New SqlConnection(strConnection)
```

3. With these changes in place, you should be able to browse to the new file and see exactly the same results we had before. The difference is that you can now add or make changes to the connection strings in the `web.config` file, giving you a single file to administrate.

How It Works

The key-value pairs that you define in an `<appSettings>` element of the `web.config` file are available to all of the ASPX files in `webroot`, and in any subfolders. In our code, we can use the `AppSettings` indexed property of the `System.Configuration.ConfigurationSettings` class to get hold of the values for use in our ASP.NET pages. There is no limit to the number of strings that it's possible to define in this way, and the `<appSettings>` element clearly has utility beyond the means for which we've used it here. Any time you have potentially volatile data that's required by a number of files on your web server, storing it in `web.config` like this is a good idea.

We'll be using this technique for specifying connection strings as our preferred option throughout the rest of the book.

Common Mistakes

When I'm teaching, I keep a log of the errors that students make in our labs. The following are things that you might want to recheck if you're having problems.

❑ **Specifying the data source incorrectly**. Depending on the database in question, the correct name, path, user ID, and password may need to be specified. The ADO.NET error message, though, is both polite and obvious – it will be something like Could not find file 'C:\BegASPNETdb\datastores\Southwind.mdb'.

❑ **Forgetting to specify namespaces, or doing so with the wrong syntax**. This creates an error such as Type OleDbConnection not found.

❑ **Using the wrong object**. Sometimes, people will try to use `strConnection.Open()` instead of `objConnection.Open()`. Once the connection object is created (`objConnection`), it is used in the rest of the page. The variable holding the connection string is only used to instantiate the connection object. This mistake produces errors such as The Open method is not a member of 'String'.

❑ **Trying to use unopened connection objects**. Connection objects must be opened (not just instantiated) before they can be used. This mistake leads to clear error messages such as To use XXX object your Connection object must be Open.

❑ **Skipping the New keyword when declaring the connection object**. This produces an error message such as Array bounds cannot appear in type specifiers.

❑   Typing errors in the syntax of the connection string. You need to be careful here, as the syntax is different from normal Visual Basic syntax (spaces are allowed, arguments are separated by semicolons). This type of mistake tends to yield unhelpful error messages pointing to the `Connection.Open()` line, rather than the line where the connection object is declared. The most common ones are as follows:

> ❑   Not putting a space in `data source` yields a message such as Could not find installable ISAM, pointing to the `Connection.Open()` line.

> ❑   Using a comma instead of a semicolon to separate arguments yields an error message such as No error information available, pointing to the `Connection.Open()` line.

> ❑   Forgetting a semicolon between arguments also yields an error message such as No error information available, pointing to the `Connection.Open()` line. This mistake might occur when you're concatenating or appending more than one argument across several lines of code.

Summary

All operations that involve data on an ASP.NET page start with a connection to the data source. Making a connection requires you to specify the data source itself, how to translate the data from that source into the ADO.NET objects you're going to use, and any necessary security information.

ADO.NET provides four different kinds of connection. The first uses the SQL Server .NET data provider, which contains a specialized set of code for connecting to Microsoft SQL Server (version 7 or higher). If you're using SQL Server as your data source, this should be your first choice.

The second type of connection, OLE DB, is very general, and allows us to connect to a wide variety of data sources – in this chapter alone, we've used it to connect to Access and Excel. We've also seen how to create a connection simply by specifying a provider that's appropriate for our data source. Remember, though, that an OLE DB connection pays a performance price in order to maintain capability with a broad range of data sources. For that reason, you should only use an OLE DB connection if there's no specialized connection available.

The third type of connection is for ODBC databases, and is not covered in this book. However, the ODBC .NET data provider supplies broadly the same functionality as the OLE DB version.

The fourth kind of 'connection' provides access to XML files or streams. This is not a true connection in the sense of the others we've looked at – there's no connection object – but the ability exists to generate a data stream that can be used by the ADO.NET objects.

In this chapter, then, we've talked in depth about how to connect to various data stores. In the next two chapters, we'll examine two ways to bring data through the connection that we've touched upon already: the data reader and dataset objects. At the same time, we'll look at some more ways to display data to your users.

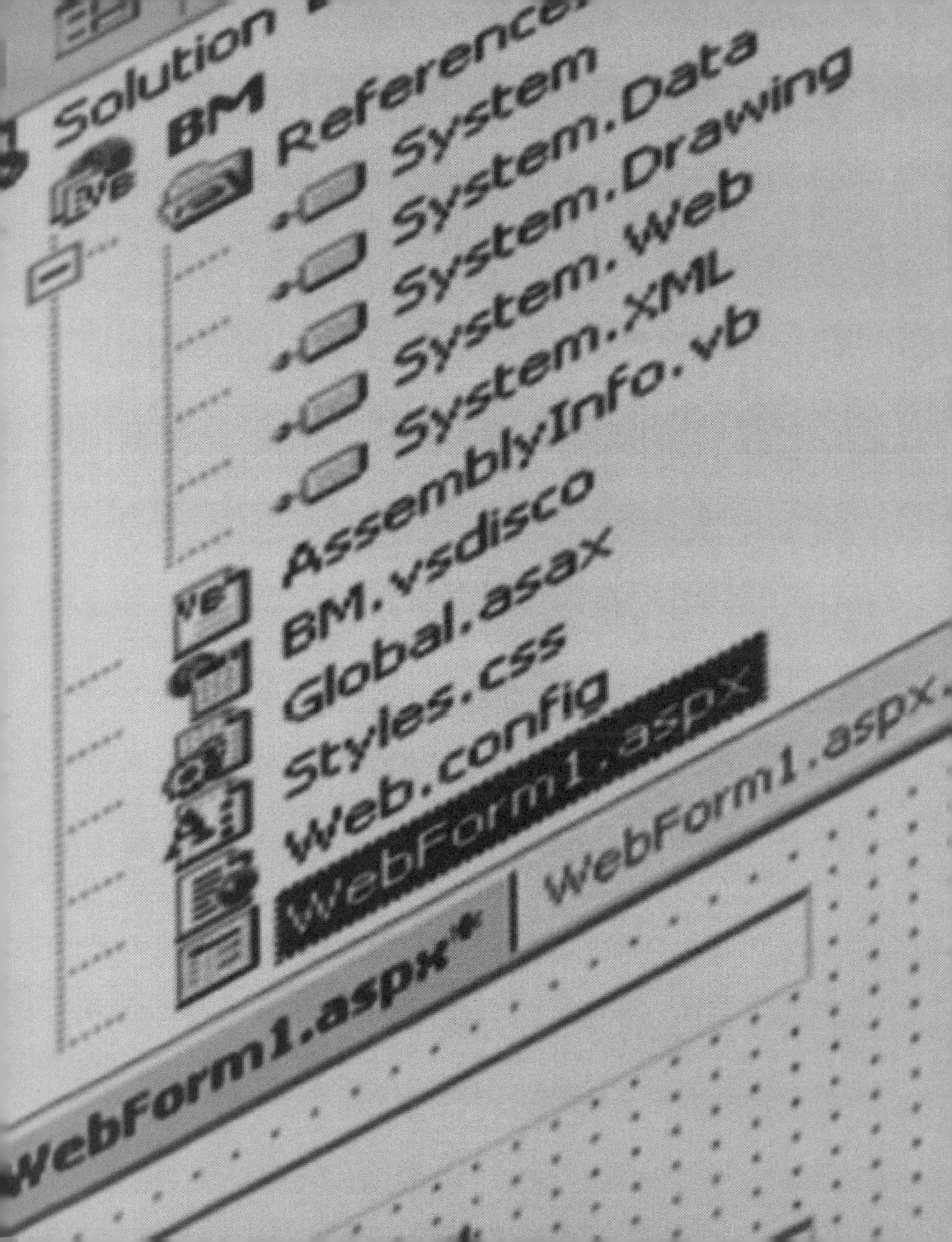

Solution

BM

References
System
System.Data
System.Drawing
System.Web
System.XML
AssemblyInfo.vb
BM.vsdisco
Global.asax
Styles.css
Web.config
WebForm1.aspx

WebForm1.aspx* | WebForm1.aspx

Data Readers,
Command Objects,
and Web Server Controls

Having spent the last chapter focusing on how to connect to different data stores, we now need to look more carefully at our options for reading data, and displaying it on a web page. As you now know, ADO.NET has two kinds of object for bringing data in through a connection: data reader classes, and the DataSet class. Once you've retrieved the data, ADO.NET offers numerous presentation options.

In this chapter, we'll start with a comparison of the two approaches to working with data. After that, we'll focus on data readers (leaving DataSet for the next chapter), and finally we'll discuss in detail the ASP.NET web server controls that display data on the page. In particular, we will extend the discussion we had in the previous chapter concerning the DataGrid, a powerful, flexible, yet easy-to-use tool for displaying data on an ASP.NET page. The running order looks something like this:

❑ The basic theory of reading and displaying information

❑ A comparison of data reader objects and the DataSet object

❑ An introduction to ADO.NET command objects

❑ ADO.NET data reader objects

❑ Four data controls that display multiple values:

    ❑ List boxes and drop-down list boxes

    ❑ Groups of radio (option) buttons

    ❑ Multiple selection controls, including check boxes and list boxes

    ❑ The ASP.NET DataGrid, and some basic formatting

Handling and Displaying Data in ADO.NET and ASP.NET

Regardless of its size or complexity, an ASP.NET page that uses data via ADO.NET will have three basic sections of code:

❑   Code to create a connection to a data source

❑   Code to read from and write to the data source, and modify data

❑   Code to display data on the ASP.NET-generated page

In the last chapter, we focused on step one: the connection. In this chapter and the one that follows it, we'll go into much more detail about steps two and three.

The second step in particular covers a lot of bases – it can be very simple, or quite complex. Broadly speaking, those two extremes will be addressed in our ASP.NET pages by data reader and dataset objects respectively; which one you choose depends on a fairly simple decision-making process. In a nutshell, you'll use data reader objects when:

❑   You are only *reading* data

❑   The data retrieved from the store is ready to be displayed without further processing

And use DataSet objects (along with helper data adapter objects) when:

❑   You might modify (edit or add new) data in the data source

❑   You want to modify the data after reading, and prior to displaying it. For example, you may want to read data into several tables, or create relationships between the data in multiple tables. You may want to constrain columns, or create multiple tables of data from multiple connections.

> A relationship **in a database describes how information from one table links to information in one or more other tables. Careful use of relationships greatly reduces the storage space, inconsistencies and maintenance costs of a database. More information on relationships is available in any database text, including** *Beginning SQL Server 2000 Programming* **(ISBN 1-8610015-23-7), also from Wrox Press.**

As stated above, this chapter will focus on data readers, leaving dataset objects until the next chapter.

Command Objects

In the last chapter, we used command objects without ever fully discussing them; it's now time for us to examine them in more detail. You'll recall from our diagrams that each .NET data provider provides its own implementation of a command object – we saw and used both `SqlCommand` and `OleDbCommand`. In terms of their behavior and their members, however, the different command objects are very similar. Unless we state otherwise, any features that we ascribe to one of them in this discussion will be present in all.

A command object holds a definition of *what* to read to or write from the data store. It sits in the middle of our flow of tasks, between connecting and displaying. The command object and the data reader object (which we'll discuss next) work together: the command object defines what to read, while the data reader defines how to use the connection object to perform the read. The most common definitions of what to read or write include:

❑ An SQL statement that reads some of the data of a table (some fields and/or some records)

❑ The name of a table in the data store

❑ An SQL statement (or stored procedure) that runs a stored procedure that returns data

❑ An SQL statement that writes to the data store

When the command object is instantiated, ADO.NET requires us to supply two arguments. The first is a string that holds the actual SQL statement (or the table name), and the second is the connection object. If we assume a connection object named `objConnection`, then we can write the following examples for SQL Server and OLE DB respectively:

```
Dim strSQL As String = "SELECT MyColumn FROM MyTable"
Dim objCommand As New SqlCommand(strSQL, objConnection)
```

```
Dim strSQL As String = "SELECT MyColumn FROM MyTable"
Dim objCommand As New OleDbCommand(strSQL, objConnection)
```

The default use of the first argument to the command object's constructor, which will be assigned to its `CommandText` property, is as an SQL statement. If you want to use a table name, or a stored procedure name, then you must change the related `CommandType` property, as follows:

```
' Read an entire table
Dim strSQL_Suppliers As String = "MyTable"
Dim objConnection As New OleDbConnection(strConnection)
Dim objCommand As New OleDbCommand(strSQL_Suppliers, objConnection)
objCommand.CommandType = CommandType.TableDirect
```

> **CommandType** can only be set to **CommandType.TableDirect** when you're using the OLE DB .NET data provider. The option is not available with the SQL Server .NET data provider.

```
' Execute a stored procedure (or a query in Access)
Dim strSQL_Suppliers As String = "MyStoredProc"
Dim objConnection As New SqlConnection(strConnection)
Dim objCommand As New SqlCommand(strSQL_Suppliers, objConnection)
objCommand.CommandType = CommandType.StoredProcedure
```

A command object's `CommandType` property can be set to one of three different values. `CommandType.TableDirect` and `CommandType.StoredProcedure` are used above; the third is the default value: `CommandType.Text`.

In this chapter, we'll just use SQL statements to read data. However, SQL can do more than just select data: it enables us to perform complicated sorting and selecting, to provide statistical information on data (such as maximums and averages), and to provide aggregate answers (such as, say, the ten records with the largest values for a particular field). To learn these kinds of syntax, consult a SQL text – for example, Beginning SQL Programming *(ISBN 1-861001-80-0), by the same authors as this book.*

Data Reader Objects

Data readers form one of the two kinds of object that define how we read data from a connection. Like the command object, they come in different versions for the different data providers, but in use they're so similar that we can consider their common functionality without fear of having to issue countless provisos. Data readers have three characteristics to keep in mind:

❑ Data readers can *only* read data. They don't provide for editing, creation, or deletion of the data in records.

❑ Data readers can only navigate forwards through data. Once you've moved to the 'next' record, there's no going back to the previous one, short of executing the SQL query all over again.

❑ Data readers do not hold data in the memory of IIS – the data goes straight to the display object (for example, the DataGrid).

By contrast, DataSet *objects create a copy of the data in the web server's memory that can be written to, or navigated around. We'll discuss* DataSet *objects in detail in the next chapter.*

The **read-only** constraint of data readers is both a blessing and a curse. The good part is that data readers are very fast and efficient in terms of the resources they consume. They're also very easy to use – the data you read goes straight to a display object such as a DataGrid. The downside, of course, is that if you *need* to edit, create, or delete data, you cannot use a data reader.

Although the fact that a data reader reads data **forward-only** sounds restrictive, in practice it's not too severe. The limitation only applies to the set of records that's defined by the command object's CommandText property (your table name or SQL statement). If your command object defines a whole table to read, then you'll get the records from first to last, as they appear in the table – but if you use a string such as "SELECT * FROM Employees ORDER BY LastName", then the data reader will go forward through these records alone, which will have already been sorted from A to Z when they were supplied by the database.

Similarly, if your CommandText is, say, "SELECT * FROM Employees ORDER BY LastName DESC", then your forward-only data reader will actually be reading out the names in reverse alphabetical order. And you can include SQL clauses like TOP or UNIQUE to get exactly the records you want. Once you understand SQL, the world is your oyster: you can supply the data to the data reader in any order, and thus overcome the constraint to a great degree. In the end, forward-only is just about navigation – you cannot move back and forth, or to a specific record, once you have read through the data.

There are two further strategies for data manipulation that can help to overcome the problems of the forward-only nature of data readers. First, you can write code to loop through the records as they are read, and apply modifications before they're displayed. Second, as you'll learn in the next chapter, there are ways to sort and select data after it has entered a DataGrid display control. Bear in mind, though, that neither of these strategies will have any effect on the data in the store – that's just not possible with a data reader.

Using a Data Reader

In the last chapter, we breezed over the actual use of data readers by employing them in the simplest way we could – we just executed the command object's ExecuteReader() method, and assigned the result straight to the DataSource property of a DataGrid control, leaving the latter to do the rest. In fact, however, this is an entirely typical way of using a data reader – we don't call its constructor, and we tend to leave the job of 'doing the reading' to another object. The purpose of this section is to spell out how data reader objects work, and to detail their close relationship with command objects.

Let's look again at the code we were using in the last chapter to place information from the Northwind database in our web pages:

```
    objConnection.Open()
    dgNameList.DataSource = objCommand.ExecuteReader()
    dgNameList.DataBind()
    objConnection.Close()
End Sub
```

This is actually an illustration of the simplest possible case: we've got just one web server control (the DataGrid object), one source of data, and one SQL query to run on that data. The data reader object is created in the second line, and destroyed when the DataGrid object goes out of scope at the end of the event handler. This neatly conceals the fact that data readers have 'open' and 'close' semantics (just like connection objects), as a slightly more involved example will demonstrate.

When you're reading data, a common requirement is to find out the number of records returned by an SQL query, for use later when we come to present the data on the page. An easy way to achieve this is to execute two SQL queries against the same data, the first being a COUNT, and the second actually doing the SELECT. The following listing assumes that we have two DataGrids named dgACount and dgAData. Notice that after the first read, we close the data reader; and after the second, we close the connection object.

```
    Dim strConnection As String = "..."
    Dim objConnection As New SqlConnection(strConnection)

    Dim strSQLcount As String
    strSQLcount = "SELECT COUNT(CategoryID) FROM Categories"
    Dim objCommand As New SqlCommand(strSQLcount, objConnection)

    objConnection.Open()
```

```
' SQL to count
Dim objReader As SqlDataReader = objCommand.ExecuteReader()
dgCount.DataSource = objReader
dgCount.DataBind()
objReader.Close()

' SQL to read data
Dim strSQLdata As String
strSQLdata = "SELECT * FROM Categories"
objCommand.CommandText = strSQLdata
objReader = objCommand.ExecuteReader()
dgData.DataSource = objReader
dgData.DataBind()

objConnection.Close()
```

Executing two queries allows us to reuse both the command object and the data reader object, but we have to remember to call the reader's `Close()` method in between the calls to `ExecuteReader()` – if we don't, we'll get an error that says, "There is already an open data reader associated with this connection." (Re)opening the data reader object is dealt with by the `ExecuteReader()` method itself.

Try It Out – Advanced use of Data Readers

We're going to use this example to pull together a few of the things that we've discussed already in this chapter. Let's imagine that we've been asked to create a page that shows a list of all the products sold by Northwind in 1997, and a count of all the records in the report. This is not *quite* as difficult as it sounds, since the SQL Server version of the Northwind database has a view that will retrieve precisely this information; it's called "Product Sales for 1997".

1. Create a new page named `Datareader.aspx` in your ch04 folder. Then add the following code (or download it from www.wrox.com).

```
<%@ Import namespace="System.Data" %>
<%@ Import namespace="System.Data.SqlClient" %>

<html>
  <head>
    <title>Data Reader</title>
  </head>
  <body>
    <h1>Data Reader</h1>
    Total Products listed =
    <asp:DataGrid id="dgCount" runat="server"
                  BorderWidth="0" ShowHeader="False" />

    <br/>
    <asp:DataGrid id="dgData" runat="server" />
  </body>
</html>

<script language="VB" runat="server">
Sub Page_Load(Source As Object, E As EventArgs)
  Dim strConnection As String = ConfigurationSettings.AppSettings("NWind")
```

```
    Dim objConnection As New SqlConnection(strConnection)
    objConnection.Open()
' Get and display count
    Dim strSQLcount As String
    strSQLcount = "SELECT COUNT(ProductName) FROM [Product Sales for 1997]"

    Dim objCommand As New SqlCommand(strSQLcount, objConnection)
    Dim objReader As SqlDataReader = objCommand.ExecuteReader()

    dgCount.DataSource = objReader
    dgCount.DataBind()

    objReader.Close()

    ' Get and display output of procedure
    Dim strProcName As String
    strProcName = "SELECT * FROM [Product Sales for 1997]"
    objCommand.CommandText = strProcName
    objReader = objCommand.ExecuteReader()

    dgData.DataSource = objReader
    dgData.DataBind()

    objConnection.Close()
End Sub
</script>
```

2. When you take a look at the above page in your browser, you'll see this:

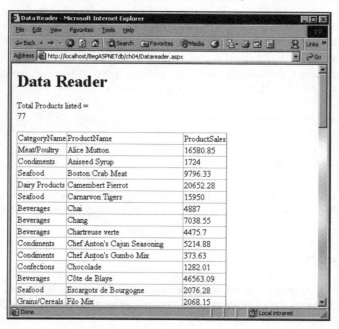

How It Works

In the HTML section, we simply create two DataGrids. The first of these will hold the count, and the second will hold the data that we'll report. It would be a little more efficient to hold the dgCount data in a label, but since we haven't looked at labels yet (you'll have to wait until the next chapter!), we just format our DataGrid to show neither borders nor a header.

```
<body>
  <h1>Data Reader</h1>
  Total Products listed =
  <asp:DataGrid id="dgCount" runat="server"
                 borderwidth=0 showheader=False />
  <br/>
  <asp:DataGrid id="dgData" runat="server" />
</body>
```

Looking at the script, there are two sections of code: the first gets the count, and the second the actual records. In the former, SQL Server does the counting, as it processes the SQL query. Note that in SQL, the COUNT keyword requires you to specify a field – we can't simply count the number of records (although you can also use the syntax COUNT(*)).

```
' Get and display count
Dim strSQLcount As String
strSQLcount = "SELECT COUNT(ProductName) FROM [Product Sales for 1997]"
```

Normally, we don't explicitly declare a data reader object, since one is created implicitly by the ExecuteReader() method. The downside of this, however, is that they're destroyed immediately after use. In this example, we intend to use the data reader object twice, which means that we must explicitly declare it so that it persists after the first use.

```
Dim objCommand As New SqlCommand(strSQLcount, objConnection)
Dim objReader As SqlDataReader = objCommand.ExecuteReader()
```

The single datum we retrieve is then put into the dgCount DataGrid:

```
dgCount.DataSource = objReader
dgCount.DataBind()
```

As we observed above, it's important, when using the same data reader object twice, to close it after the first use. Otherwise, when you use it the second time, you'll get an error stating that it's still open from the previous use.

```
objReader.Close()
```

Next, we begin work on the second task, which is to place the actual data into the second grid. We start by setting up the CommandText property, and notice that using view from a SQL Server database involves exactly the same syntax as using a table:

```
' Get and display output of procedure
Dim strProcName As String
strProcName = "SELECT * FROM [Product Sales for 1997]"
objCommand.CommandText = strProcName
```

We can then fill the data reader object, using our standard `ExecuteReader()` method. Note that there is no need to `Open()` it first.

```
objReader = objCommand.ExecuteReader()
```

Filling the second grid involves the same syntax as for the first grid:

```
dgData.DataSource = objReader
dgData.DataBind()
```

After the first use of the data reader object, we closed it. After the last use of the data reader, we can close the *connection*, safe in the knowledge that the data reader will automatically be cleaned up too.

```
objConnection.Close()
```

By no means does this example demonstrate the limits of data reader objects' capabilities. For example, and as mentioned above, it's possible to read the records returned from a query one by one, applying modifications to each before sending them to be displayed – the `Read()` method lies at the heart of this ability, as you'll soon see if you take a look at the Microsoft documentation. Our specialization in this book, however, is on ASP.NET's facilities for dealing with data, and it's with that in mind that we're going to move on.

Using Data-based Controls in ASP.NET

Now that we've discussed how to obtain data from a connection using a data reader object, we'll advance to the related subject of displaying the data on an ASP.NET page. We'll cover four data-aware controls that display multiple data values: list boxes, drop-down boxes, radio controls, and check boxes. After that, we'll examine the most commonly used options for the `DataGrid`, with the rest discussed in the next chapter. Also in the next chapter, we'll cover controls that display single values, such as text boxes and labels.

As you've seen in the examples we've looked at so far, ASP.NET offers an easy, three-step way to display data that comes from ADO.NET.

❑　Add an HTML element for a data-aware web server control (such as a text box or a data grid) to the ASP.NET page

❑　Assign an ADO.NET data reader object (or some other ADO.NET object that implements the `System.Collections.IEnumerable` interface) to the control's `DataSource` property

❑　Execute the `DataBind()` method of the control

Rather like the situation we had with data reader objects, we've already used these steps for binding to a `DataGrid` object, but we're going to take the time now to look at the technique in more detail.

If you're one of those people who spent three years on classic ASP, typing their fingernails down to the quick to display data, the ASP.NET web server controls are an answer to your prayers. In most cases, you don't have to perform any looping, and you never have to be involved in typing <TH>, <TR>, and <TD> elements.

To begin, we ought to investigate something that may have been bugging you since we first came across it: what, precisely, is binding? Given that we can simply set the control's `DataSource` property, isn't the process of binding redundant? In fact, the two steps address two different issues, as the following example will demonstrate.

Imagine that you have three text box controls that show three fields of the current record. The data source defines which *field* to display in each text box, while the binding means that the text box should display the value of the current record, and that the value should change when the current record changes. By having those three text boxes bound to the same record navigation system, when the user clicks to the next record, all three of the bound text boxes will show data from the next record.

When we're using a `DataGrid` that shows all the records at once, as we've been doing so far, this aspect of binding is not obvious – that's why we've had to clarify it. Later, however, we'll discuss `DataGrid` paging, which displays only some of the records at a time. In that situation, the fruits of binding are more obvious; it ensures that all fields display values from the same subset of records.

Keep in mind two basic points about the syntax for all of the data binding controls we'll discuss in this chapter. First, these controls are ASP.NET only – you *must* use the `<asp:>` syntax. Second, they *must* run at the server, so they need the attribute `runat="server"` in the tag.

ASP.NET provides about a dozen data-aware web server controls. These form two groups: those that display a single data value (such as a text box), and those that display multiple values (such as a list box or a data grid). The techniques for specifying the data to be displayed vary between the two types; we'll cover multiple-value controls in this chapter (because they're well suited for use with data readers), and we'll discuss the single-value controls in the next chapter (in conjunction with datasets). The most commonly used multiple-value controls are:

❑   `<asp:ListBox>` and `<asp:DropDownList>`

❑   `<asp:RadioButtonList>` and `<asp:CheckBoxList>`

❑   `<asp:DataGrid>`

And when adding any of these controls to your page, you need to follow the following four steps:

❑   Add the ASP.NET control to your page, and identify the methods that are to be run in response to user events (such as clicks on the control)

❑   Create your connection and command objects

❑   Set the `DataSource` property, and run `Bind()` for the data control

❑   Write code into the handlers for the clickable events

In the sections that follow, we'll practice this pattern in examples that illustrate each of these control types.

List Box and Drop-down List Controls

When you're creating a web site that accepts input from its users, it's important to do all that you can to minimize the number of mistakes they can make. One technique we can use is to reduce the amount of typing they have to do. For example, if you asked a visitor to enter the abbreviation for their state or country, you could expect to get numerous variations. You can imagine the kind of validation headache this creates, and the majority of visitors will leave your site rather than fool around trying to fix an error in their data. As an alternative, we'll focus in the next few sections on how to offer *choices* to your visitors, rather than having them type entries themselves.

In this particular section, we'll discuss the ListBox and DropDownList controls together, because they have essentially the same properties and syntax. The difference is in how many list items are shown.

❑ A ListBox control shows as many items as is set in its Rows property, and provides vertical scroll bars if there are additional items.

❑ A DropDownList control always shows one item, along with a drop-down arrow. When the arrow is clicked, the DropDownList control shows the items.

> There is no **Rows** property for a **DropDownList** control, so while it saves space at first, once expanded it takes up much more space than if you limited the number of rows in the **ListBox**.

Given our specific interest in this book, there's a further consideration here: we want the items in the `ListBox` to come from a data source. In other words, we'll choose a single field in the data store, and have our list control display the value of that field for every record we read from the data store. For the purposes of this illustration, we'll assume that we have a connection object, a command object, and a data reader object as described earlier in this chapter. Given those things, our SQL statement for filling the list control will generally be designed to select all or some of the records:

```
SELECT MyFieldToDisplay FROM MyTable
```

Or:

```
SELECT MyFieldToDisplay FROM MyTable WHERE SomeOtherField = Expression
```

Of course, we must add an ASP.NET `ListBox` control to the page – and since we're seeking input from the user, it must be placed inside a form, so that ASP.NET's postback feature will work. The addition of the `AutoPostBack` attribute to the element means that postback will take place immediately that a change in the selected item occurs, without the need to wait for a "submit" button to be pressed.

```
<html><body>
  <form runat="server">
    <asp:ListBox id="lbxEmployees" runat="server"
                 AutoPostBack="True" />
  </form>
</body></html>
```

With this in place, we can focus on the code that populates the list box with our values. We (implicitly) create a data reader with the command object's `ExecuteReader()` method, and declare it to be the source of data for the `ListBox`. We're going to allow our visitors to search through Northwind employees by their last names, so we also explicitly tell the `ListBox` that it needs to display the "`Lastname`" field by setting its `DataTextField` property.

```
If Not IsPostBack Then
  objConnection.Open()
    lbEmployees.DataSource = objCommand.ExecuteReader()
    lbEmployees.DataTextField = "Lastname"
    lbEMployees.DataBind()
  objConnection.Close()
End If
```

In addition to the two we've used above, there's a third important property that you may need: `DataValueField`. Unlike `DataTextField`, this won't appear in the list box, but it *will* be available in your code. To see why this could be useful, imagine that you have a list of food categories to display, but that once the visitor has clicked on one, you need to work with the category ID, not the name that was displayed. Using both properties, we get the best of both worlds: the `DataTextField` for the human interface, and the `DataValueField` for a more efficient programming interface.

It is absolutely crucial to place the code that populates the list box in an `If Not IsPostBack Then` block, so that it only runs once, when the page is first loaded. To see why, you need to understand that when a list box is first populated, its `SelectedIndex` and `SelectedItem` properties are set to -1 and `Nothing` respectively, indicating that no selection has been made. When the user makes a selection, the former changes to the position in the list of the selected item, while the latter represents the selected item itself. But when postback of the page occurs, repopulation of the list takes place, both properties revert to their original settings. In other words, you lose the user's selection.

The next question to be answered is how you *use* the visitor's selection from a list box. It turns out that it's possible to derive three different pieces of information from the selection. First, if you want to use the text that the visitor clicked on in the box, you can use the following expression, which will return the value from the field you set in the `DataTextField` property:

```
lbxMyListBox.SelectedItem.Text
```

In many cases, however, you won't want to work with the text the user clicked on, but with an associated value called the `DataValueField`, as discussed above. The second possibility, then, is to retrieve this value with the following:

```
lbxMyListBox.SelectedItem.Value
```

The third available piece of information is the index of each item in the list, via the `SelectedIndex` property. (Note that this is zero-based, so your largest index value will be one less then the number of items in the list.) The index number can be used in expressions such as the one below, where the index number is used to identify a particular item in the list:

```
lbxMyListBox.Items(x)
```

With this theory behind us, we can now move forward to using a list box in the context of an example.

Try It Out – Using List Boxes

The visitors to an internal Northwind web site might want to know a little more about particular employees. One way for us to deal with that would be to offer them a list box of employees' names, and to fill a `DataGrid` with more information when they select one. In this example, we'll do this in two steps. First, we'll display the last names of all the employees. Second, we'll write a WHERE clause that will use the visitor's selection to retrieve further information about that employee.

1. Create a new page in the `ch04` folder named `Using_listboxes.aspx`, and fill it as follows:

```
<%@ Import namespace="System.Data" %>
<%@ Import namespace="System.Data.SqlClient" %>

<html>
  <head>
    <title>Using a ListBox</title>
  </head>
  <body>
    <h3>Using a ListBox</h3>
    <form runat="server">
      <asp:ListBox id="lbxEmployees" runat="server"
                   AutoPostBack="True"
                   Rows="5"
                   OnSelectedIndexChanged="subListChange" />
    </form>
  </body>
</html>

<script language="VB" runat="server">
Sub Page_Load(Source As Object, E As EventArgs)
  If Not IsPostBack Then
    Dim strConnection As String = ConfigurationSettings.AppSettings("NWind")

    Dim strSQLforListBox As String = "SELECT LastName, EmployeeID " & _
                                     "FROM Employees ORDER BY LastName"

    Dim objConnection As New SqlConnection(strConnection)
    Dim objCommand As New SqlCommand(strSQLforListBox, objConnection)

    objConnection.Open()
    lbxEmployees.DataSource = objCommand.ExecuteReader()
    lbxEmployees.DataTextField = "LastName"
    lbxEmployees.DataValueField = "EmployeeID"
    lbxEmployees.DataBind()
    objConnection.Close()
  End If
End Sub

Sub subListChange(S As Object, E As EventArgs)
  Response.Write("subListChange triggered")
End Sub
</script>
```

2. View the above code in your browser, and you should see the following page. Try clicking on a name, and you'll see our diagnostic feedback indicate that a change in the index value of the selected item has occurred.

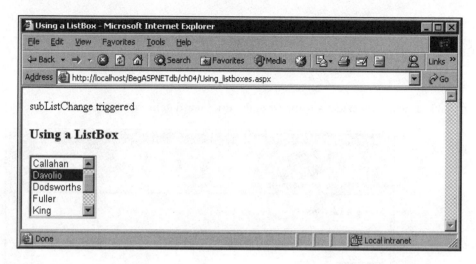

3. Next, we'll modify the code in the `subListChange()` method to do some actual work when a name is selected from the list. First, we will add a grid to display the information on the selected employee, as follows:

```
<body>
  <h3>Using a ListBox</h3>
  <form runat="server">
    <asp:ListBox id = "lbxEmployees"
                 AutoPostBack = "True"
                 Rows = "5"
                 OnSelectedIndexChanged = "subListChange"
                 runat = "server" />
    <br/><br/>
    <asp:DataGrid id="dgEmployee" runat="server" />
  </form>
</body>
```

4. Now we want to use the list box to select the information pertinent to just one employee, and to display that in the `DataGrid`. Comment out the diagnostic line, and add code as follows:

```
Sub subListChange(S As Object, E As EventArgs)
  ' Response.Write("subListChange triggered")
  Dim strConnection As String = ConfigurationSettings.AppSettings("NWind")

  Dim strSQLforGrid As String = "SELECT TitleOfCourtesy, FirstName, " & _
                "LastName, Country, Region, City, Notes " & _
                "FROM Employees WHERE EmployeeID = " & _
                lbxEmployees.SelectedItem.Value
```

109

```
    Dim objConnection As New SqlConnection(strConnection)
    Dim objCommand As New SqlCommand(strSQLforGrid, objConnection)

    objConnection.Open()
    dgEmployee.DataSource = objCommand.ExecuteReader()
    dgEmployee.DataBind()
    objConnection.Close()
End Sub
```

5. Now, when we select a name from the list, their details are displayed in a `DataGrid`:

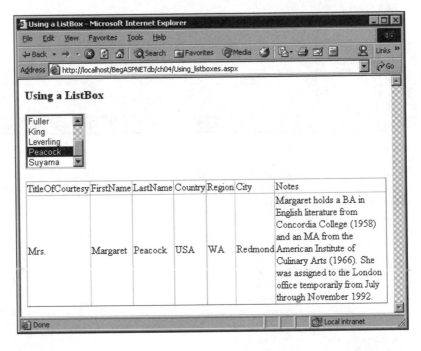

How It Works

This time, we added two ASP.NET web server controls to our page: one to display the list of employees, and another to show the employee information. We also chose to specify an `OnSelectedIndexChanged` event handler.

```
    <body>
      <h3>Using a ListBox</h3>
      <form runat="server">
```

```
                <asp:ListBox id="lbxEmployees" runat="server"
                             AutoPostBack="True"
                             Rows="5"
                             OnSelectedIndexChanged="subListChange" />
            <br/><br/>
            <asp:DataGrid id="dgEmployee" runat="server" />
        </form>
    </body>
```

With the controls in place, we use the code we studied earlier to create connection and command objects to populate the list box, and to bind the data to the list box. However, we only do this on the first occasion the page is displayed. Also, although we show the LastName (the DataTextField) to the user, for our programming purposes we will want to use the EmployeeID number (the DataValueField).

```
    Sub Page_Load(Source As Object, E As EventArgs)
      If Not IsPostBack Then
        Dim strConnection As String = ConfigurationSettings.AppSettings("NWind")

        Dim strSQLforListBox As String = "SELECT LastName, EmployeeID " & _
                                         "FROM Employees ORDER BY LastName"

        Dim objConnection As New SqlConnection(strConnection)
        Dim objCommand As New SqlCommand(strSQLforListBox, objConnection)

        objConnection.Open()
        lbxEmployees.DataSource = objCommand.ExecuteReader()
        lbxEmployees.DataTextField = "LastName"
        lbxEmployees.DataValueField = "EmployeeID"
        lbxEmployees.DataBind()
        objConnection.Close()
      End If
    End Sub
```

Last, we write code into the method that executes when the user selects a name from the list. This code repeats the data acquisition process, but does so for the DataGrid instead of the list box. Notice how we set the value of the SQL WHERE clause to be equal to the DataValueField of whichever name was selected.

```
    Sub subListChange(S As Object, E As EventArgs)
      ' Response.Write("subListChange triggered")
      Dim strConnection As String = ConfigurationSettings.AppSettings("NWind")

      Dim strSQLforGrid As String = "SELECT TitleOfCourtesy, FirstName, " & _
                    "LastName, Country, Region, City, Notes " & _
                    "FROM Employees WHERE EmployeeID = " & _
                    lbxEmployees.SelectedItem.Value

      Dim objConnection As New SqlConnection(strConnection)
      Dim objCommand As New SqlCommand(strSQLforGrid, objConnection)
```

```
    objConnection.Open()
    dgEmployee.DataSource = objCommand.ExecuteReader()
    dgEmployee.DataBind()
    objConnection.Close()
End Sub
```

You've probably encountered list boxes from which you can make multiple selections, using the Shift or Control keys. ASP.NET offers a `SelectionMode` *property for list boxes that allows multiple selections. We will cover how to interpret the data returned from such controls later in this chapter, when we look at how to handle check boxes.*

Using the Radio Button List

In a sense, radio buttons have the same logic as the list boxes (in single selection mode) that we just examined: the visitor sees many choices, but can pick only one. Even the name of the control – `RadioButtonList` – is a reminder that they're in the list family of data-aware controls. (Note that ASP.NET also supports a `RadioButton` control that behaves as an individual control, not as part of a list.) Each button in the list has a `Text` property, which is displayed next to it, and a `Value` property, which is hidden from the user but can be utilized programmatically. As with list boxes, this allows us to (for example) show the visitor a useful description of a record (such as a name), but use the record's ID number for coding purposes.

Vertical lists of more than a few radio buttons can take up a lot of precious space on a page, so ASP.NET allows a more efficient 'matrix' layout, through three "Repeat" properties. The first, `RepeatLayout`, determines how IIS will render the control into HTML: a value of `Flow` creates multiple buttons within HTML `<span>` tags, while a value of `Table` creates an HTML `<table>` structure on the page. Unless you have a CSS style that must apply to a `<span>`, the default table setting is better for a tidy appearance.

The second property in this set is `RepeatDirection`. Setting this to `Horizontal` renders the items in order from left to right, then continuing in the second row from left to right. `Vertical`, on the other hand, is the default setting, and renders the items in order running down the left column, and then continuing from the top of the next column to the right.

Third, you can set the number of columns you want with the `RepeatColumns` property. In fact, you should *always* set this property, because the default value of 0 means the buttons will all be in one line, and this may cancel out your other "Repeat" properties.

If we have selected `RepeatLayout = "Table"`, we can also set `CellSpacing` and `CellPadding` in pixel units – **spacing** refers to the distance between cells, while **padding** gives you the option to add extra space between the text and the inside of each cell. (Because there is no line defining the edge of the cells in these tables, the two options amount to more or less the same thing.) Both values of `RepeatLayout` also support the `TextAlign` property, which dictates the location of the text relative to the button itself (`Left` or `Right`). Radio buttons do not have as many formatting features as tables or data grids, but they do allow you to meet some basic design needs.

Try It Out – A Radio Button List

In the last exercise, we created a page with a list box of employees and a grid that displayed more information on a selected employee. In this exercise, we'll implement the same page, but use radio buttons instead of a list box.

1. Create a new file called `Radio_button.aspx`, and copy and paste the code from the last exercise into it.

2. Replace all instances of "`lbxEmployees`" with "`radEmployees`" (there should be five replacements).

3. Change `<asp:ListBox>` to `<asp:RadioButtonList>`.

4. Delete the `Rows` attribute, as this doesn't apply to radio buttons, and fix the title and header to say "Radio Buttons" rather than "a List Box". At this stage, your server control should look something like this:

```
<asp:RadioButtonList id="radEmployees" runat="server"
                     AutoPostBack="True"
                     OnSelectedIndexChanged="subListChange" />
```

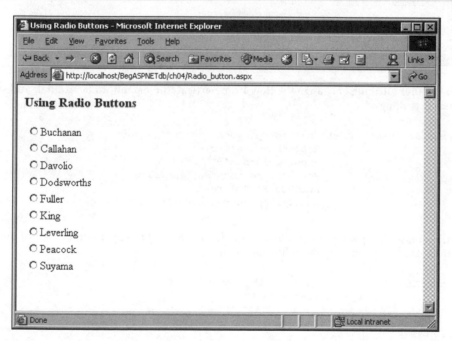

113

5. Next, let's work with the formatting of the buttons. Change the `<asp:RadioButtonList>` attributes as follows, and save the new page as `Radio_button_2.aspx`:

```
<asp:RadioButtonList id="radEmployees" runat="server"
                     RepeatLayout="Table"
                     RepeatColumns="3"
                     AutoPostBack="True"
                     OnSelectedIndexChanged="subListChange" />
```

6. View the result of the above changes, and notice that we've saved a lot of space by putting the buttons into three columns:

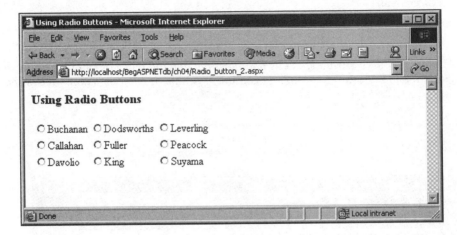

7. Add another attribute to change the flow from vertical (the default) to horizontal, and see how that affects things:

```
<asp:RadioButtonList id="radEmployees" runat="server"
                     RepeatLayout="Table"
                     RepeatColumns="3"
                     RepeatDirection="Horizontal"
                     AutoPostBack="True"
                     OnSelectedIndexChanged="subListChange" />
```

8. Last, increase the spacing and padding, and also set the text to appear on the left of the buttons. Do this by making the following changes:

```
<asp:RadioButtonList id = "radEmployees"
            RepeatLayout = "Table"
            RepeatColumns = "3"
            RepeatDirection = "Horizontal"
            CellPadding = "5"
            CellSpacing = "10"
```

```
                    TextAlign = "Left"
                    AutoPostBack = "True"
                    OnSelectedIndexChanged = "subListChange"
                    runat = "server">
        </asp:RadioButtonList>
```

How It Works

This example features no new code with regard to the connection, command, or data reader objects. In the first version of the new page, though, we can see how just a few quick changes to the page can make a big difference to the display. Open it up again, and take a look at the source code in your browser. ASP.NET has generated the `<table>` elements on our behalf, as follows:

```
<table id="radEmployees" border="0">
  <tr>
    <td>
      <input id="radEmployees_0"
             type="radio"
             name="radEmployees"
             value="5"
             onclick="__doPostBack('radEmployees_0','')"
             language="javascript" />
      <label for="radEmployees_0">Buchanan</label>
    </td>
  </tr>

  ...
```

In the second version, the layout responds to simple changes in the properties. To help you remember, you might want to look at the result of deleting the `RepeatColumns` attribute – it reverts to the default value of 0, which means back to one column, and an inefficient layout.

Multiple Selections with Check Boxes and List Boxes

Often, we'll want to display a list of choices from which our visitors can select more than one item, if they so wish – a list of subjects on which they might like to be sent information, perhaps. In many cases, these choices will be loaded dynamically from a data source, rather than being hard-coded. We have three mechanisms to offer the visitor multiple selections: a `CheckBoxList` control, or a `ListBox` or `DropDownList` control with the `SelectionMode` property set to `Multiple`. However, the way we *handle* the user's multiple selection is the same in all three cases. In this section, we'll cover the topic of multiple selection in two parts: first, how to create the display; and second, how to use the data that's returned.

Displaying Multiple Selection Controls

To start the process, you must create the `asp:CheckBoxList` (or `asp:ListBox`, or `asp:DropDownList`) control within a form in the body of the HTML block. It's important that both the form and the `asp` control must have the `runat="server"` setting.

```
<form id="MyForm" runat="server">
  <asp:CheckBoxList id="chklstMyCheckList" runat="server" />
</form>
```

Or:

```
<form id="MyForm" runat="server">
  <asp:ListBox id="lbxMyListBox" runat="server" SelectionMode="Multiple" />
</form>
```

Once the controls are on the page, populating them with data follows the familiar pattern: we open a connection, call the `ExecuteReader()` method of a command object, assign field names to the web server control's `DataTextField` and `DataTextValue` properties, perform the data bind, and close the connection. So far, so good.

Using Data from Multiple Selections

Handling multiple selections, however, requires more code and planning than the data-aware controls we've worked with so far. If you don't handle multiple selections properly, your code will tend to react only to the first item selected.

> *You can test this by making a copy of the radio button example, changing the control type to `CheckBoxList`, and making no changes to the way you handle the data. If you select Buchanan and Callahan, you'll just get the data for Buchanan.*

The correct technique is the same for `CheckBoxList`, `ListBox`, and `DropDownList` controls, and consists of two steps:

❑ Loop through each item in the list, and check if it was selected. If it *was* selected, your code must react to the selection – usually by adding the value or text to a string that will be used elsewhere in the code.

❑ Then, check if any items were selected at all – is the string longer then zero? Write code in an `If...Then...Else` structure to handle the case of a selection, and the case of no selection.

To assist in this task, ADO.NET allows enumeration over its list objects, which means that we can use a `ForEach...In` loop to test every item in the list. The syntax for the "Is this item selected?" loop could therefore be the following:

```
Dim strSelectionResult As String
Dim liThisOne As ListItem

For Each liThisOne In ckbEmployees.Items
  If liThisOne.Selected Then
    strSelectionResult &= liThisOne.Value
  End If
Next

' Remove next line prior to deployment
Response.Write("strSelectionResult = <br/>" & strSelectionResult & "<hr/>")
```

In the above code, we create a string (`strSelectionResult`) to hold the output of our loop – the values of the selected items, concatenated together. Often, though, we'll want to have some characters before and after each value in the string. Furthermore, we may have some text that goes outside of the whole list of selected values, such as the SQL WHERE keyword to start things off. You can imagine that such requirements will result in code that looks something like this:

```
For Each liThisOne In ckbEmployees.Items
  If liThisOne.Selected Then
    strSelectionResult &= "MyLeadingCharacters"
    strSelectionResult &= liThisOne.Value
    strSelectionResult &= "MyFollowingCharacters"
  End If
Next

strSelectionResult = "WHERE " & strSelectionResult
```

Once we've looped through the choices, we must check whether *any* of the items were selected. This is easy to do, since the presence of a selection will result in the length of our string *immediately after the loop* being greater than zero. The following sample assumes that you have a `DataGrid` object named `dgMyDataGrid`, and that you only want the grid to appear if a selection has been made.

```
If strSelectionResult.Length > 0 Then
  dgMyDataGrid.Visible = True

  ' Work with the strSelectionResult, perhaps
  ' in an SQL statement to fill another grid

Else
  dgMyDataGrid.Visible = False
End If
```

As a side issue – but mentioned here because SQL statements can quickly get quite complex – I find it invaluable to use trace statements in my development code. You can do this in a sophisticated way in Visual Studio, but even when you're using Notepad, it's not hard to write key troubleshooting information to the page. Bear in mind that if you do have a problem with the SQL statement, you may have to exit the method prior to making the connection, so that your trace information will show up on the page. We'll demonstrate this in the next example.

Try It Out – Multiple Selections

We're going to create a page that lists all the Northwind employees, with a check box next to each name. When one or more boxes are checked, we'll show a `DataGrid` containing information about the selected employee(s).

1. Create a new page named `Multiple_selections.aspx`, and fill it with the following code. This is the longest example we've used so far, but you should be familiar with most of its elements from the work we've already done.

```
<%@ Import namespace="System.Data" %>
<%@ Import namespace="System.Data.SqlClient" %>

<html>
  <head><title>Multiple Selections</title></head>
  <body>
    <h3>Multiple Selections</h3>
    <form runat="server">
      <asp:CheckBoxList id="ckbEmployees" runat="server"
                        RepeatLayout="table"
                        RepeatDirection="vertical"
                        RepeatColumns="3"
                        CellPadding="9"
                        CellSpacing="18"
                        TextAlign="right"
                        OnSelectedIndexChanged="subListChange"
                        AutoPostBack="true" />
      <br/><br/>
      <asp:DataGrid id="dgEmployee" runat="server" />
    </form>
  </body>
</html>

<script language="vb" runat="server">
Sub Page_Load(Source As Object, E As EventArgs)
  If Not IsPostBack Then
    Dim strConnection As String = ConfigurationSettings.AppSettings("NWind")
    Dim strSQLforCheckBoxes As String = "SELECT LastName, EmployeeID " & _
                                        "FROM Employees ORDER BY LastName;"
    Dim objConnection As New SqlConnection(strConnection)
    Dim objCommand As New SqlCommand(strSQLforCheckBoxes, objConnection)

    objConnection.Open()
```

```
        ckbEmployees.DataSource = objCommand.ExecuteReader()
        ckbEmployees.DataTextField = "LastName"
        ckbEmployees.DataValueField = "EmployeeID"
        ckbEmployees.DataBind()
        objConnection.Close()
    End If
End Sub

Sub subListChange(S As Object, E As EventArgs)

    ' Remove next line prior to deployment
    Response.Write("subListChange triggered<hr/>")

    Dim strWhereClause As String = ""
    Dim liThisOne As ListItem

    For Each liThisOne in ckbEmployees.Items
        If liThisOne.Selected Then
            strWhereClause &= "EmployeeID=" & liThisOne.Value & " OR "
        End If
    Next

    ' Remove next line prior to deployment
    Response.Write("strWhereClause = <br/>" & strWhereClause & "<hr/>")

    If strWhereClause.Length > 0 Then
        dgEmployee.Visible = True

        ' This line removes the final " OR " from the WHERE clause
        strWhereClause = Left(strWhereClause, strWhereClause.Length - 4)
        strWhereClause = "WHERE " & strWhereClause

        Dim strConnection As String = ConfigurationSettings.AppSettings("NWind")
        Dim strSQLforGrid As String = "SELECT TitleOfCourtesy, FirstName, " & _
                                "LastName, Country, Region, City, Notes " & _
                                "FROM Employees " & strWhereClause

        Dim objConnection As New SqlConnection(strConnection)
        Dim objCommand As New SqlCommand(strSQLforGrid, objConnection)

        ' Remove next line prior to deployment
        Response.Write("strSQLforGrid = <br/>" & strSQLforGrid & "<hr/>")

        objConnection.Open()
        dgEmployee.DataSource = objCommand.ExecuteReader()
        dgEmployee.DataBind()
        objConnection.Close()
    Else
        dgEmployee.Visible = False
    End If
End Sub
</script>
```

2. Take a look at the results, which (assuming that you've commented out the debugging lines) should resemble the following:

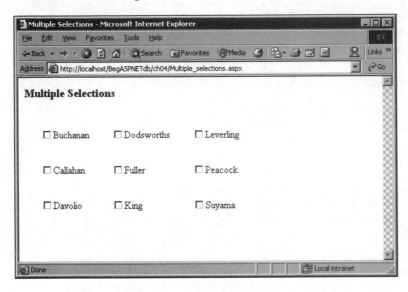

3. Then, when you make a selection of two names, you should get:

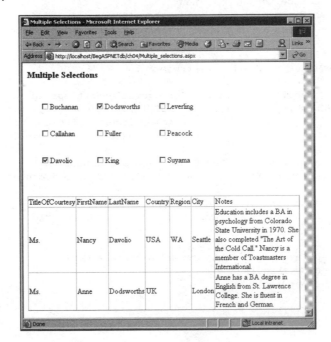

How It Works

In order of execution, what happens first is that in the Page_Load() handler, a set of check boxes is populated from a data store. Then, in subListChange(), we have code that determines what (if anything) was selected in the check boxes. Last, we have code that populates the DataGrid control. Keep clear in your mind that we connect, use a command, and bind *twice* – once for the check boxes that show the names, and then again for the DataGrid that displays the information.

Starting with the HTML, and ignoring any formatting detail, the first thing to note is that setting the AutoPostBack attribute makes a 'submit' button unnecessary – whenever a box is checked or unchecked, the DataGrid will be repopulated. Also note that we've wired up a method called subListChange() to run whenever there is a change in the selection.

```
<html>

    ...

    <form runat="server">
      <asp:CheckBoxList id="ckbEmployees" runat="server"

    ...

                        OnSelectedIndexChanged="subListChange"
                        AutoPostBack="True" />
      <br/><br/>
      <asp:DataGrid id="dgEmployee" runat="server" />
    </form>
  </body>
</html>
```

The code that places the check boxes contains nothing new – as usual, it's wrapped in the "If Not IsPostBack" syntax to make sure that the check box list isn't repopulated after every selection. When the user clicks on a check box, the list object will trigger the SelectedIndexChanged event, which calls the subListChange() method below. In it, we build up a string of values from the selected items that will form a SQL WHERE clause for the DataGrid.

```
Sub subListChange(S As Object, E As EventArgs)

  ' Remove next line prior to deployment
  Response.Write("subListChange triggered<hr/>")

  Dim strWhereClause As String = ""
  Dim liThisOne As ListItem

  For Each liThisOne in ckbEmployees.Items
    If liThisOne.Selected Then
      strWhereClause &= "EmployeeID=" & liThisOne.Value & " OR "
    End If
  Next
```

Clearly, it's possible that there will be no selection at all, if the user's action was to uncheck the only checked box. To deal with this, we take a look at the length of the string holding the WHERE clause. If selections *were* made, then we execute all of the connection, command and binding code for the DataGrid object.

```
' Remove next line prior to deployment
Response.Write("strWhereClause = <br/>" & strWhereClause & "<hr/>")

If strWhereClause.Length > 0 Then
  dgEmployee.Visible = True

  ' This line removes the final ' OR ' from the WHERE clause
  strWhereClause = Left(strWhereClause, strWhereClause.Length - 4)
  strWhereClause = "WHERE " & strWhereClause

  Dim strConnection As String = ConfigurationSettings.AppSettings("NWind")
  Dim strSQLforGrid As String = "SELECT TitleOfCourtesy, FirstName, " & _
                      "LastName, Country, Region, City, Notes " & _
                      "FROM Employees " & strWhereClause

  Dim objConnection As New SqlConnection(strConnection)
  Dim objCommand As New SqlCommand(strSQLforGrid, objConnection)

  ' Remove next line prior to deployment
  Response.Write("strSQLforGrid = <br/>" & strSQLforGrid & "<hr/>")

  objConnection.Open()
  dgEmployee.DataSource = objCommand.ExecuteReader()
  dgEmployee.DataBind()
  objConnection.Close()
```

If the check box list contained no selections, then we can just hide the DataGrid, keeping the page neat and tidy.

```
Else
  dgEmployee.Visible = False
End If
```

This works quite nicely, but to do more to improve the appearance of the data on our pages, we need to look much more closely at the behavior of the ASP.NET web server controls. We'll start doing that in the next section, in the context of a control we're already quite familiar with: the data grid.

Data Grids

In classic ASP, it was possible to spend a tremendous amount of time writing code to display, sort, hyperlink from, and otherwise work with tables of data. This author spent more time troubleshooting and maintaining such code than he did writing database queries and business logic! In ASP.NET, however, Microsoft has created the DataGrid control, which is very complex internally, but satisfyingly easy to use. Simply by setting the control's properties and child elements, you can instruct it to:

❑ Write HTML tags to create a `<table>`, automatically sensing the number of columns and rows needed to fit the data

❑ Write HTML tags to apply table-level formatting

❑ Write HTML tags to implement row styles that the programmer creates

❑ Write HTML tags to format columns, including formats such as 'buttons' and 'hyperlinks'

❑ Divide data into pages, and provide navigation tools to move through the pages

❑ Write HTML tags to implement sorting on a column selected by the visitor

❑ Write HTML tags to allow the user to edit data in a selected row

If you like, you can look at the `DataGrid` as a way either of saving you hundreds of dollars in buying third-party controls, or of saving yourself weeks of time trying to get all those features to work. In this chapter, we will cover the first three topics in the above list. In the next chapter, we'll cover column formatting, paging and sorting. In Chapter 7, we'll discuss editing data.

Formatting the Entire Grid

Having used them a number of times, you've already seen the basics of editing and filling a `DataGrid`. One of the things that we've done regularly, and is well worth remembering, is to place the grid inside a `<form>` element; this isn't always necessary, but you'll need to do it in order to have any kind of sorting or editing facilities, and it's a good habit to get into.

Moving on to its appearance, the `DataGrid` supports the traditional `BackColor` and `ForeColor` properties – either Internet Explorer's 16 basic colors (aqua, black, blue…), or Netscape's 135 colors (`AliceBlue`, `AntiqueWhite`, `AquaMarine`, etc.). You can also use the RGB system. The syntax is simple:

```
<asp:DataGrid id="dgMyDataGrid" runat="server"
            ForeColor="purple"
            BackColor="silver" />
```

Or:

```
...
ForeColor="#FF00FF"
...
```

Instead of setting a `BackColor`, we can use the `BackImageURL` attribute to specify an image – but although this sounds easy, it tends to become more problematic in real life. The image does not automatically expand to fit the grid – rather, it repeats – so you have to be careful about the image you choose.

```
backImageURL = "MyImage.gif"
```

We can set the location of the grid on the page with the `HorizontalAlign` attribute. The default value for this is `"NotSet"`, which generally means 'left'; you can change it to `"left"`, `"center"`, or `"right"` There is no property for vertical alignment of the entire grid.

As with a regular HTML table (and, therefore, as you'd hope), you can set the grid border's color, width, and style, with the latter including options like `"solid"`, `"dashed"`, and `"dotted"`. Note that the `BorderColor` affects both internal and external borders, while the width and style are only applied to the external borders of the grid. The code below illustrates this difference; color options are the same as for the background and foreground.

```
BorderStyle="dashed"
BorderWidth="5"
BorderColor="gray"
```

The above code yields the following on the browser screen, demonstrating that the border style and width only affect the outer border.

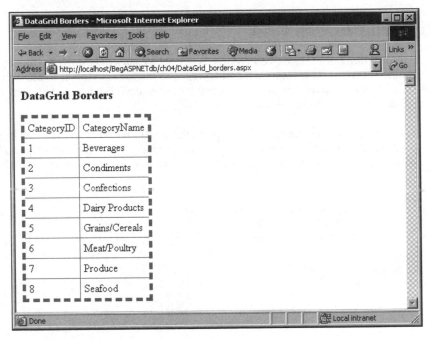

We can set standards for the content of cells with the `Font-Name`, `Font-Size`, `CellSpacing`, and `CellPadding` properties. The second pair in that list behaves in the same way as the identically named attributes of the radio button list that we saw earlier. `Font-Name` and `Font-Size` work the same as for plain HTML tags, as in the following example:

```
CellSpacing="2"
CellPadding="10"
```

```
Font-Name="verdana"
Font-Size="20"
```

The `DataGrid` control also includes `Enabled` and `Visible` properties. `Visible="False"` means that the table is hidden from the viewer (useful when you have the control on the page, but no data to display), while `Enabled` determines whether the visitor can interact with clickable items on the data grid (such as a button to begin an update process). Grids that are `Enabled="False"` will be gray.

Row Formatting

ASP.NET offers an easy, three-step technique for formatting the rows that appear in several of its web server controls. First, you need to understand how ASP.NET names the different types of rows that can appear in a grid. Second, you need to set some properties of the data grid itself. Third, you create a style for each type of row, using one of several syntactic possibilities. After that, ASP.NET does the rest.

In all, there are seven row types. The `Header` row contains the names of the columns, while the `Footer` will be added to the bottom of the grid, after the last row of data. The data itself is presented in `Item` rows, of which there are four sub-types. `Item` itself is the default, but there's also an `AlternatingItem` (which will give a horizontally striped look to the grid), a `SelectedItem` (if selection of rows is allowed), and an `EditItem` (for rows that are being edited – see Chapter 7).

That's six so far; the seventh type is the `Pager`, which we'll look at later on when we examine how to add some hyperlinks to navigate through the pages when there's too much data to fit in one grid. It's worth noting here that for paging to be possible, you need to set `AllowPaging="True"`. Similarly, in order for the header and footer rows to be displayed, the `ShowHeader` and `ShowFooter` attributes must be set to `"True"`. The former has this value by default, but the latter does not.

As you can see below, each type of row can get its own formatting. The column on the left indicates the row type name, while on the right are two columns of examples.

Header	FirstName	LastName
Item	Nancy	Davolio
AlternatingItem	Andrew	Fuller
Item	Janet	Leverling
AlternatingItem	Margaret	Peacock
Item	Steven	Buchanan
SelectedItem	Robert	King
EditItem	Laura	Callahan
Footer	Check daily for specials	
Pager	<Previous Next>	

It's in this area that ASP.NET is at its most confusing. It has two terms that can be tricky to differentiate, because each applies to the same seven kinds of rows.

❑ **Styles** determine the *formatting* of the rows, such as font size and background color. For example, you'd use a `Style` to apply a blue background to the `Header` row.

❑ **Templates** determine what *information* (HTML tags, data and text) will appear in the row. For example, you'd use a `Template` to show the words Check daily for specials in a `Footer` row.

In the `DataGrid` control, templates affect columns, rather than rows.

There are three forms of syntax that can set styles for a row. The first syntax is the most compact, and uses an attribute of the `<asp:DataGrid>` element:

```
<asp:DataGrid id="dgEmployees" runat = "server"
              HeaderStyle-backcolor="lightgray" />
```

In the second option, which is probably the most easily readable, we specify a style element within the `<asp:DataGrid>` element:

```
<asp:DataGrid id="dgEmployees" runat="server">
  <HeaderStyle backcolor="lightgray" />
</asp:DataGrid>
```

The third technique is to refer to a class that you've created in a Cascading Style Sheet (CSS). The following example assumes that you have a style named *MyHeaderStyle* in a CSS named *MyStyleSheet*.

```
<head>
  <style ref="MyStyleSheet" type="text/css">
    .MyHeaderStyle {property1: value1; property2: value2;}
  </style>
</head>
<body>
  <asp:DataGrid id="dgEmployees" runat="server"
              HeaderStyle-CssClass="MyHeaderStyle" />
  . . .
```

In ASP.NET, there are more than a dozen properties that can be set in row styles, including:

❑ `BackColor` and `ForeColor`.

❑ `Height`, `Width`, and `WordWrap` of a row. (Note: the width of the table will be determined by the widest of all the styles. In other words, don't bother setting one style to create a narrow table if another style will create a wide table. The table will end up wide.)

❑ `HorizontalAlign` and `VerticalAlign`.

❑ Font properties, such as name and size.

❑ Border width, color, and style.

❑ CSS class.

As in so many situations, it's easy to go overboard on these style properties, and to end up with a visually confusing grid. But if you set each property to implement color-coding, or to make the text easier to read, then you will improve the usability of your page.

Try It Out – DataGrid Row Styles

Let's imagine that your boss has asked you to write the ASP.NET code to display the following page. The code, which we'll analyze in full, applies styles to the header, footer, and "alternating item" rows in order to achieve its results.

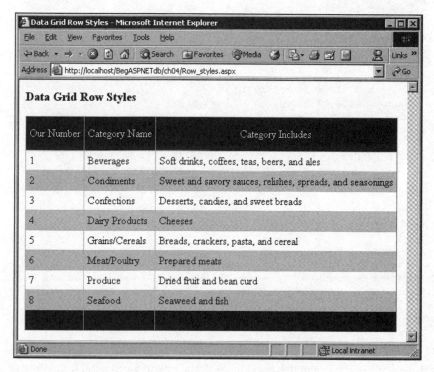

1. Open your editor, create a page named Row_styles.aspx and enter or download the following code:

```
<%@ Import namespace="System.Data" %>
<%@ Import namespace="System.Data.SqlClient" %>

<html>
  <head><title>Data Grid Row Styles</title></head>
  <body>
    <h3>Data Grid Row Styles</h3>
    <asp:DataGrid id="dgCategories" runat="server"
```

```
                         ShowHeader="True"
                         ShowFooter="True"
                         CellPadding="5">

       <HeaderStyle BackColor="black"
                    ForeColor="white"
                    HorizontalAlign="center"
                    Height="50" />

       <AlternatingItemStyle BackColor="lightgray" />

       <FooterStyle BackColor="black"
                    ForeColor="white" />
    </asp:DataGrid>
  </body>
</html>

<script language="VB" runat="server">
Sub Page_Load(Source As Object, E As EventArgs)
  Dim strConnection As String = ConfigurationSettings.AppSettings("NWind")
  Dim objConnection As New SqlConnection(strConnection)

  Dim strSQL As String = "SELECT CategoryID AS [Our Number], " & _
                         "CategoryName AS [Category Name], " & _
                         "Description AS [Category Includes] " & _
                         "FROM Categories"

  Dim objCommand As New SqlCommand(strSQL, objConnection)

  objConnection.Open()
  dgCategories.DataSource = objCommand.ExecuteReader()
  dgCategories.DataBind()
  objConnection.Close()
End Sub
</script>
```

How It Works

There are three areas of interest in this page: the SQL statement, the general formatting of the DataGrid control, and the specific row styles. We'll start with the SQL statement, which includes a feature that we haven't used before. **Aliasing** allows us to take the names of the fields in the database and change them so that they look better when displayed, without losing the link between the two.

It's worth mentioning why there's a need for aliases. Developers follow a syntax error minimization convention of not having spaces in table and column names (for instance, CategoryName). For display purposes, however, the presence of spaces makes things much more readable (Category Name). Aliases exist to bridge this gap.

The creation of aliases requires the SQL AS keyword. You write the original field name, followed by AS, followed by your chosen name. After the query has been executed, you (and ADO.NET) will refer to the fields by using the alias. If the alias has a space in it, you must use brackets, as we did here.

```
Dim strSQL As String = "SELECT CategoryID AS [Our Number], " & _
                       "CategoryName AS [Category Name], " & _
                       "Description AS [Category Includes] " & _
                       "FROM Categories"
```

Moving on to the formatting of the DataGrid control, we know that we want a header and footer, so we explicitly set the appropriate properties to "True".

```
<asp:DataGrid id="dgCategories" runat="server"
        ShowHeader="True"
        ShowFooter="True"
```

While we're at it, we also add some padding to all of the cells in the grid, making the resulting table a little easier on the eye.

```
CellPadding="5">
```

Now we get to the individual row styles. The top row will be of the HeaderStyle.

```
<HeaderStyle BackColor="black"
        ForeColor="white"
        HorizontalAlign="center"
        Height="50" />
```

We get the gray and white background stripes by setting the AlternatingItemStyle element's BackColor attribute to lightgray.

```
<AlternatingItemStyle BackColor="lightgray" />
```

And finally we format the footer to look the same as the header, even though it contains no text in this particular example.

```
<FooterStyle BackColor="black"
        ForeColor="white" />
    </asp:DataGrid>
  </body>
</html>
```

In addition to the three we've used here, the rows in DataGrids can be formatted using four other style elements: ItemStyle, EditItemStyle, SelectedItemStyle, and PagerStyle. Other controls will make different style properties available, and you should consult the documentation to discover what works with the control you're using.

Going Further with Displaying Data

In the next chapter, we'll take a look at some more ways to format the data in tables, several of which are only available when the data source for the DataGrid is a dataset object. We'll also take a look at the Calendar control, and the techniques for working with controls that bind a single value of data, such as a text box.

Common Mistakes

As in the previous chapter, We're going to conclude with a list of common pitfalls that you might encounter while experimenting with the examples presented in this chapter:

❑ The web server control in your HTML page must have an ID that matches the object name you've used in the DataSource and DataBind() statements. It must also have the runat="server" attribute set.

❑ Never instantiate a data reader object. We can let the command object's ExecuteReader() method do that job for us.

❑ As always, know your data source. If you're getting an error, double check that you have the table and field names correct in your SQL query.

❑ Your <asp:CheckBoxList> control must be in a <form> tag, and the <form> tag must also have the runat="server" attribute.

❑ If you don't assign values to the DataValueField and DataTextField properties of the web server control, you won't get an error, but all the check boxes on your screen will be labeled System.Data.Common.DbDataRecord.

❑ Note that the JET provider deletes spaces from column names, so Category ID will be displayed in the browser as CategoryID, without the space.

❑ The DataValueField and DataTextValue properties must be set before the connection object's Close() method is called. Don't try to reduce the time your connection is open by setting these properties after the connection closes.

❑ Similarly, the call to DataBind() must occur after DataValueField and DataTextField have been set.

Summary

We've covered two major areas in this chapter: how to use data reader and command objects together, and how to display data in some of the controls that display multiple records.

The data reader is one of two ways to get data from a connection; the other is the dataset. Data readers use minimal resources, because they stream data from the data store into a display control, and then sever the data connection – the data doesn't have to sit in IIS memory. However, data readers can only read data (they can never write it), and you can only navigate forwards through the records. You can't create multiple tables or relationships, or read data from more than one source. In spite of these constraints, however, data readers are very useful – there are many web pages that just display data from a single table or stored procedure.

Data reader objects are closely linked to command objects for two reasons. First, the latter's `Text` property holds a description of the data to be read. Second, it is the command object's `ExecuteReader()` method that actually creates and initializes the data reader object. The `Text` property can store a table name, an SQL statement, or a stored procedure (or an Access query).

All data-aware ASP.NET controls can be categorized into one of two groups: single-value, and multiple-value. In this chapter, we looked at the most common multiple-value controls. To use them, we must add an element for the control to the body of the page, and then set the control's data source in the code. Last, we must execute a `DataBind()`. Remember that we can associate two fields with each item in the list: the `DataTextField` appears to the user, while the `DataValueField` is available to the programmer, behind the scenes.

Multiple *selections* are available for some list controls. After the user clicks, we go to a method that loops through each item in the list to see if it has been selected. If it has, then we generally concatenate the `Value` or `Text` onto a result string for future use. We must also be prepared to react to a lack of selection.

At the end of the chapter, we began our discussion of the `DataGrid`, one of the most powerful controls in ASP.NET. The grid takes a set of data, senses the number of rows and fields, and then automatically builds an HTML table to display the information. We can set several format properties for the entire table, and ASP.NET defines row types, such as `Header` and `Item`, to which we can assign styles too.

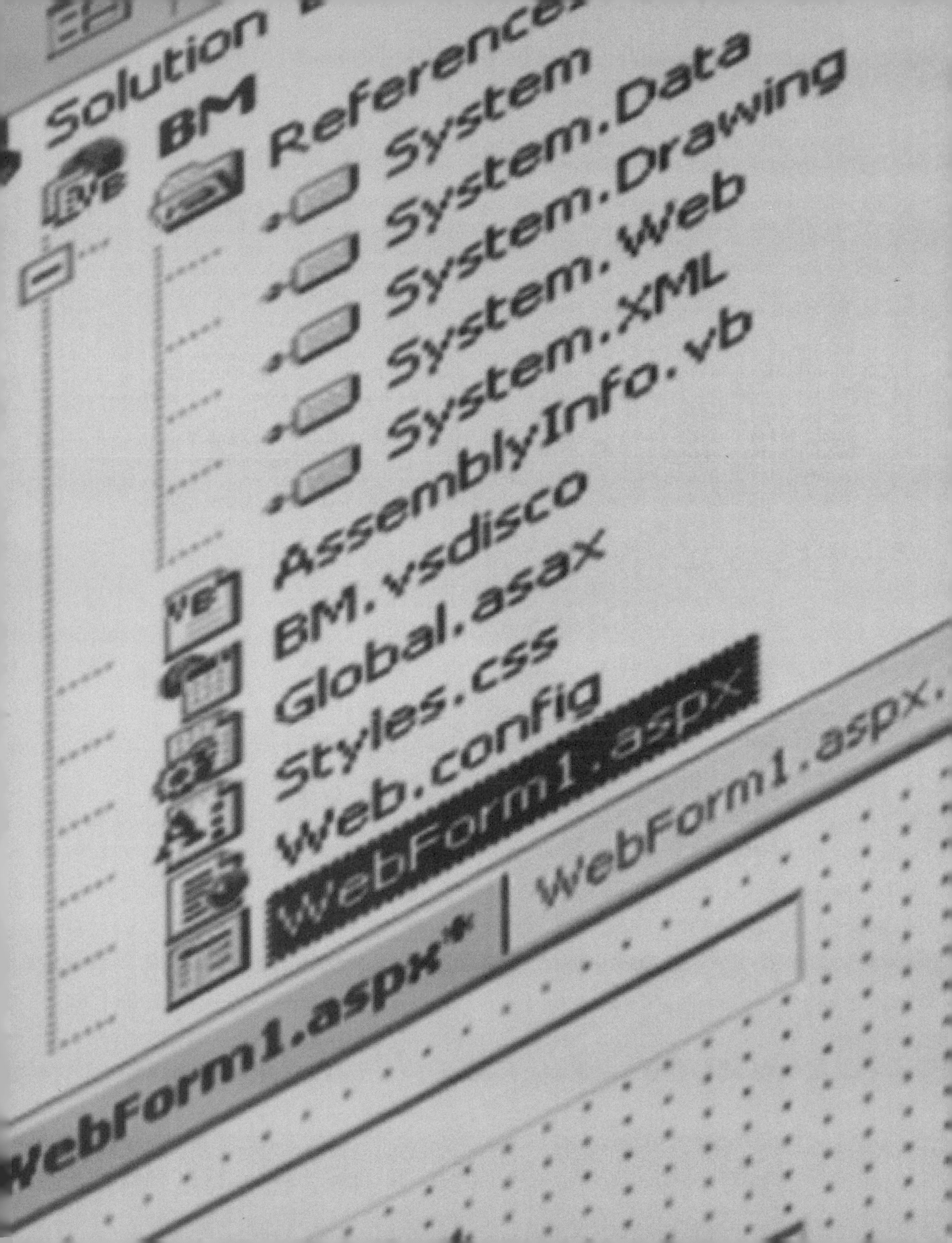

Solution
BM
References
System
System.Data
System.Drawing
System.Web
System.XML
AssemblyInfo.vb
Assembly
BM.vsdisco
Global.asax
Styles.css
Web.config
WebForm1.aspx

WebForm1.aspx* | WebForm1.aspx.

WebForm1.aspx*

Reading Data using the DataSet Object

In this chapter, we're going to discuss a huge topic: the ADO.NET `DataSet` object, which enables us to represent very complex data (should we need to do so). It contains `DataTable` objects, which may be thought of as very similar to the tables in a database. These, in turn, contain `DataColumn` and `DataRow` collections. All of these objects are rich in functionality, and have lots of properties and methods – but rather than tortuously stepping through them, we'll focus on how to use them to provide solutions to some common tasks, and look at enough theory to troubleshoot our mistakes. More specifically, you'll learn about the following:

- ❏ What a `DataSet` object is, and how it compares to a data reader
- ❏ Populating a `DataSet` with data from both a database source and an XML file
- ❏ Displaying the data within a `DataSet` by binding to a `DataGrid` control
- ❏ Accessing columns and rows within a `DataSet`
- ❏ Using a `DataSet` to work with data from different data sources
- ❏ Creating relationships within a `DataSet`
- ❏ Creating views of the data held within a `DataSet`
- ❏ Sorting, filtering, and paginating the data displayed within a `DataGrid`
- ❏ Using a `DataSet` as a source of dates for the ASP.NET `Calendar` control

This list doesn't explore every aspect of the `System.Data.DataSet` class, but it certainly includes the tools you'll require in order to tackle many of the scenarios you'll encounter. It's also a starting point to find out more information if and when you need it.

DataSet Objects

A `DataSet` object holds data in the server's memory, ready to be used to build an ASP.NET page. In some ways, we can think of a `DataSet` as being a copy of a selected part of a database, but it doesn't have to be as simple as that – the data in one `DataSet` object can come from several different sources. Furthermore, it's possible to create relationships between the stored data within a `DataSet`, regardless of where that data originated. This can be useful when you're faced with two databases that contain information about the same things, and you need to bring them together in a coherent way. We'll see an example of this a little later on.

Remember that anything we do to the data in a `DataSet`, such as sorting or modifying it, affects only the data stored in memory, not the original data source. We can *choose* to have the changes we make reflected in the data source (as we'll see in Chapter 7), but we are not compelled to do so. In other words, the `DataSet` is *disconnected* from the data source(s) whose data it contains.

Before we dig deeper into datasets, let's first compare them to the data readers of the previous chapter.

Datasets and Data Readers

You'll recall from the previous chapter that we sent data from our data reader objects directly into display controls – no data was maintained in memory. While this was happening, a connection to the database was maintained; failure to close this connection after acquiring the data could lead to excessive consumption of valuable system resources, leading potentially to the failure of the whole server. What all this means is that if you want to edit and manipulate your data, a data reader is not the right choice.

`DataSet` objects, working in harness with data adapter objects, are very different. The data we read from a data source can be held in memory and edited and manipulated freely, with no need for the resource-hungry database connection to remain. We therefore have scope to do far more with our data before we display it, or use it in some other context. What all this means is that if you simply want to push a handful of rows from a data source into a display control, a `DataSet` object is not the right choice.

The following table presents a comparison of the ADO.NET `DataSet` and data reader classes.

Data reader	Dataset
Read only.	Read and write.
Forward only.	Possible to navigate through the records forwards and backwards, and to jump to a given record.
Creates a stream of data.	Data is copied into IIS memory.
Quicker.	Slower.

Data reader	Dataset
Minimal use of resources in IIS and data source (only one record in memory at a time).	Uses more memory in IIS.
Can loop through records and display them in the order they come from the data source.	Can take various actions on the entire group of records.
Does not hold `DataTables`, and thus has no collections of rows or columns.	Holds `DataTables` and all of their properties, events and methods. In turn, the `DataTables` hold collections of columns and rows and all of their properties, events and methods.
Cannot set relationships or constraints (although it's possible to read related data if the SQL statement reading the data contains a `JOIN`).	Can create (and hold) relationships between tables, and constraints in tables, within the dataset.
Once read, there is no way to transmit data back to the source.	Changes can be made to the `DataSet` and then uploaded back to the original data source.
Limited to reading data from one source.	Can contain multiple tables from multiple data sources.
Little code required – data reader objects are created implicitly by methods of other objects.	Generally requires explicit creation of the `DataSet` and `DataTable` objects, and often some additional objects too.
Data cannot be transferred.	Can transfer data to other data sources, other tiers, or to XML streams.
Primary use: to read data to fill a data-aware control such as a label, list box, or `DataGrid`, while using minimal resources.	Primary uses: to display complex data (from multiple sources, or with relationships), or to write (edit, create, delete) data in the data store.

DataTable Objects

Having drawn what comparisons we can between datasets and data readers, we can begin to take a closer look at the various parts of a `DataSet` object that we mentioned in the opening paragraph. First, a `DataTable` object is used to hold the data within a `DataSet` – a `DataSet` can contain multiple, named `DataTable` objects, much as we can have multiple tables within a relational database. Indeed, a `DataTable` object is very similar to a database table, consisting of a set of columns with particular properties.

When we add data to a `DataSet` object, we do so by placing it into a specific `DataTable` object. During this process, not only is the actual data placed into the `DataTable`, but also the `DataTable` acquires the schema of the data. Thus, the data stored in a `DataTable` object carries type information, just like the data stored in a database table.

Once we have some data in a `DataTable`, we can perform processing on it, use it as a source for filling web server controls, or prepare it for display by passing it on to a `DataView` object (we'll examine how to use `DataView` objects a little later on).

Each `DataTable` object has, among many others, a pair of properties called `Columns` and `Rows`. Respectively, these are collections of `DataColumn` and `DataRow` objects that belong to the `DataTable` in question; they represent the columns and rows of data it holds. Once again, we'll look at these collections in more detail soon.

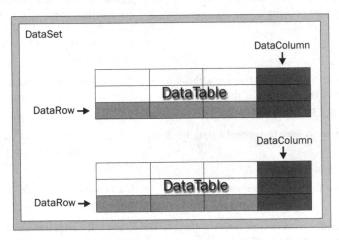

Six Steps to Data Transfer

Now that you understand at least a little of what a `DataSet` object looks like, we can start to examine what it takes to use one. The basic approach for transferring data from a data source into a `DataSet` can be set out as follows:

1. Create a connection object

2. Create a command object to hold our SQL statement

3. Create a `DataSet` object

4. Create one or more `DataTable` objects in the `DataSet`

5. Create a data adapter with the connection and command objects

6. Use the `Fill()` method of the data adapter to transfer data (and its schema) from the connection object into a `DataTable` of the `DataSet`.

The first two of these steps are unchanged from our work with data readers in the previous chapter, and you'll soon recognize them when we begin working on some examples. For now, then, you can just take it as read that we have a couple of objects called `objConnection` and `objCommand`, and we'll pick up the story at step 3.

Creating a DataSet

A `DataSet` can be created in the following way:

```
Dim dsMyDataSet As New DataSet("MyDataSetName")
```

The string that we provide to the constructor will be used as the name of the root element of any XML document we choose to generate from this dataset – if we don't provide one, the string `"NewDataSet"` will be used.

After a line of VB.NET code like this has been executed, the `DataSet` exists but contains neither data nor a schema – those will be added in the next few sections.

Creating a DataTable

We can create a `DataTable` object like this:

```
Dim dtMyTable As New DataTable("MyTableName")
```

On this occasion, the (optional) string that we pass to the constructor is a name that we can use to identify this table programmatically, after we've added it to a `DataSet` object.

After this line, the `DataTable` object isn't attached to any particular `DataSet`, and although that's not hard to do, we'll soon see how to create `DataTable` objects within a particular `DataSet` implicitly, using a data adapter. An advantage of implicit creation is that there's less code to type.

Creating a Data Adapter

Unlike the `DataSet` and `DataTable` classes, which don't have versions specific to the type of data source being accessed, data adapter classes come in flavors such as `SqlDataAdapter` and `OleDbDataAdapter`. Simply put, the purpose of a data adapter is to retrieve a set of data from a data source, and place it in a `DataTable`. That sounds easy in theory, but in practice it can become quite complex – data adapters can be used in a number of different ways.

One technique for instantiating a data adapter is the following, where we use a command object and a connection object as arguments to the constructor:

```
Dim objAdapter As New SqlDataAdapter(objCommand, objConnection)
```

However, the piece of information from the command object that the constructor is interested in is actually just the SQL query string, so it's also possible just to provide that string, rather than specifying a command object.

```
Dim strSQL As String = "SELECT * FROM Products"
Dim objAdapter As New SqlDataAdapter(strSQL, objConnection)
```

If you don't specify a command object when you create a data adapter, one will be created for you automatically – if you then need to use it, you can retrieve it using the data adapter's SelectCommand *property. Creating and passing a command object neither improves nor degrades performance.*

Filling Tables

With the data adapter created, we can use its Fill() method either to fill an existing DataTable object, or to create a new DataTable and fill it. There are numerous different ways to use Fill() – the documentation lists no fewer than eight overloads – but four are particularly common:

❑   Create a new DataTable (with the default name "Table") in the specified DataSet object:

```
objAdapter.Fill(objDataSet)
```

This creates a DataTable named "Table" in the objDataSet object, with all the same DataColumns as the data source (say, the result of an SQL query). It then populates this DataTable object.

❑   Create a new DataTable object with a customized name in the specified DataSet object:

```
objDataAdapter.Fill(objDataSet, "MyNewTableName")
```

This creates a DataTable named "MyNewTableName" in the objDataSet object. It gives the table the same DataColumns as the source (with the same DataColumn names), and then populates it.

❑   Fill a previously created DataTable:

```
Dim objTable As New DataTable("MyTableName")
objDataSet.Tables.Add(objTable)
objDataAdapter.Fill(objDataset, "MyTableName")
```

Once again, this gives the table the same DataColumns as the source (with the same DataColumn names), and then populates it.

❑   Load a range of records from a data adapter object into a specified DataSet and DataTable:

```
objDataAdapter.Fill(objDataSet, iStartRec, iNumberOfRec, "MyTableName")
```

This works identically to the previous examples, with the addition that only `iNumberOfRec` records will be loaded (rather than all the records), starting from the zero-based index represented by `iStartRec`.

> Remember that in this version of the `Fill()` method, the third parameter specifies the number of records to add, *not* the index of the last record to add.

For details of the other `Fill()` overloads, take a look at the Microsoft documentation. Among them, there's one that makes the data adapter fill one `DataTable` from another.

Regardless of the precise technique we use, the `Fill()` method is very careful in its use of the connection object. If the connection is open when the data adapter tries to initialize it, `Fill()` will leave it open. However, if the connection is closed when the data adapter tries to initialize it, it will open the connection, do its work, and then close it again. Basically, the state of the connection is left unchanged.

After the six steps described above, the data is sitting in a `DataTable` object within a `DataSet` object, and if we wish, we can bind the `DataTable` to a control to display our data. Let's start putting some of the above into practice.

Try It Out – Filling a DataSet Object and Binding to a DataGrid

For our first example, we will simply fill a `DataSet` object with some records from the `Categories` table of the Northwind database, and bind the implicitly generated `DataTable` object to a `DataGrid` for display.

1. Now that we're in Chapter 5, you can start by making a new directory named ch05 in our webroot folder. In the folder, create a file called `DataSet_filling.aspx`, and enter the following:

```
<%@ Import namespace="System.Data" %>
<%@ Import namespace="System.Data.SqlClient" %>

<html>
  <head>
    <title>Filling the DataSet and binding to the DataGrid</title>
  </head>
  <body>
    <asp:DataGrid id="dgCategories" runat="server" /><br/>
  </body>
</html>

<script language="VB" runat="server">
Sub Page_Load(Source As Object, E As EventArgs)

  ' Connection setup
  Dim strConnection As String = ConfigurationSettings.AppSettings("NWind")
```

```
      Dim objConnection As New SqlConnection(strConnection)
      Dim strSQL As String = "SELECT * FROM Categories"

      ' DataAdapter setup
      Dim objAdapter As New SqlDataAdapter(strSQL, objConnection)

      ' DataSet & Adapter & Table
      Dim objDataSet As New DataSet()
      objAdapter.Fill(objDataSet, "dtCategories")

      dgCategories.DataSource = objDataSet.Tables("dtCategories")
      dgCategories.DataBind()
   End Sub
</script>
```

2. View the above page in your browser, and you should see a result like this:

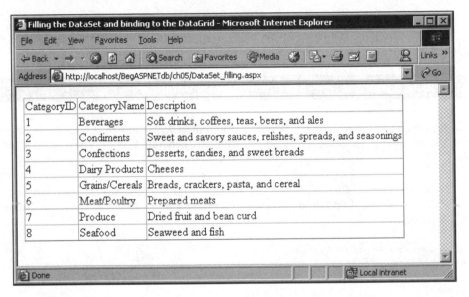

How It Works

In the `Page_Load()` event handler, we first create our connection object and the SQL query that we'll use to retrieve data from the `Categories` table:

```
Dim strConnection As String = ConfigurationSettings.AppSettings("NWind")
Dim objConnection As New SqlConnection(strConnection)
Dim strSQL As String = "SELECT * FROM Categories"
```

With those in place, we instantiate our data adapter:

```
Dim objAdapter As New SqlDataAdapter(strSQL, objConnection)
```

And once we have our data adapter, we use its `Fill()` method to create and populate a `DataTable` object in a new dataset. The table will be called `dtCategories`:

```
Dim objDataSet As New DataSet()
objAdapter.Fill(objDataSet, "dtCategories")
```

Finally, we bind the `DataTable` object called `dtCategories` to our `DataGrid`:

```
dgCategories.DataSource = objDataSet.Tables("dtCategories")
dgCategories.DataBind()
```

And that's all there is to it! The `DataTable` object we created in our `DataSet` object has been added to a collection called `Tables`, in which we can refer to it by name. But in all honesty, the *output* from this sample is nothing that we couldn't have achieved using the techniques we met in the last chapter. It's time to dig deeper into the world of datasets.

Accessing the Rows and Columns of Dataset Tables

Now that we've seen briefly how to bind a `DataTable` to a `DataGrid`, let's get our hands a little dirtier by getting direct access to the rows and columns of the `DataTable` objects contained by a `DataSet` object. This technique can be useful for returning one field of a record that's been chosen from a control, or for setting variables to the values of individual fields from records, or for setting the value of a single-valued control with a single field from a record.

Accessing Tables

Before we can get access to rows and colmuns, we have to get access to the tables that contain them. As we saw above, the `DataSet` class has a `Tables` property that returns a collection of all the `DataTable` objects in the current `DataSet`. To make that clearer, we can add a `DataTable` to the `Tables` collection with the `Add()` method, like so:

```
Dim myTable As New DataTable("MyTableName")
myDataSet.Tables.Add(myTable)
```

We can access a `DataTable` contained within this collection by using either the name of the `DataTable`:

```
myDataSet.Tables("MyTableName")
```

or the index number of the `DataTable`:

```
myDataSet.Tables(tableNumber)
```

Remember that the indices are zero-based, so the first `DataTable` in your `DataSet` will be accessed with `Tables(0)`. Now that we have accessed the tables, we can proceed into the rows.

Accessing Rows

The `DataTable` class has a `Rows` property that returns a collection of all the `DataRow` objects in the `DataTable`. Building on our techniques for accessing tables above, we can access *rows* with the index number of the `DataRow` we're interested in:

```
myDataSet.Tables("MyTableName").Rows(rowNumber)
```

Now that we can access a particular row, we can finally reach in and pluck out the value of a particular column within that row.

Accessing Columns

To access the value in a particular column within a given row, we can use either the name of the column:

```
myDataSet.Tables("MyTableName").Rows(rowNumber)("MyFavoriteField")
```

Or the index number of the column:

```
myDataSet.Tables("MyTableName").Rows(rowNumber)(columnNumber)
```

If, for example, we wished to obtain the first name of the first employee in the `Employees` table, we might use an expression like this:

```
myDataSet.Tables("Employees").Rows(0)("FirstName")
```

Alternatively, if our user picked an employee from a `ListBox` web server control, in which the `DataValueField` was set to the `EmployeeID` number that corresponds to the employee's position in the table, we might use the following to obtain the first name of the employee:

```
myDataSet.Tables("Employees").Rows(lstEmployees.DataValueField)("FirstName")
```

To make sure that these ideas are straight in your mind, it's probably a good time for a little more practice.

Try It Out – Displaying the Rows and Columns of a Table in a Dataset

In this example, we'll apply the things you've just learned in an ASP.NET page that displays the number of units in stock for each of the products in the Northwind database. Rather than using a `DataGrid` control, we'll create our own HTML table to display the results. We'll bring the data into a `DataTable` object, and then use properties of its `Columns` and `Rows` collections to extract the information we need.

1. In the ch05 folder, create a new file called `DisplayRows.aspx` and enter the following:

```
<%@ Import namespace="System.Data" %>
<%@ Import namespace="System.Data.SqlClient" %>

<html>
  <head>
    <title>Displaying Rows</title>
  </head>
  <body>
    <div id="display" runat="server">Table Will Go Here</div>
  </body>
</html>

<script language="VB" runat="server">
Sub Page_Load(Source as Object, E as EventArgs)

  ' Connection setup
  Dim strConnection As String = ConfigurationSettings.AppSettings("NWind")
  Dim objConnection As New SqlConnection(strConnection)
  Dim strSQL As String = "SELECT ProductName, UnitsInStock FROM Products"

  ' DataAdapter setup
  Dim objAdapter As New SqlDataAdapter(strSQL, objConnection)

  ' DataSet & Adapter & Table
  Dim objDataSet As New DataSet()
  objAdapter.Fill(objDataSet, "dtProducts")

  Dim strResultsHolder As String
  strResultsHolder = "<table width=80% border=1>"
  strResultsHolder &= "<tr>"

  Dim c As DataColumn
  For Each c In objDataSet.Tables("dtProducts").Columns
    strResultsHolder &= "<td>" & c.ColumnName & "</td>"
  Next
  strResultsHolder &= "</tr>"

  Dim r As DataRow
  Dim value, blankValue As Integer
  For Each r In objDataSet.Tables("dtProducts").Rows

    value = 100 * r("UnitsInStock") / 125
    blankValue = 100 - value
    strResultsHolder &= "<tr><td width=30%>" & r("ProductName") & "</td>" & _
                        "<td width=60%><table width=100%><tr>" & _
                        "<td width=" & value.ToString & "% bgcolor=#9933FF>" & _
                        " </td>" & _
                        "<td width=" & blankValue.ToString & "%> </td>" & _
                        "</tr></table></td>" & _
                        "<td width=10%>" & r("UnitsInStock").ToString & _
                        "</td></tr>"
  Next
```

```
        strResultsHolder &= "</table>"
display.InnerHTML = strResultsHolder
End Sub
</script>
```

2. View the above page in your browser to see a result like the following:

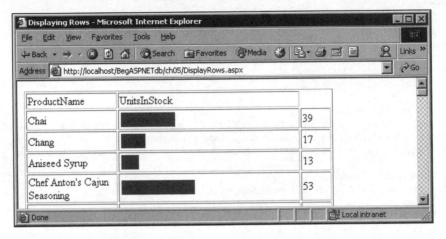

How It Works

This time, it's worth having a quick look at the HTML section, since we're using a different technique from the one we've been using so far. On this occasion, we're employing a server-side `<div>` element to hold our output:

```
<div id="display" runat="server" >Table Will Go Here</div>
```

The plan for the rest of the example is then to construct the raw HTML for a table holding our results, and to place this into the `<div>` element. We begin that process in the `Page_Load()` event handler by creating the connection object, and defining the SQL query that will retrieve the `ProductName` and `UnitsInStock` columns from the `Products` table of the Northwind database.

```
Dim strConnection As String = ConfigurationSettings.AppSettings("NWind")
Dim objConnection As New SqlConnection(strConnection)
Dim strSQL As String = "SELECT ProductName, UnitsInStock FROM Products"
```

Next, we create our data adapter and a new `DataSet`, and use the data adapter's `Fill()` method to create and populate the `dtProducts` table within that `DataSet`:

```
Dim objAdapter As New SqlDataAdapter(strSQL, objConnection)
Dim objDataSet As New DataSet()
objAdapter.Fill(objDataSet, "dtProducts")
```

We're going to hold the raw HTML for our table in a string called `strResultsHolder`; here we create it and begin the table definition:

```
Dim strResultsHolder As String
strResultsHolder = "<table width=80% border=1>"
strResultsHolder &= "<tr>"
```

The first thing we do in our table is to output the column names. To do this, we'll loop through every `DataColumn` object in `Columns` using a `For Each...Next` loop:

```
Dim c As DataColumn
For Each c In objDataSet.Tables("dtProducts").Columns
```

In the loop, we obtain the name of each column from its `ColumnName` property:

```
    strResultsHolder &= "<td>" & c.ColumnName & "</td>"
Next
strResultsHolder &= "</tr>"
```

Next, we loop through each `DataRow` object in the `Rows` collection, again using a `For Each...Next` loop:

```
Dim r As DataRow
Dim value, blankValue As Integer
For Each r In objDataSet.Tables("dtProducts").Rows
```

Note that we could not use the `For Each...Next` loop to modify any data in the `DataSet` object, since the `For Each` construct provides read-only access.

As we loop through the rows, we obtain the value of the `UnitsInStock` field in each row, and use this number to convert the units in stock for each product into a percentage, based on a maximum of 125 units:

```
value = 100 * r("UnitsInStock") / 125
blankValue = 100 - value
```

Next, we obtain the name of the product from the `ProductName` field. We'll put this in the first column of our HTML table, while the second column will contain a graphical representation of the units in stock, courtesy of our `value` variable. We add the actual number of units in stock to the final column of our table:

```
strResultsHolder &= "<tr><td width=30%>" & r("ProductName") & "</td>" & _
                    "<td width=60%><table width=100%><tr>" & _
                    "<td width=" & value.ToString & "% bgcolor=#9933FF>" & _
                    " </td>" & _
                    "<td width=" & blankValue.ToString & "%> </td>" & _
                    "</tr></table></td>" & _
                    "<td width=10%>" & r("UnitsInStock").ToString & _
                    "</td></tr>"
    Next
```

Finally, we finish our HTML table, and place the output onto our server-side `<div>` element, `display`:

```
strResultsHolder &= "</table>"
display.InnerHTML = strResultsHolder
```

In this example, we've used data from a `DataSet` object in a very immediate way – the value of that data has a direct impact on the way it gets presented. In general, of course, we're free to do anything we like with the information we retrieve, as later samples will demonstrate.

Working with Multiple Data Sources

Now that we've got rather more of a feel for how datasets (and some of their associated objects) behave, we can move on to examine another of the benefits that were laid out at the beginning of the chapter. As we stated then, `DataSet` objects are not tied (as data readers are) to a single data source. In our next example, we'll look at the simultaneous processing of data from two very different sources: the `Products` table of the Northwind database, and an XML file.

First, we'll create a `DataSet` that will contain a `DataTable` filled from an XML file. Then we'll create another `DataTable` to contain data from an RDBMS source (in this case, the `Products` table of Northwind). That should be enough to keep us occupied for the time being, but you can be assured that we'll be returning to and improving this example later in the chapter.

Try It Out – Data from Multiple Data Sources

Imagine that the Northwind employees have been sampling some of the products they sell, and making some comments about them in an XML file. We want to create a page that shows these comments in one table, and – for contrast – a list of the first four products in the database in another.

1. In the `ch05` folder, create a file called `Comments.xml` and enter the following:

```xml
<?xml version="1.0" standalone="yes"?>
<Reviews>
  <Review>
    <ReviewID>1</ReviewID>
    <ProductName>Chai</ProductName>
    <EmployeeID>6</EmployeeID>
    <Date>2001-01-01</Date>
    <Comment>"Even tastier than my mother's"</Comment>
  </Review>
  <Review>
    <ReviewID>2</ReviewID>
    <ProductName>Chang</ProductName>
    <EmployeeID>7</EmployeeID>
    <Date>2002-02-02</Date>
    <Comment>"Reminds me of my childhood school lunch"</Comment>
  </Review>
  <Review>
    <ReviewID>3</ReviewID>
```

```
      <ProductName>Aniseed Syrup</ProductName>
      <EmployeeID>8</EmployeeID>
      <Date>2003-03-03</Date>
      <Comment>"Gave me the courage to enlist in the Navy"</Comment>
  </Review>
  <Review>
      <ReviewID>4</ReviewID>
      <ProductName>Chai</ProductName>
      <EmployeeID>8</EmployeeID>
      <Date>2003-03-03</Date>
      <Comment>"Of questionable taste"</Comment>
  </Review>
</Reviews>
```

2. In the same folder, create a file named `Multiple_tables.aspx`. Enter the following code:

```
<%@ Import namespace="System.Data" %>
<%@ Import namespace="System.Data.SqlClient" %>

<html>
  <head>
    <title>Multiple Data Sources</title>
  </head>
  <body>
    <h3>Multiple Tables from Different Data Sources</h3>
    Products from Northwind and some comments
    <asp:DataGrid id="dgComments" runat="server" /><br/>
    <asp:DataGrid id="dgProducts" runat="server" /><br/>
  </body>
</html>

<script language="VB" runat="server">
Sub Page_Load(Source As Object, E As EventArgs)

  ' Connection
  Dim strConnection As String = ConfigurationSettings.AppSettings("NWind")
  Dim objConnection As New SqlConnection(strConnection)

  ' SQL query setup
  Dim strSqlProducts As String = "SELECT ProductID, ProductName FROM Products "
  strSqlProducts &= "WHERE ProductID < 5 ORDER BY ProductID"

  ' Create DataSet and data adapter
  Dim objDataSet As New DataSet("CommentsPage")
  Dim objAdapter As New SqlDataAdapter(strSqlProducts, objConnection)

  ' First Table - "Comments Table" From XML
  objDataSet.ReadXML(Server.MapPath("Comments.xml"))

  ' Second Table - "Products Table" from Northwind
  objAdapter.Fill(objDataSet, "dtProducts")
```

```
   dgComments.DataSource = objDataSet.Tables("Review")
   dgProducts.DataSource = objDataSet.Tables("dtProducts")
   Page.DataBind()
End Sub
</script>
```

3. On loading the above ASPX page into your browser, you should see the following outcome:

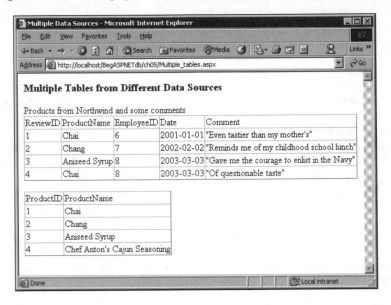

How It Works

Let's start with a quick look at the XML file. You can see that we've got a set of `<Review>` elements inside the root element, `<Reviews>`. Each review contains five elements that map to five fields in the ADO.NET `DataTable`. It is important to remember that the first level below the root is named `Review`, because that is how ADO.NET will name the `DataTable` object that you make from this XML file.

```
<?xml version="1.0" standalone="yes"?>
<Reviews>
  <Review>
    <ReviewID>1</ReviewID>
    <ProductName>Chai</ProductName>
    <EmployeeID>6</EmployeeID>
    <Date>2001-01-01</Date>
    <Comment>"Even tastier than my mother's"</Comment>
  </Review>
  ...

</Reviews>
```

Moving on to the ASP.NET page, the HTML section contains nothing new: we have two `DataGrid` controls and some caption text.

```
<body>
  <h3>Multiple Tables from Different Data Sources</h3>
  Products from Northwind and some comments
  <asp:DataGrid id="dgComments" runat="server" /><br/>
  <asp:DataGrid id="dgProducts" runat="server" /><br/>
</body>
```

The most striking thing about the `Page_Load()` event handler is the difference between our setup for reading the XML file, and that for reading from the RDBMS. We only need to create an ADO.NET connection to Northwind, because – as we saw in Chapter 3 – the XML file is handled differently. Similarly, we only need an SQL query to limit our selection of records from the RDBMS source; for the XML file, we will read every record.

```
Sub Page_Load(Source As Object, E As EventArgs)

  ' Connection
  Dim strConnection As String = ConfigurationSettings.AppSettings("NWind")
  Dim objConnection As New SqlConnection(strConnection)

  ' SQL query setup
  Dim strSqlProducts As String = "SELECT ProductID, ProductName FROM Products "
  strSqlProducts &= "WHERE ProductID < 5 ORDER BY ProductID"
```

Next, we create a `DataSet` object and the data adapter.

```
  ' Create DataSet and data adapter
  Dim objDataSet As New DataSet("CommentsPage")
  Dim objAdapter As New SqlDataAdapter(strSqlProducts, objConnection)
```

Then, as in Chapter 3, we use the `DataSet` class's `ReadXml()` method to create a new `DataTable` in `objDataSet`, and then fill this `DataTable` with the contents of the XML file. We pass the name of the XML file to the `ReadXml()` method, including the path to its physical directory.

```
  ' First Table - "Comments Table" From XML
  objDataSet.ReadXml(Server.MapPath("Comments.xml"))
```

Now we can use the data adapter's `Fill()` method to create and populate our second `DataTable` from the Northwind source. It's worth our while always to create appropriate names for a `DataTable`, so we use the overload that enables us to specify a name, rather than being stuck with whatever ADO.NET assigns (or, worse still, having to refer to the `DataTable` by its index number in the `Tables` collection).

```
  ' Second Table - "Products Table" from Northwind
  objAdapter.Fill(objDataSet, "dtProducts")
```

> **ReadXml()** creates a **DataTable** for us, and automatically names it with the name of the first element below the root in the XML file – in this case, **Review**.

At this point, we have two `DataTable` objects filled with data, so we set these to be the data sources for our `DataGrid` controls:

```
dgComments.DataSource = objDataSet.Tables("Review")
dgProducts.DataSource = objDataSet.Tables("dtProducts")
```

Finally, we bind them all at once with `Page.DataBind()`. This method binds a data source to the current page and all its child controls – for us here, it's a shorthand alternative to calling the `DataBind()` methods of both web server controls.

Structuring XML Data

Although we've been able to fill our `DataTable` with data from the `Comments.xml` file, and to bind this `DataTable` to a `DataGrid` and display it, our ability to work with data from this XML file is quite limited, because it has no explicit data type structure. The columns in the `DataTable` called `Review` are *all* of type `String` – even the ones such as `EmployeeID` that appear to be numerical. To work with XML data effectively, that data needs to have type information associated with it, and this is done through the use of an XML schema.

> *Providing type information is not the only purpose of an XML schema, but it's the one we're most interested in here. More generally, it's used to validate an XML document – it defines the elements and attributes that can be placed in a document, and the order in which they can appear. The other way to validate an XML document – a document type definition (DTD) – doesn't allow us to specify data types, and would be of limited use to us here.*

An XML schema allows us to define data types for elements and attributes, and uses an XML-compatible syntax to do so. Schemas can become very complex, and a detailed examination of them is beyond the scope of this book, so we here we'll just introduce the ideas involved, and discuss the schema that we'll be using for the `Comments.xml` file. A more in-depth look at schemas can be found in *Beginning XML 2nd Edition* (1-861005-59-8), also from Wrox Press.

XML Schemas

In the .NET Framework, there are two separate formats for schemas: **XML Schema Definition** language (XSD), and **XML-Data Reduced** (XDR) schemas. These formats are very different, and you need to be confident with XML in order to construct a schema using either of them. However, it's useful to be able to recognize the main elements, so that's what we'll look at here.

In fact, we're just going to look at the more prevalent format: XSD. The XDR schema format is proprietary to Microsoft, and typically found in documents produced by SQL Server 2000's powerful XML-handling capabilities. Rather confusingly, its syntax is almost precisely the opposite of XSD's.

You can choose to place an XSD schema inside the XML document it validates, or to keep it in a separate file. For our first look, we'll examine a sample XSD schema for our `Comments.xml` file, part of which is reproduced below. Note that within each `<Review>` element, we have `<ReviewID>`, `<ProductName>`, `<EmployeeID>`, `<Date>` and `<Comment>` elements:

```
<?xml version="1.0" standalone="yes"?>
<Reviews>
  <Review>
    <ReviewID>1</ReviewID>
    <ProductName>Chai</ProductName>
    <EmployeeID>6</EmployeeID>
    <Date>2001-01-01</Date>
    <Comment>"Even tastier than my mother's"</Comment>
  </Review>

  ...

  <Review>
    <ReviewID>4</ReviewID>
    <ProductName>Chai</ProductName>
    <EmployeeID>8</EmployeeID>
    <Date>2003-03-03</Date>
    <Comment>"Of questionable taste"</Comment>
  </Review>
</Reviews>
```

Keeping this in mind, let's see what an XSD schema for this document might look like, with the help of an example.

Try It Out – Defining an XSD Schema

In the `ch05` folder, create a file called `Comments.xsd`, and enter or copy in the following:

```
<?xml version="1.0" standalone="yes"?>
<schema xmlns="http://www.w3.org/2001/XMLSchema">
  <element name="Reviews">
    <complexType>
      <choice maxOccurs="unbounded">
        <element name="Review">
          <complexType>
            <sequence>
              <element name="ReviewID"    type="int" />
              <element name="ProductName" type="string" />
              <element name="EmployeeID"  type="int" />
              <element name="Date"        type="date" />
              <element name="Comment"     type="string" />
            </sequence>
          </complexType>
        </element>
      </choice>
    </complexType>
  </element>
</schema>
```

The key points of the body of this XSD schema are:

❑ The entire schema is contained within an element called <schema> (with a lower-case 's')

❑ Any element that can occur within the document must be represented by an <element> element. This element has a name attribute that indicates the name of the element it defines; it can also have a type attribute that indicates its data type. The <EmployeeID> element, for example, is defined as being of type int, which corresponds to a System.Int32 data type.

❑ If the element is to contain nested child elements (such as our <Review> element), we must include the <element> tags for these within a <complexType> element. Inside the latter, we specify how the child elements must occur. We can use a <choice> element to specify that the child elements can occur in any order, or <sequence> to specify that the child elements must appear in the same order as they are listed in the schema. If an element may appear more than once (as our <Review> element does), we need to include a maxOccurs attribute. Setting this to "unbounded" means that we can have as many of these elements as we like.

As suggested above, the data type of of an element, as specified by the type attribute, is *not* the .NET data type of that element – it's the W3C data type. For the majority of such data types, however, the corresponding .NET data type is clear. There is a complete list of the W3C data types and the corresponding .NET data types in the .NET Framework documentation; here are some of the most common:

XSD Type	.NET Data Type
int	System.Int32
date	System.DateTime
string	System.String
decimal	System.Decimal

Although the format of the XSD schema looks like quite complex, we have provided enough information for you to get started and maybe modify the example schema for your own XML files. In the meantime, we're going to use it in the next example.

Try It Out – Displaying Column Type Information

We can run a simple diagnostic page to check that our schema has produced the correct data types for the Comments.xml file. This facility will be very important soon, when we create a relationship between the data from the XML file, and the data from the database.

1. In the ch05 folder, create a new file called DisplayColumnInfo.aspx, and enter the following:

```
<%@ Import namespace="System.Data" %>
<%@ Import namespace="System.Data.SqlClient" %>

<html>
  <head>
<title>Display Column Information</title>
  </head>
</html>

<script language="VB" runat="server">
Sub Page_Load(Source As Object, E As EventArgs)

  ' Connection
  Dim strConnection As String = ConfigurationSettings.AppSettings("NWind")
  Dim objConnection As New SqlConnection(strConnection)

  ' SQL statements setup
  Dim strSqlProducts As String = "SELECT ProductID, ProductName FROM Products "
  strSqlProducts &= "WHERE ProductID < 5 ORDER BY ProductID;"

  ' Create dataset and data adapter with properties that apply to all tables
  Dim objDataSet As New DataSet("ProductsPage")
  Dim objAdapter As New SqlDataAdapter(strSqlProducts, objConnection)

  ' First Table - "Comments Table" From XML
  objDataSet.ReadXmlSchema(Server.MapPath("Comments.xsd"))
  objDataSet.ReadXml(Server.MapPath("Comments.xml"))

  ' Second Table - "Products Table" from Northwind
  objAdapter.Fill(objDataSet, "dtProducts")

  ' Diagnostic print of tables in objDataSet - loop through DataSet.Tables
  Dim strNames As String
  Dim c As DataColumn
  Dim iTableItem As DataTable
  For Each iTableItem In objdataSet.Tables
    strNames &= "Table Name: " & iTableItem.tableName & "<br/>"

    For Each c In iTableItem.Columns
      strNames &= "- Column " & c.ColumnName & " is of type " _
                            & c.DataType.ToString & "<br/>"
    Next

  Next
  Response.Write(strNames)
End Sub
</script>
```

Viewing this page in a browser should produce output like the following:

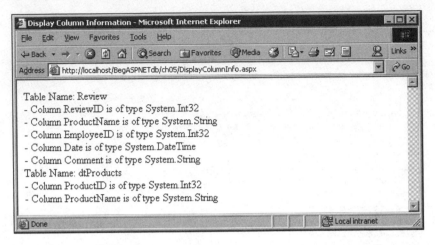

How It Works

The start of this code is the same as for the previous example: we create a connection object, a `DataSet`, and a data adapter, and then fill a `DataTable` with the `Comments.xml` file. Into this sequence, though, we insert a new step: before we fill from the XML file, we first have to read the schema from the `Comments.xsd` file (using the `ReadXmlSchema()` method), and then use the `ReadXml()` method to fill the `DataTable` in the `DataSet`.

```
' First Table - "Comments Table" From XML
objDataSet.ReadXmlSchema(Server.MapPath("Comments.xsd"))
objDataSet.ReadXml(Server.MapPath("Comments.xml"))
```

Next, we fill another `DataTable` from the `Products` table, once again giving us a `DataSet` object containing two `DataTable` objects. This allows us to loop through the `Tables` collection, displaying the names of the tables, and entering a sub-loop that runs through all the columns in each table. For each `DataColumn` object, we display the name and .NET data type, using the `DataColumn.DataType` property in the latter case. Note the use of the `ToString()` method to return this value as a string:

```
Dim strNames As String
Dim c As DataColumn
Dim iTableItem As DataTable
For Each iTableItem In objdataSet.Tables
  strNames &= "Table Name: " & iTableItem.tableName & "<br/>"

  For Each c In iTableItem.Columns
    strNames &= "- Column " & c.ColumnName & " is of type " _
                    & c.DataType.ToString & "<br/>"
  Next

Next
Response.Write(strNames)
```

This bit of script is of quite general use: you can add it to a page if you're having difficulties with the names of your DataTable objects, or the DataColumn objects within them. It also provides useful information about the data type of a DataColumn, which is very important for our next example.

Defining Relationships between DataTable Objects

As we've discussed, a great benefit of DataSet objects is their ability to create relationships between the various DataTable objects they hold, regardless of the (potentially diverse) original sources of the data in those tables. We explored the concept of a relationship between database tables in Chapter 2. In ADO.NET, the System.Data.DataRelation class allows us to implement the same idea between two DataTable objects.

The ADO.NET relationship mechanism revolves around the identification of a **parent column** in one table, and a **child column** in the other. Once that's been done, it becomes possible (among other things) to choose one of the rows in the parent table (the one that contains the parent column), and acquire a collection containing all of the rows in the child table for which the value in the child column matches the one in the parent column. The forthcoming example will demonstrate a situation in which such functionality is useful.

There are many ways to create a DataRelation object, but the one we'll look at here just needs you to specify a name for the relationship (so that it can be identified in a collection of relationships), the parent column of the relationship, and the child column of the relationship. Apart from that, there's more one more very important thing to note about creating a DataRelation object:

> The parent and child columns specified in the **DataRelation** object constructor must be of the same data type.

Creating a DataRelation Object

Let's start to formalize the above discussion by putting it in terms of some code. The process for creating a DataRelation object is straightforward:

1. Declare a DataColumn object for the parent column, and a DataColumn object for the child column:

```
Dim parentCol As DataColumn
Dim childCol As DataColumn
```

2. Specify which columns the parent and child columns will be:

```
parentCol = objDataSet.Tables("ParentTable").Columns("ParentColumn")
childCol = objDataSet.Tables("ChildTable").Columns("ChildColumn")
```

3. Create the `DataRelation` object, passing in a name for the relationship, the parent column, and the child column:

```
Dim myRelation As DataRelation
myRelation = New DataRelation("Relation", parentCol, childCol)
```

4. Finally, add the new `DataRelation` object to the `Relations` collection of of our `DataSet`:

```
objDataSet.Relations.Add(myRelation)
```

Note that when we add the relationship to the dataset, we have to use the name of the object (`myRelation`), rather than the string we passed to the constructor (`"Relation"`). The `Add()` method expects an object, not a string.

If we were writing a Windows application, we'd now have a very easy job indeed – the Windows Forms `DataGrid` control can easily display related records. The `DataGrid` web server control, on the other hand, does not have this functionality, so we'll have to retrieve and display the related records ourselves.

Retrieving Related Records

Suppose that we have a `DataRow` in our parent table, and that we wish to obtain all the rows in the child table related to this row – how do we get them? The answer is the `DataRow.GetChildRows()` method, to which we pass the name of the relationship, and from which we receive an array of `DataRow` objects in the child table that correspond to the `DataRow` in the parent table. The process for doing this is as follows:

1. Define a `DataRow` array to hold the `DataRow` objects returned by the `GetChildRows()` method:

```
Dim childr() As DataRow
```

2. Now we can actually get the child rows:

```
childr = r.GetChildRows("Relation")
```

3. We access the child rows as we would access any other array, with `childr(rowNumber)`. Once we have a child row, we can access its columns in the usual way:

```
childr(0)("MyFavoriteColumnInTheChildTable")
```

That's enough talk for now; let's get down to some action! Our next example will create a relationship between the data from the `Comments.xml` file and some data from the `Employees` table of `Northwind`, allowing us to display the comment about a product, and some more information about the employee who made the comment.

It has come to the attention of Northwind's management that some of the employees' comments about their products are less than favorable. They want to know who made those comments, so that they can get in touch with them to find out more.

1. Create a file called `DefiningRelationships.aspx` in the `ch05` folder. Enter the following code, which expands on some of the examples we've already looked at in this chapter.

```
<%@ Import namespace="System.Data" %>
<%@ Import namespace="System.Data.SqlClient" %>

<html>
  <head>
    <title>Defining Relationships</title>
  </head>
  <body>
    <h3>Defining relationships between different DataTables</h3>
    <div id=display runat="server">Table Will Go Here</div>
  </body>
</html>

<script language="VB" runat="server">
Sub Page_Load(Source As Object, E As EventArgs)

  ' Connection
  Dim strConnection As String = ConfigurationSettings.AppSettings("NWind")
  Dim objConnection As New SqlConnection(strConnection)

  ' SQL query setup
  Dim strSqlEmployees As String = "SELECT FirstName, LastName, Notes, " & _
                                  "Extension, EmployeeID " & _
                                  "FROM Employees ORDER BY EmployeeID"

  ' Create DataSet and data adapter
  Dim objDataSet As New DataSet()
  Dim objAdapter As New SqlDataAdapter(strSqlEmployees, objConnection)

  ' First Table - "Comments Table" From XML
  objDataSet.ReadXmlSchema(Server.MapPath("Comments.xsd"))
  objDataSet.ReadXml(Server.MapPath("Comments.xml"))

  ' Second Table - "Employees Table" from Northwind
  objAdapter.Fill(objDataSet, "dtEmployees")

  ' Define the Columns
  Dim parentCol As DataColumn
  Dim childCol As DataColumn
```

```
      parentCol = objDataSet.Tables("dtEmployees").Columns("EmployeeID")
      childCol = objDataSet.Tables("Review").Columns("EmployeeID")

      ' Create the relationship between the EmployeeID columns
      Dim relation As DataRelation
      relation = New DataRelation("Relation", parentCol, childCol)
      objDataSet.Relations.Add(relation)

      Dim strResultsHolder As String = "<table width=100% border=1>"
      Dim r As DataRow
      Dim c As DataColumn

      ' Create the table header
      strResultsHolder &= "<tr><td>Product<br/>Name</td><td>Comment</td>"

      For Each c In objDataSet.Tables("dtEmployees").Columns
         strResultsHolder &= "<td>" & c.ColumnName.ToString() & "</td>"
      Next

      ' Now we create the table body
      ' Loop through all the rows in Review
      For Each r In objDataSet.Tables("dtEmployees").Rows

         ' Create childr as an array of DataRow objects
         Dim childr() As DataRow

         ' Now we get the child rows from the relationship
         childr = r.GetChildRows("Relation")

         ' Now we loop through all the child rows
         Dim theChildRow As DataRow
         For Each theChildRow In childr

            ' Now we can loop through all the columns in that child row
            strResultsHolder &= "</tr><tr>"
            strResultsHolder &= "<td>" & theChildRow("ProductName") & "</td><td>" & _
                              theChildRow("Comment") & "</td>"

            For Each c In objDataSet.Tables("dtEmployees").Columns
               strResultsHolder &= "<td>" & r(c.ColumnName).ToString() & "</td>"
            Next
         Next
      Next

      display.InnerHTML = strResultsHolder
End Sub
</script>
```

2. Viewing the above page in a browser produces the following table, which displays the name of the product and the comment made about it, and also shows some information about the employee who made the comment:

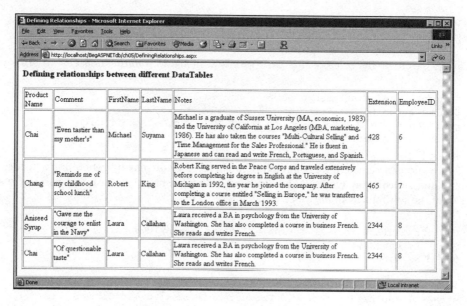

How It Works

In the `Page_Load()` event handler, we create the data adapter and `DataSet` objects, as we've done throughout this chapter. We then proceed to fill one `DataTable` in the `DataSet` from the `Comments.xml` file (first reading in the XSDL schema from `Comments.xsd`), and another from the `Employees` table of Northwind.

```
' First Table - "Comments Table" From XML
objDataSet.ReadXmlSchema(Server.MapPath("Comments.xsd"))
objDataSet.ReadXml(Server.MapPath("Comments.xml"))

' Second Table - "Employees Table" from Northwind
objAdapter.Fill(objDataSet, "dtEmployees")
```

Now that we have our `DataTable` objects, we can proceed to create the relationship following the steps we outlined earlier. First, we define `DataColumn` objects for the parent and child columns:

```
' Define the Columns
Dim parentCol As DataColumn
Dim childCol As DataColumn
```

Next, we specify the columns that will *be* the parent and child columns. The parent column will be the `EmployeeID` column of the `dtEmployees` table, and the child column will be the `EmployeeID` column of the `Review` table:

```
parentCol = objDataSet.Tables("dtEmployees").Columns("EmployeeID")
childCol = objDataSet.Tables("Review").Columns("EmployeeID")
```

That done, we create the `DataRelation` object, and then add it to the dataset's `Relations` collection:

```
' Create the relationship between the EmployeeID columns
Dim relation As DataRelation
relation = New DataRelation("Relation", parentCol, childCol)
objDataSet.Relations.Add(relation)
```

With the relationship created, we begin to prepare a table for display by generating a header containing column name information. Notice that we're hard-coding the names of the columns, since we won't be using all of the columns from the `Review` table:

```
Dim strResultsHolder As String = "<table width=100% border=1>"
Dim r As DataRow
Dim c As DataColumn

' Create the table header
strResultsHolder &= "<tr><td>Product<br/>Name</td><td>Comment</td>"

For Each c In objDataSet.Tables("dtEmployees").Columns
    strResultsHolder &= "<td>" & c.ColumnName.ToString() & "</td>"
Next
```

Now we begin to loop through each row in the `dtEmployees` table (remember: this is the table that contains our parent column). For each row, we define a `DataRow` array called `childr` to hold any associated rows from the `Review` table, and then use the `GetChildRows()` method to retrieve them.

```
For Each r In objDataSet.Tables("dtEmployees").Rows

    ' Create childr as an array of DataRow objects
    Dim childr() As DataRow

    ' Now we get the child rows from the relationship
    childr = r.GetChildRows("Relation")
```

The rows now held in the `childr` array are those containing an `EmployeeID` value that matches the one of the current row in the `dtEmployees` table. We loop through them, extracting the values of the `ProductName` and `Comment` columns:

```
' Now we loop through all the child rows
Dim theChildRow As DataRow
For Each theChildRow In childr
```

```
                ' Now we can loop through all the columns in that child row
            strResultsHolder &= "</tr><tr>"
            strResultsHolder &= "<td>" & theChildRow("ProductName") & "</td><td>" & _
                                theChildRow("Comment") & "</td>"
```

Note the "`</tr><tr>`" in the first line of the loop, which finishes the previous row of the HTML table and begins the next row. All that remains now is to loop through the columns of the parent table, `dtEmployees`, and obtain the values from the columns. Again, note the use of `ToString()` to ensure a string representation, regardless of the actual data type of the column.

```
            For Each c In objDataSet.Tables("dtEmployees").Columns
                strResultsHolder &= "<td>" & r(c.ColumnName).ToString() & "</td>"
            Next
```

Now we only have to remember to finish all our loops:

```
        Next
    Next
```

And then we simply place `strResultsHolder` onto our server-side `<div>` element, and the data is displayed.

```
        display.InnerHTML = strResultsHolder
```

That was quite a complex example, but it contained many parts that you should often find useful. For example, the code that obtains the child rows and then loops through them is more-or-less generic – the basic skeleton of this routine is below, and you can use it to navigate relationships within your own data.

```
        Dim childr() As DataRow
        childr = r.GetChildRows("Relation")

        Dim theChildRow As DataRow
        For Each theChildRow In childr

            ' Add your own code here to do things with the child rows

        Next theChildRow
```

When working with relationships between `DataTable` objects, always keep in mind that the data types of the parent and child columns must be the same. If you attempt to create a relationship between columns with different data types, you will receive the following error:

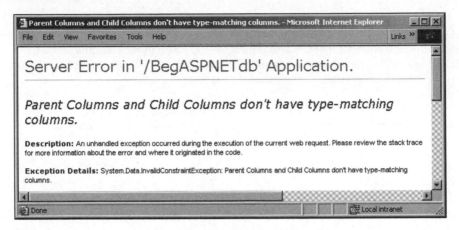

If you're in any doubt about the data types of your columns, the utility that we presented earlier in the *Displaying Column Type Information* example should help you out!

Creating Views of Data with DataView Objects

So far, when we've used `DataSet` objects and `DataGrid` controls in the same sample, we've taken every `DataRow` and `DataColumn` in our `DataTable` objects, and placed them directly into the `DataGrid`. Often, though, we'll want to display things in a different order, or just show a subset of `DataColumn` objects, or a selection of `DataRow` objects. It's possible to perform such tasks by writing a more complex SQL query, but that doesn't help if you want to create more than one presentation from a single `DataTable`.

This is where the `System.Data.DataView` class comes in. We can create any number of `DataView` objects from a `DataTable`, and each can provide a different selection of data. Once you have a `DataTable` created and populated, using a `DataView` object is quite easy: we simply create it, set the sorting or filtering criteria, and then use it as the source for the `DataGrid`.

When and Where to Sort

Since it's possible to sort and select data in an SQL statement, this raises the question of when we should sort data using SQL, and when we should do it with a `DataView` object. The first thing to consider is that a SQL statement is much faster, because the RDBMS is optimized for this type of operation, and because if only certain data is selected, fewer rows are sent to the `DataSet`. However, if your data source is not an RDBMS (if you're using a text file, for example), you may have very limited support for querying your data.

Most of the time, if you only need to sort the data once, it makes sense to use an SQL statement to do it. If you need to sort the data more than once, and make more than one selection from this sorted data, then a DataView is the right option – remembering of course that the original SQL statement must then return all of the data that you need for all of your views. If your ability to query your original data source is limited, then using a DataView object to sort and select it is an ideal solution.

SQL statements and DataView objects can be used to perform sorting and selecting on the same page – it's irrelevant to the DataSet whether a SQL statement has previously sorted the data. Frequently, your best approach is to perform one level of selecting and a default sort in a SQL statement, and then do additional selecting or re-sorting as you create multiple DataView objects.

Creating the DataView

As usual, we can break down the process of creating and using DataView objects into discrete stages. As a first step, the following snippet shows how to create a simple DataView object containing the data in a DataTable object called myTable:

```
Dim dvView As New DataView(myTable)

' Bind the DataView to a DataGrid
dgMyGrid.DataSource = dvView
dgMyGrid.DataBind()
```

Sorting Data with the Sort Property

Having created the DataView object, we can sort the data through the use of its Sort property:

```
dvView.Sort = "myField ASC"
```

Notice the ASC in the code above; it means we're sorting the rows in ascending order of the data in myField. Alternatively, we could have specified descending order with DESC, and you can use further fields to resolve any 'ties' in sorting, as follows:

```
dvView.Sort = "myField1 ASC, myField2 DESC"
```

Keep in mind that all DataView sorting and selecting operations occur on the web server. This means that they are generally slower than similar operations performed using an RDBMS. Furthermore, they will be using web server resources, as opposed to those of the RDBMS.

Filtering Data with the RowFilter Property

As well as sorting the data in a DataView object, we can use the RowFilter property to filter the data before we display, using code like this:

```
dvView.RowFilter = "MyField < 5"
```

163

In terms of its syntax, the `RowFilter` property is a bit more complex that the `Sort` property, but it's similar to an SQL `WHERE` clause. Keep in mind that the entire expression must be in double quotes, and that any literal text within must be in single quotes. The following examples demonstrate most likely situations; the asterisk in the last line is a wildcard character.

```
dvView.RowFilter = "MyIntegerField = 10"
dvView.RowFilter = "MyIntegerField <= 10"
dvView.RowFilter = "MyIntegerField <> 10"
dvView.RowFilter = "MyIntegerField IN (10, 20)"

dvView.RowFilter = "MyDateField = #1/30/2003#"
dvView.RowFilter = "MyDateField >= #1/1/1993# AND MyDateField <= #12/31/1993#"
dvView.RowFilter = "MyTextField = 'Joe'"
dvView.RowFilter = "MyTextField IN ('Joe', 'Jim', 'John')"
dvView.RowFilter = "MyTextField LIKE = '*son'"
```

It's also worth mentioning that `DataView` implements the `IEnumerable` interface, which means (among other things) that it has a `Count` property. In this case, however, it's a count of the number of records *after the RowFilter has been applied*, which might make for results that aren't quite what you were expecting.

By and large, one `DataView` object is associated with one `DataTable` object. It's difficult to use a `DataView` to bring the `DataColumn` objects from two `DataTable` objects together, as you might do in an SQL `JOIN`. For that task, it's better to write the `JOIN` into the SQL query that reads the data into the `DataTable`.

Try It Out – Using a DataView Object

For this example, suppose that we want to produce a page to display tables showing a list of Northwind employees in the UK, and a list of those in the USA. For each table, we want to include a note on how many entries there are.

1. In the `ch05` folder, create a file named `DataSet_views.aspx`. Enter the following code:

```
<%@ Import namespace="System.Data" %>
<%@ Import namespace="System.Data.SqlClient" %>

<html>
  <head>
    <title>DataSet Views</title>
  </head>
  <body>
    <h3>DataSet Views</h3>
    UK Employees:
    <asp:Label id="lblUKCount" runat="server" />
    <asp:DataGrid id="dgEmployeesUK" runat="server" /><br/>
    USA Employees:
    <asp:Label id="lblUSACount" runat="server" />
    <asp:DataGrid id="dgEmployeesUSA" runat="server" /><br/>
  </body>
</html>
```

```
<script language="VB" runat="server">
Sub Page_Load(Source as Object, E as EventArgs)

  ' Connection setup
Dim strConnection As String = ConfigurationSettings.AppSettings("NWind")
  Dim objConnection as New SqlConnection(strConnection)

  ' DataAdapter setup
  Dim strSQL as string = "SELECT FirstName, LastName, Country FROM Employees"
  Dim objAdapter As New SqlDataAdapter(strSQL, objConnection)

  ' DataSet & Adapter & Table
  Dim objDataSet As New DataSet()
  ObjAdapter.Fill(objDataSet, "dtEmployees")
  Dim dtEmployees as DataTable = objDataSet.Tables("dtEmployees")

  ' Views Setup
  Dim dvUK as New DataView(dtEmployees)
  dvUK.RowFilter = "Country = 'UK'"
  dvUK.Sort = "LastName ASC"

  Dim dvUSA as New DataView(dtEmployees)
  dvUSA.RowFilter = "Country = 'USA'"
  dvUSA.Sort = "LastName DESC"

  ' Bind
  lblUKCount.Text = dvUK.Count
  dgEmployeesUK.DataSource = dvUK

  lblUSACount.text = dvUSA.Count
  dgEmployeesUSA.DataSource=dvUSA

  Page.DataBind()
End Sub
</script>
```

2. Take a look at the page. You should see two tables of employees, as follows:

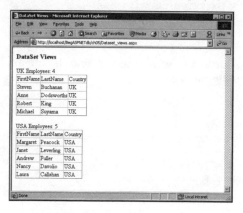

How It Works

We use a few new commands in this page, as well as giving a bit more consideration to using some old ones. As usual, let's start with a look at the HTML, so that we can see our objectives. We create two independent DataGrids, giving each an accompanying text label that will display the count.

```
UK Employees:
<asp:Label id="lblUKCount" runat="server" />
<asp:DataGrid id="dgEmployeesUK" runat="server" /><br/>
USA Employees:
<asp:Label id="lblUSACount" runat="server" />
<asp:DataGrid id="dgEmployeesUSA" runat="server" /><br/>
```

In the Page_Load() event handler, we create our connection as usual, and then use a data adapter to create and fill a DataTable object called dtEmployees.

```
' DataAdapter setup
Dim strSQL As String = "SELECT FirstName, LastName, Country FROM Employees"
Dim objAdapter As New SqlDataAdapter(strSQL, objConnection)

' DataSet & Adapter & Table
Dim objDataSet As New DataSet()
ObjAdapter.Fill(objDataSet, "dtEmployees")
Dim dtEmployees as DataTable = objDataSet.Tables("dtEmployees")
```

Now we build two DataViews from the DataTable. In each, we set a filter to select only the employees from one country. (We also reverse the sort order in one of them, just to show off the technique.)

```
' Views setup
Dim dvUK As New DataView(dtEmployees)
dvUK.RowFilter = "Country = 'UK'"
dvUK.Sort = "LastName ASC"

Dim dvUSA As New DataView(dtEmployees)
dvUSA.RowFilter = "Country = 'USA'"
dvUSA.Sort = "LastName DESC"
```

Finally, we set the data sources for our web server controls, and bind. By using Page.DataBind(), we can perform all of the binding at once.

```
' Bind
lblUKCount.Text = dvUK.Count
dgEmployeesUK.DataSource = dvUK

lblUSACount.text = dvUSA.Count
dgEmployeesUSA.DataSource = dvUSA

Page.DataBind()
```

And that's all there is to it. One dataset, one `DataTable` object, one interaction with the database, but two views – and of course, there could have been more. With that, however, our examination of reading data using a `DataSet` object comes to an end, and we can start to make good on the other promise we made in the last chapter. We're going to spend the second half of *this* chapter having a closer look at the `DataGrid` web server control, and a few of its brothers in arms.

We are by no means finished with our studies of `DataSet` objects. Chapters 6 and 7 contain information on creating, inserting, modifying, and deleting the records they can contain.

DataGrid Column Properties

To this point, we've accepted our `DataGrid` columns as they were presented to us by the data source. However, the `DataGrid` is quite capable of applying customization to each column on an individual basis, controlling such things as the column heading, the appearance of the data in a column, and even whether a column should appear at all. The techniques involved are not difficult, as long as you remember the following:

- ❑ Turn off the automatic generation of columns
- ❑ Create columns of your own, and set their properties within the `DataGrid` object
- ❑ Be careful to follow HTML element rules, and to use the correct field names
- ❑ The formatting syntax is tricky, so type carefully

Starting at the top of that list, we must set the `DataGrid`'s `AutoGenerateColumns` attribute to `False`. Then, we can add an element named `<Columns>`, and within that as many `BoundColumn` controls as we need. Each bound column can have several of its own attributes, as we will discuss below, but the most basic one is `DataField`, which specifies the actual column in the `DataTable` to bind to the `DataGrid`.

```
<asp:DataGrid id="dgProducts" runat="server"
              AutoGenerateColumns="False">
  <Columns>
    <asp:BoundColumn DataField="myField1" />
    <asp:BoundColumn DataField="myField2" />
  </Columns>
</asp:DataGrid>
```

Many field names in data stores use abbreviations, making them difficult to understand for web site visitors. To overcome this kind of problem, the `BoundColumn` control supports the `HeaderText` attribute, which can provide a more friendly column header. We can use this in the following way:

```
<asp:BoundColumn DataField="myField1" HeaderText="myCustomText" />
```

It's even possible to include HTML elements in the value you assign to the `HeaderText` attribute, as this string is sent directly to the browser.

Another likelihood is that we'll want to format the values within a column, for an easier-to-read display. For this, we use an attribute of the `BoundColumn` control called `DataFormatString`, which is always followed by a value in double quotes. The value has four parts, built around a set of braces and a colon; for a `BoundColumn` that contains price information, it might look something like this:

```
<asp:BoundColumn DataField="myField1"
                 DataFormatString="Our Price {0:C2} postpaid" />
```

To the left of the opening brace, we have literal characters (such as "`Our Price `" here). Then, inside the braces, but to the left of the colon, we have a number that's always zero for a `DataGrid` (because there's only one value in each cell of the grid). To the right of the colon, but still inside the braces, is a code that will affect the formatting of values in this column. Finally, to the right of the braces, we have some more literal characters ("`postpaid`" above).

The codes for formatting values consist of a letter followed by a number. The letter determines the general formatting, and the number determines the degree of accuracy. However, the same letter codes can mean different things, depending on the type of data you're dealing with. For example, `D` for numbers means decimal, while for dates it means 'long' (that is, verbose) output. Furthermore, upper and lower case letters can denote different patterns (`d` is a 'short' date, while `D` is a 'long' date). On top of these complexities, keep in mind that formats for dates and currency will vary according to localization (4/10/2002 means different days in Lancaster, Pennsylvania and Lancaster, England – in the US, dates are formatted month/day/year; in the UK, they're formatted day/month/year).

In the following table (which isn't exhaustive – check the documentation for the others), the raw data used for numbers and currency is 12.6789, while for dates it's midnight at the start of March 23, 2003.

Format	Syntax	Result	Notes
Numbers	`{0:N2}`	12.68	Number indicates the number of decimal places to display.
Numbers	`{0:N0}`	13	Numbers are rounded to the nearest integer.
Currency	`{0:c2}`	$12.68	No difference between `C` and `c`. Symbol will be local (server) currency symbol.
Currency	`{0:c4}`	$12.6789	Number determines the number of decimal places to display.
Currency	`"¥{0:N2}"`	¥12.68	Add currency symbols other than the server's default with literal characters, and using numeric format.
Scientific Notation	`{0:E3}`	1.27E+001	Number represents total number of significant figures.

Format	Syntax	Result	Notes
Percent	{0:P}	1,267.89%	No difference between P and p. A value of 1 will appear as 100%. A value of 0.01 will appear as 1%.
Dates	{0:D}	Sunday, March 23, 2003	Upper case gives long date (day plus date in words).
Dates	{0:d}	3/23/2003	Lower case gives short date (date in numbers).
Dates	{0:f}	Sunday, March 23, 2003 12:00 AM	Long date plus hours and minutes.
Dates	{0:F}	Sunday, March 23, 2003 12:00:00 AM	Long date plus hours, minutes, and seconds.
Date	{0:s}	2003-03-23T00:00:00	ISO 8601 sortable.
Times	{0:T}	12:00:00 AM	Time (t gives no seconds).

The last thing that we suggested might be useful to do is to show or hide DataGrid columns. This can be done by setting the Visible attribute of the column to "False":

```
<asp:BoundColumn DataField="myField1" Visible="False" />
```

As you'd expect, the default value of Visible for a column is "True". To change the value in response to a user action, we'd use the following syntax:

```
myDataGrid.Columns(myColumnIndexAsInteger).Visible = False
```

Let's put all of the above to the test, with the help of another of our worked examples.

Try It Out – DataGrid Column Properties

We will put together a page that shows the first few orders from Northwind, with modifications. For instance, we'll display the order ID number, but the CEO is planning to move to a new numbering system, and has asked us to pad them with leading zeros until they have seven digits (she also likes to see a # in front of the order number). The shipped-to address should also appear, but it'll be possible to hide it by clicking on a check box. In addition, we'll show the shipped date (but *only* the date, not the time), and some more descriptive column headings.

1. Create a file called `DataGrid_properties.aspx` and add the following code:

```
<%@ Import namespace="System.Data" %>
<%@ Import namespace="System.Data.SqlClient" %>

<html>
  <head><title>DataGrid Bound Columns</title></head>
  <body>
    <h3>DataGrid Bound Columns</h3>
    <form runat="server">
      <asp:CheckBox id="chkShowAddressee" runat="server"
                    AutoPostBack="True"
                    Text="Show Address for Shipping"
                    OnCheckedChanged="CheckChanged" />

      <asp:DataGrid id="dgOrders" runat="server"
                    AutoGenerateColumns="False">
        <Columns>
          <asp:BoundColumn DataField="OrderID"
                           HeaderText="Order<br/>Number"
                           DataFormatString="#{0:D7}" />
          <asp:BoundColumn DataField="ShipAddress"
                           HeaderText="Shipped<br/>To"
                           Visible="False" />
          <asp:BoundColumn DataField="OrderDate"
                           HeaderText="Shipped<br/>Date"
                           DataFormatString="{0:d}" />
        </Columns>
      </asp:DataGrid>
    </form>
  </body>
</html>

<script language="VB" runat="server">
Sub Page_Load(Source As Object, E As EventArgs)
   Dim strConnection As String = ConfigurationSettings.AppSettings("NWind")
   Dim objConnection As New SqlConnection(strConnection)
   Dim StrSQL As String = "SELECT * FROM Orders WHERE OrderID < 10255 " & _
                      "ORDER BY OrderID"

   Dim objAdapter As New SqlDataAdapter(strSQL, objConnection)
   Dim objDataSet As New DataSet()
   objAdapter.Fill(objDataSet)
   objConnection.Close()

   dgOrders.DataSource = objDataSet
   dgOrders.DataBind()
End Sub

Sub CheckChanged(S As Object, E As EventArgs)
   dgOrders.Columns(1).Visible = chkShowAddressee.Checked
End Sub
</script>
```

2. Viewing the above page will give the screen below. Notice the improved text in the header of each column.

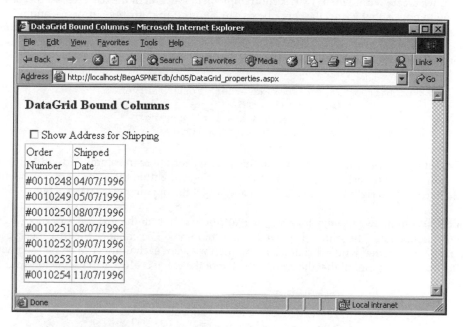

3. When we click on the check box, we get the additional column, as follows:

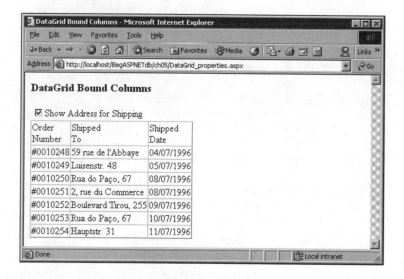

How It Works

The form we create within the HTML section implements several of the features we discussed above. The first thing to note is that we set the check box's `AutoPostBack` attribute to `True`, and wired it to the `CheckChanged()` event handler, which will control the showing and hiding of the shipping address column. It's also worth pointing out that this is a single check box, rather than the list we used in the last chapter, although the syntax for using it is very similar.

```
<asp:CheckBox id="chkShowAddressee" runat="server"
            AutoPostBack="True"
            Text="Show Address for Shipping"
            OnCheckedChanged="CheckChanged" />
```

Now we set up our `DataGrid` control, but this time we format each column individually. Take a good look at how we create each `<asp:BoundColumn>` element within the `<Columns>` element; a common mistake here is to go right to the first column and forget the opening `<Columns>` tag.

For our first column, we use the `HeaderText` attribute to output the text `Order<br/>Number` in place of the real field name. The values displayed in the column will be enhanced with a specific format: we want the data preceded with a # character, and then we want each number to be padded with leading zeros to seven digits. Recall that the zero to the left of the colon is always the same for `BoundColumn` formatting.

```
<asp:DataGrid id="dgOrders" runat="server"
            AutoGenerateColumns="False">
  <Columns>
    <asp:BoundColumn DataField="OrderID"
                  HeaderText="Order<br/>Number"
                  DataFormatString="#{0:D7}" />
```

Our second column again uses our own text instead of the field name. Also, since we start with our check box empty, we want to initialize this column to be invisible.

```
<asp:BoundColumn DataField="ShipAddress"
              HeaderText="Shipped<br/>To"
              Visible="False" />
```

The third and final column takes another format – in this case, we want a short date.

```
<asp:BoundColumn DataField="OrderDate"
              HeaderText="Shipped<br/>Date"
              DataFormatString="{0:d}" />
  </Columns>
</asp:DataGrid>
```

Moving on to the VB.NET code, we set up the connection as we've done several times before, and then provide the SQL query string. In it, you can see how we limit ourselves to the first few orders by using a `WHERE` clause. (The first order number in the table is 10248.)

```
Dim StrSQL As String = "SELECT * FROM Orders WHERE OrderID < 10255 " & _
                       "ORDER BY OrderID"
```

We use the SQL query as the first argument to instantiate our data adapter, which then fills a `DataSet` object. We finish by binding this `DataSet` to the `DataGrid`.

```
Dim objAdapter As New SqlDataAdapter(strSQL, objConnection)
Dim objDataSet As New DataSet()
objAdapter.Fill(objDataSet)
objConnection.Close()

dgOrders.DataSource = objDataSet
dgOrders.DataBind()
```

You'll remember that when we created the check box, we specified that when the status changed, the `CheckChanged()` method should be called. The logic of this method is not hard to divine: when the box is checked, we want the column to be visible; when it's unchecked, the column should disappear. Both of these properties are implemented using Boolean values, so we can just set one to the other! Since bound columns are indexed (from zero) in the order they were created, the shipped-to column is `Columns(1)`.

```
Sub CheckChanged(S As Object, E As EventArgs)
  dgOrders.Columns(1).Visible = chkShowAddressee.Checked
End Sub
```

To summarize what we've learned about bound columns, remember that you can use them to create better headings for your columns, and to configure the format of the data they contain. Bound columns can also have their `Visible` property changed at runtime.

DataGrid Sorting

Among its other abilities, the ASP.NET `DataGrid` control contains the tools you need to set up data sorting with automatic, in-grid hyperlinks for the user. You just have to understand how to set it up (it works in conjunction with `DataView` objects), and how to react to the visitors' requests. In outline, the process of sorting within a `DataGrid` has these steps:

- ❑ Create a `DataGrid` with specific properties that support sorting
- ❑ Create a single, generic `DataView` object that can accept a string for its sort order
- ❑ Create a public variable to hold the `DataView`'s sort string
- ❑ Create three procedures for:
  - ❑ Dealing with the general data binding
  - ❑ Setting the sort string on first load of the page
  - ❑ Setting the sort string when a sort has been requested by the visitor

173

The first of these steps – fixing the `DataGrid` settings – is simple. As usual, our `DataGrid` must be within a `<form>` element that's set to run at the server. In addition, we set the `AllowSorting` attribute to `True`, which will automatically change our column headings into clickable text. This is a standard format that the majority of visitors will recognize as indicating that they can sort the records by that column.

EmployeeID	FirstName	LastName	Country
5	Steven	Buchanan	UK
8	Laura	Callahan	USA

Also in the `DataGrid` control, we must set the `OnSortCommand` attribute to *MySortingSub*, where the latter is the name of the handler that will implement the sorting functionality.

In step two, you'll recall from our section on `DataView` objects that we can create a `DataView` for a particular `DataTable`, and then set its `Sort` property in a later command.

For the third step, the variable that holds the sort string must be available to all our handlers, so we'll need to place it within the `<script>` element, but outside any other code. We will also need to use the `Public` keyword, rather than `Dim`.

Last of all, we create three procedures:

- ❑ The first is called `SetData()`. It creates our connection, data adapter, `DataSet`, and `DataView` objects, and queries the database.
- ❑ The second is the `Page_Load()` event handler, which sets the `DataView` to use and then executes `SetData()`.
- ❑ The third is an event handler called `SortColumn()`. It changes the sort order and then executes `SetData()`.

The key to getting this kind of ASP.NET page to function correctly is to understand how the three handlers interact: when they're called, and how information flows between them. We'll examine exactly what goes on in our next example, but first we need to study the two arguments that have been passed to every event handler we've written so far: `Source` and `E`. We've been faithfully typing their names, but never actually using them. That's going to change here, and there are three points to be aware of:

- ❑ The `Source` parameter is the name of (and therefore a reference to) the object that called the procedure.
- ❑ In many cases, we must change the keyword `EventArgs` to be more specific to the kind of event that invoked the handler. If it were to be invoked by a `SortCommand` event, for example, then `EventArgs` should be changed to `DataGridSortCommandEventArgs`.
- ❑ An event can pass one or more arguments to a handler, as properties of the object `E`. In our case, the argument is called `SortExpression` and can be read using `E.SortExpression`.

Suppose that we want to display a table of employees that can be sorted by EmployeeID, Name, or Country. To add a little complexity, in the case of the latter we want to sort within a country by the employee's last name.

1. Create a new file named DataGrid_sorting.aspx in the ch05 folder, and then enter the following code:

```vb
<%@ Import namespace="System.Data" %>
<%@ Import namespace="System.Data.SqlClient" %>

<html>
  <head><title>DataGrid Sorting</title></head>
  <body>
    <h3>DataGrid Sorting</h3>
    <form runat="server">
      <asp:DataGrid id="dgEmployees" runat="server"
                  AllowSorting="True"
                  OnSortCommand="SortColumn" />
    </form>
  </body>
</html>

<script language="VB" runat="server">
Public strViewString As String

Sub SetData()

  ' Connection setup
  Dim strConnection As String = ConfigurationSettings.AppSettings("NWind")
  Dim objConnection As New SqlConnection(strConnection)

  ' DataAdapter setup
  Dim strSQL As string = "SELECT EmployeeID, FirstName, LastName, " & _
                    "Country FROM Employees"
  Dim objAdapter As New SqlDataAdapter(strSQL, objConnection)

  ' DataSet & Adapter & Table
  Dim objDataSet As New DataSet()
  objAdapter.Fill(objDataSet, "dtEmployees")
  Dim dtEmployees As DataTable = objDataSet.Tables("dtEmployees")

  ' Create DataView on dtEmployees
  Dim dvView As New DataView(dtEmployees)
  dvView.Sort = strViewString

  ' Bind data
  dgEmployees.DataSource = dvView
  dgEmployees.DataBind()
End Sub
```

```
Sub Page_Load(Source As Object, E As EventArgs)
  If Not Page.IsPostBack Then
    strViewString = "LastName"
    SetData()
  End If
End Sub

Sub SortColumn(Source As Object, E As DataGridSortCommandEventArgs)
  If E.SortExpression = "Country" Then
    strViewString = "Country, LastName"
  Else
    strViewString = E.SortExpression
  End If
  SetData()
End Sub
</script>
```

2. The above ASPX page yields a display that looks like the one below:

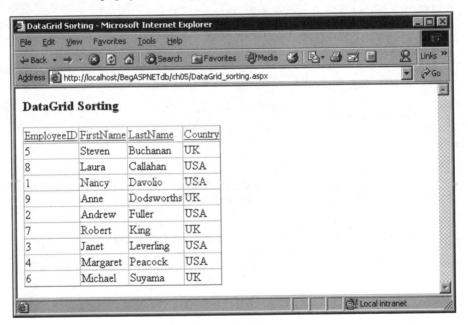

3. Clicking the Country column heading will re-sort the rows according to country:

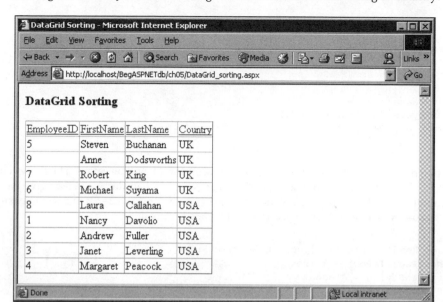

How It Works

We'll analyze this page in the same four parts that we discussed in the theory section above. First, ensuring that the DataGrid control is inside a `<form runat="server">` element, we set two properties as follows:

```
<form runat="server">
  <asp:DataGrid id="dgEmployees" runat="server"
                AllowSorting="True"
                OnSortCommand="SortColumn" />
</form>
```

Next, right inside the `<script>` element, we have the Public variable that holds our sort string. strViewString can be used from any of the three procedures that follow it – this is a level of flexibility we'll need, since the variable will hold the name of the column on which we want to sort.

```
<script language="VB" runat="server">
Public strViewString As String
```

Talking of those three procedures, let's take a look at the first. SetData() creates and uses various objects that we're now familiar with (a connection, a data adapter, a DataSet, and a DataTable called dtEmployees), and then goes on to create a DataView object, setting its Sort property to the contents of our public strViewString variable.

```
Sub SetData()

  ...

  ' Create DataView on dtEmployees
  Dim dvView As New DataView(dtEmployees)
  dvView.Sort = strViewString

  ' Bind data
  dgEmployees.DataSource = dvView
  dgEmployees.DataBind()
End Sub
```

There are two occasions in the life of the page when SetData() will be called. The first occurs when the page loads for the first time, through a call in the Page_Load() handler. There, we give the sort order string an initial value of "LastName". Notice the use of Page.IsPostBack in a test to ensure that we don't call SetData() from this code every time the page is reloaded.

```
Sub Page_Load(Source As Object, E As EventArgs)
  If Not Page.IsPostBack Then
    strViewString = "LastName"
    SetData()
  End If
End Sub
```

The other time we call SetData() is after a visitor has clicked on a re-sort link (that is, an underlined column heading). In this case, the name of the column on which we wish to sort is contained in the E.SortExpression property, which we assign to strViewString. An exception to this occurs if the SortExpression is Country, in which case we set strViewString to "Country, LastName", as defined by the requirement list for this example.

```
Sub SortColumn(Source As Object, E As DataGridSortCommandEventArgs)
  If E.SortExpression = "Country" Then
    strViewString = "Country, LastName"
  Else
    strViewString = E.SortExpression
  End If
  SetData()
End Sub
```

> If, when writing code like this, you get an error message such as 'SortExpression' is not a member of 'System.EventArgs', then you didn't change **EventArgs** to the proper object name. There are dozens of these objects, but you can always find the name of the right one by searching the documentation.

The code we've looked at so far hasn't been too difficult, so before we leave this section, we can take a look at a couple of variations that you might like to try. First, if we were to use bound columns, it would be possible to give each column an individual value for its `SortExpression` property, rather than just getting the column header. Setting a string such as "*myColumn1* ASC, *myColumn2* DESC", would avoid the need for the `If` structure in the `SortColumn()` handler – we'd just set `strViewString` to `E.SortExpression` in all cases.

Second, we could react to the click not by changing the `DataView` object's sort property, but by creating a new SQL statement. This is fundamentally different, because changing a `DataView` works on the data in the `DataSet` object, while changing the query results in the `DataSet` containing the information in a different order. Usually, the ADO.NET solution is more efficient, but it never hurts to do a little testing.

DataGrid Paging

For displaying data with a large number of rows, it makes good sense to show only a limited number of records at a time, and to allow the user to 'walk through' the pages of records. For example, if we were binding the `OrderDetails` table of Northwind (which has over 2000 records) to a `DataGrid`, we would want to display a handful of these at a time, and to offer the user navigation hyperlinks to the other pages of records. ASP.NET and ADO.NET enable us to implement this feature with a minimum of fuss – and by adding a bit more code, to make it look quite attractive. We'll take a look at how to do this in outline, and then introduce a practical example.

First, and as usual, the `DataGrid` must be within a `<form runat="server">` element. In order to navigate through the pages, we will have navigation buttons, and these buttons require the form.

Second, there are several new `DataGrid` properties that we need to work with:

❑ Setting the `AllowPaging` attribute to `True` provides us with a paging footer containing **Previous** and **Next** hyperlinks

❑ The `PageSize` attribute sets the number of rows to display on one page

❑ `CurrentPageIndex` is a zero-based index that identifies the page currently being displayed (and therefore, through simple arithmetic, the number of the row at the top of the current page)

To show the next page at any stage in the proceedings, we simply set `CurrentPageIndex` to the index of the new page, and re-bind the data. The place to do this is in a handler that executes when a `PageIndexChanged` event occurs, as specified by the `OnPageIndexChanged` attribute.

Third, we must understand some more about the passage of information from the `DataGrid` object to our event handlers. Here, for example, when the `DataGrid.PageIndexChanged` event is fired, it sends (among other things) a value called `NewPageIndex` that contains the index of the page that should be displayed next.

Fourth, we have to get the right code in the right procedure. Of the three that follow, only `Page_Load()` has a fixed name; the names of the others are up to you:

❑ `DataFiller()` creates the connection, data adapter, and `DataTable` objects, sets the data source for the `DataGrid`, and binds.

❑ `Page_Load()` needs to call `DataFiller()` on the first occasion that the page is loaded, but otherwise does nothing at all.

❑ `GridPageChanged()` sets the `CurrentPageIndex` to the index of the new page to be displayed before making a call to `DataFiller()`.

With these four points in mind, let's have an example that will allow us to see how paging actually works.

Try It Out – DataGrid Paging

Our objective is simple: we want to show a `DataGrid` of Northwind products (showing names and ID numbers), but we only want to show eight products at a time. We want to offer the user the default hyperlinks to navigate to the next and previous set of products in the list.

1. In folder `ch05`, create a file named `DataGrid_paging.aspx` and enter the following code:

```
<%@ Import namespace="System.Data" %>
<%@ Import namespace="System.Data.SqlClient" %>

<html>
  <head><title>DataGrid Paging</title></head>
  <body>
    <h3>DataGrid Paging</h3>
    <form runat="Server">
      <asp:DataGrid id="dgProducts" runat="server"
                    AllowPaging="True"
                    OnPageIndexChanged="GridPageChange"
                    PageSize="8" />
    </form>
  </body>
</html>

<script language="VB" runat="server">
Sub Page_Load(Source As Object, E As EventArgs)
  If Not Page.IsPostBack Then
    DataFiller()
  End IF
End Sub

Sub DataFiller()
  Dim strConnection As String = ConfigurationSettings.AppSettings("NWind")
  Dim objConnection As New SqlConnection(strConnection)

  Dim strSqlProducts As String = "SELECT ProductID, ProductName " & _
```

```
                                    "FROM Products ORDER BY ProductID"
    Dim objAdapter As New SqlDataAdapter(strSqlProducts, objConnection)

    Dim objDataSet As New DataSet()
    objAdapter.Fill(objDataSet, "dtProducts")

    dgProducts.PagerStyle.NextPageText = "Next"
    dgProducts.PagerStyle.PrevPageText = "Previous"

    dgProducts.DataSource = objDataSet.Tables.Item("dtProducts")
    dgProducts.DataBind()
End Sub

Sub GridPageChange(S As Object, E As DataGridPageChangedEventArgs)
    dgProducts.CurrentPageIndex = E.NewPageIndex
    DataFiller()
End Sub
</script>
```

2. When the above page is viewed, you'll see the following:

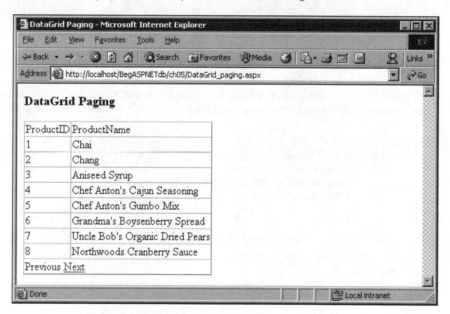

3. After clicking the **Next** hyperlink, you should the second screen:

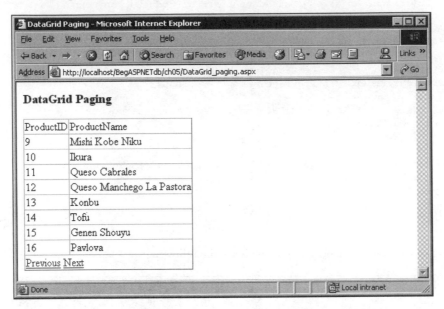

How It Works

Starting with the HTML code, our first action is to switch on paging by setting the grid's `AllowPaging` attribute to `"True"`. The default number of rows in a page is ten, but we'll change that to eight. Also, we set `GridPageChange()` to be the event handler that's called when the user goes to a different page.

```
<form runat="Server">
  <asp:DataGrid id="dgProducts" runat="server"
                AllowPaging="True"
                OnPageIndexChanged="GridPageChange"
                PageSize="8" />
</form>
```

Moving on to `DataFiller()`, recall that our objective is simply to perform all of the actions normally required to fill a `DataGrid`, just as we've done before. By default, the first row displayed will be the first `DataRow` from the `DataTable`.

```
Sub DataFiller()
   Dim strConnection As String = ConfigurationSettings.AppSettings("NWind")
   Dim objConnection As New SqlConnection(strConnection)

   Dim strSqlProducts As String = "SELECT ProductID, ProductName " & _
                                  "FROM Products ORDER BY ProductID"
   Dim objAdapter As New SqlDataAdapter(strSqlProducts, objConnection)
```

```
Dim objDataSet As New DataSet()
objAdapter.Fill(objDataSet, "dtProducts")
```

Before binding to the `DataGrid`, we set the text for the 'next page' and 'previous page' links:

```
dgProducts.PagerStyle.NextPageText = "Next"
dgProducts.PagerStyle.PrevPageText = "Previous"
```

Then we do finally bind our table to the `DataGrid`, and we're finished.

```
dgProducts.DataSource = objDataSet.Tables.Item("dtProducts")
dgProducts.DataBind()
End Sub
```

From here, things get much easier – `Page_Load()`, for example, shows few changes from its incarnations in earlier examples. On the first occasion that the page is loaded, we call `DataFiller()`; the rest of the time, we do nothing at all.

```
Sub Page_Load(Source As Object, E As EventArgs)
   If Not Page.IsPostBack Then
      DataFiller()
   End If
End Sub
```

Finally, when the user clicks on a navigation button, `GridPageChange()` is called. All we do here is set the `CurrentPageIndex` to a specific value, and then call `DataFiller()` again. The "specific value" in question is the index number passed to the handler by the `DataGrid`; it will be one higher then the index of the page currently being shown.

```
Sub GridPageChange(S As Object, E As DataGridPageChangedEventArgs)
   dgProducts.CurrentPageIndex = E.NewPageIndex
   DataFiller()
End Sub
```

To review paging, the procedure – which you'll surely have noticed to be very similar to that for sorting – is fairly straightforward, once you understand the theory. Keep in mind that several properties must be set in the `DataGrid`, and that you must separate out the `DataGrid`-filling code so that it can be executed at two junctures: when the page is first loaded, and when a navigation button is clicked.

Calendar Control and Data Sources

Many software designers are working on ASP.NET controls, just as they supplied controls for classic ASP. As a demonstration of what can be done with the .NET architecture, Microsoft has developed the `Calendar` web server control, and included it with ASP.NET – it can be used to display a one-month calendar that allows the user to select dates, and to 'move' to the next and previous months. In this section, we're going to focus on how to get dates from a data source and display them in the control.

When dealing with the `Calendar` control, there are three main points to understand. First, the control shows the current month by default, but the `VisibleDate` property can be used to change this – you can use it to specify any day you like.

Second, we have a choice of four settings for the `SelectionMode` property that will determine how many days can be selected at once. The options are the four members of the `CalendarSelectionMode` enumeration: `Day` (a single day can be selected), `DayWeek` (a single day or an entire week can be selected), `DayWeekMonth`, and `None` (no selection allowed). `Day` mode returns a single date that resides in the `SelectedDate` property; if multiple items are selected, they are put in a collection named `SelectedDates`.

Third, dates from certain data sources – including some forms of dates from a Microsoft Access database – will not have formats that are valid for the `Calendar` control. For example, if you want to use a field that was established in Access as a `date/time` type in `dd-mmm-yyyy` format, that value will be stored in a `DataSet` object in a form that the `Calendar` control does not recognize. We need to convert that value using a .NET class called `Convert`; this includes a `ToDateTime()` method that takes account of the server's localization settings for date formatting.

```
Convert.ToDateTime(MyDataSet.Tables("MyTable").Rows(MyIndex)("MyDateField"))
```

With these tips, our knowledge of how to work with `DataSet` objects, and our experience of reading specific values from a `DataSet`, we're ready to use the `Calendar` control as a front end to our data.

Try It Out – The Calendar Web Server Control

In this example, we'll create two pages. The first will be a warm-up – we'll just show the date selected from a `Calendar` control in a label. In the second version, we'll add a list box of employees, and arrange things so that when the user selects an employee, a `Calendar` will show the day and month when that employee was hired. In other words, we'll read data from Northwind and display it in a `Calendar` control.

1. Create a new page named `Calendar_1.aspx` in the `ch05` folder, and enter the following code:

```
<%@ Import namespace="System.Data" %>
<%@ Import namespace="System.Data.SqlClient" %>

<html>
  <head><title>Using the Calendar</title></head>
  <body>
    <h3>Using the Calendar</h3>
    <form runat="server">
      <asp:Label id="lblSelectedDate" runat="server" />
      <asp:Calendar id="calHire" runat="Server"
                    SelectionMode = "DayWeek"
                    OnSelectionChanged = "CalendarChange" />
    </form>
  </body>
</html>
```

```
<script language="VB" runat="server">
Sub CalendarChange(Source As Object, E As EventArgs)
  lblSelectedDate.Text = calHire.SelectedDate
End Sub
</script>
```

2. Take a look at the page and select a few dates. Also try moving to another month. You should see something like the image below:

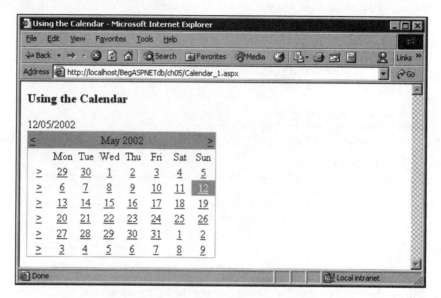

3. For our next version, we'll connect to a data store. Re-save the file as Calendar_2.aspx, and add the highlighted code, as follows:

```
<%@ Import namespace="System.Data" %>
<%@ Import namespace="System.Data.SqlClient" %>

<html>
  <head><title>Calendar: Hire Dates</title></head>
  <body>
    <h3>Calendar: Hire Dates</h3>
    <form runat="server">
      <asp:ListBox id="lstEmployees" runat="server"
                   Rows="7"
                   Autopostback="True" /><br/>
      <asp:Label id="lblSelectedDate" runat="server" />
      <asp:Calendar id="calHire" runat="server"
                    SelectionMode = "None" />
</form>
  </body>
</html>
```

```
<script language="VB" runat="server">
Sub Page_Load(Source As Object, E As EventArgs)
  Dim strConnection As String = ConfigurationSettings.AppSettings("NWind")
  Dim objConnection As New SqlConnection(strConnection)

  Dim strSQL As String = "SELECT EmployeeID, LastName, FirstName, HireDate " & _
                     "FROM Employees;"

  Dim objAdapter As New SqlDataAdapter(strSQL, objConnection)
  Dim objDataSet As New DataSet("dsEmployees")
  objAdapter.Fill(objDataSet, "dtEmployees")

  If Not IsPostBack Then
    lstEmployees.DataSource = objDataSet
    lstEmployees.DataTextField = "LastName"
    lstEmployees.DataBind()
  Else
    Dim datHireDate As Date
    datHireDate = Convert.ToDateTime( _
objDataSet.Tables("dtEmployees").Rows(lstEmployees.SelectedIndex)("HireDate"))

    lblSelectedDate.Text = _
objDataSet.Tables("dtEmployees").Rows(lstEmployees.SelectedIndex)("LastName")
    calHire.VisibleDate = datHireDate
    calHire.SelectedDate = datHireDate
    lblSelectedDate.Text &= " hired on " & datHireDate
  End If
End Sub
</script>
```

4. Now, when we run the above code, we see the following screen:

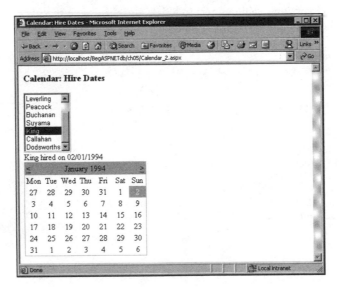

How It Works

As is our habit, let's begin with a quick look at the body of the HTML in the page. We have an ASP.NET web server `ListBox` control, a label, and a `Calendar` control with `id="calHire"`.

```
<form runat="server">
  <asp:ListBox id="lstEmployees" runat="server"
               Rows="7"
               Autopostback="True" /><br/>
  <asp:Label id="lblSelectedDate" runat="server" />
  <asp:Calendar id="calHire" runat="server"
                SelectionMode = "None" />
</form>
```

In the `Page_Load()` event handler, we begin by creating our connection and retrieving information about the employees (including their hire date) from the `Employees` table. We then fill a `DataTable` object called `dtEmployees` with this data.

The *interesting* code begins when we check to see if this the first time we are loading the page. If it is, we bind `objDataSet` to our list box to display the employees.

```
If Not IsPostBack Then
   lstEmployees.DataSource = objDataSet
   lstEmployees.DataTextField = "LastName"
   lstEmployees.DataBind()
```

If we're posting back to the page, then we wish to find the employee that has been selected from the list box, change the `Calendar` control to indicate their hire date, and change the `Text` of the label to display the hire date as well. The employee we have chosen is obtained from the `SelectedIndex` property of `lstEmployees`; this value will also indicate the `DataRow` of `dtEmployees` we need to access to obtain the `HireDate` and `LastName`. To ensure we have a correctly formatted date, we use `Convert.ToDateTime()`:

```
   Else
     Dim datHireDate As Date
     datHireDate = Convert.ToDateTime( _
objDataSet.Tables("dtEmployees").Rows(lstEmployees.SelectedIndex)("HireDate"))

     lblSelectedDate.Text = _
objDataSet.Tables("dtEmployees").Rows(lstEmployees.SelectedIndex)("LastName")
```

Finally, we update the `Calendar` control to display the hire date, and display the last name of the employee and their hire date in the label:

```
     calHire.VisibleDate = datHireDate
     calHire.SelectedDate = datHireDate
     lblSelectedDate.Text &= " hired on " & datHireDate
   End If
```

In Chapter 6 where we look at creating and inserting data, we'll see how to use the value in `calHire.SelectedDate` *to update our data source.*

Filtering from a Drop-down List

For our final example in this chapter, we'll look at binding data to a drop-down list, and using the value selected from the list to filter and provide different views of that data. This quite large sample will bring together a number of the things that we've been looking at over the last two chapters, so don't let it's length put you off. For the most part, it's things you've seen before, working in slightly different contexts.

Try It Out – Binding to a Drop-down List

We're going to implement a page that displays the products available from Northwind, and allows them to be filtered by their category (beverages, condiments, etc.), and by price range.

1. In the `ch05` folder, create a new file called `ProductFilter.aspx`, and enter the following code:

```
<%@ Import namespace="System.Data" %>
<%@ Import namespace="System.Data.SqlClient" %>

<html>
  <head><title>DataGrid Filtering</title></head>
  <body>
    <h3>DataGrid Filtering</h3>
    <form runat="server">
      <asp:Literal id="lbCategoryFilter" runat="server"
                   Text="Category:" />
      <asp:DropDownList id="ddlCategoryFilter" runat="server"
                        AutoPostBack="True"
                        OnSelectedIndexChanged="FilterChange" />
      <asp:Literal id="lbPriceFilter" runat="server"
                   Text="Price Range:" />
      <asp:DropDownList id="ddlPriceFilter" runat="server"
                        AutoPostBack="True"
                        OnSelectedIndexChanged="FilterChange">
        <asp:ListItem Value="0" Selected="True">Any Price</asp:ListItem>
        <asp:ListItem Value="1">Cheap</asp:ListItem>
        <asp:ListItem Value="2">Moderate</asp:ListItem>
        <asp:ListItem Value="3">Expensive</asp:ListItem>
        <asp:ListItem Value="4">Absurdly Expensive</asp:ListItem>
      </asp:DropDownList>
      <br/><br/>
      <asp:DataGrid id="dgProducts" runat="server">
        <HeaderStyle BackColor="#C0C0FF" />
        <ItemStyle BackColor="#F1F1F1" />
        <AlternatingItemStyle BackColor="#E8E6E6" />
      </asp:DataGrid>
    </form>
  </body>
</html>
```

In the above, the only difference between a `Literal` and the `Labels` we've worked with before is that the former doesn't allow you to apply styles to its content.

```vb
<script language="VB" runat="server">
Public strCategoryFilter As String = "CategoryID=1"
Public strPriceFilter As String = "UnitPrice>0"

Sub Page_Load(Source As Object, E As EventArgs)
  If Not Page.IsPostBack Then
    FillDropDownList()
    DataFiller()
  End If
End Sub

Sub FillDropDownList()
  Dim strConnection As String = ConfigurationSettings.AppSettings("NWind")
  Dim objConnection As New SqlConnection (strConnection)
  Dim strSqlCategories As String = "SELECT CategoryName,CategoryID " & _
                                   "FROM Categories"

  Dim objCommand As New SqlCommand(strSqlCategories, objConnection)
  Dim objReader As SqlDataReader = Nothing

  objConnection.Open()
  objReader = objCommand.ExecuteReader()

  ddlCategoryFilter.DataSource = objReader
  ddlCategoryFilter.DataTextField = "CategoryName"
  ddlCategoryFilter.DataValueField = "CategoryID"
  ddlCategoryFilter.DataBind()
  objConnection.Close()
End Sub

Sub DataFiller()
  Dim strConnection As String = ConfigurationSettings.AppSettings("NWind")
  Dim objConnection As New SqlConnection(strConnection)
  Dim strSqlProducts As String = "SELECT ProductID, ProductName, " & _
                                 "CategoryID, UnitPrice FROM Products"
  Dim objAdapter As New SqlDataAdapter(strSqlProducts, objConnection)

  Dim objDataSet As New DataSet()
  objAdapter.Fill(objDataSet, "dtProducts")

  ' Create our DataView and filter by category and price
  Dim dvUK As New DataView(objDataSet.Tables("dtProducts"))
  dvUK.RowFilter = strCategoryFilter & " AND (" & strPriceFilter & ")"

  dgProducts.DataSource = dvUK
  dgProducts.DataBind()
End Sub
```

```
Sub FilterChange(Source As Object, E As EventArgs)
FilterByPrice(ddlPriceFilter.SelectedItem.Text.ToString())
  FilterByCategory(ddlCategoryFilter.SelectedItem.Value.ToString())
  DataFiller()
End Sub

Sub FilterByPrice(strChoice As String)
  Select strChoice
    Case "Any Price"
      strPriceFilter = "UnitPrice>0"
    Case "Cheap"
      strPriceFilter = "UnitPrice<20"
    Case "Moderate"
      strPriceFilter = "UnitPrice>19 AND UnitPrice<50"
    Case "Expensive"
      strPriceFilter = "UnitPrice>=50"
    Case "Absurdly Expensive"
      strPriceFilter = "UnitPrice>100"
  End Select
End Sub

Sub FilterByCategory(strChoice As String)
  strCategoryFilter = "CategoryID = " & strChoice
End Sub
</script>
```

2. Viewing this page in a browser produces output like the following:

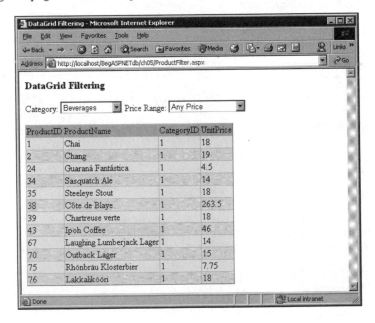

3. We can view the confections by selecting Confections from the Category drop-down list. After that, selecting Cheap from the Price Range drop-down list displays all the cheap confections available:

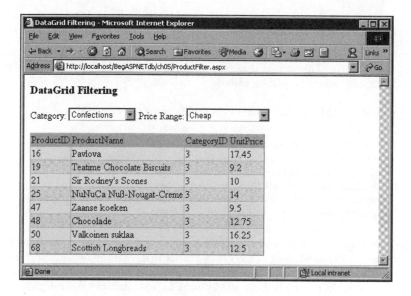

How It Works

The main points of the code in this page are:

- ❑ The DataGrid properties that give the table its visual appeal
- ❑ The use of two public strings to hold our filter expressions
- ❑ Binding data from the Categories table to a drop down list
- ❑ The use of one handler to deal with a change in *either* drop-down list
- ❑ Retaining the value selected in the Category drop-down list between pages

Let's look first at the HTML for the page, which is a little more elaborate than usual:

```
<form runat="server">
  <asp:Literal id="lbCategoryFilter" runat="server"
              Text="Category:" />
  <asp:DropDownList id="ddlCategoryFilter" runat="server"
                  AutoPostBack="True"
                  OnSelectedIndexChanged="FilterChange" />
  <asp:Literal id="lbPriceFilter" runat="server"
              Text="Price Range:" />
  <asp:DropDownList id="ddlPriceFilter" runat="server"
                  AutoPostBack="True"
                  OnSelectedIndexChanged="FilterChange">
```

We have a server-side <form> element, within which we have two labels that display the legends **Category** and **Price Range** in order to identify the two drop-down lists to the visitor. There are two things to note about those list controls here:

❑ The ddlCategoryFilter list has no items specified for it. Instead, it will be filled from the Categories table at runtime.

❑ For both list controls, the OnSelectedIndexChanged attribute is set to the same value: FilterChange. This means that whenever the user changes the selection in *either* drop-down list, FilterChange() will be called.

Continuing with the HTML, we have the items for the price filter drop-down list:

```
    <asp:ListItem Value="0" Selected="True">Any Price</asp:ListItem>
    <asp:ListItem Value="1">Cheap</asp:ListItem>
    <asp:ListItem Value="2">Moderate</asp:ListItem>
    <asp:ListItem Value="3">Expensive</asp:ListItem>
    <asp:ListItem Value="4">Absurdly Expensive</asp:ListItem>
  </asp:DropDownList>
```

Next, we have our DataGrid control. Notice that we use the BackColor attribute of the HeaderStyle element to set the background color of the grid's header row, that the background color of the rows of the grid is set through BackColor attribute of ItemStyle, and that the background color of every other row is set with the BackColor attribute of AlternatingItemStyle. This gives our DataGrid control a more pleasing appearance.

```
    <asp:DataGrid id="dgProducts" runat="server">
      <HeaderStyle BackColor="#C0C0FF" />
      <ItemStyle BackColor="#F1F1F1" />
      <AlternatingItemStyle BackColor="#E8E6E6" />
    </asp:DataGrid>
  </form>
```

In our VB.NET code, the first thing we do is to define two public strings that will hold default values for our first filter.

```
  Public strCategoryFilter As String = "CategoryID=1"
  Public strPriceFilter As String = "UnitPrice>0"
```

In Page_Load(), we use Page.IsPostBack to determine whether this is the first time the page has been loaded. If so, we populate our drop-down list with FillDropDownList(), and call DataFiller() to display our data.

```
  Sub Page_Load(Source As Object, E As EventArgs)
    If Not Page.IsPostBack Then
      FillDropDownList()
      DataFiller()
    End If
  End Sub
```

If it is not the first time the page has been loaded, `DataFiller()` will be called by `FilterChange()`, which itself will be called when the visitor selects an entry from one of the drop-down lists.

In `FillDropDownList()`, we use a data reader object to bind the categories from the `Categories` table to the `ddlCategoryFilter` drop-down list. We only have to populate the drop-down list once, when the page is first loaded – the values will persist between postbacks, so there's no need to refill it when they occur. `FillDropDownList()` begins with the usual connection and command objects, opens a connection, and uses `ExecuteReader()` to begin reading the data. This should all look quite familiar.

```
Sub FillDropDownList()
  Dim strConnection As String = ConfigurationSettings.AppSettings("NWind")
  Dim objConnection As New SqlConnection (strConnection)
  Dim strSqlCategories As String = "SELECT CategoryName,CategoryID " & _
                                   "FROM Categories"

  Dim objCommand As New SqlCommand(strSqlCategories, objConnection)
  Dim objReader As SqlDataReader = Nothing

  objConnection.Open()
  objReader = objCommand.ExecuteReader()
```

Next, we bind the incoming data from the `Categories` table of Northwind to `ddlCategoryFilter`. You'll recall that the `DataTextField` property sets the field that will actually be displayed in the list, while `DataValueField` sets the field that will be used to provide the values that will be returned.

```
  ddlCategoryFilter.DataSource = objReader
  ddlCategoryFilter.DataTextField = "CategoryName"
  ddlCategoryFilter.DataValueField = "CategoryID"
  ddlCategoryFilter.DataBind()
```

Finally (and very importantly!), we close the connection:

```
  objConnection.Close()
End Sub
```

Next up for investigation is `DataFiller()`. The first part of this is pretty standard: we create the relevant objects, and fill a `DataTable` with data from the `Products` table of Northwind.

```
Sub DataFiller()
  Dim strConnection As String = ConfigurationSettings.AppSettings("NWind")
  Dim objConnection As New SqlConnection(strConnection)
  Dim strSqlProducts As String = "SELECT ProductID, ProductName, " & _
                                 "CategoryID, UnitPrice FROM Products"
  Dim objAdapter As New SqlDataAdapter(strSqlProducts, objConnection)

  Dim objDataSet As New DataSet()
  objAdapter.Fill(objDataSet, "dtProducts")
```

Then we create our `DataView` object and set its `RowFilter` property to filter with category information *and* price information, using `strCategoryFilter` and `strPriceFilter`.

```
' Create our DataView and filter by category and price
Dim dvUK As New DataView(objDataSet.Tables("dtProducts"))
dvUK.RowFilter = strCategoryFilter & " AND (" & strPriceFilter & ")"
```

Finally, we bind the `DataView` to our `DataGrid`.

```
dgProducts.DataSource = dvUK
dgProducts.DataBind()
End Sub
```

In `FilterChange()`, we call both `FilterByPrice()` and `FilterByCategory()`. To the former, we pass the string that has been selected from `ddlPriceFilter`; to the latter, we pass a string that has been chosen from `ddlCategoryFilter`. These two procedures will set up the correct strings for filtering our data:

```
Sub FilterChange(Source As Object, E As EventArgs)
  FilterByPrice(ddlPriceFilter.SelectedItem.Text.ToString())
  FilterByCategory(ddlCategoryFilter.SelectedItem.Value.ToString())
```

Finally in `FilterChange()`, we call `DataFiller()` to redisplay our data.

```
  DataFiller()
End Sub
```

In the last two procedures, we actually set up the strings for filtering the displayed data. In `FilterByPrice()`, we use a `Select...Case` statement to set up the correct value for `strPriceFilter`:

```
Sub FilterByPrice(strChoice As String)
  Select strChoice
    Case "Any Price"
      strPriceFilter = "UnitPrice>0"
    Case "Cheap"
      strPriceFilter = "UnitPrice<20"
    Case "Moderate"
      strPriceFilter = "UnitPrice>19 AND UnitPrice<50"
    Case "Expensive"
      strPriceFilter = "UnitPrice>=50"
    Case "Absurdly Expensive"
      strPriceFilter = "UnitPrice>100"
  End Select
End Sub
```

In `FilterByCategory()`, we simply set `strCategoryFilter` to the string passed to it:

```
Sub FilterByCategory(strChoice As String)
  strCategoryFilter = "CategoryID = " & strChoice
End Sub
```

And that's all there is to it! With ASP.NET, as you can surely begin to see, you don't need to do a lot of work in order to get useful, well-presented results.

Common Mistakes

If you're having difficulty accessing the individual values within the columns of a table, you might like to use the following checklist to help identify your problem:

- ❑ Note that there is no period between the row index and the name of the field: it's `Rows(Index)("FieldName")`, not `Rows(Index).("FieldName")`.

- ❑ The names of the `DataTable` object and the field both need double quotes *and* parentheses.

- ❑ All of the web server controls you're using (as well as the form, if present) must have the `runat="server"` attribute set.

- ❑ Don't forget that the indexes of all collections – including the collection of items in a `ListBox`, and the collection of `DataRow` objects in a `DataTable` – are zero-based.

- ❑ If you're attempting to retrieve a particular row based on a number returned from (say) a `ListBox` item, and there are gaps in the sequence of `DataValues`, then the `ListBox.SelectedItem.Index` numbers may not correspond to the correct row in the data source.

Summary

This chapter has addressed a variety of real-world questions that ASP.NET pages are asked to deal with. We started by discussing the differences between the `DataReader` and `DataSet`, noting that the `DataSet` holds data in memory, and allows manipulation of this data without any further connection to the data source being maintained. We also saw that the `DataSet` is not concerned with the origin of the data, and throughout the chapter we worked comfortably with different sets of data from different sources.

A `DataSet` object contains `DataTable` objects, rather like the tables in an ordinary database, and these in turn contain `DataColumn` and `DataRow` objects. It is important to keep in mind the relationship between these objects, and the syntax necessary to refer to them. We saw how the data adapter uses a connection object and either an SQL string or a command object to fill a `DataTable` with data, and the `ReadXml()` method to fill a `DataTable` with data from an XML file.

We looked at how to bind a `DataSet` to a `DataGrid` for easy display, and then went deeper into the `DataSet`, looking at how to extract values from particular columns. We saw the importance of field data types when we looked at creating relationships between `DataTable` objects with the `DataRelation` object, and had a brief look at how an XML schema can provide this information for XML data.

ADO.NET enables us to create a `DataView` object, which provides us with a specific way to look at data within a `DataTable`. With a `DataView`, we can allow visitors to our site to sort and filter the data that is displayed in front of them, enabling a more customized view of our data.

We don't have to accept the default `DataGrid` that shows every `DataColumn` of a `DataTable`. Instead, we can describe the `DataGrid` as a set of `BoundColumns`, where we define for each column the field from which they take their data, the visibility (controllable at runtime), the heading, and other characteristics. Likewise, we don't have to show all of the rows in a `DataGrid`. With ASP.NET, it's easy to present only a set of rows at a time, with handy hyperlinks for paging through the data.

Last of all, we looked at how to link an ASP.NET `Calendar` control to a data source, and provided a more polished example of filtering our data, with options from a data source bound to a drop-down list.

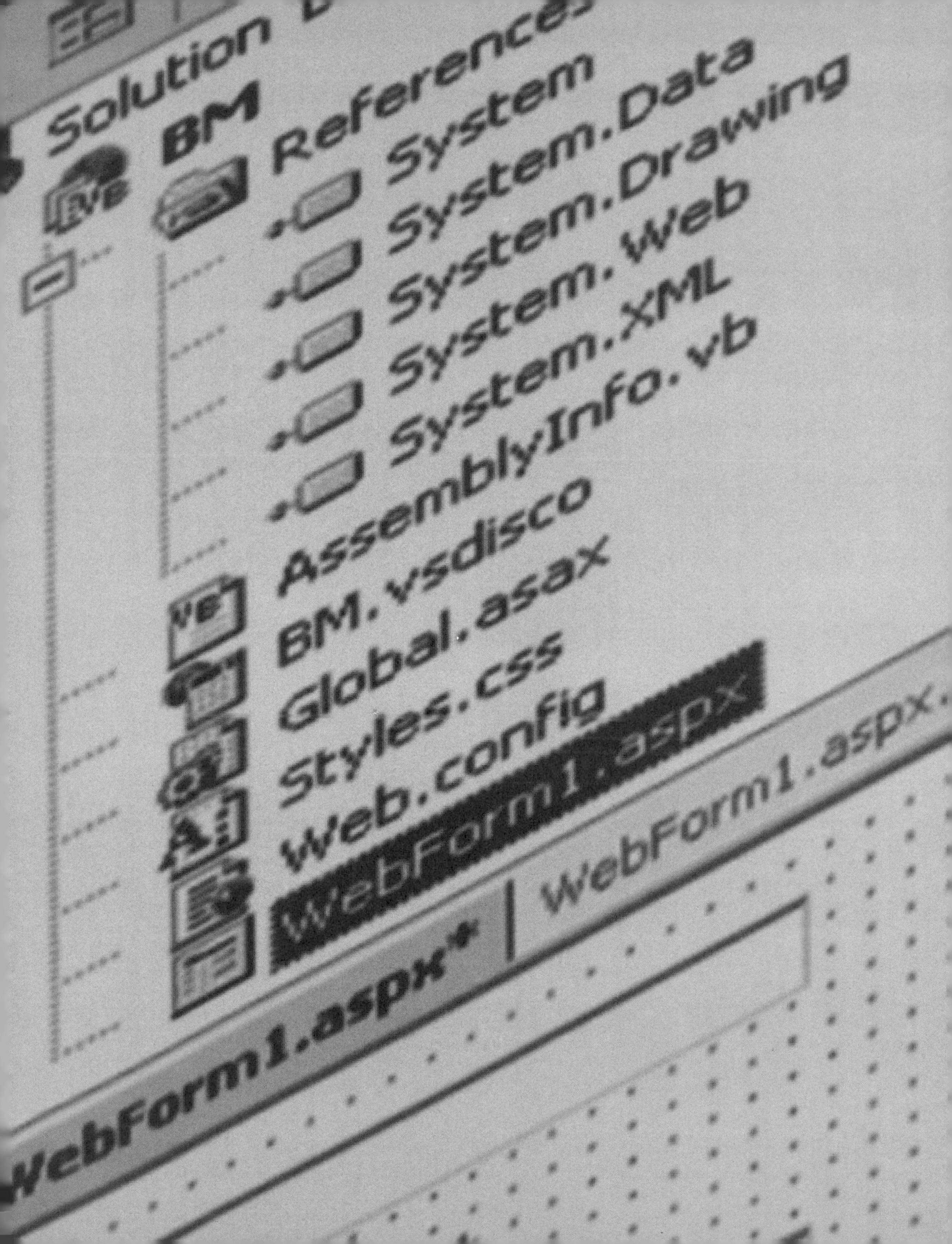

Solution [Explorer]

BM

References
System
System.Data
System.Drawing
System.Web
System.XML

AssemblyInfo.vb
BM.vsdisco
Global.asax
Styles.css
Web.config
WebForm1.aspx

WebForm1.aspx* | WebForm1.aspx.

WebForm1.aspx*

Creating and Inserting Records

In previous chapters, we've seen how to use data readers and datasets to retrieve data from a data source. In this chapter, we'll analyze how to insert new records into a database table, using SQL code that's created by and called from ADO.NET objects. In particular, we will focus on the following topics:

- ❑ The basics of inserting records
- ❑ How to use ASP.NET validation controls to prevent errors during insert operations
- ❑ How to use command and dataset objects to perform record insertions
- ❑ How to use `TextBox` and `Calendar` controls for record creation
- ❑ How command builder objects can write SQL code on our behalf

Inserting Data with ASP.NET and ADO.NET

When we use SQL statements to insert records into one or more database tables, we have to respect some rules. In this section, we'll look at some of the basic theory of inserting data with ASP.NET and ADO.NET:

- ❑ Understanding primary keys and foreign keys
- ❑ Providing mandatory fields
- ❑ Obeying the syntax of SQL's `INSERT` keyword

It All Looks so Simple

You may recall that we took a very brief look at creating and inserting records back when we first started talking about relational databases and the SQL language in Chapter 2. We even went as far as to show the syntax for a straightforward `INSERT` operation:

```
INSERT INTO Shippers
(CompanyName, Phone)
VALUES ('Wrox Deliveries', '(504) 666-6836')
```

Essentially, all we have to do in this chapter is to look at the different ways of assembling and then executing statements like this using ADO.NET code in our ASP.NET applications. Whenever you're adding new records to a database, though, there are some important considerations to bear in mind. The operation isn't quite as straightforward as it first appears.

Primary Keys

The first potential obstacle that we need to overcome is the rules concerning primary keys. As you know, a primary key uniquely identifies a record within a table, and any attempt to insert a duplicate will always cause an error. So when we insert a new record, we have to assure ourselves that we have provided that record with a valid and unique primary key.

Auto-Increment Primary Keys

Often, you'll encounter primary keys that have been defined as **auto-increment** fields. This can be very useful when the primary key doesn't contain significant data (an ISBN is an example of a primary key that *does* contain significant data), but each record still needs to have a unique identifier. If you were to take a look at the Northwind database through MS Access, you'd see that the Customers table is defined like this:

While the Categories table looks like this:

In this second table, the checkmark in the Identity column instructs the database to increment the primary key field automatically, by the value specified in the Identity Increment column. The Identity Seed represents the initial value that will be assigned to this field in the first record to be inserted.

When we're dealing with this kind of field from SQL, we can omit its name from the `INSERT` statement, safe in the knowledge that a value will be generated on our behalf:

```
INSERT INTO Categories
(CategoryName, Description)
VALUES ('Books/Magazines', 'Some books, some magazines')
```

If we actually tried to enter a value into this field, we'd get an error. If a table that you're dealing with has an auto-increment primary key, steer well clear of that field, and let the database do the work.

Foreign Keys

The second stumbling block to deal with comes when we have foreign keys to consider. As you may recall, a foreign key in one table is related to the primary key of another table, in such a way that it's only possible to create records containing the foreign key for which the value of the key field is equal to one of the values already present in the table containing the primary key. In other words, an operation that attempts to add a record to a table containing a foreign key will fail, *unless* the value of the key field matches one of the primary key values in the related table.

Relating two or more tables in this fashion can be quite advantageous. Imagine, for example, a database in which one table holds details about books: their ISBNs, titles, prices, and so on. Another table holds details of authors: their names, contact information, and the ISBNs of books they've written. By making the ISBN a primary key in the book table, and a foreign key in the author table, we introduce a useful constraint: no author can be added to the author table until a book they've written is added to the book table. To put that into SQL code, it's illegal to execute a statement like this:

```
INSERT INTO tabAuthor
(ISBN, Author)
VALUES ('1-861005-92 X', 'Fabio Claudio Ferracchiati')
```

Until you've first executed a statement like this:

```
INSERT INTO tabBook
(ISBN, Title, Price)
VALUES ('1-861005-92-X', 'Data-Centric .NET Programming with C#', '$59.99')
```

If you violate the rules of a primary key-foreign key relationship during an operation in your application, that operation will fail.

Mandatory Fields

The third and final thing to worry about when inserting new records regards mandatory fields – database columns for which we must always provide a value. Primary keys are always mandatory, but other fields can be mandatory too. Going back to our table of books in the last section, the ISBN is the primary key, but it seems quite reasonable to insist that all books should have a title, too.

In the `Categories` table of the `Northwind` database, two of the fields are mandatory, while the other two are not. In the Access screenshot below, this situation is reflected by the absence or presence of checkmarks in the **Allow Nulls** column. A field that may not be null is a mandatory field.

Column Name	Datatype	Length	Precision	Scale	Allow Nulls	Default Value	Identity	Identity Seed	Identity Increment	Is RowGuid
CategoryID	int	4	10	0			✓	1	1	
CategoryName	nvarchar	15	0	0						
Description	ntext	16	0	0	✓					
Picture	image	16	0	0	✓					

Clearly, when you're adding records to a table programmatically, you must be sure to provide values for all mandatory fields – unless, of course, you're dealing with a field whose values are generated automatically.

Formalizing the Syntax

The discussion so far has included a few snippets of SQL code, but just before we attempt our first proper example, we should take a look at the syntax of `INSERT` statements in a fairly formal way. The generic form of an `INSERT` statement may be represented as follows:

```
INSERT [INTO]
{ table_name }
{
  [(column_list)]
  {
    VALUES ( {DEFAULT | NULL | expression} [ ,...n] )
  }
}
```

Where:

- ❑ `INSERT` is the SQL command

- ❑ `[INTO]` is an optional keyword that we can include before the table name

- ❑ `table_name` is the name of the table in which we want to insert our record

- ❑ `column_list` represents a comma-separated list of column names that we'll provide values for. This list can be omitted if we provide values for every column, in the same order as they appear in the table specification. When we have an auto-increment primary key, we don't specify its value – it is inserted automatically.

- ❑ `VALUES` introduces the list of data values to be inserted. There must be one data value for each column in `column_list` or, when the column list is not provided, in the table. The comma-separated `VALUES` list must be enclosed in parentheses.

With all of these pieces in place, we can at last begin to attack the problem of creating records in a database using ADO.NET.

Using ADO.NET to Insert a New Record

Now that we've seen some basic SQL commands with which to insert new records, and taken a look at some of the rules that govern the scope of what we can do, we can start writing some code that uses ADO.NET's command objects to insert new records into our database.

The steps necessary to use an SQL INSERT command can be summarized as follows:

- ❏ Open a connection to the database
- ❏ Create a new command object
- ❏ Define an SQL command
- ❏ Execute the SQL command
- ❏ Close the connection

That at least sounds fairly straightforward, so let's try it out.

Try It Out – Adding a New Record Using a Command Object

In this exercise, we will write code that adds a new category to the Northwind database's Categories table. This table has an auto-increment primary key whose value we'll retrieve after execution of the INSERT statement. In real-world code, it's often necessary to know the value generated by the database, in order to use it as a foreign key in related tables.

1. In a directory called ch06 under our webroot folder, create a new text file called Insert_With_Return.aspx.

2. Add the following code to the file (or download it from the Wrox web site). Because the activity of adding records to databases has a high potential for error, we've wrapped the data access code in a Try...Catch...Finally block:

```
<%@ Import Namespace="System.Data" %>
<%@ Import Namespace="System.Data.SqlClient" %>

<html>
  <head>
    <title>Adding a New Record</title>
  </head>
</html>

<script language="VB" runat="server">
Sub Page_Load(Source as Object, E as EventArgs)

  ' Connection setup
  Dim strConnection As String = ConfigurationSettings.AppSettings("NWind")
  Dim objConnection As New SqlConnection(strConnection)
```

```
Dim strSQL As String = "INSERT INTO Categories (CategoryName,Description)" & _
" VALUES ('Guitars', 'Here you can find just the" & _
                    " guitar you were looking for');" & _
                    "SELECT @@IDENTITY As 'Identity'"

Dim dbComm As New SqlCommand(strSQL, objConnection)
Dim iID As Integer

Try
  objConnection.Open()
  iID = dbComm.ExecuteScalar()
Catch ex As Exception
  Response.Write(ex.Message)
  Response.End
Finally
  If objConnection.State = ConnectionState.Open Then
    objConnection.Close()
  End If
End Try

Response.Write("The ID of the new record is: " & iID.ToString())
End Sub
</script>
```

3. When you browse to this page, and assuming that you haven't previously made changes to the `Categories` table, this is what you'll see:

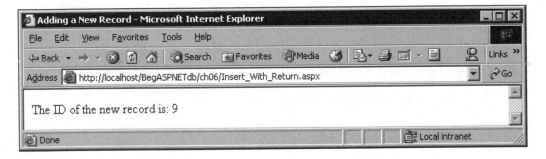

If you have previously made changes to the `Categories` table, you may find that the ID of the new record is a number greater than 9. This is not a cause for concern.

How It Works

This example progresses in similar fashion to the ones in earlier chapters – especially those in Chapter 4 – until we get to the definition of the SQL statement:

```
Dim strSQL As String = "INSERT INTO Categories (CategoryName,Description)" & _
                    " VALUES ('Guitars', 'Here you can find just the" & _
                    " guitar you were looking for');" & _
                    "SELECT @@IDENTITY As 'Identity'"
```

What you're looking at here is actually two statements in one. First is the INSERT statement itself, which looks just like the other examples of INSERT statements you've seen so far, and provides values for the mandatory CategoryName field and non-mandatory Description field of the Categories table. CategoryID is an auto-increment primary key, so we don't provide a value for that.

The second part of the string is SELECT @@IDENTITY As 'Identity'. This command asks SQL Server to return the primary key value that it just created for our new record. We retrieve it by using the command object's ExecuteScalar() method, which returns only the first value of the first row of a result set (unlike ExecuteReader(), which returns the whole thing).

```
Dim iID As Integer

Try
  objConnection.Open()
  iID = dbComm.ExecuteScalar()
```

Finally, we have to free the server's resources by closing the connection to the database, and checking for an exception that will be raised from the database should an error occur:

```
Catch ex As Exception
  Response.Write(ex.Message)
  Response.End
Finally
  If objConnection.State = ConnectionState.Open Then
    objConnection.Close()
  End If
End Try

Response.Write("The ID of the new record is: " & iID.ToString())
```

Note that if you refresh this page in your browser, another record will be added to the table. CategoryName and Description values are not checked for similarity with existing records, so the database will just generate another new primary key value, and assume that we know what we're doing.

ASP.NET Validation Controls

The example in the last section demonstrated how to insert new records into a database simply by hard-wiring an SQL INSERT statement into our code. In our ASP.NET applications, we'll often want to retrieve information from a form within the ASP.NET page, and insert those values into the database. That's what we're going to look at now.

As soon as we start allowing our users to enter data, we increase the risks of errors being introduced into the database. And if they fail to provide a value for a mandatory field, the data won't get into the database at all. The standard way of dealing with this and related problems is to add some client-side script code that informs users about their mistakes before posting data to the server, so that such mistakes can be dealt with smoothly and efficiently. ASP.NET offers convenient a solution to facilitate checking of text controls in a form: the **validation controls**.

ASP.NET validation controls can be placed anywhere you like in any page that requires them. By using attributes to set their properties, we can inform them about the controls they have to check. The following table lists the five validation controls available.

Syntax	Description
`<asp:RequiredFieldValidator>`	Checks that a specific input control contains a value.
`<asp:CompareValidator>`	Compares the contents of two input controls. A typical use is for 'password' and 'confirm password' text fields.
`<asp:RangeValidator>`	Checks that the specific input control has a value in the range of permitted values.
`<asp:RegularExpressionValidator>`	Checks the value of the specific input control against the regular expression provided.
`<asp:CustomValidator>`	Performs a custom check on an input control.

In addition to the examples in the following pages, Chapter 10 contains further demonstrations of the ASP.NET validation controls at work.

Try It Out – Using the RequiredFieldValidator Control

In this exercise, we're going to create an ASP.NET page that can add records to the Categories table of the Northwind database. Because the Categories table has a mandatory field (CategoryName), we're going to use a RequiredFieldValidator control.

1. Create a new text file in the ch06 folder, and name it Required_Field.aspx.

2. Add the following code to the file:

```
<%@ Import Namespace="System.Data" %>
<%@ Import Namespace="System.Data.SqlClient" %>

<html>
  <head>
    <title>Validating a Field</title>
  </head>
  <body>
    <form id="Form1" method="post" runat="server">
      <table id="Table1"
             style="Z-INDEX: 101; LEFT: 8px; POSITION: absolute; TOP: 8px"
             cellSpacing="0" cellPadding="0" width="300" border="0">
        <tr>
          <td style="WIDTH: 115px">
```

```
                        <asp:Label id="Label1" runat="server">CategoryName</asp:Label>
                </td>
                <td>
                    <asp:TextBox id="txtCategoryName" runat="server" width="193" />
                </td>
            </tr>
            <tr>
                <td style="WIDTH: 115px">
                    <asp:Label id="Label2" runat="server">Description</asp:Label>
                </td>
                <td>
                    <asp:TextBox id="txtDescription" runat="server" width="193" />
                </td>
            </tr>
            <tr>
                <td style="WIDTH: 115px" colSpan="2">
                    <asp:Button id="btnInsert" runat="server"
                        OnClick="btnInsert_Click" width="298" text="INSERT!" />
                </td>
            </tr>
        </table>
        <asp:RequiredFieldValidator id="rfvCategoryName" runat="server"
            style="Z-INDEX: 102; LEFT: 316px; POSITION: absolute; TOP: 14px"
            ErrorMessage="Please insert the new category name"
            ControlToValidate="txtCategoryName" />
    </form>
  </body>
</html>

<script language="VB" runat="server">
Dim objConnection As SqlConnection

Sub Page_Load(Source as Object, E as EventArgs)

  ' Create a new connection object pointing to the database
  Dim strConnection As String = ConfigurationSettings.AppSettings("NWind")
  objConnection = New SqlConnection(strConnection)
End Sub

Sub btnInsert_Click(Sender As Object, E As EventArgs)
  If Page.IsValid Then
    Dim strSQL As String="INSERT INTO Categories (CategoryName,Description)" & _
                    " VALUES (@CategoryName, @Description);" & _
                    " SELECT @@IDENTITY AS 'Identity'"

    Dim dbComm As New SqlCommand(strSQL, objConnection)
    dbComm.Parameters.Add("@CategoryName", SqlDbType.NVarChar, 15)
    dbComm.Parameters.Add("@Description", SqlDbType.NText)

    dbComm.Parameters("@CategoryName").Value = txtCategoryName.Text
    dbComm.Parameters("@Description").Value = txtDescription.Text

    Dim iID as Integer
```

```
      Try
         objConnection.Open()
         iID = dbComm.ExecuteScalar()
      Catch ex As Exception
         Response.Write(ex.Message)
         Response.End
      Finally
         If objConnection.State = ConnectionState.Open Then
            objConnection.Close()
         End If
      End Try

         Response.Write("The ID of the new record is: " & iID.ToString())
         Response.End
      End If
   End Sub
</script>
```

3. Now let's try to execute this page by pressing the Insert! button without first inserting a value into the CategoryName text field. This is what you'll see:

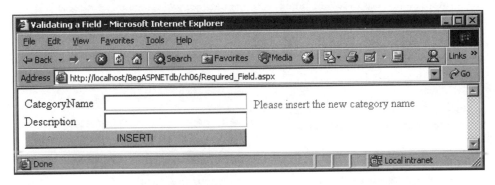

How It Works

Let's start by examining the HTML code, where the major innovation is the inclusion of the `RequiredFieldValidator` control. As you can see, we use the `ControlToValidate` attribute to link this control with the control to be validated, and specify an `ErrorMessage` attribute that represents the message to be displayed in the ASP.NET page should it be posted without a value in the mandatory input control:

```
<asp:RequiredFieldValidator id="rfvCategoryName" runat="server"
    style="Z-INDEX: 102; LEFT: 316px; POSITION: absolute; TOP: 14px"
    ErrorMessage="Please insert the new category name"
    ControlToValidate="txtCategoryName" />
```

Now we can examine what happens when the user clicks the INSERT! button. First of all, we have to check that all of the "validator" controls have validated their respective input controls successfully. We obtain this information using the IsValid property, exposed by the global Page class. When this property is True, every control has been validated successfully:

```
Sub btnInsert_Click(Sender As Object, E As EventArgs)
   If Page.IsValid Then
```

Once we know that the page is valid, we can retrieve the values from the input controls and insert them into the database. For this, as usual, we have to define a new command object, and set its properties to use the connection object that was created in the page's Page_Load() event handler. On this occasion, however, we've used a different form of syntax in the INSERT statement:

```
Dim strSQL As String="INSERT INTO Categories (CategoryName,Description)" & _
                      " VALUES (@CategoryName, @Description);" & _
                      " SELECT @@IDENTITY AS 'Identity'"
```

In the parentheses following the VALUES keyword, instead of specifying values that have to be inserted in the database, we use two placeholders: @CategoryName and @Description. Now, we *could* have used concatenation in order to construct our SQL command, but by doing things this way, we get ourselves at least two advantages:

❑   The code is easier to write and to manage

❑   We can avoid having to worry about characters such as quotation marks

For instance, if we were to insert a *description* in one of the text fields in our form, we might inadvertently use some undesirable characters, such as quotation marks. When we use string concatenation to get this information into the database, we find ourselves writing code like this:

```
Dim strSQL As String = "INSERT INTO Categories (CategoryName, Description) " & _
                       "VALUES ('" & txtCategory.Text & "', '" & _
                       txtDescription.Text & "')"
```

Now imagine that a user types a string such as "That's my category" into the txtDescription field. The strSQL string we create will effectively contain the following INSERT command:

```
Dim strSQL As String = "INSERT INTO Categories (CategoryName, Description) " & _
                       "VALUES ('category', 'That's my category')"
```

Examining the string carefully, you can see that executing this command would generate a syntax error as a result of the odd numbers of single quotation marks.

Returning to the code of the example at hand, the command object needs to know which placeholders to use during execution of the INSERT command. To this end, we have to use its Parameters collection, adding a separate entry for each placeholder. Additionally, we have to specify the data type (and, for character types, the maximum length) of each field.

```
Dim dbComm As New SqlCommand(strSQL, objConnection)
dbComm.Parameters.Add("@CategoryName", SqlDbType.NVarChar, 15)
dbComm.Parameters.Add("@Description", SqlDbType.NText)

dbComm.Parameters("@CategoryName").Value = txtCategoryName.Text
dbComm.Parameters("@Description").Value = txtDescription.Text
```

For more information about using parameters in your database queries, there's a longer discussion on the subject in Chapter 8, when we talk about using stored procedures in SQL Server databases.

Finally, we use the command object's ExecuteScalar() method to execute the INSERT statement, just as we did in the previous example.

```
Dim iID as Integer
Try
  objConnection.Open()
  iID = dbComm.ExecuteScalar()
Catch ex As Exception
  Response.Write(ex.Message)
  Response.End
Finally
  If objConnection.State = ConnectionState.Open Then
    objConnection.Close()
  End If
End Try

Response.Write("The ID of the new record is: " & iID.ToString())
Response.End
```

If you now try the application again, this time providing values for both fields, you should find that the database is updated just as it was in our first example.

Parameters Using the OLE DB Provider

Before concluding this section, it's worth taking one of our occasional detours to examine the differences between the SQL Server and OLE DB .NET data providers, for this is one situation in which they're quite significant. In particular, the way that we declare the VALUES to be provided to the INSERT statement must change, as you can see from the listing below:

```
<%@ Import namespace="System.Data" %>
<%@ Import namespace="System.Data.OleDb" %>

<!-- HTML section as before -->

<script language="VB" runat="server">
Dim objConnection As OleDbConnection
```

```
Sub Page_Load(Source As Object, E As EventArgs)
    objConnection = New OleDbConnection("Provider=Microsoft.Jet.OLEDB.4.0; " & _
    "data source=C:\BegASPNETdb\Datastores\NWind.mdb")
End Sub

Sub btnInsert_Click(Sender As Object, E As EventArgs)
    If Page.IsValid Then
        Dim strSQL As String = "INSERT INTO Categories " & _
                               "(CategoryName, Description) VALUES (?, ?)"

        Dim dbComm As New OleDbCommand(strSQL, objConnection)
        dbComm.Parameters.Add("CategoryName", OleDbType.VarChar, 32, "CategoryName")
        dbComm.Parameters.Add("Description", OleDbType.VarChar, 128, "Description")

        dbComm.Parameters("CategoryName").Value = txtCategoryName.Text
        dbComm.Parameters("Description").Value = txtDescription.Text

        Try
            objConnection.Open()
            dbComm.ExecuteNonQuery()
        Catch ex As Exception
            Response.Write(ex.Message)
            Response.End()
        Finally
            If objConnection.State = ConnectionState.Open Then
                objConnection.Close()
            End If
        End Try

        Response.Write("A new record has been added")
        Response.End()
    End If
End Sub
</script>
```

Here, we specify a question mark for each parameter that we want to pass to the INSERT command, and then we create each parameter by specifying the name, the data type, the number of characters, and the source column name. Apart from a slight simplification with regard to acquiring a return value from the SQL command, the functionality of this example is identical to that of the SQL Server example.

Inserting Records Using a DataSet Object

All this messing around with INSERT statements is all very well, and in some circumstances it can be a powerful technique, but there's another way of doing things. We saw in the last chapter that DataSet objects are very powerful, enabling us to represent part of a database in memory. In order to get information from the database into our DataSets, we had to use methods of a data adapter object – and we can use the same communication path to make information travel in the opposite direction. We can *add* records to a DataSet object, and then call the data adapter's Update() method to have them inserted into a database.

We can summarize the steps involved in inserting a new record using a `DataSet` object as follows:

❑ Create a connection object.

❑ Create a data adapter object.

❑ Inform the data adapter about the connection we want to use.

❑ Create a `DataSet` object.

❑ Use the data adapter's `Fill()` method to execute the `SELECT` command and fill the dataset.

❑ Create a new row using the `NewRow()` method exposed by the `DataTable` object.

❑ Set the data row's fields with the values we wish to insert.

❑ Add the data row to the data table with the `Add()` method of the `DataRowCollection` class.

❑ Set the data adapter class's `InsertCommand` property with the `INSERT` statement that we want to use to insert the record. (We will see later that we can use a **command builder** object to create SQL commands automatically.)

❑ Use the `Update()` method exposed by the data adapter to insert the new record into the database. Optionally, we can use the `DataSet` class's `GetChanges()` method to retrieve just the changes that occurred to the object after the filling process.

❑ Use the `AcceptChanges()` method provided by the `DataSet` class in order to align the in-memory data with the physical data within the database.

As we saw in Chapter 5, `DataSet` objects are adept at dealing with XML, and it's also possible to insert new records into a database after reading them straight from an XML file. We would do this in the following way:

❑ Create a connection object.

❑ Create a data adapter object.

❑ Inform the data adapter about the connection we want to use.

❑ Create a `DataSet` object.

❑ Use the `ReadXml()` method exposed by the `DataSet` object to bring data into the application from an XML file.

❑ Set the data adapter class's `InsertCommand` property with the `INSERT` statement that we want to use to insert the record.

❑ Use the `Update()` method exposed by the data adapter to insert the new record into the database.

We'll demonstrate this second way of using a `DataSet` object to insert information into a database in the second of the two examples that conclude this chapter.

Command Builder Classes

The ADO.NET library provides some classes that are capable of creating SQL INSERT, UPDATE, and DELETE statements automatically, based on the SELECT statement that was specified during the creation of the data adapter object. **Command builder** classes can be very useful when you have a simple SELECT statement, but sadly you can't use them when your data adapter object was created from a SELECT command that retrieves records from two or more tables joined together. In the following demonstration, you'll see how they work.

Try It Out – Inserting a New Record Using the DataSet Object

In this example, we're going to create an ASP.NET page that will be capable of adding records to the Categories table contained in the Northwind database. We'll use a DataGrid control to show the records in the table, and a DataSet object to add a new record. Thanks to the DataGrid control's DataBind() method, we'll see the new record appear in the grid after the insertion process.

1. Create a new text file in the webroot\ch06 folder, and call it DG_Insert.aspx.

2. This is quite a long listing, so we'll take it in stages. First, the HTML code, which places the DataGrid along with a couple of text boxes, a button, and a RequiredFieldValidator on the page:

```
<%@ Import namespace="System.Data" %>
<%@ Import namespace="System.Data.SqlClient" %>

<html>
  <head>
    <title>DataGrid - Insert</title>
  </head>
  <body leftMargin="0" topMargin="0">
    <form id="Form1" method="post" runat="server">
      <table id="Table1"
             style="Z-INDEX: 110; LEFT: 5px; POSITION: absolute; TOP: 5px"
             cellSpacing="0" cellPadding="0" width="300" border="0">
        <tr>
          <td colSpan="3">
            <asp:DataGrid id="dgNorthwind" runat="server"
                    Width="728" Height="234" BorderColor="#CC9966"
                    BorderStyle="None" BorderWidth="1"
                    BackColor="White" CellPadding="4" EnableViewState="False">
              <ItemStyle ForeColor="#330099" BackColor="White" />
              <HeaderStyle Font-Bold="True"
                      ForeColor="#FFFFCC" BackColor="#990000" />
              <FooterStyle ForeColor="#330099" BackColor="#FFFFCC" />
              <PagerStyle HorizontalAlign="Center"
                      ForeColor="#330099" BackColor="#FFFFCC" />
            </asp:DataGrid>
          </td>
        </tr>
```

```
            <tr>
              <td colSpan="3"></td>
            </tr>
            <tr>
              <td colSpan="3">
                <p>
                  <asp:Label id="Label1" runat="server"
                             Width="317" BackColor="Firebrick" ForeColor="White">
                    Insert a new record...
                  </asp:Label>
                </p>
              </td>
            </tr>
            <tr>
              <td colSpan="3"></td>
            </tr>
            <tr>
              <td colSpan="3">
                <asp:Label id="Label2" runat="server" Width="85px">
                  Category</asp:Label>
                <asp:TextBox id="txtCategory" runat="server" Width="220px" />
                <asp:RequiredFieldValidator id="rfvCategory" runat="server"
                        ErrorMessage="Please insert the category name..."
                        ControlToValidate="txtCategory" />
              </td>
            </tr>
            <tr>
              <td colSpan="3">
                <asp:Label id="Label3" runat="server" Width="85">
                  Description</asp:Label>
                <asp:TextBox id="txtDescription" runat="server" Width="220" />
              </td>
            </tr>
            <tr>
              <td colSpan="3">
                <asp:Button id="btnInsert" runat="server" OnClick="btnInsert_Click"
                            Width="317" Height="22"
                            BorderColor="#FFFFC0" BorderStyle="Solid"
                            BackColor="Firebrick" ForeColor="White" Text="Insert" />
              </td>
            </tr>
          </table>
        </form>
      </body>
    </html>
```

3. Next, we have the declaration of global variables for the connections, data adapter, and
dataset objects, followed by the Page_Load() event handler:

```
<script language="VB" runat="server">
Dim objConnection As SqlConnection
Dim daNorthwind As SqlDataAdapter
Dim dsNorthwind As DataSet
```

```
Sub Page_Load(Source As Object, E As EventArgs)

  Dim strConnection As String = ConfigurationSettings.AppSettings("NWind")
  objConnection = New SqlConnection(strConnection)

  Dim strSQL As String = "SELECT CategoryID, CategoryName, Description " & _
                         "FROM Categories"
  daNorthwind = New SqlDataAdapter(strSQL, objConnection)

  ' Create a command builder object in order to create
  ' INSERT, UPDATE, and DELETE SQL statements automatically
  Dim cb As New SqlCommandBuilder(daNorthwind)

  ' Is the page being loaded for the first time?
  If Not Page.IsPostBack Then
    FillDataGrid()
  End If
End Sub
```

4. Following hard on the heels of `Page_Load()` is `FillDataGrid()`, which is called by the former and performs the function its name suggests. It's not dissimilar from the procedures with similar names that you saw in the previous chapter.

```
Sub FillDataGrid()

  ' Create a new dataset to contain categories' records
  dsNorthwind = New DataSet()

  ' Fill the dataset retrieving data from the database
  daNorthwind.Fill(dsNorthwind)

  ' Set the DataSource property of the DataGrid
  dgNorthwind.DataSource = dsNorthwind.Tables(0).DefaultView

  ' Bind the dataset data to the DataGrid
  dgNorthwind.DataBind()
End Sub
```

5. Finally, we have the handler for the button being clicked, which performs validation and then enters the new category into the database.

```
Sub btnInsert_Click(Sender As Object, E As EventArgs)

  ' If user has filled every text box correctly...
  If Page.IsValid Then

    ' Create a temporary dataset to contain the new record
    Dim dsTemp As New DataSet()

    ' Fill the temporary dataset
    daNorthwind.Fill(dsTemp)
```

```
    ' Create a new row
    Dim r As DataRow = dsTemp.Tables(0).NewRow()

    ' Add the category name, reading its value from the text box
    r("CategoryName") = txtCategory.Text

    ' Add the category description, reading its value from the text box
    r("Description") = txtDescription.Text

    ' Add the new row into the dataset's rows collection
    dsTemp.Tables(0).Rows.Add(r)

    ' Update the database using the temporary dataset
    daNorthwind.Update(dsTemp)

    ' Usually, you have to call the AcceptChanges() method in order to align the
    ' dataset with records in the database. Because this is a temporary dataset,
    ' we can omit this instruction.
    ' dsTemp.AcceptChanges()

    ' Refresh the data grid to display the new record
    FillDataGrid()
  End If
End Sub
</script>
```

6. With all of this code in place, you should be able to launch the page and see this:

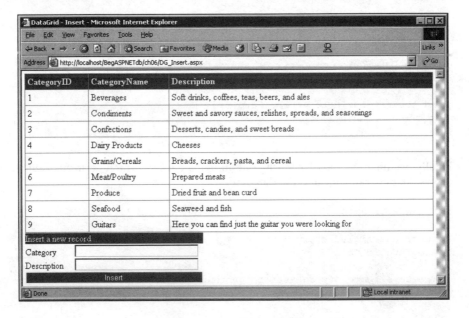

7. And after inserting a new category name and description (and pressing the Insert button), you'll see the new record appear at the bottom of the list:

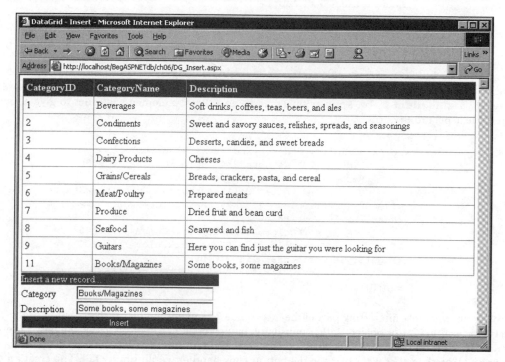

Don't worry if the CategoryID is different from the one you can see here. The value allocated by the database will vary, depending on how many times you've added and deleted categories from this table.

How It Works

In the next chapter, we'll see how the `DataGrid` control provides some properties and methods that enable users to edit the rows it contains directly – you just select the row you want to modify, and the `DataGrid` will show text box fields to receive the new data. Sadly, however, the `DataGrid` control doesn't provide an automatic way to insert a *new* record, so we have to add input controls for each value to be added into the database. This is the reason for those two text box controls in the HTML code:

```
<tr>
  <td colSpan="3">
    <asp:Label id="Label2" runat="server" Width="85px">
      Category</asp:Label>
    <asp:TextBox id="txtCategory" runat="server" Width="220px" />
    <asp:RequiredFieldValidator id="rfvCategory" runat="server"
        ErrorMessage="Please insert the category name..."
        ControlToValidate="txtCategory" />
  </td>
</tr>
<tr>
```

```
            <td colSpan="3">
              <asp:Label id="Label3" runat="server" Width="85">
                Description</asp:Label>
              <asp:TextBox id="txtDescription" runat="server" Width="220" />
            </td>
          </tr>
```

The `DataGrid` used in the example creates columns by reading their names from the `SELECT` statement we specified during creation of the data adapter object. Moreover, the `DataGrid` uses `ItemStyle`, `HeaderStyle`, `FooterStyle` and `PagerStyle` elements in order to give a more agreeable aspect to the grid.

```
        <asp:DataGrid id="dgNorthwind" runat="server"
                 Width="728" Height="234" BorderColor="#CC9966"
                 BorderStyle="None" BorderWidth="1"
                 BackColor="White" CellPadding="4" EnableViewState="False">
          <ItemStyle ForeColor="#330099" BackColor="White" />
          <HeaderStyle Font-Bold="True"
                       ForeColor="#FFFFCC" BackColor="#990000" />
          <FooterStyle ForeColor="#330099" BackColor="#FFFFCC" />
          <PagerStyle HorizontalAlign="Center"
                       ForeColor="#330099" BackColor="#FFFFCC" />
        </asp:DataGrid>
```

Moving on, the most interesting part of the `Page_Load()` event handler is the creation of the `SqlCommandBuilder` object. Rather unusually, having created the `cb` variable, we never use it again – but this line of code is essential, nonetheless. Without it, the call to the data adapter object's `Update()` method that takes place in the button-click handler would simply fail. The creation of this object, which takes our data adapter object as a parameter to its constructor, is key to the automatic creation of `UPDATE`, `INSERT`, and `DELETE` SQL statements that will result in any changes made to the dataset being reflected in the database:

```
Sub Page_Load(Source As Object, E As EventArgs)

    Dim strConnection As String = ConfigurationSettings.AppSettings("NWind")
    objConnection = New SqlConnection(strConnection)

    Dim strSQL As String = "SELECT CategoryID, CategoryName, Description " & _
                           "FROM Categories"
    daNorthwind = New SqlDataAdapter(strSQL, objConnection)

    ' Create a command builder object in order to create
    ' INSERT, UPDATE, and DELETE SQL statements automatically
    Dim cb As New SqlCommandBuilder(daNorthwind)

    ' Is the page being loaded for the first time?
    If Not Page.IsPostBack Then
        FillDataGrid()
    End If
End Sub
```

In `FillDataGrid()`, we use the `DataBind()` method that's exposed by the `DataGrid` control in order to refresh the records in the grid. Also, thanks to the `DataSource` property of the `DataGrid` object, we can inform the grid about which part of the in-memory database we want to display.

```
Sub FillDataGrid()

    ' Create a new dataset to contain categories' records
    dsNorthwind = New DataSet()

    ' Fill the dataset retrieving data from the database
    daNorthwind.Fill(dsNorthwind)

    ' Set the DataSource property of the DataGrid
    dgNorthwind.DataSource = dsNorthwind.Tables(0).DefaultView

    ' Bind the dataset data to the DataGrid
    dgNorthwind.DataBind()
End Sub
```

Finally, when the user presses the **Insert** button, our first check is to verify that the rules of the `RequiredFieldValidator` control have been met. After that, we create a temporary `DataSet` that will eventually contain the record we want to insert in the database, and fill it with the records from the `Categories` table that we earlier read into the data adapter object.

```
Sub btnInsert_Click(Sender As Object, E As EventArgs)
    ' If user has filled every text box correctly...
    If Page.IsValid Then

        ' Create a temporary dataset to contain the new record
        Dim dsTemp As New DataSet()

        ' Fill the temporary dataset
        daNorthwind.Fill(dsTemp)
```

Last of all, we have to add a new row to the temporary `DataSet`, specifying the category name and the description provided by the user on the ASP.NET page. With that done, calling the `Update()` method (now) provided by the `SqlDataAdapter` object will insert the record in the database. We don't have to open the connection and close it after the record insertion, because the `SqlDataAdapter` object manages everything automatically.

```
        ' Create a new row
        Dim r As DataRow = dsTemp.Tables(0).NewRow()

        ' Add the category name, reading its value from the text box
        r("CategoryName") = txtCategory.Text

        ' Add the category description, reading its value from the text box
        r("Description") = txtDescription.Text
```

```
    ' Add the new row into the dataset's rows collection
  dsTemp.Tables(0).Rows.Add(r)

    ' Update the database using the temporary dataset
    daNorthwind.Update(dsTemp)
```

And now we can call the `FillDataGrid()` method in order to refresh the data in the grid.

```
    ' Refresh the data grid to display the new record
    FillDataGrid()
  End If
```

By producing the necessary `INSERT` statement on our behalf, the ADO.NET `SqlCommandBuilder` object has enabled us to update the database with our new category without the need to construct another SQL query – something that you'll surely agree to be a good thing!

Try It Out – Using a Calendar, a DataSet, and XML to Insert Records

In the last example of this chapter, we'll create an ASP.NET page that displays a `DataGrid` control containing records from the `Employees` table of the `Northwind` database. Also on the page is a `Calendar` control that we'll use to specify the hiring date of a new employee. When a date has been selected, we'll use a `DataSet` to add the new employee to the database, along with two more new employees whose details will be read from an XML file.

1. The name of the ASPX file for this example will be `Cal_Insert.aspx`, so generate a new text file with that name and place it in the `ch06` folder.

2. Once again, we'll start the code listing with the HTML section, which this time has a form containing information for formatting a `DataGrid` control and a `Calendar` control. The `DataGrid` contains `BoundColumn` controls like the ones you saw in the previous chapter.

```
<%@ Import namespace="System.Data" %>
<%@ Import namespace="System.Data.SqlClient" %>

<html>
  <head>
    <title>Inserting Calendar and XML Data</title>
  </head>
  <body>
    <form id="Form1" runat="server" method="post">
      <table id="Table1"
             style="Z-INDEX: 101; LEFT: 7px; POSITION: absolute; TOP: 7px"
             cellSpacing="0" cellPadding="0" width="300" border="0">
        <tr>
          <td style="WIDTH: 681" colSpan="2">
            <asp:DataGrid id="dgNorthwind" runat="server" Width="479"
                    Height="191" BorderColor="#CC9966" BorderWidth="1"
                    BorderStyle="None" BackColor="White" CellPadding="4"
                    DataKeyField="EmployeeID" AutoGenerateColumns="False">
```

```
                        <SelectedItemStyle Font-Bold="True"
                                    ForeColor="#663399" BackColor="#FFCC66" />
                <ItemStyle ForeColor="#330099" BackColor="White" />
                <HeaderStyle Font-Bold="True"
                            ForeColor="#FFFFCC" BackColor="#990000" />
                <FooterStyle ForeColor="#330099" BackColor="#FFFFCC" />
                <Columns>
                 <asp:BoundColumn DataField="FirstName" HeaderText="First Name" />
                 <asp:BoundColumn DataField="LastName" HeaderText="Last Name" />
                 <asp:BoundColumn DataField="HireDate" HeaderText="Hire Date" />
                </Columns>
                <PagerStyle HorizontalAlign="Center"
                            ForeColor="#330099" BackColor="#FFFFCC" />
              </asp:DataGrid>
            </td>
          </tr>
          <tr>
            <td style="WIDTH: 681; HEIGHT: 49" colSpan="2">
              <asp:Label id="Label1" runat="server" Height="45" Width="480"
                        BackColor="Maroon" Font-Bold="True" ForeColor="#FFE0C0">
                By selecting a date from the calendar, you
                will insert a new record in the database.
              </asp:Label>
            </td>
          </tr>
          <tr>
            <td style="WIDTH: 681" colSpan="2">
              <asp:Calendar id="calHire" runat="server"
                    OnSelectionChanged="calHire_SelectionChanged"
                    BorderColor="#FFCC66" Height="153" Width="479"
                    BackColor="#FFFFCC" BorderWidth="1" ForeColor="#663399"
                    EnableViewState="False" ShowGridLines="True"
                    Font-Names="Verdana" Font-Size="8pt">
                <TodayDayStyle ForeColor="White" BackColor="#FFCC66" />
                <SelectorStyle BackColor="#FFCC66" />
                <NextPrevStyle Font-Size="9pt" ForeColor="#FFFFCC" />
                <DayHeaderStyle Height="1" BackColor="#FFCC66" />
                <SelectedDayStyle Font-Bold="True" BackColor="#CCCCFF" />
                <TitleStyle Font-Size="9pt" Font-Bold="True"
                            ForeColor="#FFFFCC" BackColor="#990000" />
                <OtherMonthDayStyle ForeColor="#CC9966" />
              </asp:Calendar>
            </td>
          </tr>
          <tr>
            <td style="WIDTH: 681" colSpan="2">
              <asp:Label id="lbError" runat="server" ForeColor="Red" />
            </td>
          </tr>
        </table>
      </form>
    </body>
</html>
```

3. The `Page_Load()` event handler is little changed from the one in the last example, save for the content of the initial SQL query, which retrieves employee details rather than category information.

```vb
<script language="VB" runat="server">
Dim objConnection As SqlConnection
Dim daNorthwind As SqlDataAdapter
Dim dsNorthwind As DataSet

Sub Page_Load(Source As Object, E As EventArgs)

  Dim strConnection As String = ConfigurationSettings.AppSettings("NWind")
  objConnection = New SqlConnection(strConnection)

  Dim strSQL As String = "SELECT EmployeeID, LastName, FirstName, HireDate " & _
                    "FROM Employees"
  daNorthwind = New SqlDataAdapter(strSQL, objConnection)

  Dim cb As New SqlCommandBuilder(daNorthwind)

  If Not Page.IsPostBack Then
    FillDataGrid()
  End If
End Sub
```

4. Because we've used the same variable names, the `FillDataGrid()` method for this example is exactly the same as the one we had last time, so we won't reproduce it here. Instead, we can move on to the `calHire_SelectionChanged()` event handler, where all the action takes place:

```vb
Sub calHire_SelectionChanged(Source As Object, E As EventArgs)

  ' If the user chooses a date in the future, an error message is displayed
  If calHire.SelectedDate <= Today() Then

    ' Create a temporary dataset to contain the new record
    Dim dsTemp As New DataSet()

    dsTemp.ReadXml("C:\BegAspNetDb\datastores\Employees.xml")

    ' Create a new row
    Dim r As DataRow = dsTemp.Tables(0).NewRow()
    r("LastName") = "Ferracchiati"
    r("FirstName") = "Fabio C."
    r("HireDate") = Convert.ToDateTime(calHire.SelectedDate)

    ' Add the new row into the dataset's rows collection
    dsTemp.Tables(0).Rows.Add(r)

    ' Update the database using the temporary dataset
    daNorthwind.Update(dsTemp, "EMPLOYEE")

    ' Refresh the data grid to display the new record
```

```
      FillDataGrid()
   Else
      Response.Write("Hire date can't be in the future!")
      Response.End()
   End If
End Sub
</script>
```

5. In keeping with the details of the above listing, we also need to create an XML file in our datastores folder, called Employees.xml. It takes the following form:

```xml
<?xml version="1.0" standalone="yes"?>
<EMPLOYEES>
  <EMPLOYEE>
    <LastName>Griffiths</LastName>
    <FirstName>Derek</FirstName>
    <HireDate>1996-08-13T00:00:00.0000000+01:00</HireDate>
  </EMPLOYEE>
  <EMPLOYEE>
    <LastName>Holmes</LastName>
    <FirstName>Eamonn</FirstName>
    <HireDate>1995-11-22T00:00:00.0000000+01:00</HireDate>
  </EMPLOYEE>
</EMPLOYEES>
```

6. Now, when we load our page, we should be presented with the following:

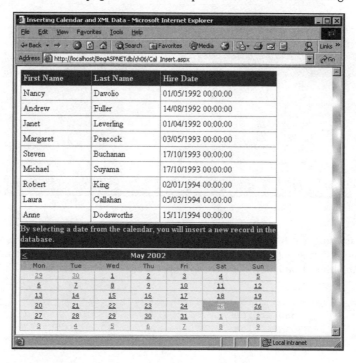

7. And when we select a date (which should be prior to the current date), three new records will be added to the database and displayed in the grid:

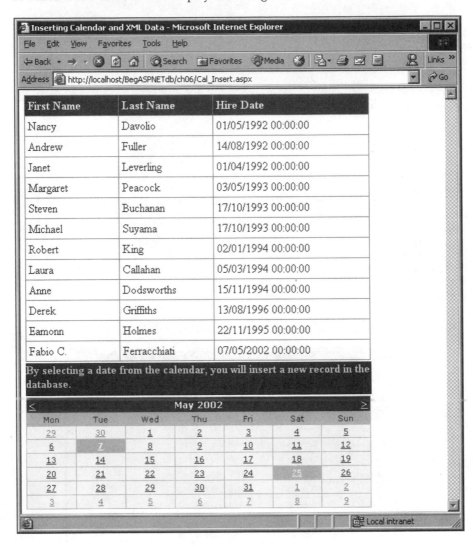

How It Works

Let's start by examining the ASP.NET `Calendar` control. We want to insert a new record when the user selects a date, so we specify a handler for the `OnSelectionChanged` event. Moreover, we've specified some attributes that change the default appearance of the calendar:

```
<asp:Calendar id="calHire" runat="server"
        OnSelectionChanged="calHire_SelectionChanged"
        BorderColor="#FFCC66" Height="153" Width="479"
        BackColor="#FFFFCC" BorderWidth="1" ForeColor="#663399"
```

```
                    EnableViewState="False" ShowGridLines="True"
                    Font-Names="Verdana" Font-Size="8pt">
        <TodayDayStyle ForeColor="White" BackColor="#FFCC66" />
        <SelectorStyle BackColor="#FFCC66" />
        <NextPrevStyle Font-Size="9pt" ForeColor="#FFFFCC" />
        <DayHeaderStyle Height="1" BackColor="#FFCC66" />
        <SelectedDayStyle Font-Bold="True" BackColor="#CCCCFF" />
        <TitleStyle Font-Size="9pt" Font-Bold="True"
                    ForeColor="#FFFFCC" BackColor="#990000" />
        <OtherMonthDayStyle ForeColor="#CC9966" />
    </asp:Calendar>
```

When the user selects a date in the calendar control, the `calHire_SelectionChanged()` event handler is called. The first operation performed is to check that the date is less than or equal to the current date; if it's not, an error will be displayed.

```
Sub calHire_SelectionChanged(Source As Object, E As EventArgs)

  ' If the user chooses a date in the future, an error message is displayed
  If calHire.SelectedDate <= Today() Then

  ' Data manipulation code, discussed in a moment.

  Else
    Response.Write("Hire date can't be in the future!")
    Response.End()
  End If
End Sub
```

In the main body of the event handler, we first fill a new `DataSet` object with the contents of the `Employees.xml` file, using the `ReadXml()` method:

```
' Create a temporary dataset to contain the new record
Dim dsTemp As New DataSet()

dsTemp.ReadXml("C:\BegAspNetDb\datastores\Employees.xml")
```

And now we can treat this `DataSet` in the same way as we treated the one in the previous example. We have to add a new row to the `Rows` collection, specify the fields we want to insert in the database, and finally call the `Update()` method specifying the name of the table contained in the XML file.

```
' Create a new row
Dim r As DataRow = dsTemp.Tables(0).NewRow()
r("LastName") = "Ferracchiati"
r("FirstName") = "Fabio C."
r("HireDate") = Convert.ToDateTime(calHire.SelectedDate)

' Add the new row into the dataset's rows collection
dsTemp.Tables(0).Rows.Add(r)

' Update the database using the temporary dataset
daNorthwind.Update(dsTemp, "EMPLOYEE")
```

In the interests of brevity, we've cut down the complexity of this demonstration by writing some of the new data into the code of the application. Hopefully, though, you can begin to see how you might assemble the techniques we've examined so far to produce something rather more complicated. For example, the hard-wired data that was entered into the database in this example could certainly be replaced by values from text boxes or drop-down list controls, if that's what you needed to do. Do experiment with the things you've seen so far, and see what you can come up with.

Summary

In this chapter, we have looked at the basic theory of inserting records into a database using standard SQL statements. You've learned how to write code in order to execute INSERT commands using ADO.NET command objects. You've also seen how, by using the Parameters collection that's exposed by command objects, you can write more readable code. Finally, we have examined how to use DataSet objects in conjunction with data adapter objects in order to insert values read from ASP.NET forms and XML files.

So: you know how to create new records, and how to insert them into a database – but that's only half the story. In the next chapter, we will look at how to modify and delete existing database records.

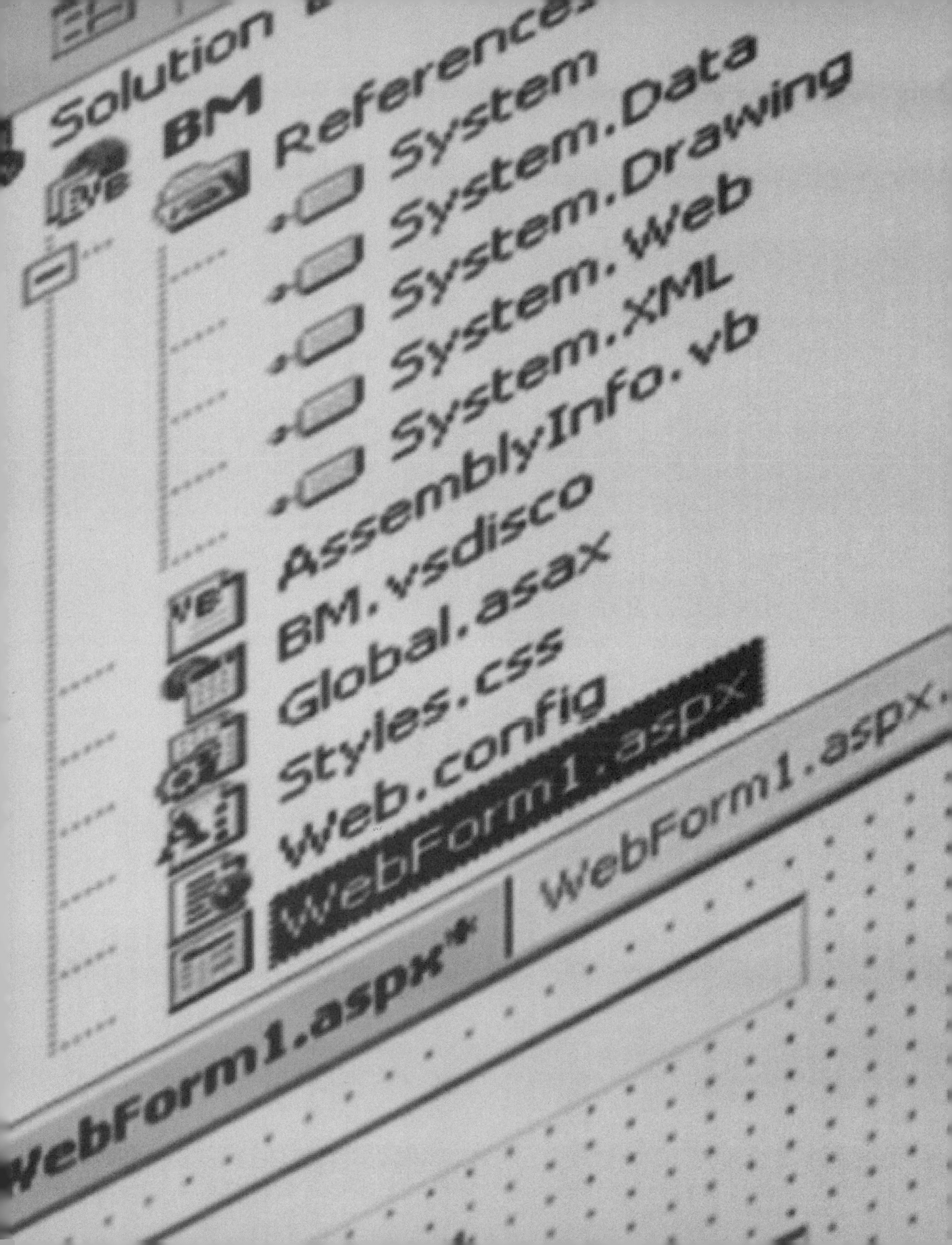

Solution
BM
References
System
System.Data
System.Drawing
System.Web
System.XML
AssemblyInfo.vb
Assembly
BM.vsdisco
Global.asax
Styles.css
Web.config
WebForm1.aspx

WebForm1.aspx* | WebForm1.aspx.

WebForm1.aspx*

Updating and Deleting Records

If you listen to conversations among database programmers, a word you might hear more frequently than you'd otherwise expect is "CRUD". That word is an acronym for Create, Read, Update, and Delete – the four basic database operations that are performed thousands of times every second, by machines all over the world. Every book about database programming covers these four operations, and this one is no exception.

In Chapters 4 and 5, we explained the different ways of reading from a database in ADO.NET. In the previous chapter, we described how you could create and then add new records to a table. That means we've got the first half of CRUD covered already; the second half – updating and deleting the records in a database – is the subject of this chapter. Specifically, you will see how to:

❑ Update and delete records in a database using SQL's UPDATE and DELETE statements

❑ Update and delete records in a database using ADO.NET command objects

❑ Create a web front end for database access using ASP.NET DataGrid control

❑ Capture user input and perform database operations using ASP.NET's event handling features

❑ Modify in-memory data and update a database using ADO.NET dataset and data adapter objects

❑ Validate data input and user actions

Updating a Database

ADO.NET provides several different ways of updating the records in a database. If you know what records need to be updated, what their new values should be, and you want to update them immediately, you can use a command object to execute an SQL UPDATE statement or a stored procedure (see the next chapter). If you need some input from your users, you can create a dataset and populate it with the records you want the users to modify. A user can then look at the records and modify them as they wish; once they're done, you create a data adapter object to push the changes back to the database.

SQL UPDATE Statements

In the last chapter, we created new records using the SQL INSERT statement. SQL also defines a UPDATE statement to update one or more existing records. The generic form of the UPDATE statement's syntax is represented below.

```
UPDATE
{ table_name }
{
  SET column1_name = expression1,
      column2_name = expression2,
      ...
      columnM_name = expressionM
  [WHERE condition1 AND|OR condition2 AND|OR ... AND|OR conditionN]
}
```

Where:

- ❑ UPDATE is the SQL command
- ❑ table_name is the name of the table containing the record(s) to be updated
- ❑ SET is a SQL keyword that starts the column update operations
- ❑ column1_name, column2_name, etc. are the name of columns in which the values will be updated
- ❑ expression1, expression2, etc. are the new values for each column
- ❑ WHERE is a SQL keyword that specifies one or more conditions that qualify the records to be updated, just as it does in SELECT statements

Syntax alone is rather dry, though, so let's look at some SQL code that would make changes to the Categories table of the Northwind database, to see how you can apply the theory in practice. If you followed the examples in the previous chapter, you now have an entry in the Categories table called Books/Magazines, created with the following INSERT statement:

```
INSERT INTO Categories
(CategoryName, Description)
VALUES ('Books/Magazines', 'Some books, some magazines')
```

Now, if you wanted to change the description associated with this category, you could use an UPDATE statement like this one:

```
UPDATE Categories
SET Description = 'Great books'
WHERE CategoryName = 'Books/Magazines'
```

What it says is, "Find all records with a CategoryName of Books/Magazines, and change their Description value to Great books." In this case, of course, there's only one record that satisfies this condition.

In addition to assigning a literal value to a column, the SET clause also allows you to assign an expression to a column, or to assign values to several columns at once. Assuming that the CategoryID of the Books/Magazines record is 9, the following UPDATE statement would update both CategoryName and Description columns:

```
UPDATE Categories
SET CategoryName = 'Magazines/Books',
    Description = 'Interesting magazines' + ' and ' + 'books'
WHERE CategoryID = 9
```

When it comes to updating records with ADO.NET, the two options available are very much like the ones we had in the last chapter when we wanted to insert records. You can use a command object to execute an UPDATE statement directly, or you can use a DataSet object to modify records in memory, and then update the database with those changes.

In the next section, we'll demonstrate how to update records using a command object. The DataSet solution will be covered after that.

Using a Command Object to Update Records

You're already familiar with a number of operations that use command objects, so extending that knowledge to cover updating a database shouldn't prove to be too tricky a task. The sequence of actions goes like this:

- ❑ Create a database connection
- ❑ Create a command object, and specify either an SQL UPDATE statement or a stored procedure
- ❑ Link the command object to the database connection
- ❑ Invoke the ExecuteNonQuery() method of the command object to execute the UPDATE query
- ❑ Close the connection

The skeleton code below shows a simple database update operation along precisely these lines. In the example that follows, we'll give it a spin.

```
Dim strConnection As String = ConfigurationSettings.AppSettings("NWind")
Dim objConnection As New SqlConnection(strConnection)
Dim strSQL As String = "UPDATE Categories " & _
                       "SET Description = 'Great books' " & _
                       "WHERE CategoryName = 'Books/Magazines'"

Dim dbComm As New SqlCommand(strSQL, objConnection)

objConnection.Open()
dbComm.ExecuteNonQuery()
objConnection.Close()
```

Try It Out – Displaying and Updating Database information with ASP.NET

For this chapter's first example, we'll create an ASP.NET page that displays the name and price of a product in the `Northwind` database, and allows the user to enter a new price for the product, thereby updating the database. For simplicity, we'll hard-wire the code to use the product with a `ProductID` of 1 from the `Products` table of the database.

1. Another chapter, another new folder. In `webroot`, create a new directory called `ch07`, and then generate a new text file called `Update_Price.aspx`.

2. As usual, we'll start our listing with the HTML code for our elementary project. It involves placing a label, a text box, and a button on the page:

```
<%@ Import namespace="System.Data" %>
<%@ Import namespace="System.Data.SqlClient" %>

<html>
  <head>
    <title>Updating a Price</title>
  </head>
  <body>
    <form method="post" runat="server">
      <asp:Label id="lblProductName" runat="server" /><br/><br/>
      <asp:TextBox id="txtPrice" runat="server" /><br/><br/>
      <asp:Button id="btnChange" runat="server" Text="Change" />
    </form>
  </body>
</html>
```

3. Our first task must be to load the first record from the database and display it on the page. We'll isolate this functionality into a procedure called `LoadProduct()` that forms the first piece of Visual Basic .NET code in our ASPX file:

```
<script language="VB" runat="server">
Sub LoadProduct()
  Dim strConnection As String = ConfigurationSettings.AppSettings("NWind")
  Dim objConnection As New SqlConnection(strConnection)
  Dim strQuery As String = "SELECT ProductName, UnitPrice " & _
                           "FROM Products WHERE ProductID = 1"
  objConnection.Open()

  Dim dbComm As New SqlCommand(strQuery, objConnection)
  Dim reader As SqlDataReader = dbComm.ExecuteReader()

  reader.Read()
  lblProductName.Text = reader.GetString(0)
  txtPrice.Text = reader.GetSqlMoney(1).ToString()

  reader.Close()
  objConnection.Close()
End Sub
```

This procedure executes the SELECT query and stores the returned records in a data reader object. It then goes to the first record (which happens to be the only record returned), and assigns the value of the ProductName and UnitPrice fields to the Text properties of the lblProductName label and the txtPrice text box respectively. With that done, it closes the reader and the connection to release the database connection.

4. The next task is to get ASP.NET to run this procedure when the user loads the page. You do this by calling it from the Page_Load() event handler, as listed below.

```
Sub Page_Load(ByVal Source As Object, ByVal E As EventArgs)
  If Not IsPostBack Then
    LoadProduct()
  End If
End Sub
</script>
```

Later in this example, we'll use a button to instruct the database to change this value, but we don't want the page to be refreshed with new data from the database as soon as that happens – we need to give the database time to make the change. The code in the If statement ensures that the database will be queried for new data only when we ask for that to happen.

5. It's a good time to give this page a run before we go any further. If you load the page into your browser, you should see something like this:

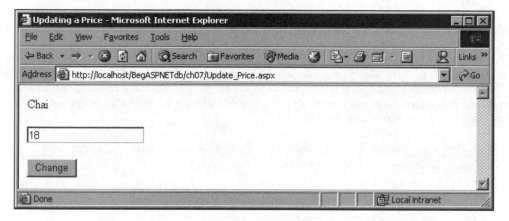

6. So far, we've just been setting the scene – there's little here that you haven't seen in previous chapters. What we really want is to be able to change the price shown in the text box, and press the Change button to update the database. We need to add a click event handler for that button to our page.

```
<asp:Button id="btnChange" runat="server"
            OnClick="btnInsert_Click" Text="Change" />
```

```
Sub btnChange_Click(ByVal Sender As Object, ByVal E As EventArgs)
  Dim strConnection As String = ConfigurationSettings.AppSettings("NWind")
Dim objConnection As New SqlConnection(strConnection)
  Dim strSQL As String = "UPDATE Products" & _
                         " SET UnitPrice = " & txtPrice.Text & _
                         " WHERE ProductID = 1"

  Dim dbComm As New SqlCommand(strSQL, objConnection)

  objConnection.Open()
  dbComm.ExecuteNonQuery()
  objConnection.Close()

  LoadProduct()
End Sub
```

How It Works

Although the SQL statement in question has changed, this is similar to the examples we've been considering elsewhere, and you should be starting to feel comfortable with this form of database access. In the btnChange_Click() event handler, we open a connection, execute a command, and close the connection. On this occasion, the command in question is an UPDATE statement that assigns whatever the user entered in the txtPrice textbox to the UnitPrice field. Once the query has run, we call the LoadProduct() procedure to reload the modified record from the database and display the new price on the page.

Before we move on, there's one more thing worth mentioning. While the code we've written so far works, it has some deficiencies that we can improve. To demonstrate the basic techniques of reading and updating database records, LoadProduct() and btnChange_Click() are self-contained – each of them has code to open and close a connection for its own use. In a production-quality application, you'd put the common code (in this case, the code for opening and closing connections) in some centralized procedures, and call it from all other places that such functionality is needed. The code below suggests one way of doing this:

```
Dim strConnection As String = ConfigurationSettings.AppSettings("NWind")
Dim objConnection As SqlConnection

Sub LoadProduct()
  Connect()
  Dim strQuery As String = "SELECT ProductName, UnitPrice " & _
                           "FROM Products WHERE ProductID = 1"

  Dim dbComm As New SqlCommand(strQuery, objConnection)
  Dim reader As SqlDataReader = dbComm.ExecuteReader()

  reader.Read()
  lblProductName.Text = reader.GetString(0)
  txtPrice.Text = reader.GetSqlMoney(1).ToString()

  reader.Close()
  Disconnect()
End Sub
```

```
Sub btnChange_Click(ByVal Sender As Object, ByVal E As EventArgs)
  UpdateProduct()
  LoadProduct()
End Sub


Private Sub UpdateProduct()
  Dim strSQL As String = "UPDATE Products" & _
                         " SET UnitPrice = " & txtPrice.Text & _
                         " WHERE ProductID = 1"
  Connect()
  Dim dbComm As New SqlCommand(strSQL, objConnection)
  dbComm.ExecuteNonQuery()
  Disconnect()
End Sub

Private Sub Connect()
  If objConnection Is Nothing Then
    objConnection = New SqlConnection(strConnection)
  End If

  If objConnection.State = ConnectionState.Closed Then
    objConnection.Open()
  End If
End Sub

Private Sub Disconnect()
  objConnection.Close()
End Sub
```

Now, the code for connecting to and disconnecting from the database is in dedicated procedures, as is the code that actually updates the product information. Such changes result in cleaner, more structured, more extensible code.

Updating Records Using a DataSet

An ADO.NET `DataSet` object provides better programmatic database update functionality. Because a `DataSet` object is always disconnected from the database, you can add to, modify, and delete any of the records it contains offline. Once you've finished making your changes, you can transfer them to the database by linking the `DataSet` to a data adapter object. In this section, we'll explore how to do that.

Firstly, assume that you've filled a `DataSet` with records from the `Products` table in the `Northwind` database, as illustrated in the code snippet below:

```
Dim strSQL As String = "SELECT ProductID, ProductName, UnitPrice FROM Products"
Dim adapter As New SqlDataAdapter(strSQL, objConnection)
Dim ds As New DataSet()
adapter.Fill(ds, "ProductTable")
```

In the last line of code here, we're naming the table in the `DataSet` that will hold these records as `ProductTable`, but in general this name can be anything you like – it certainly doesn't have to be the same as the name of a table in the database. The advantage of this feature is that you can easily separate the in-memory representation of a table from its source in the database. As far as your application is concerned, you're always dealing with the table called `ProductTable`, as in:

```
Dim tbl As DataTable = ds.Tables("ProductTable")
```

If your friendly DBA later decides that the table in the database should be named differently, the only place where you need to change your code is the `SELECT` statement. (In fact, most applications use stored procedures to execute database operations, so your DBA can modify all the stored procedures that reference the table, without you having to change your code at all.)

> After you've got hold of the **DataSet**, you should always release the connection to the database as quickly as possible, by invoking the **Close()** method of the connection object.

Modifying Records in a DataSet

With a `DataSet` object in your hands, you can modify one or more of the records it contains. The code snippet below shows how you might change the price of a product:

```
Dim tbl As DataTable = ds.Tables("ProductTable")
tbl.PrimaryKey = New DataColumn() _
                { _
                    tbl.Columns("ProductID") _
                }
Dim row As DataRow = tbl.Rows.Find(1)
row.Item("UnitPrice") = 100
```

A key element to be aware of here is that in order to *modify* a record in a `DataSet`, we've got to *find* it first, and that's something we haven't done before. The first step in this process is to set up a column (or a selection of columns) in a dataset table as a primary key into that table. We can then use the primary key as an index to the rows of the table, so that we can quickly find the record we're looking for.

As suggested above, it's sometimes the case that a single column can be used as the primary key. On other occasions, the primary key may be a composite of several columns. As a result, the `DataTable.PrimaryKey` property is defined as a collection of columns that together make up the primary key, and you initialize it with all of the columns concerned, as shown in the second statement above. By contrast, if the primary key had consisted of a composite of the `CategoryID` and `ProductID` columns, we would have had to define the primary key like this:

```
tbl.PrimaryKey = New DataColumn() _
                { _
                    tbl.Columns("CategoryID"), _
                    tbl.Columns("ProductID") _
                }
```

Moving on to the next line of our sample, the `Find()` method of the `DataRowCollection` object that's represented by the `DataTable.Rows` property accepts a primary key value, and returns the `DataRow` containing the matching key. If the primary key consists of multiple columns, you pass in an array of values. For example, if the primary key consisted of a composite of the `CategoryID` and `ProductID` columns, the code snippet below would find a row with `CategoryID` value 1 and `ProductID` value 3.

```
Dim KeyValues(1) As Object
KeyValues(0) = 1;
KeyValues(1) = 3;
Dim row As DataRow = tbl.Rows.Find(KeyValues)
```

Once you have the row, you can modify any field in the record it represents simply by assigning a new value to it. The above example modified the `UnitPrice` field by assigning it with the value 100. You can make as many changes as required to this record, and you can modify more records by searching for them and executing the same set of operations. Remember that the changes you're making here only affect the `DataSet` – the database is not being updated at this point.

Updating Records in the Database

To push the changes you make in a `DataSet` object to the database, you must first reconnect to the database, and then use the same data adapter object that you used to retrieve the data to update the database with your new information:

```
objConnection.Open()
adapter.Update(ds, "ProductTable")
objConnection.Close()
```

Just as we saw when we were inserting records into the database in the previous chapter, the call to the data adapter's `Update()` method neatly encapsulates the task of transferring the new information to the database. Then, as now, we needed to set up a command builder object in order to make the mechanism work, but this time the work going on behind the scenes is rather more involved, and it's interesting to examine exactly how it works.

ADO.NET determines which records in the database to update by examining all of the records in the specified table in the `DataSet` object – `ProductTable` in this example. When you first fill the `DataSet` with records from a database, ADO.NET saves *two* copies of each field: `Original` and `Current`. If you wish, you can get access to these values individually by specifying the one you want in expressions like these:

```
row.Item("UnitPrice", DataRowVersion.Original)
row.Item("UnitPrice", DataRowVersion.Current)
```

In addition, each row has a property called `RowState` that indicates the current state of that row. It may be one of the following five values defined in the `System.Data.DataRowState` enumeration.

Value	Description
Added	The row has been added to the table.
Deleted	The row has been deleted from the table. Note that it's only been *marked* as deleted, and has not been physically removed. This allows ADO.NET to delete the corresponding row in the database later on, as we'll shortly discuss in more detail.
Detached	The row is not in a table. This happens when you have created a new DataRow object, but have not yet added it to the table's Rows collection (or you have removed the row from the table using the Remove() method). This is also covered later on.
Modified	The row has been modified. For instance, you have assigned a new value to one of the fields in the row.
Unchanged	The row has not been changed.

When you modify a record by changing the value of a field (as we did with UnitPrice), ADO.NET changes the row's Current value to the newly assigned value, and changes the RowState property to Modified. When you then invoke the data adapter's Update() method, ADO.NET updates the corresponding field in the database with the current value.

If you wish, you can call the AcceptChanges() method of a DataRow object to change the original values of all fields to the current value. (This method also sets the RowState to Unchanged.) Alternatively, you can call the AcceptChanges() method on a DataTable to accept changes to all rows in the table.

The opposite of AcceptChanges() is RejectChanges(), which is also supported by both row and table objects, and discards any changes that you've made to the DataSet. Calling a row's RejectChanges() method changes its RowState back to Unchanged. If you call the RejectChanges() method of a table, changes to *all* rows will be lost, and the RowState of *all* rows will be reset to Unchanged. Calling the table's RejectChanges() method will also remove any rows that you've added to the table.

Using a Command Builder

We said in the last chapter – and repeated above – that the creation of a command builder object is essential to the operation of the data adapter's Update() method. Once again, though, the increase in complexity here makes it useful to explore the subject in more depth.

```
Dim cb As New SqlCommandBuilder(adapter)
```

As a result of the above line of code, the SqlCommandBuilder's constructor will create a SqlCommand object with an SQL UPDATE statement based on the adapter's SELECT command, and then assign this command object to the data adapter's UpdateCommand property. Command builder classes can build INSERT and DELETE commands as well, and do so automatically when you create instances of them.

Creating a Update Command Manually

While command builder objects are undoubtedly handy and can save you a lot of coding, they have their drawbacks – or at least, their limitations:

❑ They can only update records in a single database table only. If you have a query that pulls records from two tables or more, the command builder won't build the update command for you.

❑ The SQL statement assigned to the data adapter object's `SelectCommand` property must return a column containing values that uniquely identify the returned records.

❑ If the `SelectCommand` property changes, you must call the adapter object's `RefreshSchema()` method to update the metadata that's used to generate the insert, update, and delete commands.

If any of these describes your situation, command builder objects won't work for you, and you'll have to build the update command manually.

```
Dim cmd As New SqlCommand("UPDATE Products SET UnitPrice = @Price " & _
                          "WHERE ProductID = @ProductID", objConnection)

Dim param As SqlParameter = cmd.Parameters.Add("@ProductID", SqlDbType.Int)
param.SourceColumn = "ProductID"
param.SourceVersion = DataRowVersion.Original

param = cmd.Parameters.Add("@Price", SqlDbType.Money)
param.SourceColumn = "UnitPrice"
param.SourceVersion = DataRowVersion.Current

adapter.UpdateCommand = cmd
```

In this code, we create a command object and pass to its constructor the SQL UPDATE statement (or the stored procedure) that performs the update. Because at this point we don't know the exact record to be updated, or the price it will be updated with, we specify that the ID and price of the product will be provided later by parameterizing the statement.

The SQL statement must include every column in the table that you want to update. If you change the values of some fields, but don't include the relevant columns in the UPDATE statement, none of the changes you make will find their way to the database.

Next, we add two parameters to the command. The first, `@ProductID`, is an integer – we specify that it should be bound to the `ProductID` column in the table, and ensure that we're dealing with the right row by binding it to the *original* value of this field in the database through the parameter's `SourceVersion` property. The second parameter, `@Price`, is bound to the `UnitPrice` column, and the *current* version of the value it contains.

Having defined the command object, we then assign it to the data adapter object's `UpdateCommand` property. When we invoke the data adapter's `Update()` method, this command is executed to update the correct product record in the database.

With the theory under our belts, we can think about putting it into practice. In this exercise, we'll load all of the beverage product records from the `Products` table in the `Northwind` database, and display them in a `DataGrid` control on an ASP.NET page. The `DataGrid` control is configured in such a way that you can edit a record inline, and update it.

1. The ASPX file for this example is going to be called `ChangePrice_Datagrid.aspx`, so create a text file by that name and add it to your `ch07` folder.

2. The HTML for this example is brief, but contains some features that we haven't seen before. This is what it looks like:

```
<%@ Import namespace="System.Data" %>
<%@ Import namespace="System.Data.SqlClient" %>


<html>
  <head>
    <title>Updating Beverages</title>
  </head>
  <body>
    <form method="post" runat="server">
      <asp:DataGrid id="dgProducts" runat="server"
                    CellPadding="5" AutoGenerateColumns="False">
        <Columns>
          <asp:BoundColumn DataField="ProductID" ReadOnly="True"
                      Visible="False" />
          <asp:BoundColumn DataField="ProductName" ReadOnly="True"
                      HeaderText="Name" />
          <asp:BoundColumn DataField="UnitPrice" HeaderText="Price" />
          <asp:EditCommandColumn ButtonType="LinkButton"
                      UpdateText="Save" CancelText="Cancel" EditText="Edit" />
        </Columns>
      </asp:DataGrid>
    </form>
  </body>
</html>
```

As you can see, we've specified explicitly that the `DataGrid` should contain four columns: three `BoundColumns`, and an `EditCommandColumn`, which is new to us here. Let's look at each of these in turn.

The first column will be linked to the `ProductID` column of the table in the dataset, but while we need to keep track of this value (so that we have a link back to the table in the database), we don't need to display it to the user, and we've no intention of allowing it to be changed.

The second column will be linked to the `ProductName` column of the table in the dataset, which we certainly will display to our users. However, we don't want to allow changes to these values.

The third column will be linked to the `UnitPrice` column of the table in the dataset. We'll display this to the users too, and they'll be able to change the values it contains by clicking on the Edit button in the fourth column.

The fourth column is an ASP.NET `EditCommandColumn` control. As you'll see, these columns are specifically intended for users to interact with. After the user has chosen to Edit data, the contents of the column change to show Save and Cancel buttons that allow them to confirm or discard their changes respectively.

3. The first VB.NET procedure we'll write is, as so often, the `Page_Load()` event handler. As is our habit, we pass off the action to a helper, which on this occasion is called `LoadGrid()`.

```
Private Sub Page_Load(ByVal Sender As Object, ByVal E As EventArgs)
  If Not IsPostBack Then
    LoadGrid()
  End If
End Sub
```

4. `LoadGrid()` creates a data adapter, fills a dataset from the database, and then populates the `DataGrid` with the information it retrieved.

```
Private Sub LoadGrid()
  Connect()
  Dim adapter As New SqlDataAdapter(strSQLSelect, objConnection)
  Dim ds As New DataSet()
  adapter.Fill(ds, ProductTableName)
  Disconnect()

  With dgProducts
    .DataSource = ds.Tables(ProductTableName)
    .DataBind()
  End With
End Sub
```

5. After that, and for the time being, we move on to our little helpers, `Connect()` and `Disconnect()`.

```
Private Sub Connect()
  If objConnection Is Nothing Then
    objConnection = New SqlConnection(strConnection)
  End If

  If objConnection.State = ConnectionState.Closed Then
    objConnection.Open()
  End If
End Sub

Private Sub Disconnect()
  objConnection.Close()
End Sub
</script>
```

6. Finally, we have the definitions of the global variables we've used in the above routines, which should be placed at the top of the `<script>` block.

```
Private strConnection As String = ConfigurationSettings.AppSettings("NWind")
Private strSQLSelect As String = "SELECT ProductID, ProductName, UnitPrice " & _
                                 "FROM Products "WHERE CategoryID = 1"
Private ProductTableName As String = "ProductTable"
Private objConnection As SqlConnection
```

7. Provided that everything has gone to plan, if you run the code at this stage, you should be presented with something like this in your browser:

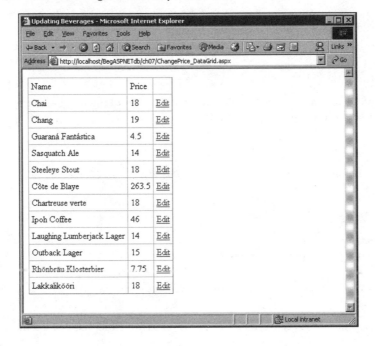

How It Works (1)

When the ASPX page is loaded for the first time, the `Page_Load()` event handler calls `LoadGrid()` to do the data binding work. In this exercise, we associate the `DataGrid` with the `ProductTable` in the `DataSet`, and then call the `DataGrid`'s `DataBind()` method to bind it. This populates the `DataGrid` with the records in the table. So far, so good.

To go further, it's interesting to take a look at how ASP.NET renders the `DataGrid`. If you take a look at the source of the generated page, each record is a row in the table, and each field is an HTML cell. The first row of the `DataGrid`, for example, looks like this:

```
<tr>
  <td>Chai</td>
  <td>18</td>
  <td>
```

```
     <a href="javascript:__doPostBack('dgProducts:_ctl2:_ctl0','')">Edit</a>
   </td>
 </tr>
```

As you can see, the Edit button is rendered as a link. When you click on the Edit link, an automatically generated JavaScript function called __doPostBack() is triggered to post the form to the server. On the server, ASP.NET checks the posted form, and generates an EditCommand event. It's now up to you to create an event handler to respond to this event, and that's where we need to go next.

8. The first step in setting up an event handler is to add a new attribute to the
<asp:DataGrid> element that specifies the procedure that will be used to handle the
EditCommand event:

```
<asp:DataGrid id="dgProducts" runat="server"
              CellPadding="5" AutoGenerateColumns="False"
              OnEditCommand="EditRecord">
```

9. With the plumbing in place, implementing the EditRecord() handler is a two-line affair:

```
Public Sub EditRecord(ByVal Sender As Object, _
                      ByVal E As DataGridCommandEventArgs)
  dgProducts.EditItemIndex = E.Item.ItemIndex
  LoadGrid()
End Sub
```

10. Now when you click on one of the Edit links, you'll see a change occur:

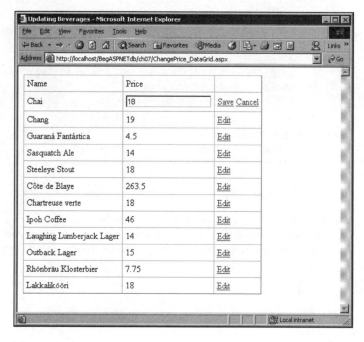

How It Works (2)

The `EditItemIndex` property of a DataGrid specifies which row should be put into edit mode. When you click an **Edit** link, ASP.NET adds the row to a `DataGridCommandEventArgs` object and exposes it as the object's `Item` property. As you can see above, the event handler gets the `DataGridCommandEventArgs` object as an argument of the `EditCommand` event. You can then retrieve the row by reading its `Item` property, which returns a `DataGridItem` object, and the row *index* with the `ItemIndex` property.

The `LoadGrid()` function will again populate the DataGrid with all of the records in the table, but this time it will behave differently, because we've assigned the DataGrid's `EditItemIndex` property with the index of a row. ASP.NET checks the DataGrid column definitions to find out which fields can be edited, and renders those fields as HTML text input controls. Our sample HTML row now looks like this:

```
<tr>
  <td>Chai</td>
  <td><input name="dgProducts:_ctl2:_ctl0" type="text" value="18" /></td>
  <td>
    <a href="javascript:__doPostBack('dgProducts:_ctl2:_ctl1','')">Save</a>
     
    <a href="javascript:__doPostBack('dgProducts:_ctl2:_ctl2','')">Cancel</a>
  </td>
</tr>
```

Now you can change the value in the **Price** column, and click either the **Save** or the **Cancel** button. These buttons raise an `UpdateCommand` and a `CancelCommand` event respectively, and to progress further with this demonstration, we need to define handlers for both of them.

11. The `CancelCommand` event handler is relatively simple. In most cases, you'll simply discard any changes that have been made, and redisplay the grid with records loaded from the database.

```
<asp:DataGrid id="dgProducts" runat="server"
              CellPadding="5" AutoGenerateColumns="False"
              OnEditCommand="EditRecord"
              OnCancelCommand="CancelEdit">
```

```
Public Sub CancelEdit(ByVal Sender As Object, _
                      ByVal E As DataGridCommandEventArgs)
  dgProducts.EditItemIndex = -1
  LoadGrid()
End Sub
```

By setting the `EditItemIndex` property to -1 (remember that the index of the first row in the grid is 0), ASP.NET will render the grid without creating any input controls. You can then call the `LoadGrid()` function to populate the grid to be displayed on the page.

12. The `UpdateCommand` event handler, on the other hand, has to do rather more than the one for `CancelCommand`. Usually, you'll want to update the database when this event fires – either by creating a command object and invoking its `ExecuteNonQuery()` method, as we did in the previous exercise, or by using the combination of a `DataSet` and data adapter object, as we explored above. Let's see how to apply the latter approach in this exercise.

```
<asp:DataGrid id="dgProducts" runat="server"
              CellPadding="5" AutoGenerateColumns="False"
              OnEditCommand="EditRecord"
              OnCancelCommand="CancelEdit"
              OnUpdateCommand="Updaterecord">
```

```
Public Sub UpdateRecord(ByVal Sender As Object, _
                        ByVal E As DataGridCommandEventArgs)

  ' Retrieve the field values in the edited row
  Dim ProductID As Int32 = Convert.ToInt32(E.Item.Cells(0).Text)
  Dim PriceTextBox As TextBox = CType(E.Item.Cells(2).Controls(0), TextBox)
  Dim Price As Decimal = Convert.ToDecimal(PriceTextBox.Text)

  dgProducts.EditItemIndex = -1
  UpdateProduct(ProductID, Price)

  dgProducts.DataSource = ds.Tables(ProductTableName)
  dgProducts.DataBind()
End Sub
```

How It Works (3)

To update the record, you need to figure out which product and field(s) have been changed. To help in this task, the `E.Item` property again returns the row that has been changed. Its `Cells` property returns a collection of cells, which is a `TableCellCollection` object. You retrieve a cell in this collection by providing its index; unfortunately, it doesn't provide a method to retrieve a cell using the column name. Once you have the cell, you can extract the value in its `Text` property.

In our event handler code, the product ID is bound to the first column, and therefore `E.Item.Cells(0).Text` returns the ID of the product being updated. Because it's an integer, we convert and assign it to an integer variable called `ProductID`.

You could also retrieve the product name by checking e.Item.Cells(1).Text, but the product name is never changed in this example, so we can safely ignore this column here.

Getting the value of the changed field requires a little more work. When it's being edited, the field is represented as an input text control inside a table cell, and you need to go via an enumeration containing the all of the controls in the cell in order to get hold of it.

```
Dim PriceTextBox As TextBox = CType(E.Item.Cells(2).Controls(0), TextBox)
Dim Price As Decimal = Convert.ToDecimal(PriceTextBox.Text)
```

Breaking this down a little, you can get to the *cell* containing the changed price with
`E.Item.Cells(2)`. Once you have the cell, you can look further into its `Controls` property to find
the input box, which is the one and only control in the cell: `E.Item.Cells(2).Controls(0)`. In
the above code, it's cast to a `TextBox` control, from which you can get the value in the `Text` property.
This value is then converted to a `Decimal` type, which maps to SQL Server's money type.

13. Once you have both the product ID and the new price, you're ready to update the database.
The `UpdateProduct()` procedure does just that.

```
Private Sub UpdateProduct(ByVal ProductID As Long, ByVal Price As Decimal)

    ' Create and load a DataSet with records from Northwind.Products table
    Connect()
    Dim adapter As New SqlDataAdapter(strSQLSelect, objConnection)
    Dim ds As New DataSet()
    adapter.Fill(ds, ProductTableName)
    Disconnect()

    ' Modify the in-memory records in the DataSet
    Dim tbl As DataTable = ds.Tables(ProductTableName)
    tbl.PrimaryKey = New DataColumn() _
                    { _
                        tbl.Columns("ProductID") _
                    }
    Dim row As DataRow = tbl.Rows.Find(ProductID)
    row.Item("UnitPrice") = Price

    ' Reconnect the DataSet and update the database
    Dim cb As New SqlCommandBuilder(adapter)
    Connect()
    adapter.Update(ds, ProductTableName)
    Disconnect()
End Sub
```

How It Works (4)

Does that look familiar? It should – this essentially contains the same code as we used to illustrate the
theory section. The first block reads an entire result set from the database, and fills a `DataSet` object.
The second block finds a record with the product ID passed to this procedure, and updates its price with
the new price. The third block builds the `UPDATE` command (plus the `INSERT` and `DELETE` commands,
which we don't use here), and then updates the record in the database. Finally, on return to
`UpdateRecord()`, the grid is re-bound to the `DataSet`. Try the application one last time, and you'll
find that it does everything we've asked of it.

And that's just about all for our discussion about updating database records. In the next section, we'll
move on to see how to *delete* records from a database.

Deleting Data

The procedure for deleting records from a database is similar to the one for updating them – in fact, it's a bit simpler. Just as you saw above, you can create a command object and use it to execute an SQL DELETE query (or stored procedure), or you can use a dataset in conjunction with a data adapter to delete some records in memory, and then perform a batch delete in the database.

SQL DELETE Statements

SQL defines a DELETE statement to delete one or more existing records, but unlike SELECT and UPDATE, we can only delete from one table at a time. The generic form of the DELETE statement's syntax is represented below:

```
DELETE [FROM]
{ table_name }
[WHERE condition1 AND|OR condition2 AND|OR ... AND|OR conditionN]
```

Where:

❑ DELETE is the SQL keyword

❑ FROM is an optional keyword that can be omitted

❑ table_name is the name of the table containing the records to be deleted

❑ WHERE is a SQL keyword that specifies one or more conditions that qualify the records to be deleted, and follows the standard format you've seen earlier in the piece

All of this being the case, the DELETE statement below will delete the category that we inserted and updated earlier in the chapter:

```
DELETE Categories WHERE CategoryName = 'Books/Magazines'
```

Specifically, this will delete *all* records in which the CategoryName field has a value of Books/Magazines. In this case, there is only one record that satisfies the condition. If you'd run the INSERT command we used earlier multiple times, you'll have several records with a CategoryName of Books/Magazines; running this DELETE operation once will delete all of them.

> If you fail to specify a **WHERE** clause in a **DELETE** SQL statement, all of the rows in the table will be deleted.

To follow the methodology of our earlier discussions, let's have a quick look at how to update records using a command object. We will then look at the DataSet solution later in the chapter.

Using a Command Object to Delete Records

The sequence of operations for using a command object to delete the records in a database is almost identical to the one for updating records:

❑ Create a database connection

❑ Create a command object and specify an SQL DELETE query (or a stored procedure)

❑ Link the command object to the database connection

❑ Invoke the ExecuteNonQuery() method of the command object to execute the DELETE query

❑ Close the connection

The skeleton code below demonstrates a simple database delete operation.

```
Dim strConnection As String = ConfigurationSettings.AppSettings("NWind")
Dim objConnection As New SqlConnection(strConnection)
Dim strSQL As String = "DELETE Categories " & _
                       "WHERE CategoryName = 'Books/Magazines'"

Dim dbComm As New SqlCommand(strSQL, objConnection)

objConnection.Open()
dbComm.ExecuteNonQuery
objConnection.Close()
```

In a nutshell, that's how you use the command object to execute a DELETE query. Rather than running through an example that would be almost identical to those we've already looked at, let's jump to see how to delete records using a DataSet and a data adapter object.

Deleting Records using a Dataset

Deleting records from a DataSet is also very similar to an update operation – you first delete them in the DataSet, and then use a data adapter to delete them physically from the database. Assuming that you've filled a DataSet with records from the Products table in the Northwind database, as illustrated in the code snippet below...

```
Dim strSQLSelect As String = "SELECT ProductID, ProductName, UnitPrice " & _
                             "FROM Products"
Dim adapter As New SqlDataAdapter(strSQLSelect, objConnection)
Dim ds As New DataSet()
adapter.Fill(ds, "ProductTable")
objConnection.Close
```

...you can then search for records in the DataSet, and delete them.

Deleting Records in a Dataset

With the DataSet in your hands, you can delete one or more of the records it contains. The code snippet below demonstrates how to delete a product:

```
Dim tbl As DataTable = ds.Tables("ProductTable")
tbl.PrimaryKey = New DataColumn() _
                { _
                    tbl.Columns("ProductID") _
                }
Dim row As DataRow = tbl.Rows.Find(1)
row.Delete()
```

The DataRow.Delete() function marks the record as deleted by changing the row.RowState property to Deleted – but the row itself remains in the table's Rows collection. An alternative is to remove a row from the Rows collection by using the Rows.Remove() method, which you could call by replacing the last line of the above code with this:

```
tbl.Rows.Remove(row)
```

This changes the row.RowState property to Detached, but once again, only the DataSet is affected. However, there is a very important difference between the two techniques we just discussed.

When you've 'deleted' a row with the DataRow.Delete() method, you can undelete it by calling the RejectChanges() method of either the DataRow object, or its parent DataTable object. Either way, the state of the row reverts to Unchanged. When a record is marked as Deleted, you can later attach a data adapter object to the DataSet, and invoke the Update() method on the data adapter. This has the result of deleting the record from the database, and the row from the DataSet.

On the other hand, once you've called the Rows.Remove() method, the row is removed from the DataSet and its RowState is changed to Detached. Importantly, however, the corresponding row will *not* be removed from the database when you invoke the Update() method of an associated data adapter object. Therefore, this method is more useful when you only need to manipulate data in memory. If you intend later to delete the record from the database, you should use DataRow.Delete().

Deleting Records in a Database

To delete the records in the database that correspond to the rows deleted from the DataSet, you must reconnect the DataSet to the database:

```
Dim cb As New SqlCommandBuilder(adapter)
objConnection.Open()
adapter.Update(ds, "ProductTable")
objConnection.Close()
```

The Update() method examines each row's RowState property. If it's Deleted, the Update() method executes the DELETE operation to remove the corresponding record from the database.

Try It Out – Deleting Records from the Database

Let's modify the ASP.NET page that we created in the last exercise to add the ability to delete a product from the database.

1. First, add a new **Delete** button column to the `dgProducts` DataGrid by adding a couple of lines to the HTML section of our ASPX file. In fact, it would be a good idea to make these changes to a new version of the file: `Delete_DataGrid.aspx`.

```
<asp:DataGrid id="dgProducts" runat="server"
              CellPadding="5" AutoGenerateColumns="False"
              OnEditCommand="EditRecord"
              OnCancelCommand="CancelEdit"
              OnUpdateCommand="UpdateRecord"
              OnDeleteCommand="DeleteRecord">
    <Columns>
      <asp:BoundColumn DataField="ProductID" ReadOnly="True"
                 Visible="False" />
      <asp:BoundColumn DataField="ProductName" ReadOnly="True"
                 HeaderText="Name" />
      <asp:BoundColumn DataField="UnitPrice" HeaderText="Price" />
      <asp:EditCommandColumn ButtonType="LinkButton"
                 UpdateText="Save" CancelText="Cancel" EditText="Edit" />
      <asp:ButtonColumn Text="Delete" CommandName="Delete" />
    </Columns>
  </asp:DataGrid>
```

2. Next, add a handler for the DataGrid's `DeleteCommand` event.

```
Public Sub DeleteRecord(ByVal Sender As Object, _
                        ByVal E As DataGridCommandEventArgs)

  ' Retrieve the ID of the product to be deleted
  Dim ProductID As Int32 = Convert.ToInt32(E.Item.Cells(0).Text)

  dgProducts.EditItemIndex = -1
  DeleteProduct(ProductID)

  ' Display the remaining items in the DataGrid
  dgProducts.DataSource = ds.Tables(ProductTableName)
  dgProducts.DataBind()
End Sub

Private Sub DeleteProduct(ByVal ProductID As Long)

  ' Create and load a DataSet with records from Northwind's Products table
  Connect()
  Dim adapter As New SqlDataAdapter(strSQLSelect, objConnection)
  Dim ds As New DataSet()
  adapter.Fill(ds, ProductTableName)
```

```
      Disconnect()

      ' Mark the product as Deleted in the DataSet
      Dim tbl As DataTable = ds.Tables(ProductTableName)
      tbl.PrimaryKey = New DataColumn() _
                      { _
                        tbl.Columns("ProductID") _
                      }
      Dim row As DataRow = tbl.Rows.Find(ProductID)
      row.Delete()

      ' Reconnect the DataSet and delete the record from the database
      Dim cb As New SqlCommandBuilder(adapter)
      Connect()
      adapter.Update(ds, ProductTableName)
      Disconnect()
    End Sub
```

3. With this new code in place, browsing to the `Delete_DataGrid.aspx` file should result in the following display:

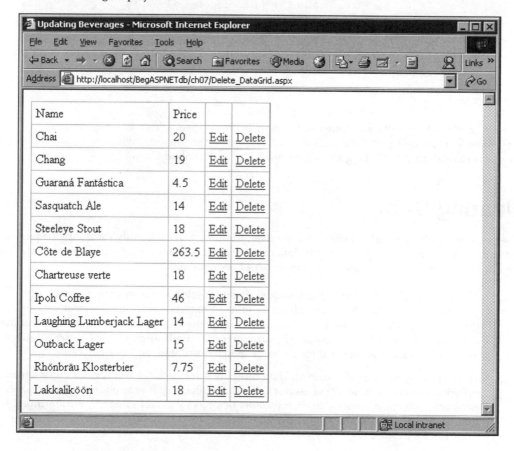

How It Works

You'll see at once that the pair of procedures we've added here is similar to the `UpdateRecord()` event handler and its associated `UpdateProduct()` procedure, but slightly simpler. If you try to click on one of the Delete links here, however, you'll get an unpleasant error:

DELETE statement conflicted with COLUMN REFERENCE constraint 'FK_Order_Details_Products'. The conflict occurred in database 'Northwind', table 'Order Details', column 'ProductID'.

In the `Northwind` database, items in the `Products` table can also appear in the `Order Details` table – and all of the beverages in the `Products` table have these kinds of relationships. Deleting them is therefore not allowed, as it will leave some order items without a related product. In production code, you'd need to catch these exceptions before they found their way to the user. In this example, to demonstrate that our code is working properly, we can use the `Page_Load()` handler to add a new entry to the `Products` table that we can be sure is legal to delete:

```
Private Sub Page_Load(ByVal Sender As Object, ByVal E As EventArgs)
    If Not IsPostBack Then
        Dim strSQL As String = "INSERT INTO Products (" & _
                               "ProductName, CategoryID, UnitPrice) " & _
                               "VALUES ('RolaBolaCola', 1, 15)"
        Connect()
        Dim dbComm As New SqlCommand(strSQL, objConnection)
        dbcomm.ExecuteNonQuery()
        Disconnect()
        LoadGrid()
    End If
End Sub
```

This new code, which will only run when the page is first loaded, adds a beverage called "RolaBolaCola" to the `Products` table that will appear in the browser. When you click Delete, the entry is removed from both the grid and the database, as described above.

Validating Data

Whenever an application allows users to enter data, it must ensure that only valid input is passed to the system beneath – and that as a result, the data in the system is always meaningful. In general, there are two criteria that describe the validity and meaning of system data:

❑ The data is valid in context. For instance, if your auction site stores users' e-mail addresses, you must ensure that the e-mail addresses that are entered into your site exist, and belong to the users who claim to own them. (A common practice here is to send a confirmation mail to the user, asking them to respond.) If your mail order application records a user's delivery address, you must ensure that the zip code matches the state and city entered.

❑ Data integrity must be maintained. Data integrity refers to the consistency of data across different areas of a system. For instance, if your online ordering application categorizes products, you must ensure that each product belongs to a valid category. Furthermore, for as long as at least one product in the database belongs to a particular category, that category must not be deleted from the database.

In the last chapter, you saw that ASP.NET offers validation controls to help with the process of data validation. For example, you could link a `RequiredFieldValidator` control to a `TextBox` control to ensure that when creating a new category, the user enters something for the category name.

In this chapter – so far – we haven't applied any validation to our exercises, but that doesn't mean it's unnecessary. When we were updating data, we used the inline editing feature of the `DataGrid` control to allow users to change the price of any product. It would be sensible only to let users enter a positive price, and only to allow numeric entries. Similarly, when the user asked to delete a product, we could have determined programmatically whether there were any orders for it. If we found that there were, we could have prevented the attempt at deletion.

However, compared to other ASP.NET web server controls (such as the aforementioned `TextBox`) the `DataGrid` is validation-unfriendly. While ASP.NET can render textboxes for inline editing, it doesn't provide an interface to link a validation control with such a text box. This limitation makes client-side validation more difficult to implement for `DataGrid` than for some of the other controls. There are several possible solutions for this problem.

❑ Perform data validation on the server – in other words, you validate the input when the page is posted back to the server. If the input is invalid, you don't update the database, and return an error message to the browser. The next exercise will implement this technique in the ASP.NET page used in the previous exercise.

❑ Create templates for inline editing. As we saw briefly in Chapter 4, the `DataGrid` control allows you to define template columns, which are a combination of ASP.NET controls and HTML code blocks that allows you to fine-tune the layout and behavior of an edit field. You could, for example, create an 'edit box' template and link it to a validation control to provide client-side validation.

For more details on this topic, take a look at Professional ASP.NET Special Edition, *also from Wrox Press (ISBN 1-86100-703-5).*

❑ Use offline editing, in which you create a second page for editing a record that would use controls such as text boxes that *can* be linked to validation controls. When the user clicks an **Edit** link, you redirect them to this edit page. This technique also provides client-side validation.

❑ In the case of our awkward **Delete** option from the last section (and therefore in others like it), the preventative approach would be simply to suppress the **Delete** button for products that may not be deleted. When you loaded records from the `Products` table into a `DataSet`, you could also query the `Order Details` table to see whether there were any order items for each product. However, you would then have to display the records in a customized data grid control because the standard `DataGrid` doesn't offer a way to display **Delete** buttons selectively.

❑ A simpler approach here would be to check whether there are orders for a product *when the page is posted back*. This is less robust, because your users can ask to delete a product only to be told later that it can't be deleted, which may annoy them. If this is not a problem, though, you could perform such checking in the handler for the `DeleteCommand` event.

Try It Out – Validating a DataGrid Control

The final exercise in this chapter will add some server-side error validation code to the ASP.NET page that we created in the previous exercise.

1. First, add a `Label` control to the top of the page, and name it `lblError`:

```
<form method="post" runat="server">
    <asp:Label id="lblError" runat="server" Width="164" /><br/><br/>
    <asp:DataGrid id="dgProducts" runat="server"
                  CellPadding="5" AutoGenerateColumns="False"
                  OnEditCommand="EditRecord"
                  OnCancelCommand="CancelEdit"
                  OnUpdateCommand="UpdateRecord"
                  OnDeleteCommand="DeleteRecord">
        <Columns>
```

2. If the user enters a negative or zero price value, this label will display an error message. Next, modify the `UpdateRecord()` function as follows.

```
Public Sub UpdateRecord(ByVal Sender As Object, _
                        ByVal E As DataGridCommandEventArgs)

    ' Retrieve the field values in the edited row
    Dim ProductID As Int32 = Convert.ToInt32(E.Item.Cells(0).Text)
    Dim PriceTextBox As TextBox = CType(E.Item.Cells(2).Controls(0), TextBox)
    Dim Price As Decimal = Convert.ToDecimal(PriceTextBox.Text)

    If Price > 0 Then
        dgProducts.EditItemIndex = -1
        lblError.Visible = False
        UpdateProduct(ProductID, Price)
    Else
        LoadGrid()
        With lblError
            .Text = "Product price must be greater than 0"
            .ForeColor = Drawing.Color.Red
            .Visible = True
        End With
    End If
End Sub
```

3. With these changes in place, any attempt to update a price with a value that's not sensible will result in a friendly error message:

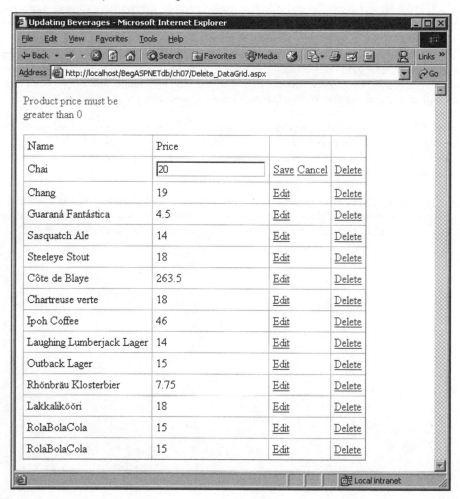

How It Works

Our code now checks whether the price entered is greater than 0. If so, it proceeds to update the product, just as before – but if not, it reloads the `DataGrid` with unchanged records, keeping the edit text box open (because the `EditItemIndex` property of the `DataGrid` is unchanged). In addition, as you saw, it displays an error message in the newly added `Label` control.

Summary

In this chapter, you've learned how to provide your users with the ability to update and delete records in ASP.NET and ADO.NET.

ADO.NET offers the ability to execute an SQL statement using either a command object, or a combination of a dataset and a data adapter. When using the latter, you can either let it build update and delete commands automatically, or you can provide them for yourself. The data adapter object can examine each record in the dataset, and use the appropriate commands to push any changes to the database.

The ASP.NET `DataGrid` control provides users with the ability to edit records inline. Users can modify or delete records and post those actions back to the database, with ASP.NET then raising events appropriate to the user action. We can then handle each event programmatically on the server to perform the operations requested by the user.

In addition, you can validate user input and actions according to business rules. While the `DataGrid` control doesn't provide easy validation (as some of the other controls do), you can use one of several techniques to ensure that data validation is done before updating the database.

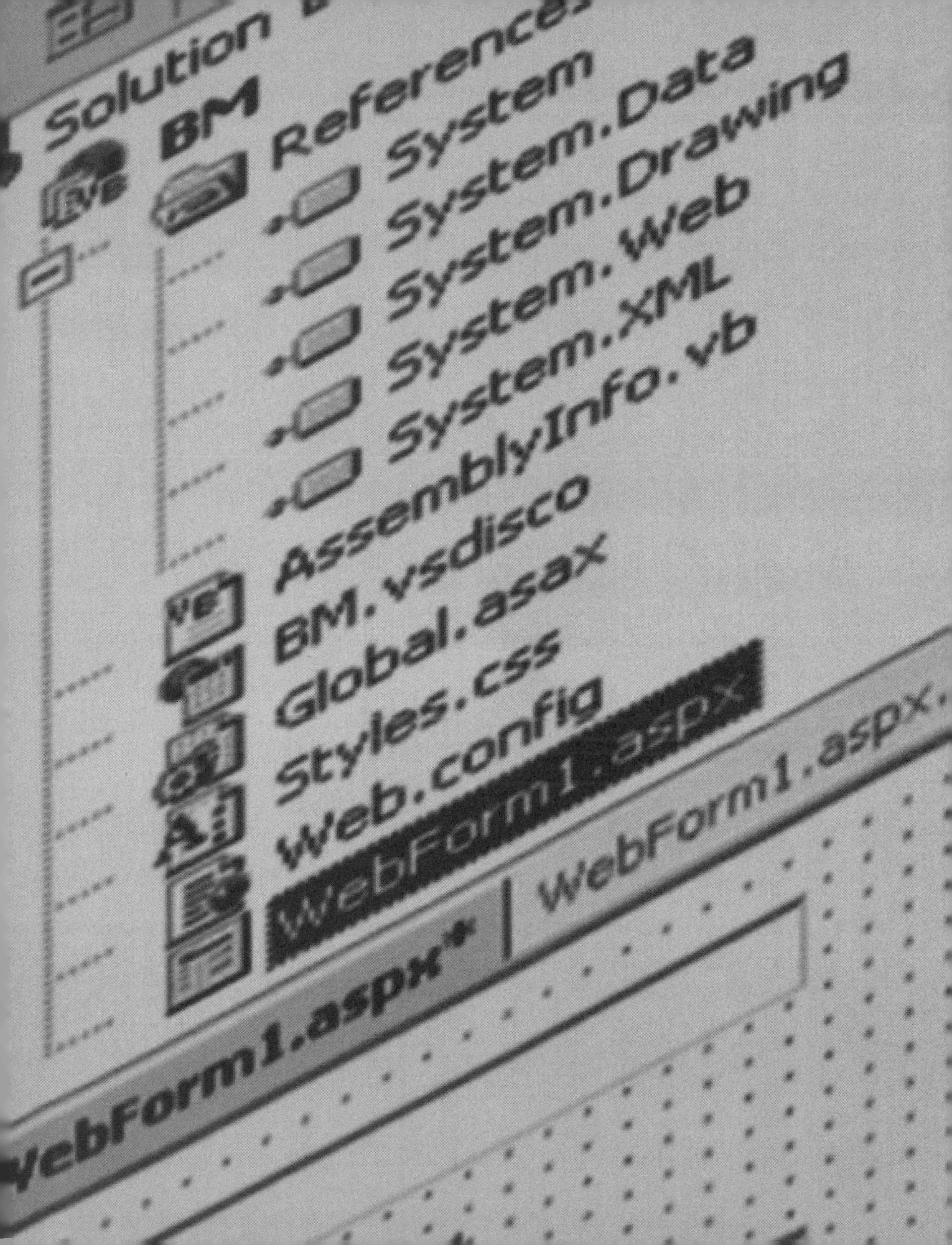

Solution
BM
References
System
System.Data
System.Drawing
System.Web
System.XML
AssemblyInfo.vb
BM.vsdisco
Global.asax
Styles.css
Web.config
WebForm1.aspx

WebForm1.aspx* | WebForm1.aspx.

WebForm1.aspx*

Using Stored Procedures

We've come a long way. In recent chapters, you've learned how to retrieve data from a database, and how to create, insert, modify, and delete the records that databases contain. In the next chapter, we'll begin to look at the place of ASP.NET code and databases in enterprise applications, but before that we have one more important subject to consider. We need to take a look at **stored procedures**.

Stored procedures are a key component of a client-server enterprise database system, providing many benefits for both performance and development. A stored procedure is a set of SQL statements that have been compiled into a single unit, and stored in the database they're intended to work with. It can be as simple as a single SELECT statement, or it can contain multiple statements that perform complex calculations and make updates to many tables. In this chapter, we'll examine:

- ❑ What stored procedures are, and why they can be so useful

- ❑ How to call stored procedures from ASP.NET code

- ❑ How to create stored procedures in an MSDE database using Visual Basic .NET

- ❑ How to pass parameters to stored procedures

- ❑ How to retrieve information from a stored procedure through the parameters you pass to it

*In this chapter, we're specifically considering SQL Server and MSDE databases. In Access, we can implement **queries**, which are similar in many ways to stored procedures.*

Advantages of Stored Procedures

To get things underway, then, we need to understand what gives stored procedures their important role in serious database-driven applications. Let's start by taking a look at some of the many advantages that stored procedures provide.

Transactions

Although a stored procedure contains SQL commands, once compiled it will interact with SQL Server very differently from the way individual SQL statements (such as those passed from an ADO.NET command object) do. One of the key changes is that the SQL commands in a stored procedure are within **transaction scope**, which means that either all of the SQL statements in a stored procedure will execute, or none will. This is known as **atomicity**.

Speed

Unlike standard SQL statements, stored procedures are compiled and optimized by the database server. This optimization involves using information about the structure of a particular database that's required at execution time by the stored procedure. This process of storing execution information (the **execution plan**) is a tremendous time saver, especially if the stored procedure is called many times.

Speed is also improved by the fact that stored procedures run entirely on the database server – there's no need to pass large chunks of SQL code over a network. For a simple SELECT statement, that might not make a big difference, but in cases where we perform a series of loops and calculations, it can have a significant effect.

Process Control

A stored procedure can take advantage of control flow statements such as IF...ELSE, and FOR and WHILE loops, that are not typically available within a basic SELECT statement. This enables us to handle some quite complex logical operations from within SQL code. Without stored procedures, we'd need to create an object in the data layer to handle looping, producing a large amount of network traffic because of the number of records that would need to be processed.

The use of control flow statements is key to any programming language, and by implementing this functionality in Transact-SQL, SQL Server bridges the gap between our code and the database.

Security

Stored procedures can also act as an additional security layer. For example, we could allow access to a stored procedure that generates an average salary for a company, while never allowing its users to see the salary information directly. If we implement security on our tables to prevent direct access, and then add a layer of stored procedures that users *can* access, we can enforce relationships and business logic that might otherwise be bypassed. A stored procedure acts a bit like a business object in component development: we don't let people call the data layer directly, instead forcing them to go through the business layer.

Providing a secure database environment in a web application is especially important, since the web server provides a convenient interface for hackers and others that would like to access areas that they have no business being in! The Web exposes our data to the outside world, so there is no such thing as a system that is too secure, or has been checked too many times. Implementing a layer of stored procedures that controls updates, insertions, and deletions can be of significant help.

Reduced Network Traffic

Using stored procedures enables a client application to pass control to a stored procedure on the database server. This allows the stored procedure to perform intermediate processing on the database server, without transmitting unnecessary data across the network.

A properly designed application that processes large amounts of data using stored procedures returns only the data that is needed by the client. This reduces the amount of data transmitted across the network.

Modularization

The modularization of code is a key aspect of using stored procedures. Modularization is not only the process of writing reusable code units; it is also the process of maximizing team talents. If there's a strong database developer on a team, then we can let them write fast and efficient database code – in stored procedures – while the component developers work on the business logic.

Stored procedures enable easier maintenance. They are centralized, so we can reuse existing stored procedures throughout a system, and from external components. They are easier to access, to maintain, and to supervise.

Calling a Stored Procedure

Stored procedures come in a number of different varieties that further confirm their similarity with the methods and functions you write in your VB.NET code. Some stored procedures accept parameters that modify their behavior or should be operated on; others don't. Similarly, not all stored procedures return result sets – if the procedure just performs some database maintenance, there will be no data to return.

The most basic kind of stored procedure doesn't accept any parameters; it's just a set of SQL statements. An example of this type can be found in the Northwind database, which contains (among others) a stored procedure called Ten Most Expensive Products. This procedure is defined as a fairly basic SELECT query, in which SQL's ROWCOUNT setting is used to limit the number of records returned. It looks like this:

```
SET ROWCOUNT 10
SELECT Products.ProductName AS TenMostExpensiveProducts, Products.UnitPrice
FROM Products
ORDER BY Products.UnitPrice DESC
```

We want to be able to execute this procedure from an ASP.NET page. In order to display the results, we'll write the information into a simple DataGrid control. The code to do this is not difficult – in fact, it's very similar to the examples we were using back in Chapters 3 and 4 – so we'll look at it all in one go.

The code we're about to write can be thought of as a basic template for executing any kind of stored procedure. As we progress in this chapter and look at some more complex examples, you'll see that we still follow the same basic techniques for connecting to the database and executing the procedures.

```
<%@ Import namespace="System.Data" %>
<%@ Import namespace="System.Data.SqlClient" %>

<html>
  <head><title>Using Stored Procedures</title></head>
  <body>
    <form runat="server" method="post">
      <asp:DataGrid id="dgOutput" runat="server" />
    </form>
  </body>
</html>

<script language="VB" runat="server">
Sub Page_Load(ByVal Source As Object, ByVal E As EventArgs)

  ' Connection setup
  Dim strConnection As String = ConfigurationSettings.AppSettings("NWind")
  Dim objConnection As New SqlConnection(strConnection)
  Dim objCommand As New SqlCommand( _
                    "[Ten Most Expensive Products]", objConnection)
  objCommand.CommandType = CommandType.StoredProcedure

  objConnection.Open()

  dgOutput.DataSource = objCommand.ExecuteReader()
  dgOutput.DataBind()

  objConnection.Close()
End Sub
</script>
```

The difference between this code and the examples you saw earlier in the book lies in the way we use the command object. Rather than a straightforward SQL query, we provide it with the name of the stored procedure we want to call.

```
Dim objCommand As New SqlCommand( _
                  "[Ten Most Expensive Products]", objConnection)
objCommand.CommandType = CommandType.StoredProcedure
```

If you were to view this page in your browser, you'd be presented with something that looks like this:

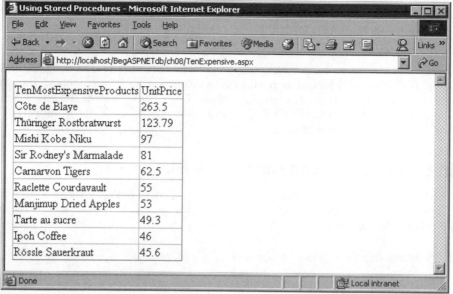

As you can see, it only took a few lines of code to make this work, and there's no SQL statement anywhere in the page itself. Admittedly, we haven't gained much from used a stored procedure on this occasion, but through the rest of the chapter we'll be creating and using some stored procedures that would be much more difficult to implement using inline SQL statements.

Creating Stored Procedures

Stored procedures are not difficult to create – at least in theory – but they do require some knowledge of the basic rules and syntax. In this section, we'll create a stored procedure and test it with MSDE. Later on, we'll put it through its paces using ASP.NET and ADO.NET.

At this point, our decision to use MSDE as our RDBMS makes things a little trickier than they could otherwise be. However, creating stored procedures still isn't very difficult, and there are no self-imposed restrictions on the range of stored procedures it's possible to create. If you have access to the Professional Edition of the Visual Basic .NET software, or the full version of SQL Server, there are a couple of visual tools that you might like to know about.

If you have the full version of SQL Server installed, the Query Analyzer is an extremely useful tool for SQL development. Among other things, it allows you to create and enter procedures directly into the database, and will check your SQL syntax too. It enables you to view database objects (such as tables, views, and stored procedures), to run SQL queries, and to test other objects.

If you have the Professional Edition of Visual Studio installed, the Server Explorer gains some features over and above those present in the Standard Edition. As we'll see shortly, the latter allows you to discover the names and execute stored procedures, but the Professional version permits viewing and editing of the procedures already present in the database, and enables you to create your own with just a few clicks of the mouse.

In this book, however, we're using MSDE, which means that we have to take a slightly different approach. Creating a stored procedure requires the execution of an SQL command, but while the tools we just discussed allow you to do that visually, with MSDE we have to write the procedures by hand, and execute them using a simple VB.NET application. Thankfully, that's not as difficult as it sounds, as you'll begin to see in the next section.

Creating a Stored Procedure in MSDE

In SQL code, a stored procedure is created in a similar fashion to a table – where a table uses CREATE TABLE, a stored procedure uses CREATE PROCEDURE. The most basic syntax for creating a stored procedure is therefore as follows:

```
CREATE PROCEDURE proc_name AS statement
```

All we need to provide is a procedure name (proc_name), and any kind of SQL statement or statements that we want the procedure to execute. As we discussed above, it is not mandatory that we have to return a result set from a stored procedure, but doing so is common, and makes for an example that's easier to grasp! The following line could be used to create a stored procedure called sp_GetCustomers that returns a result set containing all of the records in the Customers table of the Northwind database:

```
CREATE PROCEDURE sp_GetCustomers AS SELECT * FROM Customers
```

In accordance with naming conventions for stored procedures, we prefix the name of the procedure with sp_. After execution of this command, the stored procedure will have been created in the database. We could then execute the stored procedure itself by using the following SQL EXECUTE command:

```
EXECUTE sp_GetCustomers
```

Of course, this isn't the limit of what's possible with stored procedures – if it was, there would be little point in creating and using them. A significant advance from this stage is the fact that, as we've mentioned, we can provide stored procedures with parameters, just as we can do with a VB.NET function. For our first example, though, we'll keep things straightforward.

Creating Stored Procedures with MSDE

In all of the examples we've looked at so far, we've been happy to use a text editor as our development tool, as this has enabled us to see most clearly exactly what's going on. From this point, however, we're going to need some of the more advanced tools that Visual Studio brings to the party. In Visual Studio, open up the Server Explorer window, and find your way to the Northwind database. As you can see, the database comes complete with seven stored procedures, including the Ten Most Expensive Products procedure we just looked at:

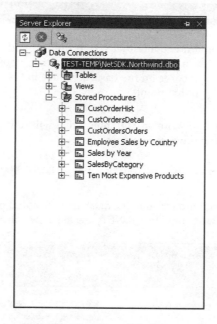

The Server Explorer window provides us with the useful ability to execute a significant proportion of stored procedures in place, without the need to construct a web page or Visual Basic application around them. To see this in action, right click on **Ten Most Expensive Products**, choose **Run Stored Procedure** from the context menu, and keep an eye on the **Output** window. Here's what you'll see:

```
Running dbo."Ten Most Expensive Products".

TenMostExpensiveProducts                 UnitPrice
---------------------------------------- ----------
Côte de Blaye                            263.5
Thüringer Rostbratwurst                  123.79
Mishi Kobe Niku                          97
Sir Rodney's Marmalade                   81
Carnarvon Tigers                         62.5
Raclette Courdavault                     55
Manjimup Dried Apples                    53
Tarte au sucre                           49.3
Ipoh Coffee                              46
Rössle Sauerkraut                        45.6
No more results.
(10 row(s) returned)
RETURN_VALUE = 0
Finished running dbo."Ten Most Expensive Products".
```

As we begin to create our own stored procedures, this facility will save time by letting us test them quickly. It's about time, then, that we gave it a try. In the following examples, we'll create and test a brand new stored procedure in the Northwind database.

Try It Out – Creating a Basic Stored Procedure

Our brief here is to write a stored procedure that selects the IDs and names of all the Northwind customers with mailing addresses in Washington State. From our knowledge of the Customers table, we know that we'll need to filter records on the basis of values in the Region field. This example will demonstrate how to proceed from that point.

1. To begin with, we need to write an SQL query that will return the CustomerID and CompanyName fields of the records in question:

```
SELECT CustomerID, CompanyName FROM Customers WHERE Region = 'WA'
```

2. Next, we need to insert this query into the database as a stored procedure – and to do that, we need to write some Visual Basic code. In VB.NET, create a new console application called CreateSP.

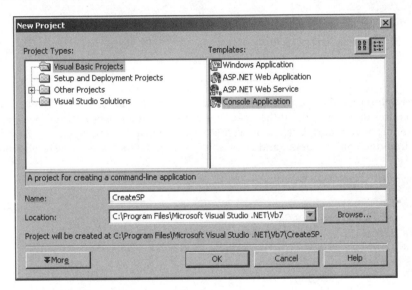

3. To the skeleton application generated by the Wizard, you need to add the following code. As you can see (and as we'll discuss later), it shares a number of features with the ASP.NET code we've been writing.

```
Imports System
Imports System.Data
Imports System.Data.SqlClient

Module Module1
  Sub Main()
    Dim cn As SqlConnection
    Dim sql As String
    Dim cmd As SqlCommand
```

```
         cn = New SqlConnection("Data Source=(local)\NetSDK;" & _
                           "Initial Catalog=Northwind;Integrated Security=SSPI")
         cn.Open()
         sql = "CREATE PROCEDURE sp_WaCustomers AS " & _
               "SELECT CustomerID, CompanyName FROM Customers WHERE Region = 'WA'"
         cmd = New SqlCommand(sql, cn)
         cmd.ExecuteNonQuery()
         Console.WriteLine("Procedure created!")
    End Sub
End Module
```

Obviously, the string that you provide as the data source can vary depending on your particular setup. Here, it's the database on the local machine that we've been using throughout our examples so far.

4. With that done, compile and run this code, and then refresh the view in the Server Explorer. You should see the new stored procedure appear in the list:

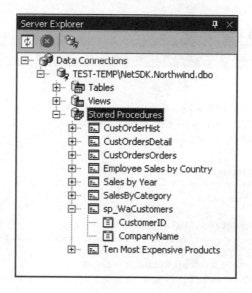

5. Finally, to prove that our stored procedure works, we can again use Visual Studio .NET to run it. When you choose Run Stored Procedure from the context menu, you'll be presented with the following:

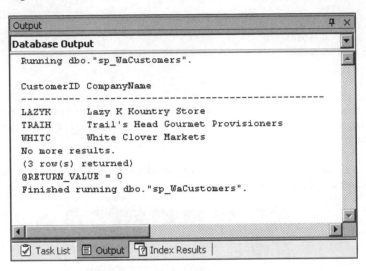

How It Works

We've already looked at most of the processes taking place here, but one aspect that merits a little further explanation is the VB.NET code that inserts the stored procedure in the database. We'll be reusing this code for the other examples in this chapter:

```
Dim cn As SqlConnection
Dim sql As String
Dim cmd As SqlCommand

cn = New SqlConnection("Data Source=(local)\NetSDK;" & _
                       "Initial Catalog=Northwind;Integrated Security=SSPI")
cn.Open()
sql = "CREATE PROCEDURE sp_WaCustomers AS " & _
      "SELECT CustomerID, CompanyName FROM Customers WHERE Region = 'WA'"
cmd = New SqlCommand(sql, cn)
cmd.ExecuteNonQuery()
Console.WriteLine("Procedure created!")
```

This familiar-looking sequence of instructions contains one significant change from our usual ASP.NET SQL-executing code: we use the command object's ExecuteNonQuery() method, rather than ExecuteReader(). As you know, the latter returns a data reader object that can be used elsewhere in your code; but when you're just performing an operation on the database, ExecuteNonQuery() is the method to use.

Amending Stored Procedures with MSDE

Fresh from your early success, you might think about trying to modify the statement so that (say) the results are ordered by CompanyName, in descending alphabetical order. A reasonable first attempt at this would surely be to make the following change to the VB.NET application:

```
sql = "CREATE PROCEDURE sp_WaCustomers AS " & _
        "SELECT CustomerID, CompanyName FROM Customers " & _
        "WHERE Region = 'WA' ORDER BY CompanyName DESC"
```

If you were to try to run this new code, however, you'd get the following error:

An unhandled exception of type 'System.Data.SqlClient.SqlException' occurred in system.data.dll

Additional information: System error.

Here, we're being told that we're trying to add a procedure that already exists; this is an illegal operation. If we want to create a new stored procedure with the same name as an old one, there are two ways of dealing with it: we can either DROP the old procedure and create a new one, or ALTER an existing procedure. Let's look at these in turn.

First, we could call DROP PROCEDURE, and then use a CREATE PROCEDURE statement to create a new stored procedure. This would delete the existing procedure and create the procedure as if it had never existed.

```
cn = New SqlConnection("Data Source=(local)\NetSDK;" & _
                        "Initial Catalog=Northwind;Integrated Security=SSPI")
cn.Open()
sql = "DROP PROCEDURE sp_WaCustomers"
cmd = New SqlCommand(sql, cn)
cmd.ExecuteNonQuery()
Console.WriteLine("Procedure deleted!")
sql = "CREATE PROCEDURE sp_WaCustomers AS " & _
        "SELECT CustomerID, CompanyName FROM Customers " & _
        "WHERE Region = 'WA' ORDER BY CompanyName DESC"

cmd = New SqlCommand(sql, cn)
cmd.ExecuteNonQuery()
Console.WriteLine("Procedure created!")
```

This method does have a side effect: if we've assigned permissions to the procedure, we'll lose them as a result of the DROP PROCEDURE statement. If we really want to start from scratch, DROP is the way to go, but if we want to retain permissions on the procedure, it's better to alter it using an ALTER PROCEDURE statement, like this:

```
cn = New SqlConnection("Data Source=(local)\NetSDK;" & _
                        "Initial Catalog=Northwind;Integrated Security=SSPI")
cn.Open()
sql = "ALTER PROCEDURE sp_WaCustomers AS " & _
        "SELECT CustomerID, CompanyName FROM Customers " & _
        "WHERE Region = 'WA' ORDER BY CompanyName ASC"
```

```
cmd = New SqlCommand(sql, cn)
cmd.ExecuteNonQuery()
Console.WriteLine("Procedure created!")
```

This should reverse the order of the data rows back again – test it yourself, if you like. Finally, you need to be aware that you'll get an error if you try to use either of these techniques when sp_WaCustomers does not exist. You've got to create the stored procedure in the first place.

Versions of Visual Studio .NET above the Standard Edition have a Delete option in the Server Explorer's context menu, but here we've looked at SQL solutions that are applicable regardless of the development environment you're using.

Passing Parameters to a Stored Procedure

In this section, we'll continue to develop the sp_WaCustomers stored procedure. It might be nice to know about the customers in Washington customers, but what about the ones in Oregon? Do we have to create a procedure called sp_OrCustomers as well? Actually, we don't. By rewriting the stored procedure to accept the state code as a parameter, we can create a much more manageable and flexible solution.

The first order of business is to create the new stored procedure, and as a starting point we can use something even simpler than sp_WaCustomers. The following SQL statement creates a stored procedure called sp_CustomersByState that returns all of the customers in the database, in alphabetical order of their company names.

```
CREATE PROCEDURE sp_CustomersByState AS
SELECT CustomerID, CompanyName FROM Customers ORDER BY CompanyName
```

We seem to have moved further away from our goal, but don't worry. In order to get the list of customers filtered correctly, we're going to change this procedure to use an SQL variable. As you're about to see, variables in SQL work in much the same way as they do in other programming languages.

SQL Variables

SQL variables are declared using the DECLARE statement. For SQL Server (and MSDE) databases, the full syntax is:

```
DECLARE @var_name As data_type
```

All variable names must be preceded with an @ symbol in order to be valid. Global variables are denoted with two such symbols (@@). The data type must be a valid SQL Server data type, such as int, datetime, char, varchar, or money.

> **Every DBMS has its own rules for variables. Both DB2 and Oracle use a different syntax from SQL Server.**

The purpose of the variable we're creating is to represent the code of the region we're interested in, so we might declare it with code like this:

```
DECLARE @region as nvarchar(15)
```

What's an `nvarchar`? To find the answer to that, we need to take a couple of steps backwards. An SQL `char` deals with character data – the number in parentheses specifies how many characters the variable can contain. If we were to declare a `char(10)`, enough space to hold ten characters would always be allocated for the data, even we chose only to store one.

Moving on, an SQL `varchar` also stores character data, but only uses as much space as it needs. If we declared a variable as a `varchar(10)`, but assigned a single character to it, only the space required to hold that character would be allocated.

These two data types work just fine, as long as we never have to deal with non-roman character sets. If we need to use a character set such as Kanji, on the other hand, we need to use a Unicode character set, in which every character requires twice as much space to store it compared with the schemes outlined above. Since Northwind Traders is a global company, they need to use international character sets, and therefore they need to store characters in Unicode format. We declare our `@region` variable as an `nvarchar(15)` because the `Customers` table defines the region as being that long.

Now that we have the `@region` variable, we can use it in the SQL statement. For ease of testing, let's set the value of `@region` to `'WA'` by using the `SET` statement to define the value of our variable:

```
CREATE PROCEDURE sp_CustomersByState AS

DECLARE @region nvarchar(15)
SET @region = 'WA'

SELECT CustomerID, CompanyName FROM Customers
WHERE region = @region ORDER BY CompanyName
```

With these changes in place, we can get hold of our Washington customers again, but we're also much closer to a final solution. We need to make a final change so that we can pass a value for the `@region` variable into the procedure, and we do this by turning the `DECLARE` statement into a parameter definition, like so:

```
CREATE PROCEDURE sp_CustomersByState @region nvarchar(15) AS
SELECT CustomerID, CompanyName FROM Customers
WHERE region = @region ORDER BY CompanyName
```

We can test this procedure by including it in a new VB.NET application called `CreateByState`, which follows the same pattern as the stored procedure-creating application we used earlier. The only change you need to make is to put the new stored procedure in the `sql` string:

```
cn = New SqlConnection("Data Source=(local)\NetSDK;" & _
                       "Initial Catalog=Northwind;Integrated Security=SSPI")
cn.Open()
sql = "CREATE PROCEDURE sp_CustomersByState @region nvarchar(15) AS " & _
      "SELECT CustomerID, CompanyName FROM Customers " & _
      "WHERE region = @region ORDER BY CompanyName"
cmd = New SqlCommand(sql, cn)
cmd.ExecuteNonQuery()
Console.WriteLine("Procedure created!")
```

In order to test that this works, compile and execute the code, and then right-click on the new stored procedure in the Server Explorer and run it. When you do this, you'll see something new: Visual Studio will ask you for the value of the parameter, via the following message box:

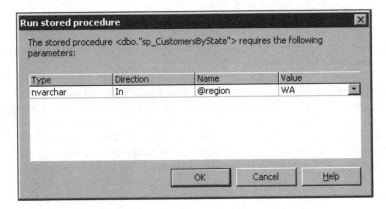

If we pass WA as a parameter, this gets us the Washington customers:

```
CustomerID CompanyName
---------- ----------------------------------------
LAZYK      Lazy K Kountry Store
TRAIH      Trail's Head Gourmet Provisioners
WHITC      White Clover Markets
```

But we can also find the Oregon customers by using the same procedure but entering OR into the dialog box:

```
CustomerID CompanyName
---------- ----------------------------------------
GREAL      Great Lakes Food Market
HUNGC      Hungry Coyote Import Store
LONEP      Lonesome Pine Restaurant
THEBI      The Big Cheese
```

As you can begin to see, we now have a reusable stored procedure that we can use to find Northwind's customers in any given state.

Passing Parameters from Web Pages

The next step is to create a web page that allows the user to enter a state code, and then performs the lookup for this information. We will need a text box and a button, in addition to our usual data grid. Assuming that you've set up the `sp_CustomersByState` stored procedure as detailed above, you should have no trouble assembling the following example.

Try It Out – Passing a Parameter to a Stored Procedure

What we want to be able to do is to key in a state and then press the button to re-filter the data grid. With that in mind, the text box will hold our parameter information, and we'll be sending that back first to the web server, and then to MSDE.

1. Here's the HTML section of the ASPX page we're working on. Enter it into a new text file, and save it in your `ch08` folder, with the name `StateFilter.aspx`:

```
<%@ Import namespace="System.Data" %>
<%@ Import namespace="System.Data.SqlClient" %>

<html>
  <head><title>Using Stored Procedures With Parameters</title></head>
  <body>
    <form runat="server" method="post">
      Enter a State Code:
      <asp:Textbox id="txtRegion" runat="server" />
      <asp:Button id="btnSubmit" runat="server"
                  Text="Search" OnClick="Submit" />
      <br/><br/>
      <asp:DataGrid id="dgOutput" runat="server" />
    </form>
  </body>
</html>
```

2. In our VB.NET code, we'll need to use a new class called `System.Data.SqlClient.SqlParameter`. Objects of this class are designed to represent a parameter in a stored procedure, and the constructor therefore needs to be told about the name, the data type, and the size of the parameter in question.

We know all of this information already. The name is `@region` (don't forget the @ symbol), the type is `nvarchar`, and the size is 15 characters. Before we can execute our stored procedure, however, we need to take an extra step to add the parameter to the collection that's maintained by the command object. Let's look at the VB.NET code, which should be placed after the HTML in the `StateFilter.aspx` file, and step through this process.

```
<script language="VB" runat="server">
Sub Submit(ByVal Source As Object, ByVal E As EventArgs)

  Dim strConnection As String = ConfigurationSettings.AppSettings("NWind")
  Dim objConnection As New SqlConnection(strConnection)
  Dim objCommand As New SqlCommand("sp_CustomersByState", objConnection)
  objCommand.CommandType = CommandType.StoredProcedure
```

3. So far, that should all be looking pretty familiar. Next, though, we need to create a parameter object, and add it to the command object's `Parameters` collection.

```
Dim objParameter As New SqlParameter("@region", SqlDbType.NVarChar, 15)
objCommand.Parameters.Add(objParameter)
objParameter.Direction = ParameterDirection.Input
objParameter.Value = txtRegion.Text
```

4. At this point, we can open the database connection, execute the reader, and then populate the data grid. The code here is exactly the same as the code we've been using elsewhere for this purpose.

```
objConnection.Open()

dgOutput.DataSource = objCommand.ExecuteReader()
dgOutput.DataBind()

objConnection.Close()
End Sub
</script>
```

5. If we run this page and search for all of Northwind's Oregon-based customers, we can see that it works as we intended:

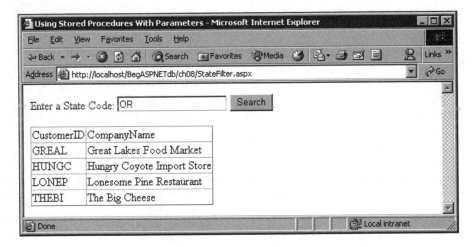

How It Works

The lines of code that set this example apart from the others we've looked at are those that deal with passing the parameter:

```
Dim objParameter As New SqlParameter("@region", SqlDbType.NVarChar, 15)
objCommand.Parameters.Add(objParameter)
objParameter.Direction = ParameterDirection.Input
objParameter.Value = txtRegion.Text
```

The first line here creates a new parameter called @region declared as an nvarchar(15), matching our declaration in the stored procedure. The second argument to this version of the constructor is always a member of the System.Data.SqlDbType enumeration, which has 24 members for representing all the data types you could ever need.

The second line then adds the parameter to the Parameters collection of the command object – forgetting to do this is an easy mistake to make! On the third line, we set the parameter object's Direction property, which determines whether it will be used to pass information to the stored procedure, or to receive information from it. ParameterDirection.Input is actually the default for this property, but from a maintenance and readability standpoint, it's helpful to put it in the code. Finally, we set the Value property of the parameter to the text property of our txtRegion text box.

When you enter a code into the text box and press the **Search** button, the form is submitted back to the ASPX page. The value in the text box is then passed as a parameter to the stored procedure; we execute the code, rebind to the data grid, and our filtered results are displayed. If the stored procedure in question were to support additional parameters, you'd just need to add further SqlParameter objects to your VB.NET code.

Try It Out – Passing a Parameter to a Built-in Procedure

To make sure that this technique is clear in your mind, we'll create an ASPX page that executes one of the Northwind database's built-in stored procedures, with a bit of a twist. We're going to create a list box that shows the names of all the customers in the system, and make arrangements so that when we select one, it will be passed as a parameter to the CustOrdersOrders stored procedure. This returns a list of all the orders for the chosen customer, which we'll present to the user.

1. First, create a new ASPX file called StoredprocParam.aspx, and save it in the ch08 folder.

2. After importing the appropriate namespaces, we need to create the input page. A simple list box, a button, and a data grid will do the trick:

```
<%@ Import Namespace="System.Data" %>
<%@ Import Namespace="System.Data.SqlClient" %>

<html>
  <head><title>Using a Built-in Stored Procedure With Parameters</title></head>
  <body>
    <form runat="server" method="post">
      <asp:ListBox id="lbCustomers" runat="server" Size="1" />
      <asp:Button id="btnSubmit" runat="server"
                  Text="Submit" OnClick="Submit" />
      <br/><br/>
      <asp:DataGrid id="dgOutput" runat="server" />
    </form>
  </body>
</html>
```

3. Next, the VB.NET code in our `Page_Load()` handler needs to populate the list box (`lbCustomers`) with customer names:

```
Sub Page_Load(Source As Object, E As EventArgs)
  If Not IsPostBack Then
    Dim strConnection As String = ConfigurationSettings.AppSettings("NWind")
    Dim objConnection As New SqlConnection(strConnection)
    Dim objCommand As New SqlCommand("SELECT CustomerID, CompanyName " & _
                                     "FROM Customers", objConnection)

    objConnection.Open()

    lbCustomers.DataSource = objCommand.ExecuteReader()
    lbCustomers.DataTextField = "CompanyName"
    lbCustomers.DataValueField = "CustomerID"
    lbCustomers.DataBind()

    objConnection.Close()
  End If
End Sub
```

4. In response to the button being clicked, we need to submit the form and execute a stored procedure that takes the value of the list box as its input parameter. This `Submit()` procedure differs from the one in the previous example only by the name of the procedure being called, and the setup of the `Parameters` collection:

```
Dim objConnection As New SqlConnection(strConnection)
Dim objCommand As New SqlCommand("CustOrdersOrders", objConnection)
objCommand.CommandType = CommandType.StoredProcedure

Dim objParameter As New SqlParameter("@customerid", SqlDbType.NChar, 5)
objCommand.Parameters.Add(objParameter)
objParameter.Direction = ParameterDirection.Input
objParameter.Value = lbCustomers.SelectedItem.Value

objConnection.Open()
```

5. When you run this page for the first time, you'll see a list box and a button:

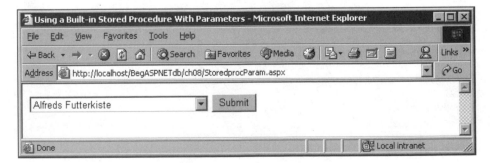

6. After selecting the first entry and pressing the Submit button, the data grid will be populated with these results:

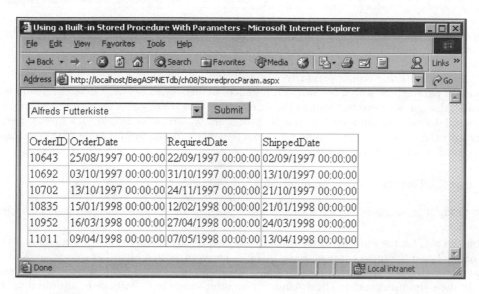

How It Works

As you probably noticed while we were going through the code above, there's very little in this example that you haven't seen before in this or earlier chapters. Apart from the difference in the way data gets sent to the stored procedure (a list box, rather than a text box), the new feature is the change to the name and type of the parameter when we set up the `SqlParameter` object:

```
Dim objParameter as new SqlParameter("@customerID", SqlDbType.NChar, 5)
objCommand.Parameters.Add(objParameter)
objParameter.Direction = ParameterDirection.Input
objParameter.Value = lbCustomers.SelectedItem.Value
```

This time, the parameter is called `@customerID`, and its type is `nchar(5)`, which corresponds to the `SqlDbType.NChar` argument passed to the constructor in the code above.

Stored Procedure Output Parameters

So far, we've seen examples of using stored procedures without parameters, and stored procedures with input parameters. Logically, then, the next step in dealing with stored procedures is to develop one that uses output parameters. If you like, you can think of an output parameter as being like using a `ByRef` parameter in a VB.NET function: it's an input parameter whose value can be changed from within the procedure.

Output parameters can come in handy when we're looking for a single value, rather than a full result set. If, for example, we want to discover the name of a product whose ID we already know, we *could* use `SELECT ProductName FROM Products WHERE ProductID = @ProductID`, but that would force us to process a result set containing a single column and a single row. While this is valid, it is also slow. Using output parameters, we can return the `ProductName` by itself, without any result set being returned to the client.

The technique for using output parameters in ASP.NET code is almost identical to the technique for using input parameters, with a few minor differences in the way things are declared. Before we look at that code, though, we need to examine the stored procedure we're going to create. (Unfortunately, Northwind doesn't contain a suitable sample procedure on this occasion.) We'll write a stored procedure that returns the name of a company in an output parameter, based on the value of the `CustomerID` that we send as an input parameter.

```
CREATE PROCEDURE sp_GetCompanyName @CustomerID nchar(5),
                                   @CompanyName nvarchar(40) OUTPUT AS
SELECT @CompanyName = CompanyName FROM Customers WHERE CustomerID = @CustomerID
```

As you can see, for the most part this procedure is little different from some of the others we've been looking at. The differences come with the `OUTPUT` keyword, which identifies `@CompanyName` as an output parameter, and the form of the `SELECT` statement, in which the first term involves assigning a value to the output parameter. These features are common to the definitions of all stored procedures that involve output parameters, and while you may encounter more complex examples, the syntax will always be the same.

Having created the stored procedure in the database by using the same basic code template that we've used to create our other procedures (see the `CreateOutput` project in the downloadable code), we can proceed to testing it. At this point, however, things start to become a little trickier. When you right-click on its name in the Server Explorer and run it, you'll be presented with more awkward dialog box:

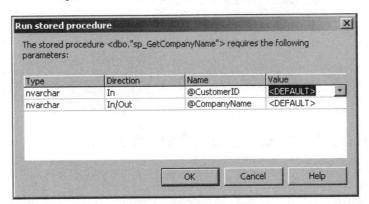

Remember: this procedure doesn't return a result set, so even if we provide a value for the input parameter to this dialog, we won't see any results. Instead, we'll just have to go ahead and create an ASP.NET page that does the job properly. What we want is to use the list box from the last example (but this time filling it with customer IDs, rather than their full names), and to have that execute the stored procedure. The value of the output parameter will then be displayed in a label control. This is `OutputParam.aspx`:

```
<%@ Import Namespace="System.Data" %>
<%@ Import Namespace="System.Data.SqlClient" %>

<html>
  <head><title>Using Stored Procedures With Output Parameters</title></head>
  <body>
    <form runat="server" method="post">
      <asp:ListBox id="lbCustomers" runat="server" Size="1" />
      <asp:Button id="btnSubmit" runat="server"
                  Text="Submit" OnClick="Submit" />
      <br/><br/>
      <asp:Label id="lblOutput" runat="server" />
    </form>
  </body>
</html>

<script language="VB" runat="server">
Sub Page_Load(Source As Object, E As EventArgs)
  If Not IsPostBack Then
    Dim strConnection As String = ConfigurationSettings.AppSettings("NWind")
    Dim objConnection As New SqlConnection(strConnection)
    Dim objCommand As New SqlCommand("SELECT CustomerID " & _
                                "FROM Customers", objConnection)

    objConnection.Open()

    lbCustomers.DataSource = objCommand.ExecuteReader()
    lbCustomers.DataTextField = "CustomerID"
    lbCustomers.DataValueField = "CustomerID"
    lbCustomers.DataBind()

    objConnection.Close()
  End If
End Sub

Sub Submit(Source As Object, E As EventArgs)

  Dim strConnection As String = ConfigurationSettings.AppSettings("NWind")
  Dim objConnection As New SqlConnection(strConnection)
  Dim objCommand As New SqlCommand("sp_GetCompanyName", objConnection)
  objCommand.CommandType = CommandType.StoredProcedure

  Dim objParameter As New SqlParameter("@customerid", SqlDbType.NChar, 5)
  objCommand.Parameters.Add(objParameter)
  objParameter.Direction = ParameterDirection.Input
  objParameter.Value = lbCustomers.Selecteditem.Value
```

So far, we've seen precious little change from the previous example. Now, however, we need to create the output parameter that will hold the output value from the stored procedure. It's a simple matter of setting the Direction property accordingly:

```
        Dim objOutputParameter as new SqlParameter("@CompanyName", _
                                         SqlDbType.NVarChar, 40)
     objCommand.Parameters.Add(objOutputParameter)
     objOutputParameter.Direction = ParameterDirection.Output
```

We then open our connection and execute our stored procedure, but this time we don't need to return a reader object – there is no result set. Be aware, though, that it's quite acceptable for a stored procedure to return a result set *and* have an output parameter; we just haven't chosen to do that here.

```
        objConnection.Open()
     objCommand.ExecuteReader()
```

At this stage, we can set the text of the label either by using the named object – in this case `objOutputParameter.Value` – or by accessing the `Parameters` collection through the use of an expression like `objCommand.Parameters("@CompanyName").Value`. Both of these approaches achieve the same results, so it comes down to personal preference.

```
        lblOutput.Text = objOutputParameter.Value
     objConnection.Close()
  End Sub
  </script>
```

When you run this example, you'll have a label that changes depending on the ID that's picked from the list box.

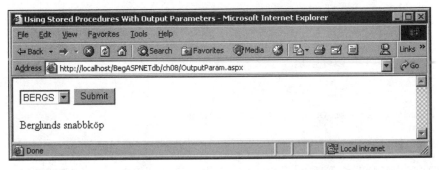

At this point, you should be able to use both input and output parameters with confidence, but let's try one last example just to make sure that we're all comfortable.

Try It Out – Calling a Stored Procedure with Output Parameters

In this final example, we'll create a stored procedure that's very similar to the one we used earlier to return customer names from selected states. However, we will adapt it so that it also returns the number of rows that were displayed for a particular state.

1. We're going to use a built-in global variable called `@@rowcount` to determine the number of rows returned by our procedure. In programming terms, this means adding an additional parameter, and setting that parameter to `@@rowcount`. Our stored procedure will therefore look like this:

```
CREATE PROCEDURE sp_CustomersByStateWithCount @region nvarchar(15),
                                       @matches int OUTPUT AS
SELECT CustomerID, CompanyName FROM Customers
WHERE region = @region ORDER BY CompanyName
SET @matches = @@rowcount
```

Once again, we can build a quick VB.NET application to create this stored procedure in exactly the same way as we've done for all the other examples.

2. We can now look at the ASPX page we will create to execute and display the results of this procedure. Again, this page is very similar to the page we created earlier, but there are a few important additions:

❑ We need to display the number of matches returned from the stored procedure.

❑ We need to add a label control to handle the output, and we also need to change the `Submit()` procedure to accept the output parameter.

❑ We also need to change the name of the stored procedure that we want to execute, and create the corresponding output parameter.

```
<%@ Import Namespace="System.Data" %>
<%@ Import Namespace="System.Data.SqlClient" %>
```

```
<html>
  <head><title>Using Stored Procedures With Output Parameters</title></head>
  <body>
    <form runat="server" method="post">
      Enter a State Code:
      <asp:Textbox id="txtRegion" runat="server" />
      <asp:Button id="btnSubmit" runat="server"
                  Text="Search" OnClick="Submit" />
      <br/><br/>
      <asp:label id="lblRecords" runat="server" />
      <br/><br/>
      <asp:DataGrid id="dgOutput" runat="server" />
    </form>
  </body>
</html>
```

```
<script language="VB" runat="server">
Sub Submit(Source As Object, E As EventArgs)

  Dim strConnection As String = ConfigurationSettings.AppSettings("NWind")
  Dim objConnection As New SqlConnection(strConnection)
  Dim objCommand As New SqlCommand("sp_CustomersByStateWithCount",objConnection)
  objCommand.CommandType = CommandType.StoredProcedure
```

```
Dim objParameter As New SqlParameter("@region", SqlDbType.NVarChar, 15)
objCommand.Parameters.Add(objParameter)
objParameter.Direction = ParameterDirection.Input
objParameter.Value = txtRegion.text

Dim objOutputParameter As New SqlParameter("@matches", SqlDbType.Int)
objCommand.Parameters.Add(objOutputParameter)
objOutputParameter.Direction = ParameterDirection.Output

objConnection.Open()

Dim objDataReader As SqlDataReader
objDataReader = objCommand.ExecuteReader()

dgOutput.DataSource = objDataReader
dgOutput.DataBind()

objCommand.Connection.Close()
objCommand.Connection.Open()
objCommand.ExecuteNonQuery()
lblRecords.Text = "Matches: " & CInt(objCommand.Parameters(1).Value)

objConnection.close()
End Sub
</script>
```

Save or download the above listing as `OutputStates.aspx`, and save it in your `ch08` folder.

3. When you run this code and enter the abbreviation for a US state in the text box, you'll see something like the following:

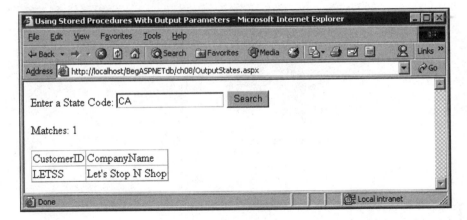

How It Works

As always, the keys to dealing with output parameters are to remember to set the parameter to an output direction, to set the correct data type, and to add them to the command object's `Parameters` collection. With that done, we can continue processing the command object, and return the result set and the output parameter. The final step is to output the `@matches` variable into the label control for display.

```
lblRecords.Text = "Matches: " & CInt(objCommand.Parameters(1).Value)
```

Essentially, this example works just like the previous one, with the addition of the output parameter. When the stored procedure is called, the output parameter is populated and returned. From that point, it's just a matter of getting access to the parameter through the command object's `Parameters` collection, as above.

Summary

This chapter has covered one of the fundamental techniques used in an enterprise database server: executing stored procedures. Having worked through the examples it contains, you should have begun to get a feel for their value, from both a maintenance and an efficiency perspective. Learning to create stored procedures provides an additional development tool that you can use in creating highly scalable systems that perform well even in peak usage times.

Stored procedures are used extensively in most database systems, so it is to your advantage to keep working with procedures and getting familiar with them, as it will give you an additional edge when working on projects. In the chapters to come, we'll see some practical applications that will further demonstrate their value.

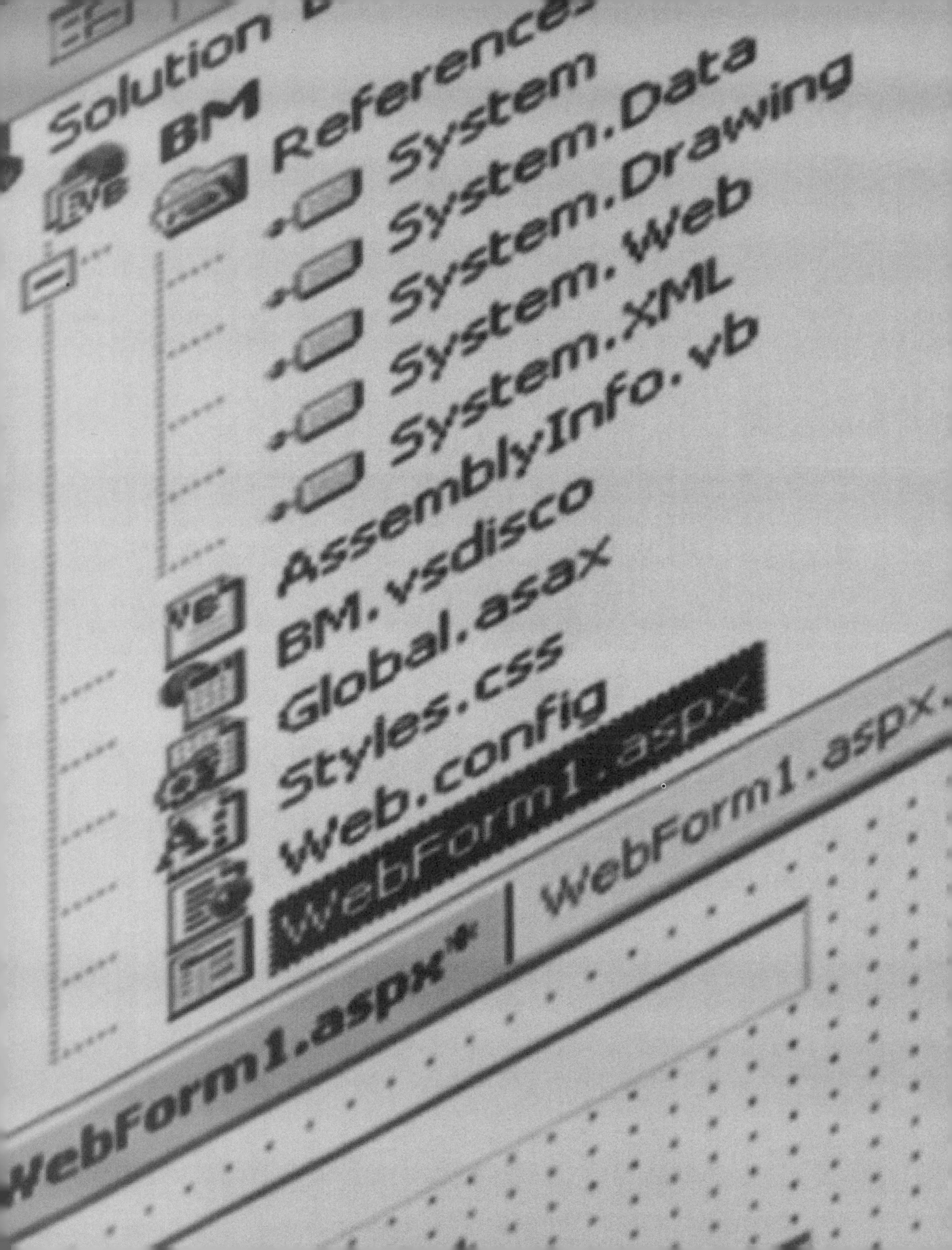

Solution
BM
References
System
System.Data
System.Drawing
System.Web
System.XML
AssemblyInfo.vb
BM.vsdisco
Global.asax
Styles.css
Web.config
WebForm1.aspx

WebForm1.aspx* | WebForm1.aspx

WebForm1.aspx

Data-Driven ASP.NET Applications in the Real World

Until now, we've been writing code without taking into account how many users would be accessing our application. However, applications are put on the Web because we *want* lots of people to use them. In most cases, the more people accessing a web site, the more successful it's deemed to be.

Now that you've learned the basic aspects of data-driven application development, we need to start talking about how to use what you've learned to create applications that can support the number of users you hope to have. If your application crashes because one half of an update your user makes is successfully written to the database but the other half fails, users are going to go elsewhere. If, for example, you have an online ticket-ordering application and an error occurs after reserving the tickets in a customer's name, but before charging their credit card, you have lost money.

In this chapter, we're going to cover the following areas:

- ❑ Ways to handle errors

- ❑ Reasons for and uses of transactions

- ❑ Techniques for organizing our .NET and database code

- ❑ Suggestions for securing the access to your database

Handling Database Errors

At some point, an error is going to occur in your web application. Maybe it's your code, maybe it's the SQL statement that's being executed, or maybe it's the network that's preventing proper communication between your web server and the database itself – but whatever the situation, you must be able to handle it in such a way that the user feels as if they are still in control. If the user can't recover, or failing that, if they can't exit the error situation gracefully, they're going to feel as though the application has failed them.

Using @@ERROR

SQL Server and MSDE provide a system global variable called @@ERROR that you can use to check for errors from within your stored procedure code (there are many other useful global variables – check out MSDN for details). The variable contains 0 if the most recent SQL statement completed successfully; if it didn't, it contains an error number.

To use @@ERROR effectively, you must capture its value after every SQL statement in your stored procedure (use a local variable of type INT to do this), because if any statement completes successfully after an earlier one has failed, @@ERROR will return 0, the value that signifies success.

To show you how this works, we need to create a situation within the database in which errors are likely to occur. One such situation is when there's an attempt to insert a non-unique record into a table that uses a unique index to prevent such an action. Let's see @@ERROR in action now.

Try It Out – @@ERROR

In the last chapter, we created a number of Visual Basic console applications for the purpose of inserting stored procedures into the Northwind database. You can use that same skeleton code to execute the sample SQL code in this chapter.

1. Listed below is some SQL code that creates a new unique index in the Employees table of the Northwind database. This unique index prevents multiple employees with the same first and last names from being entered. Use your skeleton VB.NET code to execute it.

```
CREATE UNIQUE NONCLUSTERED INDEX IX_Employees ON dbo.Employees
(LastName, FirstName) ON [PRIMARY]
```

2. Next, create a stored procedure that inserts a new record into the Employees table.

```
CREATE PROCEDURE InsertEmployee(@FirstName nvarchar(10),
                                @LastName nvarchar(20)) AS
INSERT INTO Employees (firstname, lastname) VALUES (@FirstName, @LastName)
RETURN @@ERROR
```

3. Still using the same skeleton code, execute the following SQL to ensure that no employee with the name Joe Smith currently exists.

```
DELETE FROM Employees WHERE firstname = 'joe' and lastname = 'smith'
```

4. At this point, we have to use a tool that ships with SQL Server, but doesn't come with MSDE. In later examples, we'll be using ASP.NET to show our results, but for the time being we're going to use the **Query Analyzer**. If you don't have access to this tool, don't worry – we'll reproduce and explain all the results of using it here.

Using the Query Analyzer, execute the following SQL script against the Northwind database:

```
DECLARE @errnum int
EXECUTE @errnum = insertemployee 'joe', 'smith'
PRINT 'Error number: ' + CONVERT(varchar, @errnum)
```

When you run the script for the first time, the result will be:

(1 row(s) affected)

Error number: 0

This means that the employee was inserted without error.

How It Works

The stored procedure that we created in Step 2 will take a first name and last name, and insert a new employee in the Employees table using those values. Its return value will be the last error that occurred. If the action was successful, 0 is returned.

In Step 3, we execute a SQL DELETE statement to ensure that an employee by the name of Joe Smith doesn't yet exist.

Let's run the SQL script in Step 4 again, to see what happens when you try to insert an employee that already exists. Because we created the unique index in Step 1, we get the following error, along with its error number:

Server: Msg 2601, Level 14, State 3, Procedure InsertEmployee, Line 4
Cannot insert duplicate key row in object 'Employees' with unique index 'IX_Employees'.
The statement has been terminated.
Error number: 2601

While we're here, we can test something else that we stated above. Keep the Joe Smith record in the database, but change the stored procedure to include a SELECT command immediately after the INSERT command:

```
ALTER PROCEDURE InsertEmployee(@FirstName nvarchar(10),
                              @LastName nvarchar(20)) AS
INSERT INTO employees (firstname, lastname) VALUES (@FirstName, @LastName)
SELECT TOP 1 * FROM employees
RETURN @@ERROR
```

Now re-run Step 4. Even though the record insertion still fails, as you can see from the result below, the returned message is Error number: 0, as our last statement (SELECT) was successful. (Note that the first employee returned from your Northwind database may be different from the one below.)

Server: Msg 2601, Level 14, State 3, Procedure InsertEmployee, Line 3
Cannot insert duplicate key row in object 'Employees' with unique index 'IX_Employees'.
The statement has been terminated.

EmployeeID	LastName	FirstName	Title	TitleOfCourtesy
1	Davolio	Nancy	Sales Representative	Ms.

(1 row(s) affected)

Error number: 0

As mentioned before, you *must* check for an error condition *before* the next SQL statement is executed. Otherwise, whatever the old error value was is overwritten by the most recently executed statement's error value. In this case, since the SELECT statement executed successfully, the @@ERROR value is 0.

Finally, let's change the InsertEmployee procedure one more time to return the error value correctly:

```
ALTER PROCEDURE InsertEmployee(@FirstName nvarchar(10),
                              @LastName nvarchar(20)) AS

DECLARE @errnum int
INSERT INTO employees (firstname, lastname) VALUES (@FirstName, @LastName)
SET @errnum = @@ERROR
SELECT TOP 1 * FROM employees
RETURN @errnum
```

What we're now doing is capturing the @@ERROR global variable's value to a local variable of type int named @errnum, so that we can use it later. Execute Step 4 one last time, and you'll see the correct error value returned, as shown below.

```
Server: Msg 2601, Level 14, State 3, Procedure InsertEmployee, Line 3
Cannot insert duplicate key row in object 'Employees' with unique index 'IX_Employees'.
The statement has been terminated.
```

EmployeeID	LastName	FirstName	Title	TitleOfCourtesy
1	Davolio	Nancy	Sales Representative	Ms.

(1 row(s) affected)

Error number: 2601

Making @@ERROR Useful

Application troubleshooting can be a troublesome thing. Often, one of the most frustrating aspects of troubleshooting is trying to understand what went wrong. Usually, it's your users, not you, who experience errors when they occur – and users are infamous for telling you that there was an error, but not bothering to record specific details about it.

One way to minimize the frustration is to log error information automatically. There are many approaches to this, one of which is to have the database itself record an error when it happens. You can do this in your stored procedures by checking the @@ERROR value after each statement within the procedure, and logging any error that occurs.

Try It Out – Using @@ERROR in a stored procedure

Let's work through an example that does exactly what we just described. We'll execute a command, and then see if an error occurred. If it did, we'll write an error log entry into a new table that we'll create.

1. Modify the `InsertEmployee` stored procedure as follows:

```
ALTER PROCEDURE InsertEmployee(@FirstName nvarchar(10),
                              @LastName nvarchar(20)) AS
INSERT INTO Employees (firstname, lastname) VALUES (@FirstName, @LastName)
IF @@ERROR <> 0
BEGIN
  INSERT INTO tblErrorLog (ErrType, Msg)
  VALUES ('Duplicate record', 'Employee duplicate record couldn''t be created.')
END
```

2. Create the `tblErrorLog` table:

```
CREATE TABLE [tblErrorLog] (
  [ErrorID] [int] IDENTITY (1, 1) NOT NULL,
  [ErrType] [varchar] (20) NOT NULL,
  [Msg] [varchar] (100) NULL,
  [ErrorDate] [datetime] NULL
    CONSTRAINT [DF_tblErrors_ErrorDate] DEFAULT (getdate()),
  CONSTRAINT [PK_tblErrors] PRIMARY KEY CLUSTERED
  (
    [ErrorID]
  ) ON [PRIMARY]
) ON [PRIMARY]
```

3. In a new directory called `webroot\ch09`, create a web page called `Insert_Employee.aspx`, as shown below:

```
<%@ Import namespace="system.data" %>
<%@ Import namespace="system.data.sqlclient" %>

<script language="vb" runat="server">
Private Sub Page_Load(ByVal Source As Object, ByVal E As EventArgs)

  Dim sql As String = "InsertEmployee"
  Dim strConnection As String = ConfigurationSettings.AppSettings("NWind")
  Dim conn As New SqlConnection(strConnection)

  conn.Open()

  Dim cmd As New SqlCommand(sql, conn)
  cmd.CommandType = CommandType.StoredProcedure
```

```
    cmd.Parameters.Add("@FirstName", "Mark")
    cmd.Parameters.Add("@LastName", "Seeley")

    Try
      cmd.ExecuteNonQuery()
    Catch ex As Exception
      Response.Write("Error: " & ex.Message & "<br/>")
    End Try

    cmd.Connection.Close()
  End Sub
</script>
```

4. Run `Insert_Employee.aspx` several times. The first time, it will run successfully, with the resulting page being blank. The second and successive times, however, you'll see this:

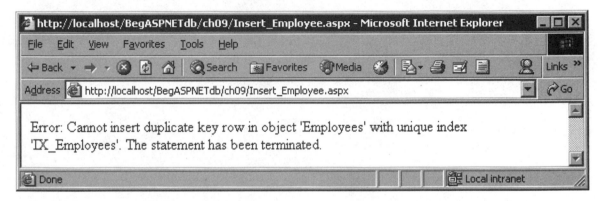

5. If you use Visual Studio .NET to take a look at the contents of the `tblErrorLog` table, your results should be similar to this:

	ErrorID	ErrType	Msg	ErrorDate
▶	1	Duplicate record	Employee duplicate record couldn't be created.	05/06/2002 16:36:51
	2	Duplicate record	Employee duplicate record couldn't be created.	05/06/2002 16:39:53
	3	Duplicate record	Employee duplicate record couldn't be created.	05/06/2002 16:39:55
✱				

How It Works

Let's step through the stored procedure to understand how it works. First, we execute the `INSERT` statement.

```
INSERT INTO employees (firstname, lastname) VALUES (@FirstName, @LastName)
```

If there has been an error,

```
IF @errnum <> 0
```

we insert a record into `tblErrorLog`, stating what the problem was:

```
BEGIN
  INSERT INTO tblErrorLog (ErrType, Msg)
  VALUES ('Duplicate record', 'Employee duplicate record couldn''t be created.')
END
```

The key to the ASPX page, meanwhile, lies in our `Try...Catch` block.

```
Try
   cmd.ExecuteNonQuery()
Catch ex As Exception
   Response.Write("Error: " & ex.Message & "<br>")
End Try
```

Since the `ExecuteNonQuery()` method call is within the `Try` section, the `Catch` section will be executed if it fails. Logging an error from within the stored procedure does not remove the need to handle the error from within our code, and your users still need to be notified that an error occurred in a way that doesn't mean the application crashing. We do that in the `Catch` section, where we simply echo the exception message out to the user.

```
Response.Write("Error: " & ex.Message & "<br/>")
```

This way, the user knows that an error has occurred, and when they call and tell you about it, you can look in the `tblErrorLog` table and see the specifics!

Raising Your Own Database Errors with RAISERROR

What if you have multiple steps within a stored procedure, and you'd like some way of communicating to your ASP.NET application which *step* within the stored procedure caused an error? One way of doing this would be to use return values, but capturing those after every statement is a time-consuming business, and we really don't want to write more code than we absolutely have to. We want a way to know that a problem occurred, and at exactly what step, without using a return value.

In this case, the T-SQL `RAISERROR` statement will fit our requirements. It allows you to raise a user-specific error in place of the actual database error that has occurred. By raising a user-specific error, you can write your .NET code to handle the error better, or you can give more explanation to your user about the error. Normally, SQL error messages are pretty cryptic about exactly what happened, but `RAISERROR` gives you complete flexibility in describing the error to your user. The complete syntax of `RAISERROR` is as follows:

```
RAISERROR ( { msg_id | msg_str} {, severity, state} [, argument [,…n] ] )
[WITH option [,…n] ]
```

As you can see from the syntax, RAISERROR has a number of options. For our purposes here, we're just going to look at the most common parameters, which are shown below:

Argument	Description
msg_id	If you want to use messages that are stored in the sysmessages table, specify the value in the 'error' field here. Note that you can only use error messages numbered 13,000 or above.
msg_str	This is the error text. If you specify this instead of msg_id, a default value for msg_id of 50,000 will be used. Any error message with an ID of 50,000 or above is considered to be user-defined.
severity	This value specifies the relative severity of the error that you're raising. You can specify a value between 0 and 18 (where 18 is the most severe); values outside this range are reserved by SQL. You will see this called the "level" of the error in some places.
state	This is an arbitrary number between 1 and 127 that represents the state of the error at the time it occurred.

Try It Out – Using RAISERROR

1. Let's change our InsertEmployee stored procedure to use the RAISERROR statement.

```
ALTER PROCEDURE InsertEmployee(@FirstName nvarchar(10),
                              @LastName nvarchar(20)) AS
INSERT INTO Employees (firstname, lastname) VALUES (@FirstName, @LastName)
IF @@ERROR <> 0
BEGIN
  RAISERROR('Employee duplicate record couldn''t be created.', 1, 1)
  INSERT INTO tblErrorLog (ErrType, Msg)
  VALUES ('Duplicate record', 'Employee duplicate record couldn''t be created.')
  IF @@ERROR <> 0
  BEGIN
    RAISERROR('Error log couldn''t be updated.', 1, 1)
  END
END
```

2. Then, let's run it with the following SQL **twice** in Query Analyzer, and examine the results.

```
EXEC InsertEmployee 'brian', 'jones'
```

The first time, it should execute correctly. However, the second time you should get the following result.

```
Server: Msg 2601, Level 14, State 3, Procedure InsertEmployee, Line 4
Cannot insert duplicate key row in object 'Employees' with unique index 'IX_Employees'.
The statement has been terminated.
Msg 50000, Level 1, State 50000
Employee duplicate record couldn't be created.

(1 row(s) affected)
```

Note that SQL Server automatically raises the error 2601 again. Next, our custom error is raised. The message (1 row(s) affected) indicates that the record in the tblErrorLog was written.

How It Works

As usual, the first thing we attempt to do in this stored procedure is to insert the new record into the Employees table:

```
INSERT INTO employees (firstname, lastname) VALUES (@FirstName, @LastName)
```

After that, we check to see whether an error occurred. If it did, we raise an error stating that the duplicate record couldn't be created. We use a severity of 1 and a state of 1 as arbitrary values, since our code doesn't care about them.

```
IF @@ERROR <> 0
BEGIN
  RAISERROR('Employee duplicate record couldn''t be created.', 1, 1)
```

If an error occurred, we also attempt to insert a new record into tblErrorLog.

```
INSERT INTO tblErrorLog (ErrType, Msg)
VALUES ('Duplicate record', 'Employee duplicate record couldn''t be created.')
```

Finally, we check to see if yet another error occurred. If it did, we raise another error stating that the error log couldn't be updated.

```
IF @@ERROR <> 0
BEGIN
  RAISERROR('Error log couldn''t be updated.', 1, 1)
END
```

Now let's create an artificial situation where an error will also occur while updating tblErrorLog. For that, we need to modify the InsertEmployee stored procedure yet again.

293

```
ALTER PROCEDURE InsertEmployee(@FirstName nvarchar(10),
                              @LastName nvarchar(20)) AS
INSERT INTO Employees (firstname, lastname) VALUES (@FirstName, @LastName)
IF @@ERROR <> 0
BEGIN
  RAISERROR('Employee duplicate record couldn''t be created.', 1, 1)
  INSERT INTO tblErrorLog (ErrType, Msg)
  VALUES (NULL, 'Employee duplicate record couldn''t be created.')
  IF @@ERROR <> 0
  BEGIN
    RAISERROR('Error log couldn''t be updated.', 1, 1)
  END
END
```

The only change we've made is that we're now attempting to insert NULL into the ErrType field, which does not allow nulls. Let's look at the results in Query Analyzer after we've run Step 2 again.

Server: Msg 2601, Level 14, State 3, Procedure InsertEmployee, Line 4
Cannot insert duplicate key row in object 'Employees' with unique index 'IX_Employees'.
The statement has been terminated.
Msg 50000, Level 1, State 50000
Employee duplicate record couldn't be created.
Server: Msg 515, Level 16, State 2, Procedure InsertEmployee, Line 8
Cannot insert the value NULL into column 'ErrType', table 'Northwind.dbo.tblErrorLog'; column does not allow nulls. INSERT fails.
The statement has been terminated.
Msg 50000, Level 1, State 50000
Error log couldn't be updated.

Notice that four errors are now raised: the original error 2601, the Employee duplicate record couldn't be created error, error 515, and the Error log couldn't be updated error.

Handling Errors in .NET

When an error occurs, it's important to give your application's users as much information as possible, so that they can handle it more effectively. To do this, you need error messages that are as descriptive as possible within your .NET code. This is where RAISERROR really shines. In the examples above, we took a relatively cryptic error and raised another one that was much more descriptive and specific to our application.

When an error occurs within the database during execution via ADO.NET, a .NET exception of type System.Data.SqlClient.SqlException occurs. Before we get into an example, let's look at some of the members that System.Data.SqlClient.SqlException provides that override or augment those that it inherits from the Exception class.

Member	Description
Class	The severity of the first error that occurred during execution of the SQL statement.
Errors	An instance of the `SqlErrorCollection` class that contains `SqlError` objects. As you'll see later in this section, SQL can return more than one error message – when it comes across some errors, it continues with execution, meaning that more than one error condition is possible. You can use this collection to enumerate through all of them.
Message	The text of the errors that occurred. If multiple errors occurred, all of the text is appended, with carriage returns between them.
Number	The message ID for the first error in the `Errors` collection. If you specified the error via the SQL `RAISERROR` statement, the `Number` will default to 50000.
State	This is the value of the state for the first error in the `Errors` collection.

Try It Out – ASP.NET with RAISERROR

1. Let's create an ASP.NET example that actually shows the error messages created by the most recent version of our `InsertEmployee` stored procedure on a web page. Call this new file `Use_Raiserror.aspx`.

```vb
<%@ Import namespace="system.data" %>
<%@ Import namespace="system.data.sqlclient" %>

<script language="vb" runat="server">
Private Sub Page_Load(ByVal Source As Object, ByVal E As EventArgs)

  Dim sql As String = "InsertEmployee"
  Dim strConnection As String = ConfigurationSettings.AppSettings("NWind")
  Dim conn As New SqlConnection(strConnection)

  conn.Open()


  Dim cmd As New SqlCommand(sql, conn)
  cmd.CommandType = CommandType.StoredProcedure

  cmd.Parameters.Add("@FirstName", "Jane")
  cmd.Parameters.Add("@LastName", "Zerdeni")

  Try
    cmd.ExecuteNonQuery()
  Catch ex As System.Data.SqlClient.SqlException
    Response.Write("- SQLException -<br/>")
    Response.Write("Message: ")
    Response.Write(replace(ex.Message, controlchars.lf, "<br/>") & "<br>")
```

```
      Response.Write("Class: " & ex.class & "<br/>")
      Response.Write("State: " & ex.state & "<br/>")
      Response.Write("<br/>- Errors collection -<br/>")

      Dim sErr As SqlError
      For Each sErr In ex.Errors
        Response.Write("#: " & sErr.Number & " - Class: ")
        Response.Write(sErr.Class & " - State: " & sErr.State)
        Response.Write(" - Message: ")
        Response.Write(replace(sErr.Message, controlchars.lf, "<br/>"))
        Response.Write("<br/><br/>")
      Next
    End Try

    cmd.Connection.Close()
  End Sub
</script>
```

2. Run the example *twice*. Here are the results you'll see when trying to insert the user during the second execution attempt.

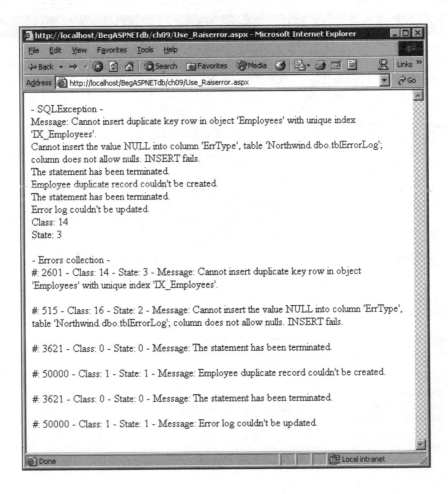

How It Works

Taking all of the familiar code as read, we catch the `SqlException` through this line:

```
Catch ex As System.Data.SqlClient.SqlException
```

Now we have the `SqlException` within the variable ex, and the next lines can display the `state`, the severity (the member that returns the severity is called `class`), and the `message` of the `SqlException`.

```
Response.Write("- SQLException -<br/>")
Response.Write("Message: ")
Response.Write(replace(ex.Message, controlchars.lf, "<br/>") & "<br>")
Response.Write("Class: " & ex.class & "<br/>")
Response.Write("State: " & ex.state & "<br/>")
```

While using the `SqlException` object is enough to know that an error occurred, it's not enough to know the exact details of each error. There are times when knowing the severity and state of each error, and not just the first one, is important. For that, you have to enumerate through the `Errors` collection:

```
Dim sErr As SqlError
For Each sErr In ex.Errors
   Response.Write("#: " & sErr.Number & " - Class: ")
   Response.Write(sErr.Class & " - State: " & sErr.State)
   Response.Write(" - Message: ")
   Response.Write(replace(sErr.Message, controlchars.lf, "<br/>"))
   Response.Write("<br/><br/>")
Next
```

For each error, the error number, severity, state, and message are returned, and you can use this information to display friendly error information to your users. Let's clean up the example above so that it displays only the custom error messages that we generate via RAISERROR in the `InsertEmployee` stored procedure. The changes to the code are highlighted.

```
<%@ Import namespace="system.data" %>
<%@ Import namespace="system.data.sqlclient" %>

<script language="vb" runat="server">
Private Sub Page_Load(ByVal Source As Object, ByVal E As EventArgs)

   Dim sql As String = "InsertEmployee"
   Dim strConnection As String = ConfigurationSettings.AppSettings("NWind")
   Dim conn As New SqlConnection(strConnection)

   Response.Write("Attempting to add an employee to the database...<br>")
   conn.Open()

   Dim cmd As New SqlCommand(sql, conn)
   cmd.CommandType = CommandType.StoredProcedure
```

```
cmd.Parameters.Add("@FirstName", "Jane")
cmd.Parameters.Add("@LastName", "Zerdeni")

Try
  cmd.ExecuteNonQuery()
Catch ex As System.Data.SqlClient.SqlException
  Dim sErr As SqlError
  For Each sErr In ex.Errors
    If sErr.Number = 50000 Then
      Response.Write(sErr.Message & "<br/>")
    End If
  Next
End Try

cmd.Connection.Close()
End Sub
</script>
```

The results are shown below.

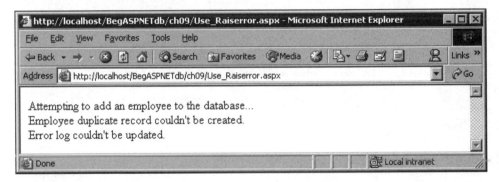

This time, when errors occur, we enumerate through each one and display only those with a message ID of 50000. As mentioned previously, this is the message ID that's generated when you specify a custom message string using RAISERROR. This is our way of knowing that these are the friendly error messages.

```
For Each sErr In ex.Errors
  If sErr.Number = 50000 Then
    Response.Write(sErr.Message & "<br/>")
  End If
Next
```

In this example, we're simply showing the user what went wrong. In your production code, you should try to do more. For instance, you'd probably want to allow them to try the operation again, or make changes to their data. In fact, in a production application, you wouldn't want execution to get to the point where it tries to insert a duplicate record. Instead, you should verify that no duplicate exists prior to attempting the insert.

Transactions

Transactions are groups of database commands that execute as a package. When dealing with real-world applications, you may need to ensure that multiple actions within the application either succeed in their entirety, or fail in their entirety. In other words, all actions should succeed, or none of them should. Transactions help you to accomplish this. You **begin** a transaction, and then, if all actions are successful, you **commit** it. Committing a transaction causes the actions to be saved to the data source. Otherwise, you **roll it back**, which puts the database back to its state was prior to the transaction beginning.

As so often, there's an acronym for the concepts that make up transaction processing. The word is **ACID**, and it works like this:

Term	Description
Atomicity	This describes the concept that all actions within the transaction should either fail or succeed. A classic example is a bank transfer from one account to another. You either want the debit from account A and the credit to account B both to be written, or you want neither of them to be written. If one is written and the other isn't, one account will end up with more or less money than it should have.
Consistency	The results of the actions that occur during the transaction should not be changed in any way by the transaction processing itself.
Isolation	The idea that multiple transactions occurring at the same time will not conflict with each other. One transaction will never see the results of another transaction until that other transaction is committed. This ensures that transactions don't read data involved in other transactions that may be rolled back, or that might not yet be completely written.
Durability	The results of the actions, once committed, should remain even if system errors occur after the commitment. Usually, transaction logs such as those used by SQL Server ensure durability: at the exact moment of commitment, the transaction is written to the log, before an attempt to update the database is made. Even if a system error occurs immediately after the log is written to, the transaction still exists and can be processed after the system is restored.

Transactions can be handled in three places within .NET database applications.

Location	Description
Database	SQL Server has T-SQL statements that allow you to group related actions into a transaction. They are BEGIN TRANSACTION, COMMIT TRANSACTION, and ROLLBACK TRANSACTION.

Table continued on following page

Location	Description
ADO.NET	ADO.NET allows you to create transactions through the use of the `Connection` object, the `Transaction` object, and the `Command` object. If you're using a SQL Server database, `TRANSACTION` T-SQL statements will be used behind the scenes. For other DBMS systems, the transaction statements that they support will be used.
Enterprise Services	.NET components can run within the COM+ space by inheriting from the `System.EnterpriseServices.ServicedComponent` class or a derived class. `EnterpriseServices` allows you to utilize the COM+ services for transaction handling. This is beyond the scope of this book.

Transactions *do* affect performance – they keep resources locked until the transaction is committed or rolled back. Because of this, other applications will have to wait if they need to access these resources. You should therefore be prudent when deciding whether you need transactions. Also, you should start transactions as late as possible within your code, and then commit them or roll them back as soon as possible, to make the lock time as short as possible.

Transactions in SQL

As stated above, transactions in SQL are handled through the use of the BEGIN TRANSACTION, COMMIT TRANSACTION, and ROLLBACK TRANSACTION statements, whose names are self-explanatory. If you wish, you can shorten them to use the keyword TRANS instead of TRANSACTION.

❑   BEGIN TRANSACTION begins the **transaction context**. Any statements after this one are a part of the transaction, until it is committed or rolled back.

❑   COMMIT TRANSACTION commits all the changes that occurred during the transaction to the database. At this point, the changes are permanent, they cannot be undone, and the transaction no longer exists.

❑   ROLLBACK TRANSACTION causes all changes that have occurred within the transaction context to be canceled, and the transaction context to end.

Any statements executed after a COMMIT TRANSACTION or a ROLLBACK TRANSACTION are no longer a part of a transaction, unless a new transaction is begun.

Try It Out – Transactions in SQL

Let's start putting transactions to use. A good example of a situation where you need transactions within a stored procedure is when you're auditing the various data changes taking place within your database. Auditing is important when you need accountability for the changes that are made to an application. If you have multiple users maintaining employee records, for example, and someone creates an employee with erroneous data, you need to be able to look at an audit entry and find out exactly who performed the operation, so that the erroneous data can be corrected.

1. Before we can do this type of auditing in our example, we need an audit log table. Here's the SQL code to create it:

```
CREATE TABLE [tblAuditLog] (
  [AuditLogID] [int] IDENTITY (1, 1) NOT NULL ,
  [Action] [varchar] (20) NOT NULL ,
  [Msg] [varchar] (100) NULL ,
  [AuditDate] [datetime] NULL
    CONSTRAINT [DF_tblAuditLog_ErrorDate] DEFAULT (getdate()),
  CONSTRAINT [PK_tblAuditLog] PRIMARY KEY CLUSTERED
  (
    [AuditLogID]
  ) ON [PRIMARY]
) ON [PRIMARY]
```

2. Next, let's modify our `InsertEmployee` stored procedure to use transactions. If the employee is successfully created, we'll insert a record into `tblAuditLog` to reflect this.

```
ALTER PROCEDURE InsertEmployee(@FirstName nvarchar(10),
                              @LastName nvarchar(20)) AS
BEGIN TRANSACTION
INSERT INTO employees (firstname, lastname) VALUES (@FirstName, @LastName)
IF @@ERROR = 0
BEGIN
  INSERT INTO tblAuditLog (Action, Msg)
    VALUES ('New employee created', 'Employee''s name is ' +
           @FirstName + ' ' + @LastName)
  IF @@ERROR = 0
  BEGIN
    COMMIT TRANSACTION
  END
  ELSE
  BEGIN
    ROLLBACK TRANSACTION
    RAISERROR('Audit of employee creation failed.', 1, 1)
    INSERT INTO tblErrorLog (ErrType, Msg)
      VALUES ('Audit Failure', 'Audit of employee creation failed.')
    IF @@ERROR <> 0
    BEGIN
      RAISERROR('Error log couldn''t be updated.', 1, 1)
    END
  END
END
ELSE
BEGIN
  ROLLBACK TRANSACTION
  RAISERROR('Employee duplicate record couldn''t be created.', 1, 1)
  INSERT INTO tblErrorLog (ErrType, Msg)
    VALUES ('Duplicate record',
           'Employee duplicate record couldn''t be created.')
```

```
    IF @@ERROR <> 0
    BEGIN
      RAISERROR('Error log couldn''t be updated.', 1, 1)
    END
END
```

3. Before we execute this, we'll clear the old records in `tblErrorLog` that were created during previous examples.

```
DELETE FROM tblErrorLog
```

4. Now, use Visual Studio .NET to execute the `InserteEmployee` stored procedure, passing "Judd" and "Pipes" as the values for `@FirstName` and `@LastName`. If you then examine the `tblAuditLog` and `tblErrorLog` tables, you should see the following:

	AuditLogID	Action	Msg	AuditDate
▶	1	New employee created	Employee's name is Judd Pipes	05/06/2002 19:12:46
✱				

	ErrorID	ErrType	Msg	ErrorDate
▶				

In these tables, you can see the audit log record that was created when the new employee was added, and the fact that we don't have an error.

How It Works

All of the interest here lies in the revisions to the stored procedure. The first change happens right at the start, where we begin the transaction.

```
BEGIN TRANSACTION
```

Next, as usual, we attempt to insert the new employee record, and then check to see whether that attempt was successful:

```
INSERT INTO employees (firstname, lastname) VALUES (@FirstName, @LastName)
IF @@ERROR = 0
```

If `@@ERROR = 0`, we know that the attempt was successful, and we can insert an entry into the audit log.

```
BEGIN
  INSERT INTO tblAuditLog (Action, Msg)
    VALUES ('New employee created', 'Employee''s name is ' +
            @FirstName + ' ' + @LastName)
```

But we now have to check to see if the audit log entry itself was successful.

```
IF @@ERROR = 0
BEGIN
```

And if it was, then we commit the transaction.

```
    COMMIT TRANSACTION
END
```

However, if the audit log entry *wasn't* successfully created, we roll back the transaction. This will cause the employee record that we created above to be removed. We don't want a new employee added without its associated audit log entry.

```
ELSE
BEGIN
   ROLLBACK TRANSACTION
```

We also raise a custom error message, and create an entry in the error log. It's important to note that since the transaction has been rolled back, any commands following the rollback are executed outside of the transaction scope.

```
    RAISERROR('Audit of employee creation failed.', 1, 1)
    INSERT INTO tblErrorLog (ErrType, Msg)
      VALUES ('Audit Failure', 'Audit of employee creation failed.')
```

As seen in previous examples, if an error occurrs while creating the entry in the error log, we raise another error.

```
    IF @@ERROR <> 0
    BEGIN
       RAISERROR('Error log couldn''t be updated.', 1, 1)
    END
  END
END
```

If the attempt to insert a new employee wasn't successful, we come to this code block:

```
ELSE
BEGIN
```

The first thing we do after an unsuccessful attempt to insert a new employee is to roll back the transaction.

```
    ROLLBACK TRANSACTION
```

Then, finally, we raise our error and create an entry in the audit log.

```
RAISERROR('Employee duplicate record couldn''t be created.', 1, 1)
INSERT INTO tblErrorLog (ErrType, Msg)
  VALUES ('Duplicate record',
          'Employee duplicate record couldn''t be created.')
IF @@ERROR <> 0
BEGIN
  RAISERROR('Error log couldn''t be updated.', 1, 1)
END
END
```

To complete this example, let's create a situation where the audit log entry can't be created. As we've done before, we'll change one line in the stored procedure so that a null value is specified for the `Action` field, which doesn't allow nulls. Here's the changed line.

```
INSERT INTO tblAuditLog (Action, Msg)
  VALUES (NULL, 'Employee''s name is ' + @FirstName + ' ' + @LastName)
```

Now when we try to insert a new employee – say, Sharon Pipes – we get an error that says we can't insert our record into the `tblAuditLog` table. And if we look at the `tblErrorLog` table, that's exactly what we find:

	ErrorID	ErrType	Msg	ErrorDate
▶	12	Audit Failure	Audit of employee creation failed.	05/06/2002 19:38:39
*				

The important thing to look out for here, however, is that even though the original insert into the `Employees` table succeeded, it was rolled back because no entry could be placed into `tblAuditLog`. Take a look at the `Employees` table, and you'll find that no new entry exists. Moreover, as we mentioned in the walkthrough of the stored procedure, the entry in `tblErrorLog` was successful because the transaction was over by the time the insert into that table took place.

Transactions in ADO.NET

Transactions in ADO.NET work the same way as they do in SQL: you begin a transaction and then, depending on the circumstances, you either commit that transaction or roll it back.

When you need a transaction in your ADO.NET code, the connection object is used to provide a transaction object. This object is then used with each command object that you want to include in the transaction. The diagram below shows the relationship between the three object types.

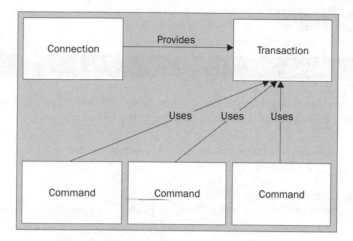

Here's how you use transactions within your ASP.NET applications:

1. Create your connection object.

2. Obtain a transaction object through the use of the connection object's BeginTransaction() method.

3. Create a command object.

4. Set the command object's Transaction property to the transaction object created in Step 2.

5. Execute the command.

6. Repeat steps 3-5 for each command you want included in the transaction.

7. If all commands execute successfully, execute the Commit() method on the transaction object created in Step 2.

8. If any commands don't execute successfully, execute the `Rollback()` method on the transaction object created in Step 2.

9. Regardless of whether the transaction was committed or rolled back, be sure to close the connection object.

Try It Out – Transactions in ADO.NET

Let's create a new example that uses the `Employees` table and the `tblAuditLog` table we created earlier. We're going to create a new employee named Brian Berry.

1. First up, delete any existing employees by that name, as well as all audit log entries, with the following SQL statements:

```
DELETE FROM tblAuditLog
DELETE FROM Employees WHERE FirstName = 'Brian' And LastName = 'Berry'
```

2. Create the ASPX page below, naming it `Trans.aspx`. You'll notice immediately that we're adding the audit log entry first. This lets us show that an insert action (in this case, the audit log entry) was executed successfully, and yet was rolled back when the employee insert failed.

```
<%@ Import namespace="system.data" %>
<%@ Import namespace="system.data.sqlclient" %>

<script language="vb" runat="server">
Private Sub Page_Load(ByVal Source As Object, ByVal E As EventArgs)

  Dim strConnection As String = ConfigurationSettings.AppSettings("NWind")
  Dim conn As New SqlConnection(strConnection)

  Dim Tran As SqlTransaction
  Dim cmd1, cmd2 As SqlCommand
  Dim sql As String

  conn.Open()
  Tran = conn.BeginTransaction()

  Try
    sql = "INSERT INTO tblAuditLog (Action, Msg) " & _
          "VALUES ('Insert the man', 'Brian Berry')"
    cmd1 = New SqlCommand(sql, conn)
    cmd1.Transaction = Tran
    cmd1.ExecuteNonQuery()
    Response.Write("Audit Log entry added<br/>")

    sql = "INSERT INTO Employees (FirstName, LastName) " & _
          "VALUES (@FirstName, @LastName)"
    cmd2 = New SqlCommand(sql, conn)
    cmd2.Transaction = Tran
```

```
        cmd2.Parameters.Add("@FirstName", "Brian")
        cmd2.Parameters.Add("@LastName", "Berry")
        cmd2.ExecuteNonQuery()
        Response.Write("Employee added<br/>")

      Tran.Commit()
    Catch
      Tran.Rollback()
      Response.Write("There was an error<br/>")
    Finally
      conn.Close()
    End Try
  End Sub
</script>
```

The first time you run this, you'll see the following messages:

Audit Log entry added
Employee added

However, the second time it's run, the employee insert will fail because an employee called Brian Berry already exists. Therefore, you'll see the error message:

Audit Log entry added
There was an error

When you look at the database, however, you'll only see one audit log entry:

	AuditLogID	Action	Msg	AuditDate
▶	3	Insert the man	Brian Berry	05/06/2002 20:01:58
*				

As you can see, when we ran it the second time, the successful audit entry that was inserted was rolled back, leaving only the first audit log entry that was created during the first run.

How It Works

What are the important parts of this code? It starts right after we open the connection to the database, when we create a `SqlTransaction` object through the use of the connection's `BeginTransaction()` method:

```
    conn.Open()
    Tran = conn.BeginTransaction()
```

We then create the (first) command object. On this occasion, we've created a variable to hold the SQL query, and passed this variable to the command's constructor, along with the connection object.

```
Try
    sql = "INSERT INTO tblAuditLog (Action, Msg) " & _
          "VALUES ('Insert the man', 'Brian Berry')"
    cmd1 = New SqlCommand(sql, conn)
```

Next, we set the command to be a part of the transaction. cmd1 is now within the Tran transaction object.

```
    cmd1.Transaction = Tran
```

We then attempt to execute the command. If this takes place successfully, we should display the message below.

```
    cmd1.ExecuteNonQuery()
    Response.Write("Audit Log entry added<br/>")
```

Now we create another command and attempt to execute it. Notice that we assign cmd2 to the same Tran transaction object.

```
    sql = "INSERT INTO Employees (FirstName, LastName) " & _
          "VALUES (@FirstName, @LastName)"
    cmd2 = New SqlCommand(sql, conn)
    cmd2.Transaction = Tran
    cmd2.Parameters.Add("@FirstName", "Brian")
    cmd2.Parameters.Add("@LastName", "Berry")
    cmd2.ExecuteNonQuery()
```

If this is successful, we display the message below, and then commit the transaction.

```
    Response.Write("Employee added<br/>")
    Tran.Commit()
```

But if any of the statements within the Try section above fail, we catch the exception and roll back the transaction, letting the user know there was an error.

```
Catch
    Tran.Rollback()
    Response.Write("There was an error<br/>")
```

Finally, regardless of whether we were successful or not, we need to close the connection.

```
Finally
    conn.Close()
End Try
```

> You've seen how to use **BEGIN TRANS**, **COMMIT TRANS**, and **ROLLBACK TRANS** from within stored procedures. When you use transactions within ADO.NET, these same statements are still being used. For the most part, you can let them do their work without worry. However, if you use ADO.NET to manage a transaction, and during that transaction you execute a stored procedure that uses SQL's transactions, they can conflict.

To see a performance comparison of the different ways of handling transactions, take a look at this article on MSDN: http://msdn.microsoft.com/library/default.asp?url=/library/en-us/dnbda/html/bdadotnetarch13.asp.

Code Organization

To this point in the book, we've been putting our Visual Basic .NET code in the same ASPX pages as the ASP.NET controls and HTML code that display the information we retrieve from the database. While this technique certainly works, there are advantages to maintaining clear separation between these two entities. In this section, we'll explain what those advantages are, and how to write code that capitalizes on them.

Benefits of Code Separation

There are several good reasons for keeping your page layout separate from the rest of your code. Let's look at them in detail:

1. The IDE is more user-friendly.
When you use Visual Studio .NET to place your Visual Basic .NET code in separate files (called **code-behind files**), the development experience is richer. You get features such as IntelliSense, improved debugging capabilities, and better compiler functionality (VB.NET's compiler runs behind the scenes as you write code, and flags any compile-time errors with a blue line).

2. Separation allows layout to be modified without recompiling code.
Keeping your page layout separate from your code allows you to change the look and feel of your pages without having to recompile. This is because of the way ASP.NET can handle ASPX pages. All the VB.NET classes within your application are compiled into a DLL when you build your web project. However, the content of the ASPX page is not compiled until the page is accessed for the first time. Each time the page changes, it is simply recompiled again, which means that you can change the ASPX page without changing the underlying code. If you wanted to change the width of a table, or the background of the page, or anything else within your page layout, you can do it without having to recompile your VB.NET event handlers.

Of course, there are limitations. If you add server controls to the page layout, they won't be recognized within the application, because the application was compiled before the server control existed. If, on the other hand, you delete a server control from the page, and yet the code tries to reference it, you'll get errors. The rule of thumb is that it's fine to change your HTML, and even the positioning or stylistic aspects of server controls, but be cautious when adding and removing elements. If in doubt, rebuild the entire project anyway.

3. Designers can focus on the look and feel, while the coder focuses on the functionality.

There are some coders who are also good at designing the look and feel of an application. For the rest of us, there are professional web designers to do that job. If you've worked in the old ASP model, and you let designers modify your ASP pages, you've probably been frustrated more than once when they've accidentally made changes to the code and broken the page. In ASP.NET, since no code needs to exist in your page layout file, they can make the changes they need to make without worry. They'll be able to focus on the page, not the code. Another key benefit is that the designer and the coder don't have to worry about stepping on each other's toes when they need to make changes at the same time. The page layout and code are in separate files, so they can both have the files they need open in their workspace, without having to worry about overwriting each other's changes.

4. Your code won't be accessible on a production server.

If you resell your application, or have a lot of proprietary business logic in it, you don't want it to be accessible to end users. With .NET, you only have to deploy the ASPX pages and the single DLL that's created when you compile your application. You don't have to place the code files themselves on your production server. Again, if you've worked in the old ASP world for any length of time, you've no doubt heard about various hacks that allowed the contents of the ASP pages to be viewed over the Internet. This should never be a problem again.

Try It Out – Separating Your Page Layout from Your Code

The beauty of using Visual Studio .NET is that it takes care of setting up the separation of your page layout and code automatically. Still, it's important to understand what it's doing behind the scenes. Let's create an ASP.NET web application in Visual Basic .NET and explain what's going on.

1. Go to the Visual Studio's **File | New Project** menu, choose **Visual Basic Projects**, and opt to create an **ASP.NET Web Application** called `CodeSep`.

2. When VS.NET finishes its machinations, you'll see the following display. Our ASP.NET page is called `WebForm1.aspx`, and by default we see the design view for that page:

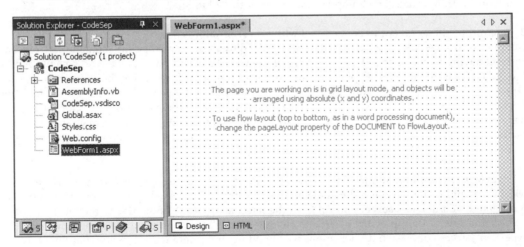

How It Works

You can alternate the page layout between the design view and the HTML view by clicking on either Design or HTML at the bottom of the screen. Here's what you'll see in the HTML view:

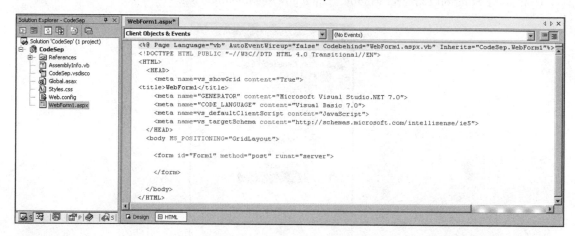

The @Page directive at the top of the page is what makes it all work. Let's look at the attributes used, noting as we do so that this list is by no means exhaustive. Refer to the documentation for a complete reference.

Attribute	Description
Language	If you use inline code (code within <% and %> blocks), this is the language used. This ensures that the correct compiler is called for this inline code.
AutoEventWireup	This attribute determines whether or not events that take place on the client cause the associated event handlers within the application to execute on the server side automatically.
	If set to true, which is the default, an event on the client causes the application to look for an event handler with a specific name, which is based on the name of the control raising the event and the type of event. If this event handler is found, it's executed.
	If set to false, you must use the Handles keyword within your code to associate a handler with an event.
CodeBehind	This is for Visual Studio .NET's benefit. It uses this to know what physical file the code for this page resides in.
Inherits	When using code-behind, this represents the class that the page itself will derive from.

Having examined these attributes, you might be wondering why you don't see a file named `WebForm1.aspx.vb` in the Solution Explorer. This is because Visual Studio .NET tries to make the environment more 'friendly' by hiding the code-behind pages! To see them, click on the **Show all files** icon in the Solution Explorer window. You'll now see the following:

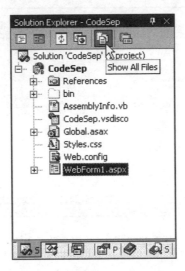

To see the `WebForm1.aspx.vb` file, expand the + sign to the left of the `WebForm1.aspx` file. You'll see the `WebForm1.aspx.vb` file where all the code is kept for your page.

Let's take a look at the code now. Visual Studio .NET gives you several ways to access the code without having to click the **Show all files** icon. You can right-click on the page in the **Solution Explorer** and click **View Code**, you can right-click on the page in HTML view and choose **View Code**, or you can just press *F7* when on the page. However you get there, though, this is the code:

```
Public Class WebForm1
    Inherits System.Web.UI.Page

#Region " Web Form Designer Generated Code "

    'This call is required by the Web Form Designer.
    <System.Diagnostics.DebuggerStepThrough()> Private Sub InitializeComponent()

    End Sub

    Private Sub Page_Init(ByVal sender As System.Object, _
                        ByVal e As System.EventArgs) Handles MyBase.Init
        'CODEGEN: This method call is required by the Web Form Designer.
        'Do not modify it using the code editor.
        InitializeComponent()
    End Sub

#End Region
```

```
        Private Sub Page_Load(ByVal sender As System.Object, _
                        ByVal e As System.EventArgs) Handles MyBase.Load
            'Put user code to initialize the page here
        End Sub

    End Class
```

There are several key things to understand about the default code created by Visual Studio .NET:

1. The fully qualified class name is the same as that specified in the `@Page Inherits` attribute. In this example, the fully qualified class name is `CodeSep.WebForm1`. You only see the name as `WebForm1` here because the namespace `CodeSep` is specified within the project's properties.

If you rename the ASPX page, the code-behind file will be renamed as well. However, the class itself won't be renamed. In most cases you'll be fine, because the ASPX page still references the correct class through the `@Page Inherits` attribute. However, it's good programming practice to name your code-behind web form classes the same as the file in which they're located.

2. All web forms derive from `System.Web.UI.Page`, or a class that inherits from it.

3. A special code region called **Web Form Designer Generated Code** is created. This allows the Visual Studio .NET designer to interact with the page. As the comment mentions, you should never change this code. However, there will be times where you may need to add code to the `Page_Init` subroutine.

When developing professional applications, take advantage of the benefits of page layout and code separation. It may seem more complicated at first, but after you get used to it, you'll be glad you did. In the remaining chapters of this book, we'll be using Visual Studio .NET's facilities to enhance our coding efforts.

Data Security Tips

It's critical that you prevent unauthorized users from accessing the information in your database. Hackers are constantly trying to find ways to steal data from online data sources, or simply to foul up systems in any way possible for the joy of it. There are books written on the subject of security in reference to web applications, and you should study the many techniques thoroughly. In this section, we're going to look at just one example of how a hacker could abuse poor programming techniques to control your data source in a way you never expected. Also, we'll point out the need to secure the 'sa' account, and to use accounts that have only the privileges they need for the tasks they are to perform on behalf of the application for which they're used.

Use Querystring Values Cautiously

Passing querystring values that will be used within SQL statements can be extremely dangerous. SQL allows you to append multiple statements together for execution by separating them with semicolons. This means that a malicious hacker can do the same, depending on how your code is constructed.

Try It Out – Hacking Querystring Values

Create the page below; it's called `Read_Employee.aspx`.

```vb
<%@ Import namespace="system.data" %>
<%@ Import namespace="system.data.sqlclient" %>

<script language="vb" runat="server">
Private Sub Page_Load(ByVal Source As Object, ByVal E As EventArgs)

  Dim sql As String = "SELECT * FROM Employees WHERE EmployeeID = " & _
                      Request.QueryString("EmployeeID")
  Dim strConnection As String = ConfigurationSettings.AppSettings("NWind")
  Dim conn As New SqlConnection(strConnection)

  conn.Open()

  Dim cmd As New SqlCommand(sql, conn)
  Response.Write("SQL: " & sql & "<br/>")

  Dim dr As SqlDataReader
  dr = cmd.ExecuteReader()

  Do While dr.Read()
    Response.Write(dr("FirstName").ToString & " " & dr("LastName").ToString)
  Loop

  conn.Close()
End Sub
</script>
```

What we're doing in this code is passing an employee's ID number, and returning the employee's name. We do this by appending the `EmployeeID` querystring value to the SQL query in the statement shown below:

```vb
Dim sql As String = "SELECT * FROM Employees WHERE EmployeeID = " & _
                    Request.QueryString("EmployeeID")
```

Let's see an example of this when it's run as it's supposed to be run. The URL on our server is http://localhost/BegASPNETdb/ch09/Read_Employee.aspx?EmployeeID=5. This returns the following result, which may be different for you, depending on the state of your sample database.

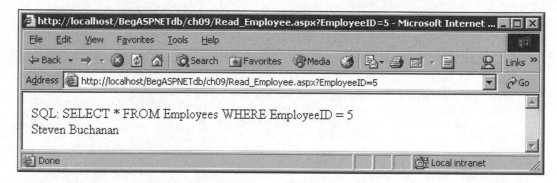

Now let's look at an example of a malicious querystring value:

http://localhost/BegASPNETdb/ch09/Read_Employee.aspx?EmployeeID=6;INSERT+INTO+E
mployees(FirstName,LastName)+VALUES+('Tom','Hacker')

Here are the results:

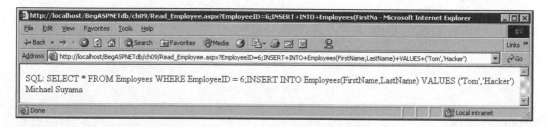

Unbeknown to you, a hacker just successfully inserted a bogus record into your database! There are two ways around this vulnerability. The first is to use a stored procedure to return the data you need. Here's an example.

```
CREATE PROCEDURE ReadEmployee(@EmployeeID as integer) AS
SELECT * FROM Employees WHERE EmployeeID = @EmployeeID
```

This prevents your code from being used to pass any extraneous information to the SQL Server, since the SQL Server will return an error if the passed value isn't an integer.

The second way, if you still want to generate the SQL statement within your code dynamically, is to use a parameter. Here's how we'd change the above example to do this.

```
<%@ Import namespace="system.data" %>
<%@ Import namespace="system.data.sqlclient" %>
```

```vb
<script language="vb" runat="server">
Private Sub Page_Load(ByVal Source As Object, ByVal E As EventArgs)

    Dim EmployeeID As Integer
    Dim sql As String = "SELECT * FROM Employees WHERE EmployeeID = @EmployeeID"
    Dim strConnection As String = ConfigurationSettings.AppSettings("NWind")
    Dim conn As New SqlConnection(strConnection)

    conn.Open()

    Dim cmd As New SqlCommand(sql, conn)
    EmployeeID = CInt(Request.Querystring("EmployeeID"))
    cmd.Parameters.Add("@EmployeeID", EmployeeID)
    Response.Write("SQL: " & sql & "<br/>")

    Dim dr As SqlDataReader
    dr = cmd.ExecuteReader()

    Do While dr.Read()
       Response.Write(dr("FirstName").ToString & " " & dr("LastName").ToString)
    Loop

    conn.Close()
End Sub
</script>
```

Now, an attempt to pass anything other than an integer will cause an error in the statement that converts the querystring value to an integer:

```vb
EmployeeID = CInt(Request.querystring("EmployeeID"))
```

Even if the hacker could somehow get past this, SQL would cause an error if the parameter's value weren't numeric.

Don't use the System Administrator (sa) Account

It shouldn't need saying again, but time and again we come across people using the 'sa' account for database access from their web applications. *Don't do it!* If a hacker finds a way to execute unauthorized SQL through your application, using the 'sa' user is like confronting a robber that's broken into your house and giving them the keys to the safe and the car in the garage as well.

> Make sure that your 'sa' account doesn't have a blank password, and make sure that the password it does have is difficult to guess.

Create Multiple SQL Users Depending on your Needs

If you have an application that your employees use, and you're also creating other applications that use the same data for different user populations, such as vendors and customers, don't use the same SQL user. Create a separate user for each user population, and give them only the rights they need. In many projects, you'll have an intranet site and an extranet site that makes a subset of the intranet site's data available. In a case like this, create two users, one called something like `Intranet_App_User`, and the other called `Extranet_App_User`.

These are tips from the real world. Hopefully, they'll spur you to keep security in the forefront of your thoughts as you develop your own web applications.

Summary

In this chapter, we've talked about a selection of subjects that should help you to create more professional applications. We didn't cover any of these topics exhaustively, but we talked enough about them to make you aware of how to take advantage of them, and how to get started. We looked at:

❑ How to deal with errors in your application to give the user the best experience possible

❑ How to make use of transactions to ensure that critical data updates are either all written successfully, or not written at all

❑ What the benefits of separation page layout and code are, and how Visual Studio .NET makes it easy to implement

❑ How security considerations should be a part of everything you do

In the next chapter, we'll look more closely at the options available to you when you decide to separate code and layout, when we discuss the topic of componentization.

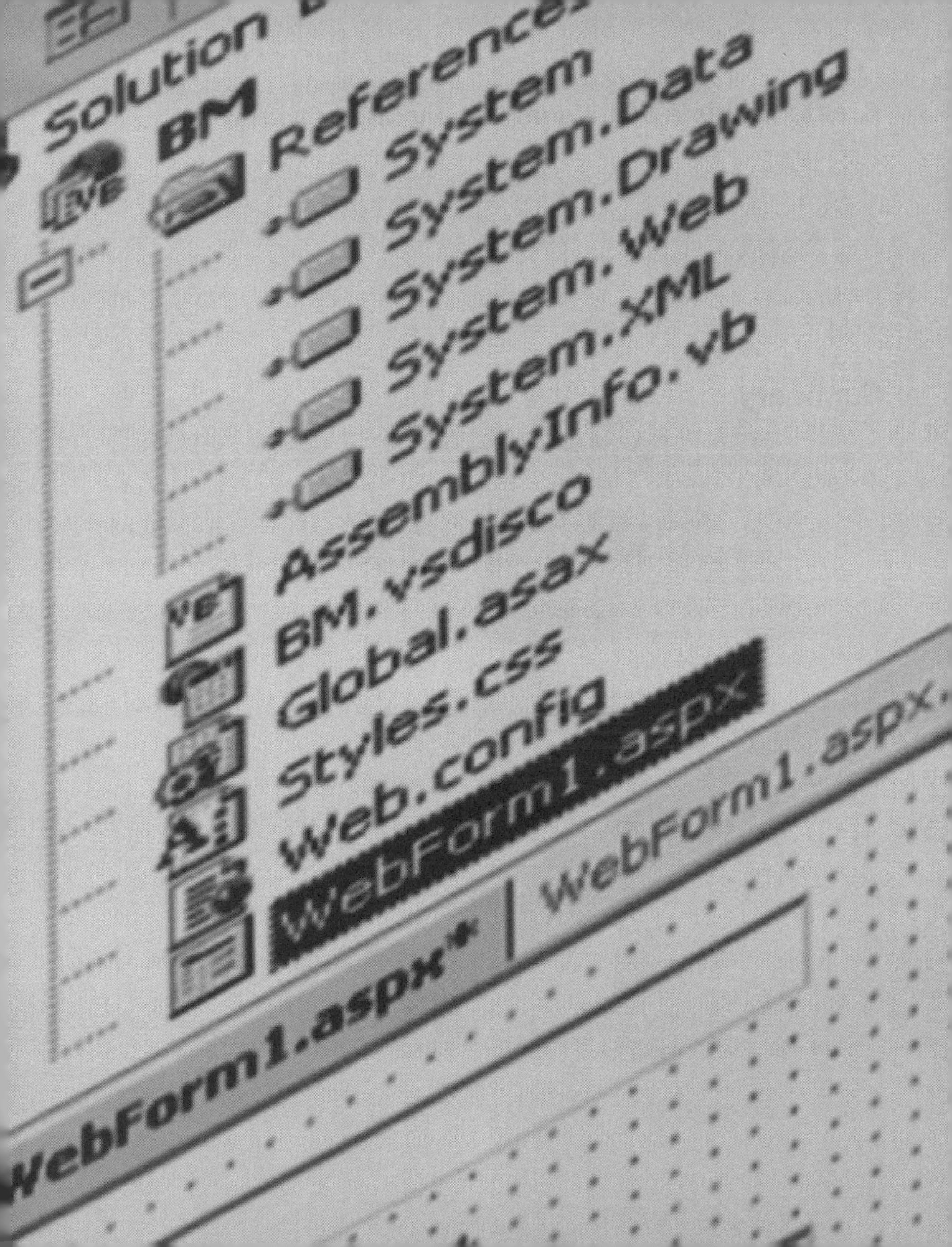

Solution
BM
References
System
System.Data
System.Drawing
System.Web
System.XML
AssemblyInfo.vb
BM.vsdisco
Global.asax
Styles.css
Web.config
WebForm1.aspx

WebForm1.aspx* | WebForm1.aspx.

WebForm1.aspx*

Componentization

Having reached this stage of the book, you've already have made a great deal of progress towards mastering database programming with ASP.NET. In this chapter, we won't be examining any new features of ASP.NET, or of ADO.NET, but we will be practicing some techniques that should help you to improve the applications you write using those technologies. We're going to look at **componentization**, which will allow you to reuse your code more efficiently, and to improve the scalability and maintainability of your applications. Specifically, we'll cover:

❑ The benefits of using componentization in .NET

❑ The creation of a simple, non-database class library, and seeing how it can be used in an ASP.NET web page

❑ A walkthrough of some ASP.NET web pages that are designed for different uses, where each page uses the same class library

❑ Some important notes about the componentization of ASP.NET web applications

❑ The practical implications of componentization

To accomplish all of this, we will be looking at solutions to the kinds of business requests that might be posed to us by Northwind Traders. These requests are similar to those you might encounter in your real-world programming efforts.

What is Componentization?

We've chosen to start talking about "componentization" rather than "components" in this chapter because in the software industry, the latter has become a somewhat overloaded term that is frequently interpreted differently by different people. We'll try to address some of this confusion as we progress, but we'll start out on firmer ground with a discussion of what these terms mean in everyday life.

In the broadest possible terms, a system that has been 'componentized' is one that's made up of units of specific functionality that work together to form the whole. Consider, for example, a personal computer. Typically, these consist of (among other things) a motherboard, a CPU, a hard drive, some memory, a video adapter, a keyboard, a mouse, and a display. All of these 'components' work together to accomplish a task. However, while there's clearly a relationship between (say) the CPU and the mouse, they:

❑   Serve different purposes

❑   Provide distinct functionality

❑   Are implemented differently

❑   Interact with each other according to specific rules

❑   Are unaware of the specific nature of each other

For the consumer, one of the chief benefits of the existence of standardized PC components is that they can, for example, replace their mouse at any time, and be confident that the new one will work in the same way as the old one. Another benefit, this time for the companies creating personal computers, is that once the way that (say) the motherboard and the CPU will interact has been decided, the teams working on those two components can do so in parallel, and independently. As we'll see, both of these have direct analogies in the world of software components.

Component Confusion

When we talk about 'componentizing' software, we do so with the aim of achieving similar benefits as those described above. When we update a part of an application, we want to be confident that the change will not have an adverse effect on the rest of the software. When software is being developed, we want to assign different parts of the effort to different teams, but to know that the pieces will work together in the end. In practice, this can be done in a number of different ways, not all of which involve things that a software engineer might call a "component".

Consider, for example, a Visual Basic .NET code-behind file for an ASP.NET page that displays the result of an SQL query in a `DataGrid`. The code-behind file interacts with a C++-based COM+ DLL that manages the process of connecting to the database, executing the query, dealing with any database problems, and cleaning up memory. Clearly, this solution has three 'components', but only one of them – the COM+ DLL – might actually be *called* a software component, at least at first. The `DataGrid` is more correctly termed a **control**, while the code-behind file is... well, just that. All the same, there are well-defined rules governing the way these three entities interact, and as long as they're followed, none of them needs to know anything about the internal workings of the others.

Class Libraries

So, having established that there are many different entities that might reasonably be described as components, we should introduce the technique that we've chosen to illustrate and demonstrate componentization in this chapter. The examples that we'll present in the pages to follow will employ DLLs containing **class libraries** that were originally written in Visual Basic .NET.

In Visual Basic .NET, a class library is the DLL that's produced when a class library project is compiled. The classes contained in the class libraries you write are similar to those in the .NET Framework class library, in that objects of these classes may be instantiated and used from within other applications. Class libraries are straightforward to write and easy to reference (that is, to make use of), and they meet all of the rules we previously set out for entities that take part in componentization.

Why Use Class Libraries?

The language-neutral architecture of .NET has made the creation of class libraries a more useful proposition than ever before – classes written in one .NET language can be used from any other .NET language, without the need for any special considerations. With the language obstacle out of the way, the benefits of using class libraries in (ASP).NET development are broadly the same as the traditional benefits of using classes in single-language development. In this section, we'll enumerate those advantages, and give some suitably themed examples.

Simplified Programming

By putting complex functionality into classes with well-defined programming interfaces, other programmers only have to worry about dealing with those interfaces. To see how this works, consider ADO.NET itself as an example. When we use ADO.NET with SQL Server or Access, we don't have to worry about the intricacies of the Tabular Data Stream or OLE DB. As Microsoft likes to say, "It just works."

You can write your class libraries in the same way. For example, it's quite easy to have one class that manages the details of loading data into collections for processing, and another that performs some checking on any attempted changes to that data before they're written back to the database. Other programmers can then just call your methods for loading, validating, and saving the data, without having to know anything about database programming.

Encapsulation

Encapsulation is the ability of a class to hide its internal data and methods, and to present a carefully designed interface to its users. In this way, only the parts of the class that you want to *be* accessible *are* accessible. For example, when we use the Fill() method of a data adapter, we're really asking for the computer to work its way through a result set and put the data into a DataTable object. But to do our job, we don't know or need to know exactly how it does that.

As a further demonstration, imagine we have a class whose objects will represent individual employees. Such a class could include a GetTaxID() method that might look something like this:

```
GetTaxID(strEmployeeID As String) As String
```

Given this definition, we would expect to provide a strEmployeeID variable as a string, and to get a string back – but we don't know anything else about how it works. There might be a database query, or a message could be sent off to a BizTalk server, but in the end we really don't care. Such processes are hidden from us by the class's programming interface.

A further benefit of encapsulation is that it allows you to present a simple interface to a potentially difficult operation. For example, suppose that we've created an instance of the employee class that we've been talking about, and that it's important for users of this class to be able to get hold of the employee's name. If the employee class has a member field like this:

```
Private mGivenName As String
```

Then we can expose it to the outside world using a property, like this:

```
Public Property GivenName As String
  Get
    Return mGivenName
  End Get
  Set(ByVal Value As String)
    If Value.Length > 0 Then
      mGivenName = Value
    Else
      Throw New ArgumentException("Given Name cannot be blank.")
    End If
  End Set
End Property
```

The property is a part of the public interface of the class, while the field, being private, is not. Using a property allows us fine control over programmatic access to the value – by not including a 'set' section, for example, we could have made this a read-only value. Also, the property allows us to perform validation when some other code attempts to change its value; this would not have been possible had we just used a public field.

In general, taking advantage of encapsulation in the design of your classes provides the following benefits to you and other users of your class libraries:

❑   It offers **data hiding**. In the above case, the programmer who is using your class cannot directly change mGivenName – they must do it through the property. Data hiding means that you can enforce rules about the data without directly exposing that logic to the class's user. You can also control when and how the value of the given name is updated in its store, be that a database or some other system.

❑   It offers the ability to modify or extend the internal code of the class at a later date, without affecting its use through others' applications. In other words, you can add functionality to a class without having to modify the other classes that use the modified class, as long as the original interface continues to be supported.

Reuse

Class libraries promote the reuse of code by allowing different applications with similar needs to reuse a common set of classes. Suppose, for example, that you have three applications that all need to access employee information – one for a phone directory, one for processing insurance claims, and one for tracking helpdesk requests. Each of these applications may need to access different information about the employee – phone number, hire date, or perhaps office location. If our employee class were to expose this information as part of its interface, then each application could use it, rather than having to create its own.

A further advantage of reuse is that classes that get used a lot also tend to get tested a lot. Classes that are well tested mean a boost to the reliability of applications that use them, and represent a time saving for you when you come to test such an application.

Enhanced Sustainability

Sustainability measures the degree to which a class or an application adapts to changes in its environment. These changes could be in the structure or sources of data that the class works with, or in how other classes or applications use it. Highly sustainable applications adapt to changes quickly and with a minimum of effort.

Designing good classes can become something of a balancing act. You want to provide as much information and functionality as is appropriate, knowing that this will promote simplicity and reuse in many projects. However, it's very difficult to anticipate every possible use, so it's hard to know exactly what interfaces you should provide. A good way to cope with this is to expose your information as generically as possible, and then let the consumer transform it into what they need.

For example, suppose that your employee class provides a method that returns the employee's name and phone number formatted into an HTML table row, ready for output in an online telephone directory. That's great for the phone directory application – all it has to do is call your method and display the results – but it's not so great if the application needs to send its output to a WAP-enabled mobile phone. If you're designing for maximum sustainability, your class shouldn't provide such a method as the only way to get the phone number. Rather, it should provide the information in a generic format (say, an XML document) and let the consumer transform that into the desired output form.

Writing a Class Library

Hopefully, we've begun to persuade you of the benefits of writing classes and class libraries for use in your applications – and particularly, for your ASP.NET database applications. In this section, we're going to look at how to write a simple class library. To help make our examples realistic, we will look at the solutions to the kinds of business problems that might be posed to us by Northwind Traders. Once the problem has been explained, we'll explain our solution, and then walk through the code.

Northwind's Business Requests

As can be seen from a quick look at the Customers table in the Northwind database, the company does business with clients in several different countries – in fact, the 91 customers are drawn from 21 different nations.

Now, in the past, Northwind didn't carefully manage the costs of shipping goods to its overseas customers, but now its auditors have recommended that it implement an additional shipping charge for such orders. After working with its shipping partner, Northwind has decided on a two-part international shipping charge:

❑ A flat amount to be charged regardless of the number of items to be shipped

❑ A per-item amount to cover increased expenses when shipping to some countries

The sum of these additional charges needs to be expressed in the currency used by the country being shipped to, on the date the order was shipped. Note that many of the European countries will now be using euros rather than their original native currency. (The Excel worksheet provided with the code download shows the shipping charges by country.) To keep things simple, the conversion rates and fees won't be changed more than twice a year, and Northwind would like to start by having this information available on its intranet site, which is called `NwtNet`.

Structuring our Solution

Our solution to this problem is fairly simple. We'll create a class library that offers two classes: one for *representing* the international shipping charge, and one for *computing* the charge based on the country the items are being shipped to, the number of items, and the date on which shipping occurred. Later on, we'll use an ASP.NET web page to collect the shipping parameters and display the results.

Try It Out – Building a Simple Class Library

Due to the amount of code in the full version of this example, we will restrict the number of countries we deal with. Following the instructions here will result in a functional application, but for the complete application you'll need to download the code from **www.wrox.com**.

Unfortunately, the Standard Edition of Visual Basic .NET does not support the creation of Class Library projects. However, it can *open such projects that have been created elsewhere. If you're using the Standard Edition, the files available for download include a skeleton project for you to use in this example.*

1. In Visual Studio .NET, create a new VB.NET Class Library project called `NwtSimple`:

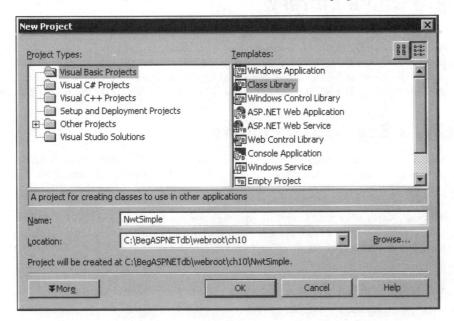

2. In the Solution Explorer, rename `Class1.vb` to `InternationalShippingCharge.vb`:

3. Now type the following code into the `InternationalShippingCharge.vb` file:

```vb
Option Explicit On
Option Strict On

Public Class ShippingCharge

  ' Class field definitions
  Private _CurrencySymbol As String
  Private _ChargeAmount As Decimal

  ' Name of the currency symbol
  Public Property CurrencySymbol() As String
    Get
      CurrencySymbol = _CurrencySymbol
    End Get
    Set(ByVal Value As String)
      _CurrencySymbol = Value
    End Set
  End Property

  ' Total amount of international shipping charge
  Public Property ChargeAmount() As Decimal
    Get
      ChargeAmount = _ChargeAmount
    End Get
    Set(ByVal Value As Decimal)
      _ChargeAmount = Value
    End Set
  End Property

  ' Class constructor
  Public Sub New()
    _CurrencySymbol = "USD"
    _ChargeAmount = 0D
  End Sub
End Class
```

```vbnet
Public Class ShippingChargeCalculator
' GetCountryList returns a DataBind-friendly list of countries
  Public Function GetCountryList() As ArrayList

    Dim CountryList As New ArrayList()
    Dim ListOfCountries As String
    Dim chra(1) As Char

    ListOfCountries = "Canada,Sweden"

    ' Define the delimiting character
    chra(0) = Convert.ToChar(",")

    ' Parse the list of countries into an array, then add to the ArrayList
    CountryList.AddRange(ListOfCountries.Split(chra))

    ' Sort the CountryList before returning it
    CountryList.Sort()

    Return CountryList
  End Function

  Public Function CalculateInternationalCharges( _
                    ByVal CountryShippingTo As String, _
                    ByVal NumberOfItems As Integer, _
                    ByVal EffectiveShipDate As Date) As ShippingCharge

    Dim sc As New ShippingCharge()
    Dim CurrencySymbol As String = "USD"
    Dim ConversionRate As Decimal = 1D

    Dim FlatCharge As Decimal = 0D
    Dim PerItemCharge As Decimal = 0D

    ' If the country has converted to the euro, then UseEuro will be true
    ' and EuroDate will define the date after which the euro must be used
    Dim UsesEuro As Boolean = False
    Dim EuroDate As New Date(DateTime.MaxValue.Ticks)

    Select Case CountryShippingTo.ToUpper()
      Case "CANADA"
        CurrencySymbol = "CAN"
        ConversionRate = 1.61189D
        FlatCharge = 0D
        PerItemCharge = 0D

      Case "SWEDEN"
        CurrencySymbol = "SEK"
        ConversionRate = 10.4909D
        FlatCharge = 25D
        PerItemCharge = 1D
```

```
      Case Else
        CurrencySymbol = "USD"
        ConversionRate = 1D
        FlatCharge = 50D
        PerItemCharge = 2.5D
    End Select


    ' Update the shipping charge
    If UsesEuro And (EffectiveShipDate > EuroDate) Then
      CurrencySymbol = "EUR"
      ConversionRate = 1.13491D
    End If


    sc.CurrencySymbol = CurrencySymbol
    sc.ChargeAmount = FlatCharge
    sc.ChargeAmount += Decimal.Round(PerItemCharge * NumberOfItems, 2)
    sc.ChargeAmount = Decimal.Round(sc.ChargeAmount * ConversionRate, 2)


    Return sc
  End Function
End Class
```

4. Select Build | Build Solution. This builds the class library, ready for the next step. It really is that easy.

How It Works

The first line of code simply starts the `ShippingCharge` class, objects of which will be created by the `ShippingChargeCalculator` class and used to represent the amount of the shipping charge.

```
Public Class ShippingCharge
```

We add two class-level variables: one to hold the name of the currency as a `String`, and a `Decimal` value to hold the charge amount.

```
Private _CurrencySymbol As String
Private _ChargeAmount As Decimal
```

Next, we expose the private class-level variables as properties of the `ShippingCharge` class.

```
Public Property CurrencySymbol() As String
  Get
    CurrencySymbol = _CurrencySymbol
  End Get
  Set(ByVal Value As String)
    _CurrencySymbol = Value
  End Set
End Property
```

```
Public Property ChargeAmount() As Decimal
  Get
    ChargeAmount = _ChargeAmount
  End Get
  Set(ByVal Value As Decimal)
    _ChargeAmount = Value
  End Set
End Property
```

As the last member in this class, the constructor simply sets some default values for the private variable. It is a good idea to do this, just in case somebody decides to create an instance of this class without using our shipping charge routine.

```
Public Sub New()
  _CurrencySymbol = "USD"
  _ChargeAmount = 0D
End Sub
End Class
```

Moving on to the second class, `ShippingChargeCalculator` contains two public functions:

❑ GetCountryList() returns an ArrayList containing the name of each country that Northwind has shipped products to. This method will be used on our web page to select a shipping destination.

❑ CalculateInternationalCharges() takes a string containing the name of the country being shipped to, an integer representing the number of items being shipped, and the date that shipping occurred. It returns an instance of the ShippingCharge class.

Let's turn our attention first to `GetCountryList()`, which returns an `ArrayList` instance of the country names, sorted into alphabetical order. We've used an `ArrayList` specifically because it works well with ASP.NET web controls' data binding features (for simplicity, we have only shown two countries here).

```
Public Function GetCountryList() As ArrayList

  Dim CountryList As New ArrayList()
  Dim ListOfCountries As String
  Dim chra(1) As Char

  ListOfCountries = "Canada,Sweden"
```

As we intend to store the country names in a simple, comma-delimited string, we can use the `String` object's `Split()` method to parse it into the `ArrayList` object. The `Split()` method expects an array of characters to represent the delimiters, for which we use the `chra` variable. To use the comma character as the delimiter, we just set the first element of `chra` to be a comma.

```
chra(0) = Convert.ToChar(",")
```

Next, we call the `Split()` method on the country list string, passing the result to the `AddRange()` method of the `ArrayList` object. `AddRange()` simply appends an array to an `ArrayList`.

```
CountryList.AddRange(ListOfCountries.Split(chra))
```

Then, to sort the list of countries alphabetically, we can call the `ArrayList.Sort()` method without any parameters. (This may seem like a wasted step here, because the string we parsed already had the countries in alphabetical order. However, with this statement in place, we could insert a new country at the end of the `ListOfCountries` string without worrying about it breaking the sort order.) We then return the `ArrayList` object.

```
    CountryList.Sort()

    Return CountryList
End Function
```

The function that actually determines the international shipping charge is `CalculateInternationalCharges()`, which starts like this, and returns an instance of the `ShippingCharge` class.

```
    Public Function CalculateInternationalCharges( _
                ByVal CountryShippingTo As String, _
                ByVal NumberOfItems As Integer, _
                ByVal EffectiveShipDate As Date) As ShippingCharge
```

First, we need to create a `ShippingCharge` instance to work with. We also prepare a few local variables to hold the values needed in our calculations, and set them to the defaults for the US market. We'll also need to declare the standardized (see www.iso.org/iso/en/ISOOnline.frontpage) currency symbol, the conversion rate, the flat rate charges, and the total number of items being shipped. The number of items being shipped is based on their packaging; so one case of 24 cans counts as one item, not 24.

```
    Dim sc As New ShippingCharge()
    Dim CurrencySymbol As String = "USD"
    Dim ConversionRate As Decimal = 1D

    Dim FlatCharge As Decimal = 0D
    Dim PerItemCharge As Decimal = 0D
```

We know that Northwind ships products to customers in Europe, and we also know that some of the countries in Europe have started using a common currency: the euro. However, it's possible that some more countries will switch to the euro at a later date, so we'll need to check to see whether the current system time is before or after the date when the country in question switched to the new currency. In order to avoid computing the shipping charge in euros when we shouldn't, we'll simply set the default value of the `EuroDate` variable to the maximum possible system date and time (the end of 9999!).

```
    Dim UsesEuro As Boolean = False
    Dim EuroDate As New Date(DateTime.MaxValue.Ticks)
```

With these in place, we start the calculation by determining which country is being shipped to. Note that we use the `ToUpper()` method on the `CountryShippingTo` string, to avoid any problems with the case of the characters in the string.

```
Select Case CountryShippingTo.ToUpper()
```

Based on the country, we assign the currency symbol, the conversion rate, the flat rate charge, and the per-item charge in US dollars. If the country is scheduled to switch to the euro, we can also set the `UsesEuro` flag and the switch date. We are giving free shipping to Canada.

```
    Case "CANADA"
        CurrencySymbol = "CAN"
        ConversionRate = 1.61189D
        FlatCharge = 0D
        PerItemCharge = 0D

    Case "SWEDEN"
        CurrencySymbol = "SEK"
        ConversionRate = 10.4909D
        FlatCharge = 25D
        PerItemCharge = 1D
```

Finally, if the country cannot be determined, we'll ask for payment in US dollars. We'll charge $50.00 as the flat charge, and $2.50 per item.

```
    Case Else
        CurrencySymbol = "USD"
        ConversionRate = 1D
        FlatCharge = 50D
        PerItemCharge = 2.5D
End Select
```

If the country being shipped to uses the euro, we need to check whether the shipping date exceeds the conversion date. If so, we need to compute the shipping charge in euros.

```
'  Update the shipping charge
If UsesEuro And (EffectiveShipDate > EuroDate) Then
    CurrencySymbol = "EUR"
    ConversionRate = 1.13491D
End If
```

Finally, we populate the `ShippingCharge` object. We calculate the actual shipping charge by initializing it with the flat charge amount, then adding the total per-item charges. This returns the charge expressed in US dollars. To convert it to the correct currency, we simply multiply by the conversion rate. After the calculations are done, we can return the populated `ShippingCharge` instance.

```
sc.CurrencySymbol = CurrencySymbol
sc.ChargeAmount = FlatCharge
sc.ChargeAmount += Decimal.Round(PerItemCharge * NumberOfItems, 2)
```

```
        sc.ChargeAmount = Decimal.Round(sc.ChargeAmount * ConversionRate, 2)

    '  Return the shipping charges
        Return sc

    End Function
End Class
```

Of course, having our new class library ready for use is only half the battle. We also need a way to specify the three values required by the calculation – the country, the ship date, and the number of items being shipped. We'll accomplish this using an ASP.NET page.

Using the Class Library in a Web Page

There are three steps involved in using our new class library from a web page. We have to create a web application, add a reference to the class library to the web application project, and finally use the library from ASP.NET. Let's see how we can do that.

Try It Out – Creating a Web Application

1. To begin this part of the process, return to Visual Studio .NET and – without closing our first solution – create a new Visual Basic ASP.NET Web Application.

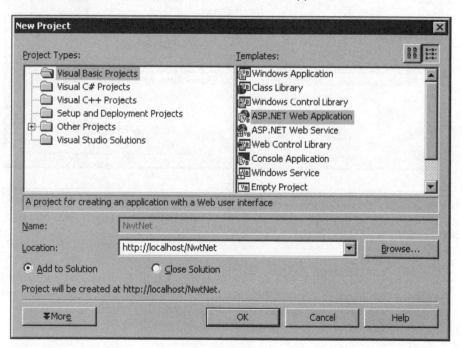

Make sure that the **Add to Solution** radio button remains selected. We want this project to be part of the same solution as the last one.

2. Next, rename the file `WebForm1.aspx` to `InternationalShippingCharge.aspx`, and save all changed files.

3. In order to use our component in the web application, we need to add a reference to it. First, ensure that the `NwtNet` project is highlighted, and then choose **Project | Add Reference...** In the **Add Reference** dialog that appears, click on the **Projects** tab, make sure that **NwtSimple** is highlighted, and then click the **Select** button. Click the **OK** button to continue.

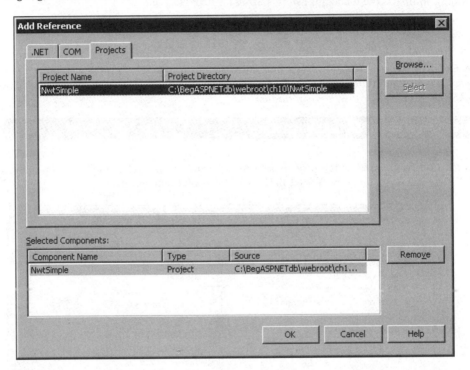

> It's good to use project references while you're developing and testing your code. Before deployment, however, you must switch to the .NET tab and reference the DLL that contains your class library.

4. If you now go to the Solution Explorer and expand the folder named **References** under the `NwtNet` project, you should see the `NwtSimple` class library listed. We're now ready to work on the ASP.NET form that uses it.

5. The `InternationalShippingCharge.aspx` page should still be open in the editor. (If it's not, then open it!) In the Design window, we need to add a `DropDownList` control, a `TextBox` control, a `Calendar` control, some `Label` controls, and a `Button`. We also need to place a `RequiredFieldValidator` and a `RangeValidator` in the cells for the `DropDownList` and the `TextBox` controls.

We can add these controls by dragging them from the toolbox and placing them inside an HTML table, as shown here. You can also add a label for the title of the page: Shipping Charge Calculator.

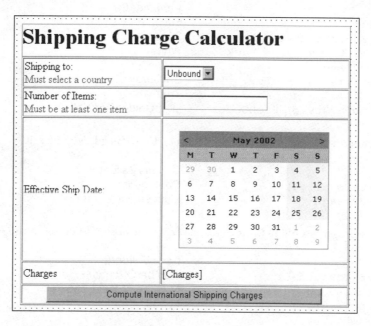

6. Set the IDs of these controls as follows:

- ❑ `DropDownList` set to `CountryList`
- ❑ `TextBox` set is `NumberOfItems`
- ❑ `Button` set to `Calculate`
- ❑ `Label` (cell adjacent to **Charges:**) set to `Charges`

7. The `Calendar` properties should be set as below:

ID	EffectiveShipDate
BackColor	White
BorderColor	DarkGray
CellPadding	4
DayHeaderStyle | BackColor	LightGray
DayHeaderStyle | Font | Bold	True
DayNameFormat	FirstLetter
Font	Verdana, 8pt
ForeColor	Black
OtherMonthDayStyle | ForeColor	Silver
OtherMonthDayStyle | BackColor	White
SeletedDate	01/04/2002
TitleStyle | Backcolor	DarkGray
TitleStyle | Font | Bold	True
WeekendDayStyle | BackColor	LightGoldenRodYellow

8. The properties of the `RequiredFieldValidator` need to be like this:

ID	CountryValidator
ControlToValidate	CountryList
ErrorMessage	Must select a country

9. And the properties of the `RangeValidator` control should be set as shown here:

ID	ItemsValidator
ControlToValidate	NumberOfItems
ErrorMessage	Must be at least one item
MaximumValue	65535
MinimumValue	1
Type	Integer

(To see the HTML that our controls generate at any point, select HTML Source from the View menu.)

10. We're now ready to work on the code behind this page – this will be stored in a file called `InternationalShippingCharge.aspx.vb`. Select View | Code from the main menu, and you can then type in the following code (or paste it from the code download).

```
Option Explicit On
Option Strict On

Imports NwtSimple

Namespace NwtNet
  Public Class InternationalShippingCharges
    Inherits System.Web.UI.Page
```

```vb
        Protected WithEvents CountryList _
            As System.Web.UI.WebControls.DropDownList
        Protected WithEvents NumberOfItems As System.Web.UI.WebControls.TextBox
        Protected WithEvents Charges As System.Web.UI.WebControls.Label
        Protected WithEvents CountryValidator _
            As System.Web.UI.WebControls.RequiredFieldValidator
        Protected WithEvents ItemsValidator _
            As System.Web.UI.WebControls.RangeValidator
        Protected WithEvents Calculate As System.Web.UI.WebControls.Button
        Protected WithEvents EffectiveShipDate _
            As System.Web.UI.WebControls.Calendar

        Private sc As New ShippingChargeCalculator()

#Region " Web Form Designer Generated Code "

    'This call is required by the Web Form Designer.
    <System.Diagnostics.DebuggerStepThrough()> _
            Private Sub InitializeComponent()

    End Sub

    Private Sub Page_Init(ByVal sender As System.Object, _
            ByVal e As System.EventArgs) Handles MyBase.Init
            'CODEGEN: This method call is required by the Web Form Designer
            'Do not modify it using the code editor.
        InitializeComponent()
    End Sub

#End Region

    Private Sub Page_Load(ByVal sender As System.Object, _
        ByVal e As System.EventArgs) Handles MyBase.Load

        If Not IsPostBack Then
          CountryList.DataSource = sc.GetCountryList
          CountryList.DataBind()
          EffectiveShipDate.SelectedDate = Date.Now
        End If
    End Sub

    Private Sub Calculate_Click(ByVal sender As System.Object, _
        ByVal e As System.EventArgs) Handles Calculate.Click
      Dim sch As ShippingCharge

      sch = sc.CalculateInternationalCharges( _
          CountryList.SelectedItem.Value, _
          Convert.ToInt32(NumberOfItems.Text), _
          EffectiveShipDate.SelectedDate)

      Charges.Text = sch.ChargeAmount.ToString() & " " & sch.CurrencySymbol
    End Sub
  End Class
End Namespace
```

11. In the Solution Explorer, right-click on the `NwtNet` project, and select **Set as StartUp Project** from the context menu.

12. Again in the Solution Explorer, right click on `InternationalShippingCharge.aspx` and select **Set As Start Page**.

13. Now select **Debug | Start**, or just press *F5*. Once our small application is running, you should see the following:

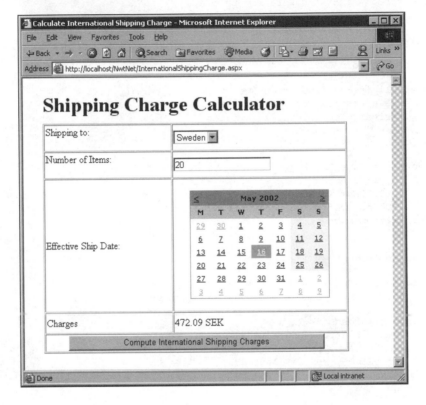

How It Works

The ASPX page that was assembled by Visual Studio on our behalf starts with a `Page` directive specifying the language, that events should be automatically posted back, the name of the file that contains the code that supports this page, and what class the page builds on:

```
<%@ Page Language="vb" AutoEventWireup="True"
        Codebehind="InternationalShippingCharge.aspx.vb"
        Inherits="NwtNet.NwtNet.InternationalShippingCharges"%>
```

After the header, we define a form to host our interactive web controls. The first control we use is a simple `Label` for the caption for the drop-down list of countries. This is tied to a `RequiredFieldValidator` control that makes sure that a country is selected:

```
<asp:Label id="Label1" runat="server">Shipping to:</asp:Label>

<asp:RequiredFieldValidator id="CountryValidator" runat="server"
                            ErrorMessage="Must select a country"
                            ControlToValidate="CountryList">
</asp:RequiredFieldValidator>
```

The actual `DropDownList` control is placed in the next table cell; we'll populate it 'behind the scenes' in our code-behind file, in the `Page_Load()` event handler:

```
<asp:DropDownList id="CountryList" runat="server"></asp:DropDownList>
```

We then have a further `Label` control and a `RangeValidator` for the number of items being shipped. At least one item must be shipped, but no more than 65,535 can be shipped. The `TextBox` control for the quantity is in the next cell:

```
<asp:Label id="Label2" runat="server">Number of Items:</asp:Label>

<asp:RangeValidator id="ItemsValidator" runat="server"
                    ErrorMessage="Must be at least one item"
                    ControlToValidate="NumberOfItems"
                    MaximumValue="65535" MinimumValue="1" Type="Integer">
</asp:RangeValidator></TD><TD style="HEIGHT: 32px">

<asp:TextBox id="NumberOfItems" runat="server"></asp:TextBox>
```

On the next row of the table, we have another caption and an ASP `Calendar` control. `Calendar` controls have a number of display-related properties, which are shown here. The settings here reflect the choices we made in Visual Studio's **Properties** window.

```
<TD style="WIDTH: 201px; HEIGHT: 211px">
<asp:Label id="Label3" runat="server">Effective Ship Date:</asp:Label>
</TD>

<TD style="HEIGHT: 211px" align=middle>
<asp:Calendar id="EffectiveShipDate" runat="server"
              Height="72px" Width="223px"
              BorderColor="DarkGray" BackColor="White"
              CellPadding="4" DayNameFormat="FirstLetter"
              ForeColor="Black" SelectedDate="2002-04-01"
              Font-Names="Verdana" Font-Size="8pt">
  <DayHeaderStyle Font-Bold="True" BackColor="LightGray"></DayHeaderStyle>
  <TitleStyle Font-Bold="True" BackColor="DarkGray"></TitleStyle>
  <WeekendDayStyle BackColor="LightGoldenrodYellow"></WeekendDayStyle>
  <OtherMonthDayStyle ForeColor="Silver" BackColor="White">
  </OtherMonthDayStyle>
</asp:Calendar>
</TD>
```

The next row has two `Label` controls: one for a caption on the charge amount, and one that will actually show the amount of the charge. Again, we will populate this 'behind the scenes'.

```
<TD style="WIDTH: 201px; HEIGHT: 33px">
<asp:Label id="Label4" runat="server">Charges</asp:Label>
</TD>
<TD style="HEIGHT: 33px">
<asp:Label id="Charges" runat="server"></asp:Label>
</TD>
```

Finally, in the last row of the table, we have the button that will trigger calculation of the charge:

```
<TD align="middle" colSpan="2">
<asp:Button id="Calculate" runat="server"
            Width="410px" Text="Compute International Shipping Charges">
</asp:Button>
</TD>
```

Having looked at the display code, we now need to examine the code-behind file. We start by enabling strict code checking, and then import the class library that we're going to use through an `Imports` statement. The next lines then define a namespace for this class (as well as the class name), and specify that it inherits from the .NET Framework class, `Page`.

```
Option Explicit On
Option Strict On

Imports NwtSimple

Namespace NwtNet
   Public Class InternationalShippingCharges
      Inherits System.Web.UI.Page
```

Next come some lines that Visual Studio has added, in which the variables for the controls on the page are declared, and then we create an instance of our `ShippingChargeCalculator` class that's available for use by all of the other procedures in the `InternationalShippingCharges` class:

```
Private sc As New ShippingChargeCalculator()
```

We then have a block of code generated by Visual Studio .NET. Although it's absolutely required, it's not something we should spend our time on here.

Two things that we do need to look at closely are the `Page_Load()` and `Calculate_Click()` event handlers. In the former, we use the familiar `If Not IsPostBack Then` syntax to ensure that the drop-down control and the date on the calendar are set just once, when the page is first loaded:

```
If Not IsPostBack Then
   CountryList.DataSource = sc.GetCountryList
   CountryList.DataBind()
   EffectiveShipDate.SelectedDate = Date.Now
End If
```

In `Calculate_Click()`, we calculate the shipping charges by calling the `CalculateInternationalCharges()` method of the `ShippingChargeCalculator` object we set up earlier, and assigning the result to an instance of the other class in our library, `ShippingCharge`. Then we just display it by assembling a string to be placed in the label control called `Charges`.

```
        Private Sub Calculate_Click(ByVal sender As System.Object, _
                    ByVal e As System.EventArgs) Handles Calculate.Click
            Dim sch As ShippingCharge

            sch = sc.CalculateInternationalCharges( _
                    CountryList.SelectedItem.Value, _
                    Convert.ToInt32(NumberOfItems.Text), _
                    EffectiveShipDate.SelectedDate)

            Charges.Text = sch.ChargeAmount.ToString() & " " & sch.CurrencySymbol
        End Sub
```

And that's all there is to it. Do take a look at the longer example in the download code, and if you like, you could think about ways to change and improve this application. For instance, you might like to try using ADO.NET to bring in the list of countries and shipping costs from the Excel spreadsheet. For the time being, however, we'll move on.

Summary

We usually save our summaries for the end of the chapter, but we've covered enough ground here to make it worth reiterating a few points. In particular, there are three things worth bearing in mind:

❑ Well-written classes make programming simpler. Our ASP.NET page didn't need to know anything about conversion rates or currency symbols – it relied on the ShippingChargeCalculator class to do that. We also encapsulated the shipping charge itself, in the ShippingCharge class.

❑ We have created a reusable class library for calculating international shipping charges that we could use equally well in a Windows Forms application, or a web service.

❑ We have a sustainable design. Suppose, for example, that Northwind were to start selling to customers in Egypt or Japan. All we would need to do is to add those countries to the ListOfCountries string in the class, and then add cases for those countries to the calculation steps. The ASP.NET pages themselves need never be touched.

Writing a Class Library for Database Access

We've learned how to write and use a class library, so now we'll examine how to involve ADO.NET in such development. In this section, we'll be examining a class library called `ProductInfo` that you'll find in the code download in a file called `ProductInfo.vb`. Due to its size, we won't be presenting all of its code in this text. Instead, we will:

❑ Cover a brief introduction to the theories involved in designing a database access class

❑ Review the key parts of a class designed to hold data values as an in-memory cache, including the sections that manage the cache and provide data that can be used in ASP.NET pages

❑ Show the class library being used in an ASP.NET page

If you're using the Access version of the Northwind *database, please refer to* ProductInfo_Access.vb *instead. That class file has a few comments in it that you will need to follow before using it as a replacement for the class presented in the book. The classes are, more or less, logically the same – but there are a number of small changes needed to make the code work with both Access and SQL Server databases.*

Designing Classes for Database Access

In this section, we'll talk about designing classes for database access. Such classes could be used exclusively to manage interactions between an application and a database, or just as one of several classes for working with data at various levels in an application. Our sample class library combines pure data access with some simple presentation support; however, the bulk of the presentation logic is left to ASP.NET pages.

If you've been asked to work with a database that already exists (like, say, Northwind), there's a standard approach to structuring your classes that will work well on most occasions. The rule is to represent each table in the database with a separate class, and to have properties in each class that correspond to the columns of the table in question. However, this won't *always* be the right approach, since there's some dependence on how the database was designed and normalized. There may also be some disagreement on exactly where the methods should go.

Some developers will say, "Keep the methods with the class." In this design, a method that updates the table will be in the class that represents that table. The advantage of this is that it promotes encapsulation and abstraction. The disadvantage is that it can make the object model more complex, and will not help to produce the simplest programming solution.

Other developers will say that a root class should hold most of the functionality, while the classes representing the tables should essentially just be 'property bags' (classes that encapsulate the columns of the table, but have little functionality beyond this). The advantage of this approach is that it tends to make for the simplest object model, but it tends to under-use abstraction and encapsulation. We're going to use this plan for our example, simply because it helps to keep the programming easy.

NwtLibrary Overview

We're going to construct quite a complex class library: the NwtLibrary. The purpose of the classes in this library is to load and cache data from three tables in the Northwind database: Suppliers, Categories, and Products. The cache will enhance the performance of our web applications by holding data in memory, rather than issuing a query to the database for each web page transition. This particular cache also allows for products, categories, or suppliers to be added, changed, or removed, and propagates these changes back to the database for permanent storage.

In an entity-relationship diagram, the parts of the database we need to use look like this:

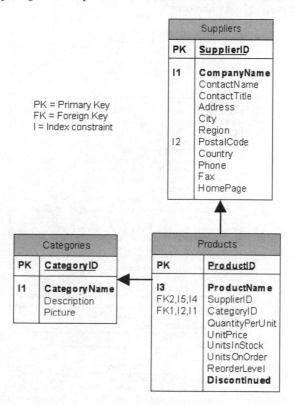

A slightly simplified diagram of the relationships between the classes in the library, represented in UML (Unified Modeling Language), looks like this:

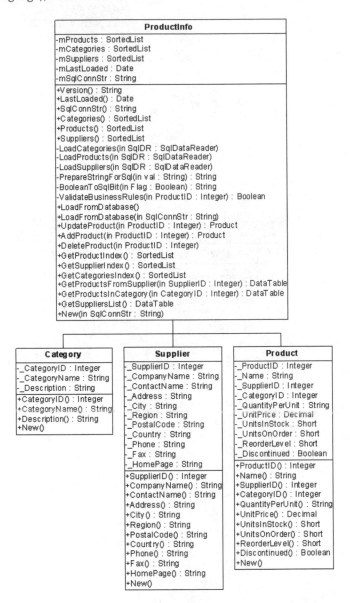

We've provided this view to help you see how the library will be structured, and how we'll go about using it in our ASP.NET pages. We won't be presenting all of the code in the chapter, but the full version is of course available in the download code for this book.

The Category, Product, and Supplier Classes

As you can see from the above diagram, the three subclasses of the main `ProductInfo` class are used to represent individual categories, products, and suppliers. Each of the classes is fairly simple, and uses the same three-part structure:

❑   Private variables to hold the actual values being stored

❑   Public properties to allow the other classes to read or change one of the private variables

❑   A class constructor with one parameter for each of the private variables

Try It Out – Constructing the Category Class

Let's put together the simplest of these classes – `Category` – to get an idea of what this structure actually looks like.

1. In Visual Studio, create a blank new solution called `NwtLibrary` in the `C:\BegASPDB\webroot\Ch10` directory. Then, add a new Visual Basic **Class Library** project, also called `NwtLibrary`. Lastly, to the project you just created, add a Visual Basic class file called `Category.vb`.

2. The first part of the class definition should be familiar: we simply import the `System` namespace:

```
Imports System

Public Class Category
```

3. We said that each class has private variables for holding the actual values in the database. In this example, we will give these variables the same names as the database columns, so that we can easily remember which value represents what data. The underscores that precede each name are there to help distinguish them from the properties we're about to look at.

```
Private _CategoryID As Integer
Private _CategoryName As String
Private _Description As String
```

4. Because we're storing the values in private variables, we need some way of providing public access to them. The most common way to do that is through the use of properties; there should be one property for each variable you need to expose.

```
Public Property CategoryID() As Integer
   Get
      Return _CategoryID
   End Get
   Set(ByVal Value As Integer)
      _CategoryID = Value
```

343

```
      End Set
   End Property

   Public Property CategoryName() As String
      Get
         Return _CategoryName
      End Get
      Set(ByVal Value As String)
         _CategoryName = Value
      End Set
   End Property

   Public Property Description() As String
      Get
         Return _Description
      End Get
      Set(ByVal Value As String)
         _Description = Value
      End Set
   End Property
```

5.   Implementing the properties like this means that we could, if we wished, add some data validation rules to the 'get' and 'set' methods. We know, for example, that the category name is limited to fifteen double-byte characters, and cannot be null. We *could* have written this:

```
Public Property CategoryName() As String
   Get
      Return _CategoryName
   End Get
   Set(ByVal Value As String)
      If Value.Length > 15 Then
         Throw New OverflowException("The category name can't exceed" & _
                                     " 15 characters in length.")
      End If
      If Value.Length = 0 Then
         Throw New NoNullAllowedException("The category name can't be null.")
      End If
      _CategoryName = Value
   End Set
End Property
```

6.   On this occasion, however, we're going to have a centralized function at a higher level for validating data as it's being changed – and we'll look at that in the next section. The last part of this class, then, defines its two constructors: one that has no parameters, and one that has three – one for each of the private variables. Having the second constructor allows us to create and populate an object in one operation.

```
Public Sub New()
End Sub
```

```
      Public Sub New(ByVal CategoryID As Integer, _
                     ByVal CategoryName As String, _
                     ByVal Description As String)
         MyBase.New()
         _CategoryID = CategoryID
         _CategoryName = CategoryName
         _Description = Description
      End Sub
   End Class
```

7. To check that this class will build properly, go to Build | Build Solution. Provided that goes well, we can move on to the next stage.

Try It Out – Constructing the ProductInfo Class

We will now construct the ProductInfo class, which holds collections of Category, Product, and Supplier objects that are created in its constructor. It loads data from the database into the cache, and has methods for saving it back. It also has methods for adding, updating, and removing a product from the cache and the database, and a few utility methods that will make developing our web applications easier.

1. Create a new Visual Basic class file in the NwtLibrary project, and call it ProductInfo.vb.

2. This class contains a great deal of code, and to get the examples to work you'll need to download the complete file from the Wrox web site. Here, we'll focus on some of its most important members, starting with the function that's responsible for getting the data from the database into the cache. Its name is LoadFromDatabase(), and it looks like this:

```
Public Sub LoadFromDatabase()
  Dim conn As New SqlConnection(mSqlConnStr)
  Dim cmd As SqlCommand
  Dim sqlDR As SqlDataReader

  If mCategories.Count > 0 Then
    mCategories.Clear()
  End If
  If mProducts.Count > 0 Then
    mProducts.Clear()
  End If
  If mSuppliers.Count > 0 Then
    mSuppliers.Clear()
  End If

  Try
    If mSqlConnStr.Length = 0 Then
      Throw New Exception("SQL Connection string cannot be zero-length")
    End If

    cmd = New SqlCommand(LOADSTATEMENT, conn)
    cmd.CommandType = CommandType.Text
```

LOADSTATEMENT is defined at the top of the file as a VB.NET string that holds a set of SQL statements, as follows:

```
Private Const LOADSTATEMENT As String = "SET NOCOUNT ON;" & _
  "SELECT CategoryID, CategoryName, Description FROM Categories " & _
  "ORDER BY CategoryID;" & _
  "SELECT ProductID, ProductName, SupplierID, CategoryID, " & _
  "QuantityPerUnit, UnitPrice, UnitsInStock, UnitsOnOrder, " & _
  "ReorderLevel, Discontinued FROM Products ORDER BY ProductID;" & _
  "SELECT SupplierID, CompanyName, ContactName, Address, City, " & _
  "Region, PostalCode, Country, Phone, Fax, HomePage FROM Suppliers " & _
  "ORDER BY SupplierID;"
```

3. The following call opens a connection to the database; after that, we can use the ExecuteReader() method of a SqlCommand object to return an instance of the SqlDataReader class. We can then pass the SqlDataReader object to other functions in order to load specific columns of the result set into the appropriate collections.

```
conn.Open()

sqlDR = cmd.ExecuteReader(CommandBehavior.CloseConnection)

LoadCategories(sqlDR)
LoadProducts(sqlDR)
LoadSuppliers(sqlDR)
```

4. It's almost always helpful to use the CommandBehavior.CloseConnection option on the ExecuteReader() method call. When the command is executed, the associated Connection object is closed when the DataReader object is closed. This frees the resources used by the database connection for you automatically, just in case you forget to add code to do so.

```
    mLastLoaded = DateTime.Now

Catch SqlExc As SqlException
  ' Error handling code
Catch Exc As Exception
  ' Error handling code
Finally
  If Not cmd Is Nothing Then
    cmd.Cancel()
  End If

  If Not conn Is Nothing Then
    If conn.State <> ConnectionState.Closed Then
      conn.Close()
    End If
  End If
End Try
End Sub
```

5. The code for loading the various columns into memory is fairly straightforward. As long as data remains to be read, we pull each of the fields out in sequence, and then use those values to create a new instance of the underlying collection type. The new instance is then added to the appropriate collection.

The listing below shows the `LoadCategories()` method; the `LoadProducts()` and `LoadSuppliers()` methods are entirely analogous to this one.

```
Private Sub LoadCategories(ByVal SqlDR As SqlDataReader)
  Try
    While SqlDR.Read

      ' Provide some default values
      Dim CategoryID As Integer = 0
      Dim CategoryName As String = ""
      Dim Description As String = ""

      If Not SqlDR.IsDBNull(0) Then
        CategoryID = SqlDR.GetInt32(0)
      End If
      If Not SqlDR.IsDBNull(1) Then
        CategoryName = SqlDR.GetString(1)
      End If
      If Not SqlDR.IsDBNull(2) Then
        Description = SqlDR.GetString(2)
      End If

      mCategories.Add(CategoryID, _
                New Category(CategoryID, CategoryName, Description))
    End While

    SqlDR.NextResult()

  Catch SqlExc As SqlException
    ' Error handling code
  Catch Exc As Exception
    ' Error handling code
  End Try
End Sub
```

6. Products in the cache can be updated or deleted, and a new product can be added to the cache. The functions that perform these tasks are fairly similar to one another, so here we will just look at the one that updates a product. Here's how it begins:

```
Public Function UpdateProduct(ByVal ProductID As Integer, _
                        ByVal Name As String, _
                        ByVal SupplierID As Integer, _
                        ByVal CategoryID As Integer, _
                        ByVal QuantityPerUnit As String, _
                        ByVal UnitPrice As Decimal, _
```

```
                              ByVal UnitsInStock As Short, _
                              ByVal UnitsOnOrder As Short, _
                              ByVal ReorderLevel As Short, _
                              ByVal Discontinued As Boolean) As Product
        Dim conn As SqlConnection
        Dim cmd As SqlCommand
        Dim prod As Product
```

7. This function knows what server, database, and credentials are used, as these are stored in the `mSqlConnStr` variable that was set up in the constructor and is available throughout the class.

```
If mSqlConnStr.Length = 0 Then
   Throw New Exception("SQL Connection string cannot be zero-length")
End If


If Not mProducts.Contains(ProductID) Then
   Throw New Exception("Unknown and non-updateable ProductID of " & _
                      ProductID.ToString() & " used.")
End If
```

8. Before we update the product, we need to make sure its data is valid. The `ValidateBusinessRules()` function does exactly that.

```
Try
    If ValidateBusinessRules(ProductID, Name, SupplierID, CategoryID, _
                            QuantityPerUnit, Discontinued) Then
```

9. In the next part of the function, we use basic ADO.NET functions to create a `Command` object and populate it with an appropriate T-SQL `UPDATE` command.

```
        cmd = New SqlCommand()
        cmd.CommandType = CommandType.Text

        cmd.CommandText = "SET NOCOUNT ON;" & _
          "UPDATE Products SET " & _
          "ProductName = '" & PrepareStringForSql(Name.ToString()) & "'," &_
          "SupplierID = " & SupplierID.ToString() & "," & _
          "CategoryID = " & CategoryID.ToString() & "," & _
          "QuantityPerUnit = '" & _
                  PrepareStringForSql(QuantityPerUnit.ToString()) & "'," & _
          "UnitPrice = " & UnitPrice.ToString() & "," & _
          "UnitsInStock = " & UnitsInStock.ToString() & "," & _
          "UnitsOnOrder = " & UnitsOnOrder.ToString() & "," & _
          "ReorderLevel = " & ReorderLevel.ToString() & "," & _
          "Discontinued = " & BooleanToSqlBit(Discontinued) & " " & _
          "WHERE ProductID = " & ProductID.ToString() & ";"
```

10. We then create and open a connection to the database, and associate it with the command object we just set up. Then we can execute the command.

```
conn = New SqlConnection(mSqlConnStr)
conn.Open()

cmd.Connection = conn

cmd.ExecuteNonQuery()
```

11. Finally, we need to update the cached version of the product. To do that, we need to find out where in the collection the updated product is. With that information, we can update its properties, and then drop the updated product into the collection.

```
prod = CType(Products(ProductID), Product)

prod.CategoryID = CategoryID
prod.Discontinued = Discontinued
prod.Name = Name
prod.QuantityPerUnit = QuantityPerUnit
prod.ReorderLevel = ReorderLevel
prod.SupplierID = SupplierID
prod.UnitPrice = UnitPrice
prod.UnitsInStock = UnitsInStock
prod.UnitsOnOrder = UnitsOnOrder

Products(ProductID) = prod

Return prod
End If

Catch SqlExc As SqlException
' Error handling code
Catch Exc As Exception
' Error handling code
Finally
If Not cmd Is Nothing Then
cmd.Cancel()
End If

If Not conn Is Nothing Then
If conn.State <> ConnectionState.Closed Then
conn.Close()
End If
End If
End Try
End Function
```

12. There are three public functions that return `SortedList` objects containing the names of the products, suppliers and categories respectively. One of these, `GetSupplierIndex()`, returns a `SortedList` that's keyed by the `SupplierID`. This is rather useful for populating a drop-down list, as you'll soon see.

```
Public Function GetSupplierIndex() As SortedList
  Dim sl As New SortedList()
  Dim sup As Supplier

  For Each sup In mSuppliers.Values
    sl.Add(sup.SupplierID, sup.CompanyName)
  Next
  Return sl
End Function
```

13. The `GetProductsFromSupplier()` function takes a `SupplierID` as a parameter and returns an ADO.NET `DataTable`. This is an ideal way to get a list of all of the products that Northwind offers from a particular vendor, because it can be bound to an ASP.NET `DataGrid` web control. The function starts by creating a new `DataTable` and then adds the desired columns to it.

```
Public Function GetProductsFromSupplier(ByVal SupplierID As Integer) _
    As DataTable
  Dim dt As New DataTable("Products")
  Dim prod As Product
  Dim cat As Category
  Dim dr As DataRow

  Try

    dt.Columns.Add(New DataColumn("ProductName", GetType(String)))
    dt.Columns.Add(New DataColumn("CategoryName", GetType(String)))
    dt.Columns.Add(New DataColumn("QuantityPerUnit", GetType(String)))
    dt.Columns.Add(New DataColumn("UnitPrice", GetType(String)))
    dt.Columns.Add(New DataColumn("UnitsInStock", GetType(Short)))
    dt.Columns.Add(New DataColumn("UnitsOnOrder", GetType(Short)))
    dt.Columns.Add(New DataColumn("ReorderLevel", GetType(Short)))
    dt.Columns.Add(New DataColumn("Discontinued", GetType(Boolean)))
```

14. Then it becomes a simple matter to iterate through the products collection, find products from the given supplier, and populate its values into a `DataRow`. The `DataRow` can then be appended to the `DataTable`.

```
    For Each prod In mProducts.Values
      If prod.SupplierID = SupplierID Then

        dr = dt.NewRow()

        dr("ProductName") = prod.Name
        cat = CType(mCategories(prod.CategoryID), Category)
```

```
            dr("CategoryName") = cat.CategoryName
            dr("QuantityPerUnit") = prod.QuantityPerUnit
            dr("UnitPrice") = prod.UnitPrice.ToString("c")
            dr("UnitsOnOrder") = prod.UnitsOnOrder.ToString
            dr("UnitsInStock") = prod.UnitsInStock.ToString
            dr("ReorderLevel") = prod.ReorderLevel.ToString
            dr("Discontinued") = prod.Discontinued.ToString

            dt.Rows.Add(dr)
        End If
    Next
    Return dt
  Catch Exc As Exception
     ' Error handling code
  End Try
End Function
```

15. Now that we've completed our review of the component class, let's see it in action. The best place to start is to make sure that you've loaded and compiled the `NwtLibrary` project into the `NwtLibrary` solution. Ensure that you've added the `Product` and `Supplier` classes from the download to your solution, and you'll be ready to go.

Using the Class Library in a Web Application

In this section, we'll use the class library that we just reviewed in a fairly straightforward ASP.NET web application that will present the user with a drop-down list of suppliers, and list the products supplied by whichever one they choose.

Try It Out – Creating Another Web Application

1. In the `NwtLibrary` solution, create a new Visual Basic **ASP.NET Web Application**, calling it `Nwt`.

2. Delete the **WebForm1.aspx** page from the newly created project.

3. From the Visual Studio .NET main menu, select **Project | Add Reference**.

4. Select the **Projects** tab, then select the `NwtLibrary` project, and add that as a reference.

5. In the **Solution Explorer**, right-click on `Nwt` and select **Set as StartUp Project**.

Just like an Internet application, we want to make the best use of the available computing resources on the intranet servers. With that in mind, we'll use the familiar technique of placing an instance of our class into the ASP.NET `Application` object. To do this, we will make a change to `global.asax` file in the `Nwt` project.

6. Update the `Application_Start()` procedure in the `global.asax` file of `Nwt` as follows:

```
Sub Application_Start(ByVal sender As Object, ByVal e As EventArgs)
' Fires when the application is started
' Put the database connection string into the application space
Application.Add("ConnStr", _
                "Data Source=localhost;Initial Catalog=Northwind;" & _
                "User ID=sa;Password=password;Persist Security Info=True")

' Create a new instance of the ProductInfo class based on the given
' connection string, then put the instance into the application space
Application.Add("ProductInfo", _
                New NwtLibrary.ProductInfo(CStr(Application("ConnStr"))))
End Sub
```

7. Add a new Web Form to the `Nwt` project and call it `ProductsFromSupplier.aspx`.

8. Add the following code as the HTML for this page. There's nothing in this that you haven't seen before; we're just placing a drop-down list and a data grid on the page, ready to receive data from the code-behind file.

```
<%@ Page Language="vb" AutoEventWireup="true"
        Codebehind="ProductsFromSupplier.aspx.vb"
        Inherits="Nwt.NwtNet.ProductsBySupplier"%>
<!DOCTYPE html PUBLIC "-//W3C//DTD HTML 4.0 Transitional//EN">
<html>
  <head>
    <title>Products From Supplier</title>
    <meta name="GENERATOR" content="Microsoft Visual Studio.NET 7.0">
    <meta name="CODE_LANGUAGE" content="Visual Basic 7.0">
    <meta name="vs_defaultClientScript" content="JavaScript">
    <meta name="vs_targetSchema"
          content="http://schemas.microsoft.com/intellisense/ie5">
    <link rel="stylesheet" href="wrox6195.css">
  </head>
  <body>
    <form id="Form1" method="post" runat="server">
      <h1>NwtNET - Products From Suppliers</h1>
      <p>Please select a supplier:
        <asp:DropDownList id="SupplierSelector" runat="server"
                          AutoPostBack="True">
        </asp:DropDownList>
      </p>
      <p>
        <hr/>
        <asp:DataGrid id="ProductsGrid" runat="server" Font-Size="9pt"
                      CellPadding="2" CellSpacing="2" BorderWidth="0px">
          <AlternatingItemStyle VerticalAlign="Top" BackColor="#E0E0E0">
          </AlternatingItemStyle>
          <HeaderStyle Font-Bold="True"></HeaderStyle>
        </asp:DataGrid>
```

```
      </p>
      <p>
        Data as of:
        <asp:Label id="LastLoaded" runat="server"></asp:Label>
        <br/>
        Component Version:
        <asp:Label id="ComponentVersion" runat="server"></asp:Label>
        <br/>
      </p>
    </form>
  </body>
</html>
```

9. Next, we need to add code to the automatically generated code-behind file. Much of this is located in the `Page_Load()` event handler, which creates a `ProductInfo` object, places it in the ASP.NET `Application` object, and then uses it to populate the drop-down list.

```
Imports NwtLibrary

Namespace NwtNet
  Public Class ProductsFromSupplier
    Inherits System.Web.UI.Page
    Protected WithEvents SupplierSelector _
        As System.Web.UI.WebControls.DropDownList
    Protected WithEvents ProductsGrid As System.Web.UI.WebControls.DataGrid
    Protected WithEvents LastLoaded As System.Web.UI.WebControls.Label

#Region " Web Form Designer Generated Code "

    <System.Diagnostics.DebuggerStepThrough()> _
        Private Sub InitializeComponent()

    End Sub

    Private Sub Page_Init(ByVal sender As System.Object, _
                          ByVal e As System.EventArgs) Handles MyBase.Init
      'CODEGEN: This method call is required by the Web Form Designer
      'Do not modify it using the code editor.
      InitializeComponent()
    End Sub

#End Region

    Private Sub Page_Load(ByVal sender As System.Object, _
                          ByVal e As System.EventArgs) Handles MyBase.Load
      Dim pi As ProductInfo
      Dim sl As SortedList
      Dim key As Integer
      Dim str As String
```

```
        If Not IsPostBack Then
          pi = Application("ProductInfo")
          sl = pi.GetSupplierIndex()

          SupplierSelector.Items.Add( _
                New ListItem("Please select a supplier", "0"))

          For Each key In sl.Keys
            SupplierSelector.Items.Add(New ListItem(CStr(sl(key)), _
                                        key.ToString))
          Next

          LastLoaded.Text = pi.LastLoaded.ToString("u")
        End If
      End Sub
```

10. The `SupplierSelector_SelectedIndexChanged()` handler responds to changes in the user's selection from the drop-down list by re-calling the `ProductInfo` object's `GetProductsFromSupplier()` method with the new information:

```
      Private Sub SupplierSelector_SelectedIndexChanged( _
          ByVal sender As System.Object, ByVal e As System.EventArgs) _
          Handles SupplierSelector.SelectedIndexChanged
        Dim SelectedItem As Integer
        Dim pi As ProductInfo

        SelectedITem = Convert.ToInt32(SupplierSelector.SelectedItem.Value)

        If SelectedITem > 0 Then
          pi = Application("ProductInfo")
          ProductsGrid.DataSource = pi.GetProductsFromSupplier(SelectedItem)
          ProductsGrid.DataBind()

        Else
          ProductsGrid.DataSource = Nothing
          ProductsGrid.DataBind()
        End If

      End Sub
    End Class
End Namespace
```

11. Finally, in the Solution Explorer, right-click on this Web Form, and select **Build and Browse** to run this page. When executed, the page should look something like this:

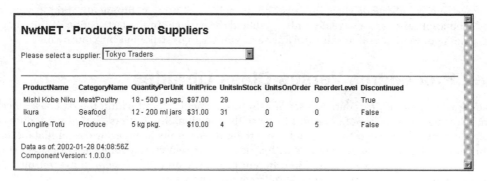

What we've Learned

In truth, there's not very much that's new here... we've just taken what you already knew about database access with ASP.NET and ADO.NET, and combined it with the fruits of this chapter's research into class libraries, to produce this application. Let's take a few moments to review the key points:

❑ We've simplified our ASP.NET pages, which no longer have to make database connections for themselves. In addition, we've simplified access to the data itself. We don't have to deal with tables and columns directly, and there are no SQL statements in the ASP.NET pages, either.

❑ We've given a double boost to the performance of our ASP.NET applications by caching the product data in the Application space. The first boost comes from having just one load of the data take place, when the application starts. Any subsequent request can just fetch the in-memory values of data from the component instead of from the database. Second, by putting the component into the Application object, all pages can share that one instance, saving the additional queries that would come from having that code in every web page.

❑ We've encapsulated the data within the classes in our class library. Any changes to the cached data must be made through properties of the classes. Changes to these values are managed through well-defined interfaces that make sure Northwind's business rules are adhered to.

❑ We have a somewhat sustainable design. If Northwind decides to change to a different database – perhaps MySQL, or DB/2 – we should be able to update the component to use the OLE DB versions of ADO.NET's connection and command objects to read the data from these sources, without necessitating a change to our ASP.NET pages.

You'll doubtless have noticed that our sample application here doesn't use all of the functionality of the class library – the `ProductInfo` class has a number of methods that we haven't called. However, this is entirely consistent with designing our libraries to be reusable. By anticipating the needs that users are likely to have, but being careful not to include inappropriate functionality, we're hoping that the library will become an attractive proposition. When you've finished examining the worked examples in this chapter, you could try building some applications that make further use of it.

What Else Do We Need to Know?

While we've certainly made some inroads into the subject of using componentization in your ASP.NET-based web applications, we've really only scratched the surface. In the last section of this chapter, we'll look at some of the issues that will surely arise as you begin to strike out on your own.

Stored Procedures Versus Class Libraries

As you know, a stored procedure is a set of T-SQL statements stored within the database in compiled form, allowing any number of programs to reuse the functionality it offers. Stored procedures can be helpful in controlling access to data, and using them often results in superior overall database and application performance. Compare this with a class library, which is a collection of classes stored in a compiled form. They too can be used in different programs, and can be helpful in controlling access to data and application logic. Which then should we use, and when?

The principal difference between these two lies in the scope within which each is used. Because stored procedures are stored and executed on the SQL Server, they tend to be used only by those classes that directly interact with the database. A class library, on the other hand, may be used by any class that can 'see' it. In practice, it's quite common to see components that manage database access use stored procedures, allowing the developer to separate data operations from business operations. We'll have more to say on this subject in the later sub section called *Complexity*.

Compatibility

It's a sure thing that at some stage after you've written a class library you'll need to update it – to add functionality, or to improve its performance, or to fix that bug you never quite got to grips with first time around. When you do so, you need to be careful to ensure that the changes you make have no adverse effects on the applications that have been happily using your library so far.

Suppose, for example, that you have a function that expects three strings in its parameter list:

```
Public Function GetSummary(Msg As String, Val As String, Amt As String) _
    As String
  Return Msg & ": " & Val & " = " & Amt
End Function
```

If, in some ASP.NET page, you have a statement like:

```
ThisTextBox.Text = GetSummary("Notice", "Balance Due", BalDue.ToString("c"))
```

Then clearly, this will assign "Notice: Balance Due = $150.25" to the Text property of ThisTextBox. Now, suppose that for some reason you replace the GetSummary() function with a new version, as follows:

```
Public Function GetSummary(Msg as String, Val as String, Amt as Decimal) _
    As String
  Return Msg & ": " & Val & " = " & Amt.ToString("c")
End Function
```

If you don't remember to update the web page to:

```
ThisTextBox.Text = GetSummary("Notice", "Balance Due", BalDue)
```

Your users will likely see an ugly error complaining about the type of `BalDue`, instead of the expected page. This occurs because you didn't recompile the ASP.NET web page (where you would have caught this error); you only recompiled the class library.

Typically, it won't be you that suffers the ill effects of your changes. Rather, it will be the developers who reused your class library. Unless you have good documentation, they won't know that you changed the function, and they won't expect to have to update their pages. Here are three rules of thumb for writing good components that avoid compatibility problems:

❑ As far as possible, consider all non-private interfaces as 'set in stone'.
That is, you should design your classes as completely as possible before releasing them for use. It's acceptable to expose new interfaces at a later date, but don't remove or change existing ones.

❑ If you must change the interface of a public method, don't replace it.
Rather, you should use overloading. For example, if we just added the new version of GetSummary() and changed the previous version as follows:

```
Public Function GetSummary(Msg As String, Val As String, Amt As Decimal) _
    As String
  Return Msg & ": " & Val & " = " & Amt.ToString("c")
End Function

Public Function GetSummary(Msg as String, Val as String, Amt as String) _
    As String
  Return GetSummary(Msg, Val, Convert.ToDecimal(Amt))
End Function
```

The developers who didn't update their pages wouldn't get errors, and those who did update would be able to use your library as well. Keep in mind, though, that some users may be using implicit data type conversions, so they may find themselves calling the wrong version of the method unexpectedly.

❑ Document and distribute documentation about your changes on a before-and-after basis.
Ideally, when you add a new method to a class, it's best to state how it worked before and how it will work after your change. If you replace a method with a new-but-similarly-named method, show both the old interface and the new one. This will make it easier for other developers to update their pages and programs that use your class library, because they will be better able to understand the changes they have to make.

Complexity

Although the use of classes and class libraries produces simpler code in the end, it can be a challenge to get the design right first time. From a functional perspective, the approach we took with `NwtLibrary` is perhaps not the best solution, because we've tried to do a lot of things in one place. Our `ProductInfo` class not only handles the task of getting data into and out of the database, but it also validates business rules and provides elements for use in the user interface. As it stands, if we needed to change any of these elements, we would have to redistribute the whole component after compiling (and testing) it.

An alternative design would be to have multiple specialized classes. We could have one class that deals only with the loading and updating of data in the database; another for building the objects needed for presentation in our web pages; and yet another for checking and assuring the integrity of the data according to Northwind's business rules. These three layers – *database access*, *business rules*, and *presentation* – are commonly used boundaries in good componentized software. If we focus our database access class purely on getting data to and from the database, then our business rules and presentation rules can interface with that. If we subsequently need to change the database hosting our data, we can just focus on changing and updating that class, without affecting the other two.

That's not to say that we should aim for a goal of having only one or two methods in each class, resulting in dozens of components supporting one design goal. This greatly increases the complexity for developers who need to figure out which class they should use, and increases the chances that a bad change will go undetected. It's a balancing act, but ideally you should try to keep the number of classes (and class libraries) as low as possible, without sacrificing too much flexibility.

A very important issue related to complexity is that class libraries act like multipliers – if a 'bad' change is made to a class library, it can break several applications simultaneously, multiplying the impact of that change by the number of affected pages. An apparently innocent change can result in an avalanche of problems that you have to dig through in order to find the cause. The best way to combat this effect is to write a set of pages that you know will test your classes thoroughly, and to adhere to a thorough testing procedure before releasing a new version.

Documentation

A cost of using class libraries that's often overlooked is that their documentation generally needs to be more detailed than one might expect. This is largely because many developers want to understand how your classes work (particularly the data flow through them) in order to use them properly. You will also need to provide a clear set of statements about what the component does in normal situations, and how it reacts to exceptions. Also consider providing documentation of the attributes of each exposed method, in addition to traditional documentation. More often than not, the developer will open the object browser to see a brief description of what a method does and how to use it, before they crack open 'real' documentation.

Having this level of documentation also benefits you when, six months or more after you've released a library, you need to make a change. Rather than trying to remember how it worked, you can start by reviewing your own documentation. When making a change to a class, remember our rules of thumb: overload rather than replace, show the before-and-after state of the component, and be careful of issues relating to automatic type conversion.

Summary

Let's finish up by reviewing what we set out to accomplish. At the beginning of this chapter, we said that you would learn how to:

❑ Write and use class libraries in your ASP.NET applications

❑ Write and use database access classes in your ASP.NET applications

❑ Understand when and why to use componentization in your applications

We've shown you how to accomplish the first goal in our international shipping charge calculator, and the second by writing a fairly complex data access library. Over the course of the chapter, we've spoken at length about the benefits and costs of componentized designs. At this stage, we pass the baton to you. Experiment with the full versions of the sample projects, and see whether you can improve on them. And remember that in the .NET Framework class library, you have an enormous, well-documented example of what it's possible to achieve.

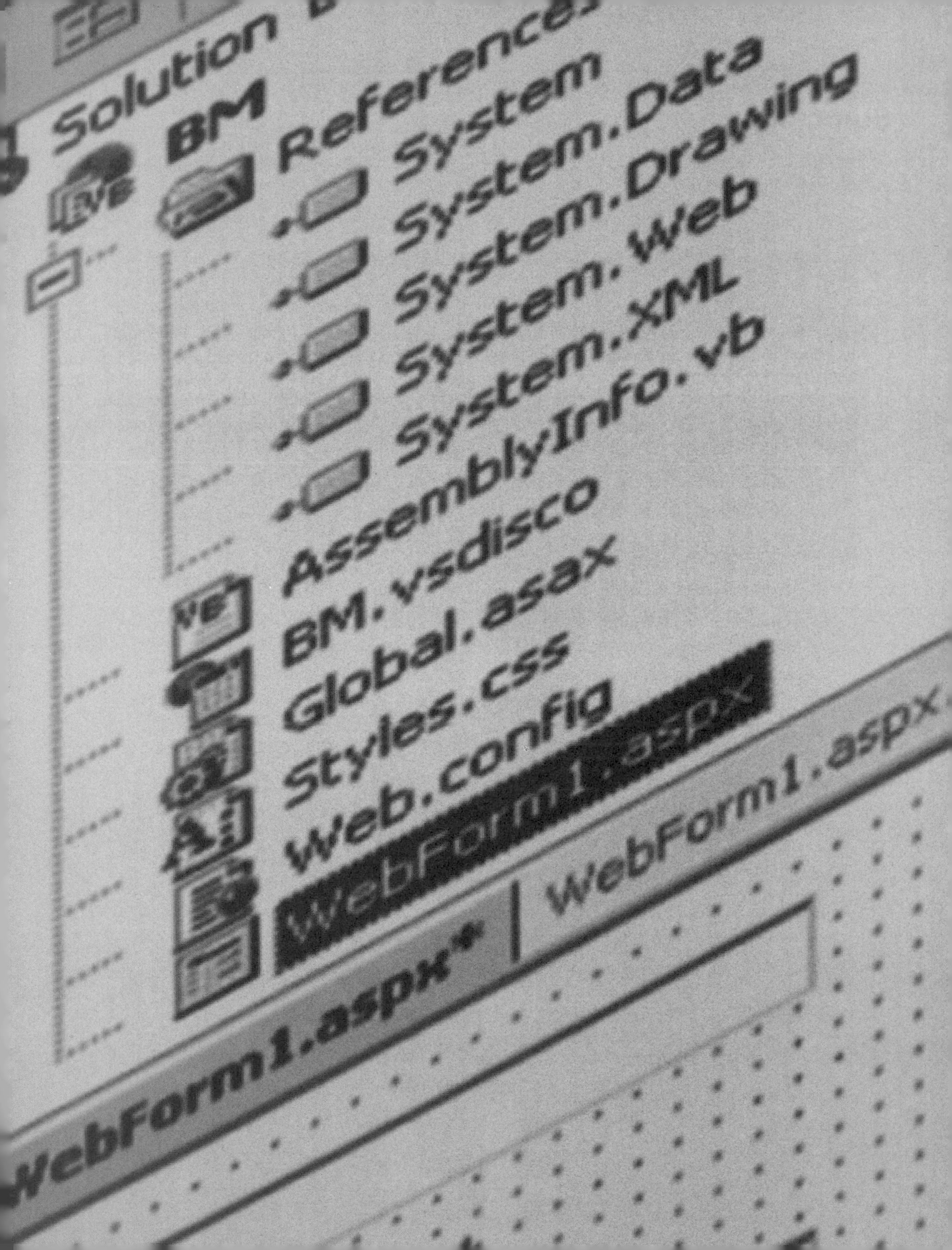

Solution
BM
References
System
System.Data
System.Drawing
System. Web
System.XML
AssemblyInfo.vb
Assembly
BM.vsdisco
Global.asax
Styles.css
Web.config
WebForm1.aspx
WebForm1.aspx* | WebForm1.aspx
WebForm1.aspx*

Performance

Given enough time and resources, a skilled development team should be able to develop an ASP.NET application that retrieves data in an efficient manner. To address performance properly, however, is to recognize that the tasks of developing and coding the end product must both be optimized. At the end of this chapter, we'll present a series of strategies for good and efficient development practices that ultimately result in good and efficient code for accessing data using ADO.NET.

To get there from here, however, we need to undertake a survey of different technologies and techniques, and come up with some objective tests. For the purpose of this exercise, the focus will be on data access performance, rather than on the performance of ASP.NET. We will cover topics such as:

- ❑ Handling connections and understanding pooling.

- ❑ Using performance counters and the PerfMon utility to measure performance and detect limits on scalability.

- ❑ Evaluating the usefulness of the .NET CLR Data, ASP.NET Application, and ASP.NET System performance counters.

- ❑ Determining the right situations in which to use a data reader rather than a dataset.

- ❑ Determining if and when it is best to migrate from existing ADO code to .NET, rather than upgrading to ADO.NET.

- ❑ Determining what style of access is best for retrieving information from a dataset and a data reader.

- ❑ Determining the performance gains (or otherwise) from using a typed dataset compared to a late-bound dataset.

Performance Measurement

Before we can start testing, we need a means of extracting useful information from those tests. For our first experiments that measure data access performance, we'll adopt a straightforward technique that uses a simple plan. We'll:

- ❑ Determine the current time (DateTime.Now)

- ❑ Run the data access task to be examined

- ❑ Determine the current time again, and subtract the start time from the end time

Subtracting one `DateTime` object from another results in a `TimeSpan` object. This exposes a `TotalMilliseconds()` method that returns the number of milliseconds in the time span. (Even in this era of GHz CPUs, milliseconds are a precise enough measure of performance.) The code we'll be using to test performance will therefore look something like this:

```
Dim startTime As DateTime
Dim howLong As TimeSpan
Dim result As String

startTime = DateTime.Now

' Perform database task to monitor here

howLong = DateTime.Now.Subtract(startTime)
result = String.Format("{0} ms", howLong.TotalMilliseconds)
```

> ASP.NET's **`Trace.Write()`** method is one way to display the result string (the **`result`** variable) so generated. The perk of using **`Trace.Write()`** is that its functionality can be turned on and off by using the **`web.config`** file in combination with the **`Trace`** attribute of the **`@Page`** directive:
>
> `<% @Page Trace="true" %>`

The results of performance tests like these – especially in one-off trials – should not be viewed as gospel. To determine the results in this chapter, each test was run several times in order to reduce the chances of an external process interfering with performance. The numbers should be compared relative to one another, and certainly do not reflect every environment; the machine used to generate the performance numbers for this chapter was a 1.2GHz PIII with 1GB of RAM.

Connection Pooling

With our timing strategy in place, we can move on. It's well known that connecting to a database can be a slow process, and that connection pools can reduce the length of time it takes. A **connection pool** is simply a set of connections with like connection strings. The idea is that if a connection is made with one set of attributes, this connection is *not* immediately closed when the `Close()` method of the connection object is called. Rather, it's placed in a pool. If another connection is then opened with exactly the same set of connection string parameters, the pooled connection is returned, rather than going to all the work of creating an entirely new connection from scratch. If the system becomes less loaded, this pooled connection will reach a timeout threshold and will be truly be closed. Connection pooling improves performance and facilitates the scalability of an application that accesses data.

OLE DB and Connection Pooling

By default, an OLE DB .NET connection object takes advantage of connection pooling. To be technically correct, connection pooling is implemented in OLE DB using **resource pooling**, which ties it to a couple of other performance enhancers: automatic transaction enlistment, and a client-side cursor engine. These services are ultimately controlled by the OLE DB Services connection attribute, which has a default value of -1. However, a variety of permutations exist:

Services Provided	OLE DB Services
Connection pooling, transaction enlistment, client-side cursors	-1
Transaction enlistment, client-side cursors	-2
Client-side cursors	-4
Connection pooling, transaction enlistment	-5
Transaction enlistment	-6
No services provided	0

> *The various permutations associated with the OLE DB Services connection attribute are a little unintuitive, and beyond the scope of the current discussion. For more information, take a look at the MSDN article entitled* Overriding Provider Service Defaults, *which you'll find at ms-help://MS.VSCC/MS.MSDNVS/oledb/htm/oledboverriding_provider_service_defaults.htm*

What's pertinent to our performance discussion is simply that the OLE DB Services connection attribute *can* be used to disable connection pooling. For best results, this should take place when connections do not need to be reused, meaning that resources should be cleaned up with deliberate immediacy.

SQL Server and Connection Pooling

The developers of SQL Server's .NET data provider were so certain that connection pooling was important that it's the default behavior exhibited by SqlConnection objects. The following example demonstrates this.

Try it Out – Evaluating Connection Pooling using SqlConnection

1. In Visual Basic .NET, start a new web application project called WXSinglePool.

2. Using Visual Studio .NET's **Toolbox**, drag-and-drop a Button (which should be named ButtonTestConnection), a TextBox (which should be named TextBoxNumIterations), a Label (which should be named LabelResults), and a CheckBox (which should be named CheckBoxCloseConnection). The TextBoxNumIterations box will used to determine the number of SqlConnection objects to open during a test.

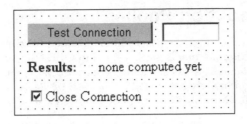

3. View the code behind the `WebForm1.aspx` file by choosing the **View | Code** menu item.

4. Since we're using the SQL Server .NET data provider, it makes sense to add an `Imports` declaration to the top of our source code file:

```
Imports System.Data.SqlClient
```

5. Finally, add the following event handler to help us evaluate how `SqlConnection` objects utilize pooling:

```
Private Sub ButtonTestConnection_Click(ByVal sender As System.Object, _
              ByVal e As System.EventArgs) Handles ButtonTestConnection.Click

  Dim numTests As Integer = Int32.Parse(TextBoxNumIterations.Text)
  Dim count As Integer = 0
  Dim connString As String
  Dim startTime = DateTime.Now
  Dim howLong As TimeSpan = New TimeSpan()

  Try
    connString = "server=localhost;database=northwind;" & _
                 "uid=sa;pwd=;"
    startTime = DateTime.Now
    For count = 1 To numTests
      Dim conn As New SqlConnection(connString)
      conn.Open()
      If CheckBoxCloseConnection.Checked Then
        conn.Close()
      End If
    Next

    howLong = DateTime.Now.Subtract(startTime)
    LabelResults.Text = String.Format("{0} ms", howLong.TotalMilliseconds)

  Catch ex As System.InvalidOperationException
    howLong = DateTime.Now.Subtract(startTime)
    GC.Collect()
    LabelResults.Text = String.Format("Pool count exceeded ({0} ms): {1}", _
                                  howLong.TotalMilliseconds, count)
  Catch ex As Exception
    LabelResults.Text = String.Format("Exception: " & ex.ToString())
  End Try
End Sub
```

How It Works

The previous code sample opens and closes an `SqlConnection` object repeatedly. On the system under test, the time taken to open and close one million connections is a little less than thirty-five seconds, which translates to 35 microseconds per connection! Clearly there is some kind of pooling going on.

By default, the `SqlConnection` class's `Pooling` connection string attribute is set to `true`, but it can be set to `false`, thus disabling pooling. An example of a connection string with connection pooling disabled would be as follows:

```
connString = "server=localhost;database=northwind;" & _
             "uid=sa;pwd=;pooling=false"
```

After disabling pooling, opening and closing a thousand database connections takes approximately three seconds (3 ms per connection). This is much longer than the pooling case. Also, this number was generated with the ASP.NET application and SQL Server database residing on the same machine. If the SQL Server database had resided on a remote host, the performance difference between using and not using connection pools would have been amplified further still.

In our code above, a `CheckBox` control is used to disable the closing of the connection:

```
If CheckBoxCloseConnection.Checked Then
  conn.Close()
End If
```

The purpose of disabling the closing of the connection is to demonstrate that connection pooling has an upper bound with respect to the number of connections pooled. When this number is exceeded, an `InvalidOperationException` is raised and the following error text is generated (as the `Message` property of the exception):

Timeout expired. The timeout period elapsed prior to obtaining a connection from the pool. This may have occurred because all pooled connections were in use and max pool size was reached.

The code that handles this exception inside our form is as follows:

```
Catch ex As System.InvalidOperationException
  howLong = DateTime.Now.Subtract(startTime)
  GC.Collect()
  LabelResults.Text = String.Format("Pool count exceeded ({0} ms): {1}", _
                              howLong.TotalMilliseconds, count)
```

Note that garbage collection is initiated here using the GC class's `Collect()` method. This step is performed in order to ensure that all of the orphaned database connections are closed; the garbage collector closes these connections as part of object finalization.

The previous error-handling code snippet can be used to demonstrate that the upper bound on connections in the connection pool is 100, but it's not quite as simple as that. The upper bound of 100 applies to the number of pooled connections *per different connection string*. A connection string is 'different' if it contains a different host, database catalog, user, or security type. For example, the following two connection strings are different because their database attributes are associated with different values:

```
conn1 = "server=localhost; database=northwind; uid=sa; pwd=;"
conn2 = "server=localhost; database=nobreezeatall; uid=sa; pwd=;"
```

Sometimes, development projects can inadvertently create different connection strings, and therefore inflate the number of pooled connections. To demonstrate this, consider a team of three developers, each of whom uses the same basic connection string, except that they use different values for the Connection Timeout connection attribute. This would cause three separate connection pools to be created, and each such pool would have a default maximum of 100 connections. The worst-case scenario would be three hundred connections. Scaling up, if twenty developers each accessed five different databases, and each developer used a different timeout setting, the worst case would get worse very quickly: 20 developers times five databases times 100 in the pool means up to ten thousand connections, and an enormous drain on resources.

Try It Out – Creating Separate Connection Pools

The WXMultiPool application, which is available for download from www.wrox.com along with the rest of the code for this book, demonstrates a variety of connection options that can result in the creation of separate connection pools.

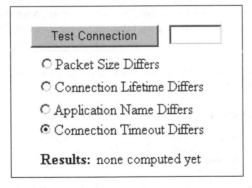

This ASP.NET form contains four RadioButton instances that correspond to specifying different values for the following connection attributes: Packet Size, Connection Timeout, Connection Lifetime, and Application Name; and a Test Connection Button. Feel free to have a look around the code before we discuss this example.

How It Works

When the Test Connection button is clicked, SQL Server connections are opened but not closed. When the upper bound is reached with respect to the number of connections pooled, the application ceases running. In order to demonstrate that the esoteric connection attributes discussed above really can cause multiple connection pools, the application behaves differently for even iterations and odd iterations. When the Connection Timeout Differs box is checked, for example, odd iterations are given a timeout value of 15, while even ones get a value of 16. The following table shows a full list of these different settings:

	Odd Iteration	Even Iteration
Packet Size	8,192	16,384
Connection Timeout	15	16
Connection Lifetime	1	2
Application Name	Name2	Name1

The WXMultiPool application demonstrates that differences in a variety of connection attributes cause multiple connection pools to be used, leading to the consumption of a large amount of resources. Furthermore, when each area of the program is using a slightly different connection string, the connection pools themselves are not being used efficiently.

Other Pooling Attributes

The control that it's possible to exert over connection pooling extends to more than just switching it on and off; it's also possible to specify how many connections there should be in a pool. The maximum number of connections in a given pool can be set using the Max Pool Size connection attribute, while the minimum number of connections in a given pool can be set using the Min Pool Size connection attribute. The defaults for these attributes are 100 and zero respectively.

In an environment where a particular connection will be used a lot, the Min Pool Size should be set to a number larger than its default value. Once the minimum number of connections has been created, that number of connections will then remain for the lifetime of the application. Raising Max Pool Size can also aid performance, while lowering it can be used to enforce a connection restriction. If the range of options, and the difficulty of determining what's best for your application, is beginning to sound dizzying, fear not: there is a mechanism that can be used to determine the peak number of connections used, the current number of pooled connections, and the current number of non-pooled connections. That mechanism is **performance counters**, and we'll be seeing all about those shortly.

While we're on the subject of connection pool attributes, though, the WXMultiPool application introduced Connection Lifetime. Each time a connection is returned to a pool, the Connection Lifetime value is compared against the number of seconds the connection has been alive. If the connection has been alive for longer than the Connection Lifetime, the connection is removed from the pool. Note that a value of zero, which is the default for this attribute, corresponds to the longest possible timeout, rather than the shortest.

Finally, if you're using the SQL Server .NET data provider with SQL Server 7.0 (or MSDE), you might need to know about the `Connection Reset` connection attribute. By default, this is set to `true`, indicating that the connection state is reset each time a connection is returned to the pool. To understand the implications of this, consider the case in which a connection is initially set to the `Northwind` database, but changed while in use to the `Pubs` database. In this scenario, returning the connection to the pool would cause the connection to be reset, and therefore the database to be reset to `Northwind`. The implication of this reset is a roundtrip to the database that you can avoid by setting the `Connection Reset` attribute to `false`, and remembering that you'll need to program for this change in behavior.

Performance Counters

Since the earliest days of Windows NT, the Windows operating system has provided performance counters as a means by which to view certain categories of performance-related information. The values of these counters can be viewed administratively using the `PerfMon` utility, but programmatic access has taken some effort – at first, they were only available by parsing complex data structures retrieved from the Windows registry, or by using a DLL that only shipped with the Windows SDK. In .NET, however, performance counters are laid bare to all developers through the classes of the `System.Diagnostics` namespace, which include `PerformanceCounterManager`, `PerformanceCounterCategory`, and `PerformanceCounter`.

Since performance counters originated on Windows NT, they are not supported on Windows 98 and Windows ME. Windows NT, 2000, and XP do support performance counters.

The complete set of performance counters is broken down into categories, and since each category is exposed as a performance counter object, the two terms "object" and "category" will get used interchangeably in this discussion. For ASP.NET, performance counters can be broken down into the following categories:

❑ **ASP.NET Application.** This category includes a variety of counters that can be used to gauge the performance of an ASP.NET application. Such counters include (but certainly are not limited to) Cache Total Hits, Cache Total Misses, Cache Total Hit Ratio, Sessions Active, and Sessions Timed Out. For the most part, the name of each counter is self-documenting. Exhibiting similarly self-documenting behavior are the ASP.NET application performance counters that can be used to determine database performance. Counters in this genre include Transactions Aborted, Transactions Committed, Transactions Pending, Transactions Total, and Transactions/Sec.

❑ **ASP.NET System.** This category's performance counters do not apply to a single ASP.NET application, but instead represent the state of all ASP.NET applications presently executing on a given web server. These counters include Application Running, Requests Queued, Request Wait Time, and State Server Session Active.

The .NET Framework also exposes a variety of different categories of counters that deal with aspects such as memory, networking, remoting, and security. More relevant to the present subject, however, is the **.NET CLR Data** category, which includes counters that demonstrate various performance aspects of the SQL Server .NET data provider. These counters can provide insight into a particular application that uses this data provider, or all the applications that use it. The specific counters within this category are:

❑ **Current # connection pools** – the total number of current connection pools for a specific instance. We've already discussed how connection string attributes can affect connection pools, and this particular counter is indispensable in tracking down issues related to inadvertently creating additional ones.

❑ **Current # pooled and nonpooled connections** – the total number of database connections presently open. This counter provides a quick way to check whether an application has circumvented the default behavior, which is to use connection pooling.

❑ **Current # pooled connections** – the total number of database connections that are presently open and associated with a connection pool.

❑ **Peak # pooled connections** – the maximum number of connections open during peak execution. Recall that the `Max Pool Size` connection attribute can be used by a connection string to increase the upper bound on the number of connections maintained in a given pool. Knowing the peak number of pooled connections should influence the value you associate with the `Max Pool Size` connection attribute.

❑ **Total # failed commands** – the total number of commands that have failed, regardless of the reason for the failure.

❑ **Total # failed connects** – the total number of connections that have failed, regardless of the reason for the failure. Included in this total are connection attempts that timed out because the maximum number of connections in the pool was exceeded – but remember that the `Max Pool Size` connection attribute is just one possible cause of a failed connection. Another variable in the equation is the `Connection Timeout` connection attribute, which can be increased so that waiting connections do not time out as readily.

The true value of performance counters is that they can be accessed either using the `PerfMon` utility (Control Panel | Administrative Tools | Performance), or programmatically. It's even possible for developers to create their own performance counter objects in order to provide data that's exactly right for their own specific application, but this topic is beyond the scope of this chapter.

An example of the `PerfMon` tool being used to monitor .NET data performance counters is shown below:

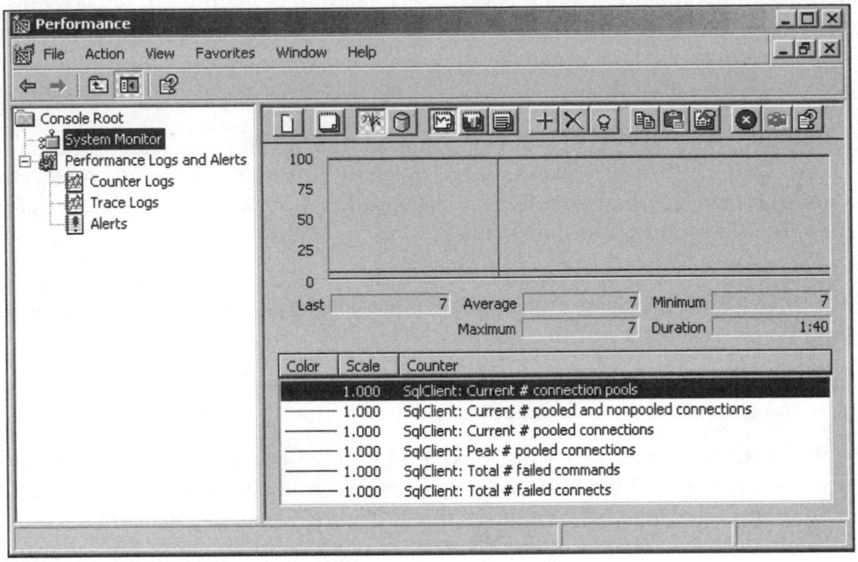

An **Add** counter icon (+) is provided on `PerfMon`'s toolbar. Clicking on this icon allows:

❑ A machine (host) to be selected, so that the performance counters on that host can be accessed.

❑ A performance counter object to be selected, such as the .NET CLR Data counter object.

❑ A specific instance to be selected. You can choose to monitor one application, or use `_global_` to specify all applications using the SQL Server .NET data provider.

❑ A specific counter to be selected. The above screenshot shows selected counters such as **Current # connection pools** and **Current # pooled and nonpooled connections**.

When you're using a large number of performance counters, the `PerfMon` utility provides a useful graphical display in the area beneath the toolbar containing the **Add** icon. Underneath this graphical display, data is presented that pertains to the counter currently highlighted. In the previous screenshot, they deal with the **Current # connection pools** counter. The values displayed include the **Last** value for this counter, the **Average** number for this counter, the **Minimum** number for this counter, the **Maximum** number for this counter, and the length of time over which performance was measured (**Duration**).

Programmatic Performance Counter Access

As mentioned above, the `System.Diagnostics` namespace provides a variety of classes that can be used to access performance objects and performance counters. These classes include:

❑ `PerformanceCounterCategory`, which is used to retrieve performance objects and their counters

❑ `PerformanceCounter`, which is used to access information (name, value, help string, etc.) from a specific performance counter

The `PerformanceCounterCategory` class exposes a shared method called `GetCategories()` that retrieves the name of all the performance counter objects for the present host, or a specific remote host. Once an instance of the `PerformanceCounterCategory` class has been created for a given performance counter category (such as .NET CLR Data), information specific to this category can be retrieved. For example, the `GetInstanceNames()` method can be called to retrieve the names of applications with a current interest in this category, and `GetCounters()` can be used to retrieve the counters associated with the category. The `GetCounters()` method returns an array of type `PerformanceCounter`.

The `PerformanceCounter` class exposes properties and methods that can be used to access a performance counter's value, and to manipulate that value. Among these is the `NextValue()` method, which retrieves the 'next' value (the method is designed to be called iteratively) as a `Float`. In the world of connection pools, however, there are no decimal values (you can't have half a connection), so we'll safely be able to cast it to an `Integer`. `PerformanceCounter` also implements properties that allow the counter's name (`CounterName`), type (`CounterType`), and help information (`CounterHelp`) properties to be queried.

The `WXPerfCount` application, which you can download from www.wrox.com, makes use of the `PerformanceCounter` class in order to display information about the counters associated with the .NET CLR Data performance counter object. The basic premise of the application is to create a slew of connection pools, connections, failed connection attempts, and failed commands. Once this is done, the .NET CLR Data performance counters are retrieved and displayed.

Without getting into detail, the `WXPerfCount` application creates each `PerformanceCounter` object by passing the category name and application instance that the counter is associated with to the object's constructor. Also passed to the constructor is the performance counter's category name. Once the performance counter instance is created, its `CounterName` property and `NextValue()` method are used to display a string indicating the value associated with the performance counter.

Try It Out – Using Performance Counters to Evaluate Performance

1. Create a new Visual Basic ASP.NET Web Application project named `WXPerfCount`.

2. Add some `Label` controls to `WebForm1.aspx` that will be used to display our performance counter results. The labels that should be added are `LabelNumCPools`, `LabelTotalCons`, `LabelPooledCons`, `LabelPeakCons`, `LabelFailedCom`, and `LabelFailedCons`. You'll end up with something like this:

```
Connection pools:     [LabelNumCPools]
No. of connections:   [LabelTotalCons]
Pooled connections:   [LabelPooledCons]
Connections at peak:  [LabelPeakCons]
Failed commands:      [LabelFailedCom]
Failed connections:   [LabelFailedCons]
```

3. Moving on to the code-behind file, we know that we'll be using objects of the `PerformanceCounter` class that's located in the `System.Diagnostics` namespace. With that in mind, we need to add an `Imports` statement right at the top:

```
Imports System.Diagnostics
```

4. Next, we add a function to the `WebForm1` class that will retrieve the next value from a performance counter that's passed to it by name. The function returns the value of the counter formatted as a string, ready for display:

```
' Permissible values for counterName include:
' "SqlClient: Current # connection pools"
' "SqlClient: Current # pooled and nonpooled connections"
' "SqlClient: Current # pooled connections"
' "SqlClient: Peak # pooled connections"
' "SqlClient: Total # failed commands"
' "SqlClient: Total # failed connects"
Function WXGetPerfCountValue(ByVal counterName As String) As String
  Dim category As String = ".NET CLR Data"
  Dim instance As String = "_global_"
  Dim pc As PerformanceCounter = Nothing

  pc = New PerformanceCounter(category, counterName, instance)
  Return pc.NextValue().ToString()
End Function
```

5. In order to give these controls something to display, we need to do some work with a database. First of all, add a `Button` called `ButtonPerf` to the form, and double-click on it to add a click event handler to the code-behind file.

6. The version of this project that's available for download tests a number of different connection strings in order to provide values for all of our label controls; here, we'll substitute something a little simpler:

```
Private Sub ButtonPerf_Click(ByVal sender As System.Object, _
                    ByVal e As System.EventArgs) Handles ButtonPerf.Click
  Dim count As Integer = 0
  Dim tempConn As SqlConnection

  For count = 1 To 100
    tempConn = New SqlConnection("server=localhost; database=northwind;" & _
                            "uid=sa; pwd=; Connection TimeOut=" & _
                            count.ToString())

    tempConn.Open()
  Next
End Sub
```

7. To the same handler, add code that reads the performance counters and displays their values in the labels we created earlier:

```
LabelNumCPools.Text = _
  WXGetPerfCountValue("SqlClient: Current # connection pools")
LabelTotalCons.Text = _
  WXGetPerfCountValue("SqlClient: Current # pooled and nonpooled connections")
LabelPooledCons.Text = _
  WXGetPerfCountValue("SqlClient: Current # pooled connections")
LabelPeakCons.Text = _
  WXGetPerfCountValue("SqlClient: Peak # pooled connections")
LabelFailedCom.Text = _
  WXGetPerfCountValue("SqlClient: Total # failed commands")
LabelFailedCons.Text = _
  WXGetPerfCountValue("SqlClient: Total # failed connects")
```

8. If you run the code as presented in this book, you find yourself faced with output that looks something like the screenshot below. The longer sample that comes with the code download allows you finer control over the database connections that are created. As you can see, it's further confirmation that providing different timeout values results in the creation of separate connection pools.

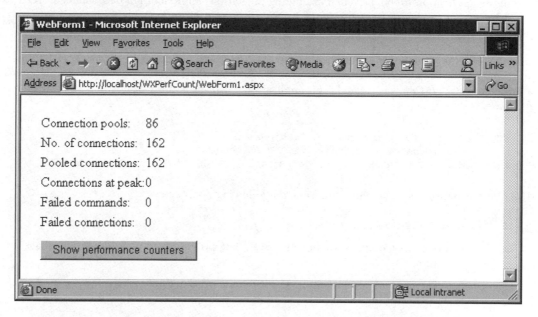

If you have problems running this example, the likely cause is a problem with your security settings – Windows won't allow users below a certain privilege level to use the facilities of the System.Diagnostics *namespace. Should you run into difficulties, go to* Control Panel / Users and Passwords, *and change the group of the user called* ASPNET *to* Administrators. *Be aware that there is a security risk inherent in this operation, which you should only perform on a development machine.*

In truth, although it's provided a demonstration of how to use performance counters programmatically, the code in the `WXGetPerfCountValue()` method is not the best way to use the `PerformanceCounter` class. More typically, instances of such counters are created and accessed repeatedly. By calling the `NextValue()` method of a performance counter repeatedly over a period of time, a histogram of performance information can be retrieved. When you're looking for erroneously created connection pools, or the peak number of connections, a histogram is a valuable tool for diagnosing the bottleneck.

DataSets, Data Readers, and Recordsets

Once a connection to a database has been established, whether it belongs to a connection pool or not, our focus passes to the range of objects available for communicating with the data source. In this section, we'll compare and contrast the choices before us.

The title of this section includes a word that is practically taboo when writing texts about .NET: `Recordset`. A `Recordset` is an ADO (rather than an ADO.NET) object, but it still has to be given the proper respect. Right now, there are millions of lines of ADO code out there, and developers are debating the best way to move that code over to .NET. Should the data access portion be rewritten (that is, converted from ADO to ADO.NET) immediately, or should it be left as ADO while upgrading the rest of the application to .NET? When examining the various approaches to data access in .NET, we should also analyze the performance of the `Recordset` in order to see whether it measures up to the performance of contemporary approaches.

In order better to understand the differences between each style of data access (ADO.NET's data reader and data set objects, and ADO's `Recordset`), the `WXTestSelectPerf` application (which we'll look at in the next *Try It Out*) was created. This application performs a query against the `Northwind` database:

```
SELECT O.OrderID, O.CustomerID, O.ShipName,
       O.ShipAddress, OD.UnitPrice, OD.Discount
FROM Orders AS O INNER JOIN [Order Details] AS OD ON O.OrderID=OD.OrderID
```

The query is performed multiple times, using the following approaches:

❑ Using an `SqlDataReader` object

❑ Using a `DataSet` object with the .NET SQL data provider and querying the database for each iteration

❑ Using a `DataSet` object with the .NET SQL data provider but performing the query only once

❑ Using an ADO `Recordset` object and querying the database for each iteration

❑ Using an ADO `Recordset` object but performing the query only once

Try It Out – Evaluating Data Reader Performance

Once again, the full version of this application is available for download from the Wrox web site, but it's quite large and fairly repetitive. In this section, rather than sifting through the complete listing, we'll just look at the key areas and then analyze the results.

First, as stated, all five approaches share the same connection string, so that's declared at the top of the class definition in the code-behind file:

```
Private _commandText As String = & _
            "SELECT O.OrderID, O.CustomerID, "O.ShipName, " & _
                "O.ShipAddress, OD.UnitPrice, OD.Discount " & _
            "FROM Orders AS O INNER JOIN [Order Details] " & _
            "AS OD ON O.OrderID=OD.OrderID"
```

After this declaration come the private methods that test the performance of the various data access technologies. They necessarily vary a little, but by and large they perform the same task. The listing that follows contains the method for testing a SqlDataReader object; the performance values computed (howLongTotal and howLongSQL) are returned as ByRef parameters:

```
Private Sub WXTestDataReader(ByVal conn As SqlConnection, _
                            ByRef howLongTotal As TimeSpan, _
                            ByRef howLongSQL As TimeSpan)
   Dim startTime As DateTime
   Dim executeStartTime As DateTime
   Dim command As SqlCommand
   Dim dataReader As SqlDataReader

   startTime = DateTime.Now
   command = New SqlCommand(_commandText, conn)
   executeStartTime = DateTime.Now
   dataReader = command.ExecuteReader()
   howLongSQL = DateTime.Now.Subtract(executeStartTime)

   Dim fieldCount As Integer = dataReader.FieldCount - 1
   Dim count As Integer
   Dim s As String

   While dataReader.Read()
     For count = 0 To fieldCount
       s = dataReader.GetValue(count).ToString()
     Next
   End While

   howLongTotal = DateTime.Now.Subtract(startTime)
   dataReader.Close()
End Sub
```

The basic idea behind this example (and the methods that test `DataSet` and `Recordset` objects) is to query repeatedly using one approach, and then measure performance. When you execute the `WXTestSelectPerf` application, you'll see something like this:

Total Duration: 3,785.44, Total SQL: 50.07

⊙ DataReader

○ DataSet re-select   ○ DataSet Select Once

○ Recordset re-select   ○ Recordset Select Once

Number of iterations: `100`

[Activate]

Based on performing the query one hundred times, the following results were generated, where the time is in milliseconds:

	Non-query time	Time in Query	Total Time
`SqlDataReader`	3,735	50	3,785
`DataSet` (re-select)	1,973	5,137	7,010
`DataSet` (select once)	1,663	170	1,833
`Recordset` (re-select)	44,364	220	44,584
`Recordset` (select once)	39,833	280	44,013

The 'winner' here seems to be the ADO.NET `DataSet`, when we performed the query once and then iterated through the result set (every row, every column) 100 times – but we need to analyze that a little more closely. *Why* did this approach win?

A `DataSet` contains the results of a query, which on this occasion just so happens to contain 2,155 rows. The footprint of this `DataSet` is not particularly taxing for the web server, so it just kept re-reading the entire cached set of data. From the point of view of a web application, though, this might not make a great deal of sense – many such applications are stateless, and would not be able to exploit the caching provided by the `DataSet`. (In fact, the `DataSet` might be better used as a *client-side* representation of data.) Also, it's important to recognize that retrieving a query's result set in its entirety, which is the `DataSet` model, could be prohibitive for queries that generate large result sets.

The second-best approach appears to be to use a data reader object, which provides fast, forward-only row traversal. The idea is to get the data one row at a time and move through it quickly in a single pass – and this is how a great many real-world web applications behave. They request data, traverse it so that it can be displayed, and then return control back to the client.

In third place, `DataSet` objects are clearly not meant to be set up 100 times (repeating the query 100 times) and then traversed once per query. This approach really calls for use of a data reader. It only makes sense to use `DataSet` objects in a situation where the cached data can be reused.

The two examples of using an ADO `Recordset` to access data were included to demonstrate the overhead associated with calling a COM component from .NET. There will be a large number of companies who are tempted to upgrade to .NET, but to leave their data access code in ADO because it simplifies the upgrade. However, you have to remember that ADO is accessed from .NET using a wrapper DLL that translates each ADO call from .NET (a managed call) to an unmanaged call. This overhead adds dozens of instructions per method or property accessed.

We could dwell on the reasons why ADO performance is *so* much worse than ADO.NET performance, but in the final analysis, it doesn't really matter. The life lesson here is: move to ADO.NET. The data access constructs (datasets and data readers) used by ADO.NET do not permit many of the performance hampering configuration settings supported by ADO. In addition, the ADO.NET programming model is simpler – you have the cached representation of data offered by datasets, or the fast, forward-only access provided by data readers.

Typed DataSets vs Late Bound DataSets

In the examples we've looked at so far, the datasets have been **late bound**. In other words, the `Dataset` instance determines which table it's going to be associated with at runtime. An alternative option is to use a **typed** dataset, in which case the association takes place when the application is compiled. From a programmatic standpoint, a typed `DataSet` is simpler to use, and your developer's instinct might lead you to expect it to be faster than its un-typed counterpart. In fact, as we'll see, a typed data set is really just a programmer-friendly wrapper around a late bound `DataSet`, and the performance change is negligible.

Try It Out – Creating a Typed DataSet

The steps required to develop a typed `DataSet` are as follows:

1. In code, create a `DataSet` and associate it with a particular SQL query (that is, use late binding, as normal).

2. Call the `DataSet`'s `GetXmlSchema()` method in order to retrieve the schema. Save this schema in a file called `WXEmployee.xsd`.

3. Using the schema file, run the xsd command-line utility to create a file containing the definition of a typed DataSet. An example of this is as follows, where the /d option specifies that a typed DataSet is being generated, the /1:VB option specifies that a VB.NET source file will be generated, and /n specifies the namespace used within the generated VB.NET file.

```
> xsd /d /1:VB WXEmployee.xsd /n:WXDBPerfDemo
```

4. The previous command creates a file called WXEmployee.vb that can be added to our project using the Project | Add Existing Item menu item in Visual Studio .NET. The class contained in WXEmployee.vb is derived from DataSet:

```
Public Class WXEmployeeDataSet Inherits DataSet
End Class
```

5. For a given DataSet, create an SqlDataAdapter and a SqlCommandBuilder object that can be used to update information in that DataSet. The WXSetupDataSet() method below demonstrates how to create a SqlCommandBuilder associated with a SqlDataAdapter, and how to use the SqlDataAdapter to fill a DataSet:

```
Const _selectAll As String = _
    "SELECT CustomerID, CompanyName, ContactName, ContactTitle, " & _
    "Address, City, Region, PostalCode, Country, Phone, Fax " & _
    "FROM WXCustomers"

Private Sub WXSetupDataSet(ByVal command As SqlCommand, _
                           ByVal ds As DataSet, _
                           ByRef da As SqlDataAdapter, _
                           ByRef cb As SqlCommandBuilder)

    command.CommandText = _selectAll
    command.CommandType = CommandType.Text
    da = New SqlDataAdapter(command)
    cb = New SqlCommandBuilder(da)
    da.Fill(ds, "WXCustomers")
End Sub
```

6. To test code that demonstrates a late bound DataSet, simply create a DataSet and pass it to WXSetupDataSet():

```
Dim da As SqlDataAdapter
Dim cb As SqlCommandBuilder
Dim ds As new DataSet()

WXSetupDataSet(command, ds, da, cb)
```

7. To test code that demonstrates a typed `DataSet`, create a typed `DataSet` instance (such as an object of the `WXEmployeeDataSet` class created earlier), and pass *that* to `WXSetupDataSet()`:

```
Dim da As SqlDataAdapter
Dim cb As SqlCommandBuilder
Dim ds As New WXDBPerfDemo.WXEmployeeDataSet()

WXSetupDataSet(command, ds, da, cb)
```

The code we actually used to evaluate typed versus late bound `DataSet` instances can be found in the `WXDataSetModify` project in the download files – it's not dissimilar from the code we used for our earlier trial involving different data access objects. What we're interested in here is the result of the evaluation, which was that a typed `Dataset` is actually couple of percentage points *slower* than a late bound `DataSet`.

You probably find that surprising at first blush, but a typed `DataSet` is really just a `DataSet` with some wrapper code to simplify programming and perform some error handling, the combined result of which is a slight performance degradation. Frankly, had the late bound `DataSet` code used in `WXDataSetModify.aspx` been as thorough with its error handling, performance would likely be identical.

The conclusion here is that while there's no raw performance issue surrounding the use of typed versus late bound `DataSet` instances, there are still good reasons to prefer the former. The extra facilities they provide make writing code faster, and should result in fewer bugs. This gives developers more time to address performance issues elsewhere in their applications.

Fine Tuning Datasets and Data Readers

Earlier, we established that using ADO with the .NET Framework is fraught with performance pitfalls that result in an order-of-magnitude performance degradation. However, ADO.NET has a few pitfalls of its own that we'll address in this last section of the chapter. For example, the elements within a data reader object can be accessed by:

❑ Indexer ordinal position
  `dataReaderInstance(0)` or `dataReaderInstance(8)`

❑ Indexer name
  `dataReaderInstance("EmployeeID")` or `dataReaderInstance("SSN")`

❑ Using an ordinal with a 'get' method
  `dataReaderInstance.GetValue(0)` or `dataReaderInstance.GetValue(12)`

Which one provides the fastest access? You'd expect providing an ordinal to be faster than a by-name lookup, but is it fast enough that it significantly affects performance? To help in the attempt to find an answer, the following enumeration was created in the code-behind file for the `WXFineTune` ASP.NET application:

```
Enum WXColumns
  OrderID
  CustomerID
  ShipName
  ShipAddress
  UnitPrice
  Discount
  MaxColumn
End Enum
```

This enumeration maps to the following SQL query, where the column names and positions correspond to values in the enumeration:

```
Private _commandText As String = _
    "SELECT O.OrderID AS OrderID, O.CustomerID AS CustomerID, " & _
        "O.ShipName AS ShipName, O.ShipAddress AS ShipAddress, " & _
            "OD.UnitPrice AS UnitPrice, OD.Discount AS Discount " & _
    "FROM Orders AS O INNER JOIN [Order Details] AS OD ON O.OrderID=OD.OrderID"
```

The beauty of an enumeration value is that it can represent either an ordinal (enumValue) or a name (enumValue.ToString()). We can therefore use the WXColumns enumeration to determine empirically whether there is a performance difference in by-name and by-value lookup.

The form in the WXFineTune application uses RadioButton controls to determine which type of lookup should be performed. The code specific to how a data reader object looks up data is as follows:

```
Dim s As String
Dim count As WXColumns

While dataReader.Read()
  For count = 0 To WXColumns.MaxColumn
    If RadiobuttonDataReaderByName.Checked Then
      s = dataReader(count.ToString()).ToString()
    ElseIf RadioButtonDataReaderOrd.Checked Then
      s = dataReader(CType(count, Integer)).ToString()
    Else
      s = dataReader.GetValue(CType(count, Integer)).ToString()
    End If
  Next
End While
```

The results of running the WXFineTune application for 100 iterations of the query in conjunction with complete traversal of the data are as follows:

	Execution Time (ms)
Data reader, indexer, ordinal	4,887
Data reader, ordinal, 'get' method	4,786

	Execution Time (ms)
Data reader, index, by name	17,264
Dataset, indexer, ordinal	2,253
Dataset, indexer, by name	12,608

This table demonstrates quite clearly that by-name lookup incurs a significant overhead when compared to by-ordinal lookup (2,253 seconds for `DataSet` by-ordinal, compared with 12,608 for `DataSet` by-name).

Last of all, you know that it's possible to execute multiple SQL statements with both dataset and data reader objects. For example, running the following four `SELECT` statements together would produce four result sets:

```
SELECT * FROM Customers;SELECT * FROM [Order Details];
SELECT * FROM Orders;SELECT * FROM Products
```

The `DataSet` object handles multiple result sets by placing each result set in a separate table, which is straightforward enough. However, since a data reader provides forward-only traversal, it must take a different tack. When the data reader's `Read()` method returns `False` (meaning that all rows of a result set have been read), the `NextResult()` method can be called in order to start reading from the next result set. At this stage, the `Read()` method can again be called to traverse the new result set. An example of this in action is as follows:

```
Dim dataReader As SqlDataReader = command.ExecuteReader()
Dim count As Integer
Dim fieldCount = dataReader.FieldCount - 1

Do
  While dataReader.Read()
    For count = 0 To fieldCount
      s = dataReader.GetValue(count).ToString()
    Next
  End While
Loop While dataReader.NextResult()
```

It turns out that a data reader object can traverse multiple result sets from a single command about as quickly as it could traverse the commands if they had been submitted separately. In a situation where SQL Server was deployed on a separate machine, however, there would be an advantage to sending over multiple queries to the database as part of a single command. The comparable tradeoff for a `DataSet` would be in reduced network handshaking against having memory consumed, because multiple result sets are cached at the same time.

Summary

Usually, a summary will provide some closure on the disparate topics that have been presented throughout a chapter. This being a chapter on performance, however, a different approach will be taken: we'll list a series of good practices that you're encouraged to follow.

The following suggestions could readily lead to improved performance with respect to establishing database connections:

❑ The .NET data providers for SQL Server and OLE DB implement connection pools automatically, so developers need not attempt to enable what is already enabled.

❑ Create connections in a single location, so that superfluous connection pools are not created by mistake in other parts of your application.

❑ Do not change innocuous connection string attributes, or you risk creating superfluous connection pools (see previous bullet).

❑ Use `PerfMon` and the .NET CLR Data performance counter to ensure that connection pools are behaving as anticipated, and to ensure that appropriate maximum and minimum values are specified for each connection pool.

Consider the following suggestions when migrating legacy code that uses ADO to run under .NET:

❑ Recognize that migrating legacy ADO code to .NET will impact performance.

❑ Where possible, upgrade ADO to use ADO.NET.

Use `DataSet` instances:

❑ Where caching is convenient (which might not be the case for a stateless application).

❑ Where memory is sufficient to handle the size of the cached data.

❑ In order to enable a client or other application tiers to manipulate data locally (especially since clients are not stateless).

❑ When the disconnected data must still maintain tables and relationships between tables.

❑ When data must be modified.

❑ When data can be shared as XML (imported to a `DataSet`, exported from a `DataSet`).

Use data reader instances where:

❑ Data access is read-only, fast, and forward-only.

❑ Data access may only require accessing part of a dataset, or where only a row of data at a time is required for processing.

When accessing data using either a `DataSet` or a data reader:

❑ Use ordinal values to look up specific data within `DataSets` and data readers.

❑ Enumerations provide a simple way to look up by ordinal, and can easily fall back to lookup by name.

There is no perfect way to guarantee good performance. Probably the most important rule is the good old 80/20 – eighty percent of the work is done by twenty percent of the code. Don't spend all of your time improving the performance of a large action that happens only once; instead, focus on small things that take place numerous times, and have a greater overall impact on performance.

Regardless of how you approach performance, ADO.NET has simplified the process by the simple expedient of preventing you from stepping in a variety of hazards. Connections pools, performance measurement counters, no cursors, and data access patterns are gift wrapped and handed to the developer. The result should be faster, more reliable data access code.

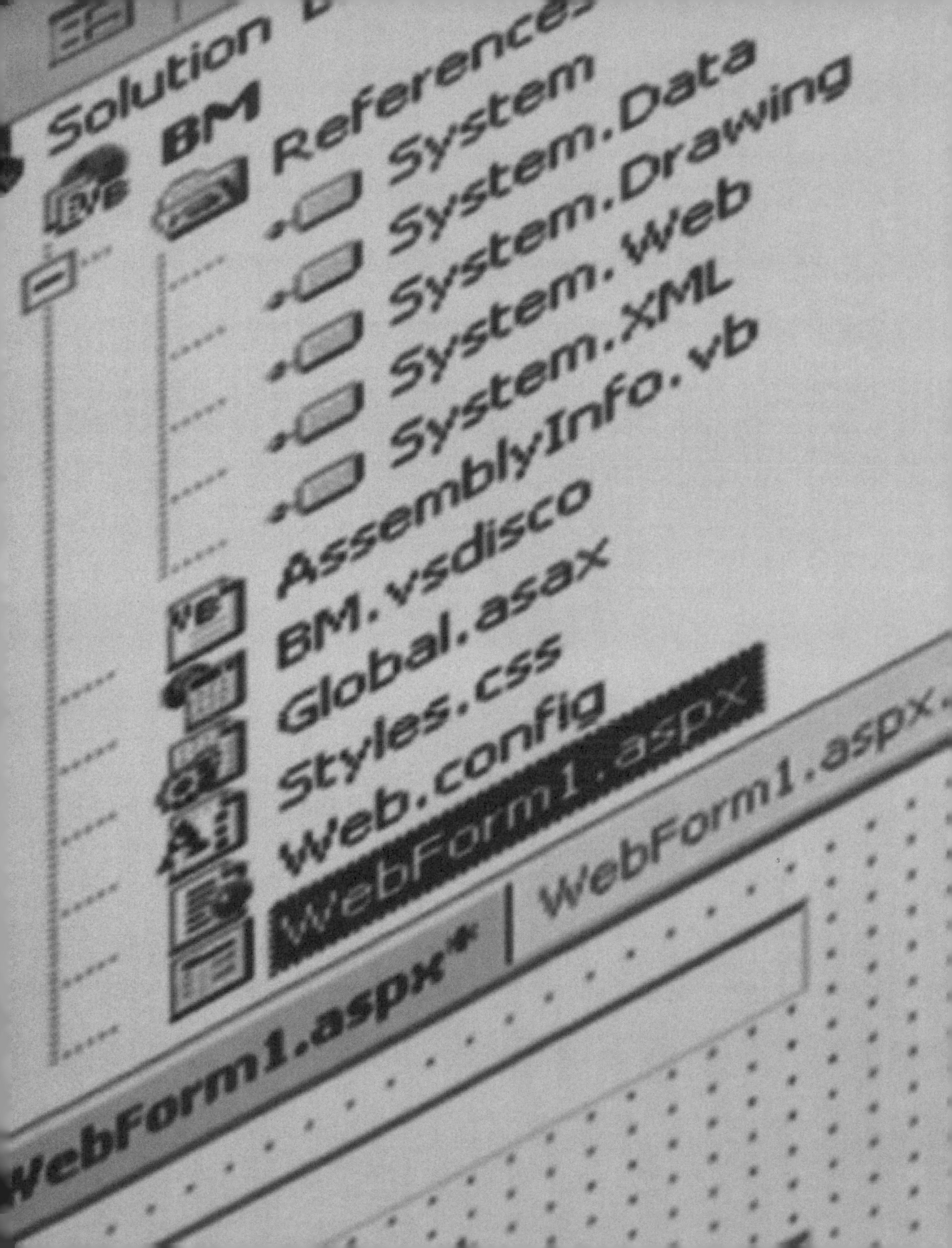

Solution Explorer

BM
References
System
System.Data
System.Drawing
System.Web
System.XML
AssemblyInfo.vb
Assembly
BM.vsdisco
Global.asax
Styles.css
Web.config
WebForm1.aspx

WebForm1.aspx* | WebForm1.aspx.

WebForm1.aspx

Writing an Application

In the first 11 chapters of this book, we've covered many aspects of the interaction between ASP.NET and ADO.NET, and practiced using many of the techniques involved in getting the two to work together. To this point, we've been demonstrating those ideas through relatively small, self-contained examples. In this chapter, we'll set out to write a much larger database-oriented application using ASP.NET techniques.

This application will make use of many of the different ideas that we've already discussed in this book. For example, we'll be using:

- ❑ Client-side scripting with JavaScript
- ❑ Code-behind concepts (with VB.NET)
- ❑ The ASP.NET web server controls
- ❑ Database access components
- ❑ ASP.NET request and response objects
- ❑ Stored procedures within the database

We'll build our application from the ground up, and as we do so we'll be able to see how these different aspects interact with each other in a 'real-life' environment. While this chapter won't explain every single line of code in detail, it *will* provide you with sufficient information to allow you to implement the application as it is, and to modify it to suit your needs. You might also use it as a starting point or a guide to writing your own applications.

Introducing the Wrox Auction Site

The tenet of e-commerce is that the Internet is able to take the place of a traditional bricks-and-mortar store, playing the role of the retailer who sits between buyer and vendor. For very little overhead, people are now able to sell their products electronically. The Internet has enabled the buyer and the seller to be brought together in a virtual (rather than a physical) manner.

Let's consider a simple example of commerce between two people, involving the kind of classified advertisements that are traditionally to be found in a local newspaper. In such a listing, advertisers will place small advertisements that list the items they wish to sell, and provide a means (usually a telephone number) by which prospective buyers can contact them.

Before we begin, we should consider the nature of a sale via a newspaper classified advertisement. During the course of the sale, the information flows in different directions at different stages. First, there is a downstream flow of information (from seller to buyer) – the listing in print in the newspaper. (Thus, the classified ad listing is just a way of bringing a buyer and seller together.) When a potential purchaser's interest has been raised, that interest must be relayed upstream (from buyer to seller) – usually by telephone or in person. Finally, there should be a face-to-face meeting in which the two parties are able to negotiate to finalize the sale – if the sale can be agreed. In our electronic world, this (the face-to-face meeting, not the agreement!) is unlikely to happen.

A Web-based Classifieds System

We'll implement a web-based classified ad system. Any user who is trying to buy an item can:

- **View** items for sale.
- **Bid** for an item they wish to purchase.

In addition, any user who is trying to sell an item can:

- **Place** a new item for sale.
- **Browse** a list of the items that they're trying to sell, and examine the bids that have been made on each of those items.
- **Accept** a bid on an item that they're selling. When the seller is satisfied about the bid for his item, he will accept the bid – and the sale will be *half* complete. Then, the buyer must **acknowledge** the acceptance, and then the sale will be finalized.

This system will also allow users to do other tasks, such as:

- **Browse** the listings to see what's for sale.
- **Register** with the system (users can browse without registering; but they must register if they want to sell an item or bid for an item).
- **Log on** to the system.
- **Change** their registration details.

If our web site takes off, we'll have a large user base – some will be buyers, some will be sellers, and (hopefully) some will be both. In order to carry out either activity, a user must register with us.

Advantages over a Print-based Classifieds System

Our Internet-based classified ad system provides certain advantages to the seller over traditional printed classifieds:

❑ When a seller submits an item for sale, it's immediately viewable by potential buyers. There's no time delay while we all wait for the newspaper to be printed.

❑ Responses from potential buyers are held by the system's data store, rather than being passed directly back to the seller. This means that the seller doesn't have to be available to respond 24 hours a day.

❑ The seller can dynamically adjust the price, based on the amount of responses an item receives.

❑ The global nature of the Internet means that the potential audience for each advert is global – it's not limited to the catchment area of a printed newspaper

The Internet classified ad system also provides advantages for potential buyers:

❑ Shoppers can see the level of interest in an item before determining the price they are willing to pay.

❑ When a shopper makes a bid, he is told whether the bid is the highest bid made on that item.

Building the Application

We'll build our application in stages. Each stage will build on the previous ones, and will add a new piece of functionality to the application. The sequence we'll follow in this chapter is:

❑ Database setup

❑ Home page construction

❑ User registration and login

❑ Adding items to the sale listings

❑ Browsing the listings and bidding for items

❑ Accepting a bid and completing the sale

Once we've created the tables and the stored procedures – which, as we'll discuss shortly, we're going to do through a pre-written setup file – the next step is to write the ASP.NET pages and database components. To get us started, let's take a look at the ASP.NET pages that will feature in our application – there are ten of them altogether. Each of these pages serves a different function, and contains the code for carrying out certain tasks. The pages are given names that reflect their functionality:

Page	Purpose
`Default.aspx`	The home page. Provides links to the login, registration and browse pages.
`BrowseListing.aspx`	This page shows a table containing brief details of each item that's currently available for purchase. From this page, registered users will be also able to select a particular product for sale, and click through to `BidItem.aspx` (to bid on the item).
`Login.aspx`	Enables a registered user to enter a username and password, and hence login to the system.
`Register.aspx`	Contains a form that enables new users to enter the necessary registration details. Also used to enable existing users to change their registration details.
`MenuForRegisteredUsers.aspx`	This is the first page that users see once they've logged in – it welcomes registered users to the site, presenting a simple menu of options that they can choose from. The menu in this page allows the user to navigate to other pages that can only be accessed by registered users.
	Sometimes, this page performs a second function: if the user placed bids on items during previous visits to the site, they will be displayed. Furthermore, if the vendor of an item has subsequently accepted a bid, the page will alert the user to the fact that their bid was successful.
`ViewMySaleItems.aspx`	Allows registered users to view the details of all of the items that they have made available for sale. From this page, the user can click-through to `Items.aspx` and edit these details. The 'highest bid' for each item is also displayed, and the user can accept a bid on an item via this page.
`Items.aspx`	Allows registered users to enter details of an item that they wish to make available for sale.
`BidItem.aspx`	Allows a potential buyer to view the details of a sale item, and to enter a bid.
`AcceptBid.aspx`	When a potential buyer's bid has been accepted, the buyer is alerted via `MenuForRegisteredUsers.aspx` (as described above). At this stage, the buyer can click through to `AcceptBid.aspx` and acknowledge the alert, and thus complete the sale.
`Logout.aspx`	Logs out the currently logged in user.

Setting up the Application

Like many web-based applications, the underlying structure of this project is dependent on the ability to store and retrieve information. Therefore, we need to support some form of data storage. For the purposes of this application, as we have throughout the book so far, we'll be using an MSDE relational database to store all of the application's data.

All of the files for this application are available from http://www.wrox.com. When you've got them, you should run the `setup.exe` program, which will create a virtual directory in IIS, and create the database along with its associated tables and stored procedures. The name of the virtual directory is `bid`, which allows you to access the application using an address of http://localhost/bid/.

The Setup Program

The setup program has no options, and all you have to do is hit the button. When setup is complete, you'll see a dialog that looks like this:

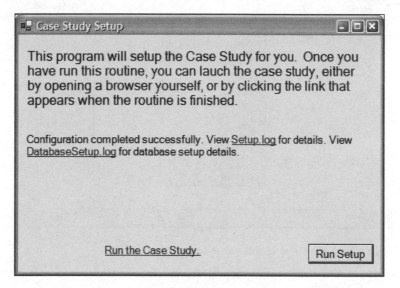

Here, you have the chance to view the log files for the creation of both the application and the database. If there were no errors, you also get the option to run the case study. This allows you to examine a finished version of the application.

The Database Model

The diagram below shows the relationships between the tables that we're using in our system. In it, you can see that there are five tables in the database:

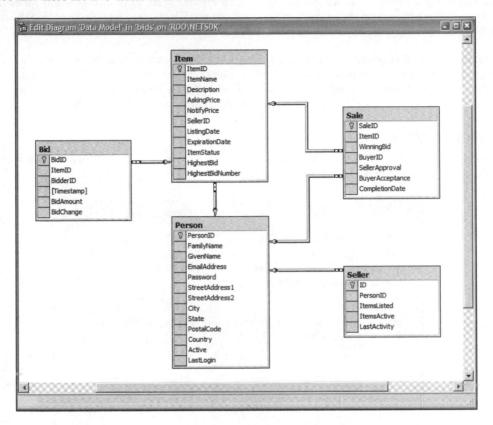

The purposes of each of these five tables are as follows:

Table	Description
Person	Contains details of all the registered users in the system.
Item	Contains details of each item that is for sale, or has been sold.
Bid	Contains details of each bid on an Item.
Sale	Contains details of each sale, including the item bought and who bought it.
Seller	Contains details of the items a Person has for sale.

Accessing the Database

To follow good design principles, we've abstracted all of our access to these tables in two ways. First, we've created a set of stored procedures. The application will talk to the stored procedures, and the stored procedures will talk to the tables. This means that if we ever need to change the tables (for example, by adding or changing columns), all we have to do is ensure that the stored procedure still works in the same way – this will ensure that the application will continue working. Moreover, access using stored procedures can be faster than accessing the tables directly.

Second, we'll use a **Data Access Layer** (DAL) in our application. The DAL is a layer of code that wraps up all of the complexities of accessing databases – it's another layer of abstraction. We will call the DAL from our ASP.NET pages, and the DAL will talk to the stored procedures. The reason for creating a DAL is similar to that for using stored procedures: it allows changes to be managed easily. It also allows us to keep all of the data code in a single place. In this example, the DAL is simply a set of classes with a number of data-related methods that we can call from our pages. Using a DAL has the added advantage of making our pages simpler, too.

In the sample code, the DAL comprises two VB.NET files, `Item.vb` and `Person.vb`, which are held in the `Components` subdirectory. We won't reproduce or examine the code for these files here, however, because we want to concentrate on the ASP.NET pages. You can examine the copies of these files that are included in the download at your leisure.

Flow of ASP.NET Pages

So: we now have the database and our components ready. What we need next is a way to communicate with the components and the users. In this section, we'll look at the flow of the ASP.NET pages used in our application. Once we've got that sorted out, we'll see how these pages can be created in Visual Studio .NET.

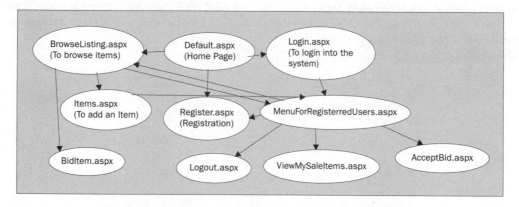

The above diagram shows how the flow of control passes between the ASPX pages. For example, after users get into the home page, they can go to the login page or the registration page, or they can browse the listings. The direction of the arrow indicates the movement from page to page.

Now we can *really* see the purpose of each page. `Default.aspx` is the home page where *every* user first comes in. There are no database calls here; its' just a stopping off point where users can choose where they want to go next. Once the user has logged in, they never return to this page – instead, their home page becomes `MenuForRegisteredUsers.aspx`, which has different menus. It's from here that users can manage the items they have for sale, accept bids, and so on.

One thing to notice is that, as specified earlier, users can browse items for sale whether or not they are logged in. `BrowseListings.aspx` identifies logged-in users and changes its appearance accordingly, allowing these users to bid on items. Otherwise, just the details of the various items for sale are shown.

Creating our Application

Having run the setup routine, you've got a running application under the URL http://localhost/bid. At this stage, you've got two options:

1. You can open the downloaded solution in Visual Studio .NET (by picking Open Solution from the File menu, or by double-clicking the `Bid.sln` file in Windows Explorer). This gives you a complete working set of code that you can examine, using the remainder of this chapter for explanations.

2. You can create a new project in Visual Studio .NET and use the code listings in the remainder of this chapter to build the application for yourself. This involves more work, but it does give you more experience of using Visual Studio .NET.

Creating a New Application

In Visual Studio .NET, open the File | New | Project dialog, and ensure that you have Visual Basic Projects selected as your Project Type. Then, click on ASP.NET Web Application as your Template, and enter http://localhost/MyBid in the Location box. We've had to pick a new name here, because the downloaded application uses the name Bid.

When you click **OK**, Visual Studio .NET will create the project, and after that our project is ready to be coded. All we have to do now is write the code!

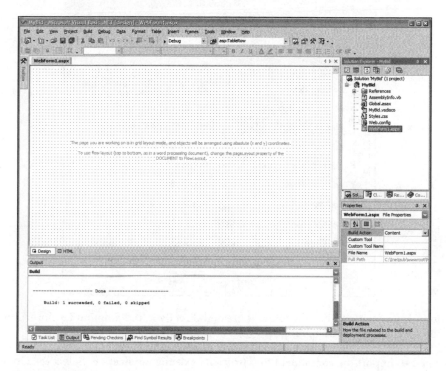

If the Solution Explorer showing these files is not visible, you can press Ctrl+Alt+L, select View | Solution Explorer, or click the Solution Explorer button on your VS .NET toolbar.

Preloading Code

Since we aren't *actually* going to code everything in this application from scratch, we need to copy some of the code from the downloaded sample. First, you need to create a directory in which to store the components. In the Solution Explorer, right-click on **MyBid**, choose **Add** from the context menu, and then select **New Folder**:

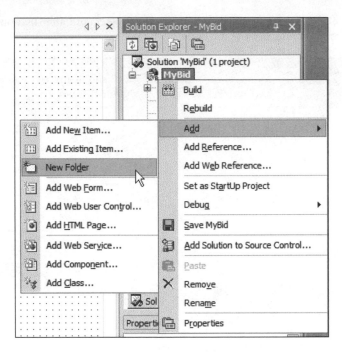

As a result of this operation, the new folder is created directly in the Solution Explorer. Just make sure that you change its name to Components.

Next, we need to import the component files from the existing application. Select the Components directory, right mouse click and select Add again, but this time pick Add Existing Item. From the next dialog, navigate to the directory where you installed the sample, and select all four files from the Components directory there. Click the Open button, and these files will be copied into our new project.

We've mentioned two of these files before – they contain the DAL components that provide the interface between our application and the database. The file with the .resx suffix is a resource file used by VS.NET, while the last one is Tools.vb, which contains the following:

```vb
Imports System.Web

Public Class Tools

  Public Shared Function IsLoggedIn() As Boolean

    Dim ctx As HttpContext = HttpContext.Current

    If ctx.Request.Cookies("email") Is Nothing OrElse _
       ctx.Request.Cookies("email").Value = "" Then
      Return False
    Else
      Return True
    End If
```

```
   End Function
End Class
```

This class just provides a central function to see whether a user is logged in or not. It accesses the current HTTP context – you don't need to worry especially about this, but it's required if you need to access the HTTP objects from within a component. From the context, we access the `Request` object, and from there the `Cookies` collection, and the cookie called `email`. This cookie contains the e-mail address of a logged-in user. If it's empty, the user isn't logged in.

Setting the Configuration

Now that the components are installed, we need to set the configuration details. For this application, this simply consists of the information required to connect to the database, which we can store in the `web.config` file. Just add the following between the `<configuration>` and `<system.web>` elements, save the file, and close it:

```
<appSettings>
  <add key="ConnectionString"
       value="server=(local)\NetSDK;database=bids;Trusted_Connection=true" />
</appSettings>
```

Coding the Application

We have built the foundations for the application. The next step is to create the ASP.NET pages that make up its superstructure. During the rest of the chapter, we will be using HTML mode for editing the pages – while VS.NET has great support for drag and drop, it doesn't help us to show you exactly what each page requires. We *could* show you the design view, but then you'd have to guess what each element is!

The first page that we will create is, reasonably enough, the starting point of the application: the home page.

The Home Page

The home page of the application is responsible for welcoming the user to the application, providing some information about what the application is for, and displaying the top-level menu selections that will enable the user to:

❑   Browse the items that are for sale

❑   Log into the system

❑   Register with the system

We'll call the home page `Default.aspx` (we'll see how to do this in a moment), which means that the user can simply type in the URL of a virtual directory on our web server, and they'll automatically be directed to this page.

Try It Out – Creating the Home Page

1. Let's start by renaming the `WebForm1.aspx` file. In the Solution Explorer, right click on this file, and then select **Rename**. As stated above, the new name is `Default.aspx`.

2. Click the HTML tab, and you'll see the code for `Default.aspx`. We need to change this, so delete everything apart from the first two lines, and replace it with the following:

```html
<html>
  <head>
    <title>Wrox Classifieds</title>
  </head>
  <body style="FONT-SIZE: 13px; FONT-FAMILY: Verdana">
    <h3 align="center">Wrox Classifieds</h3>
    <h3 align="center">Main Menu</h3>
    Thank you for visiting the Wrox Classifieds website.
    We offer you the opportunity to:
    <ol>
      <li>Browse for items on sale</li>
      <li>Bid for Items on Sale</li>
      <li>Sell your items</li>
    </ol>
    <p align="justify">
      Feel free to browse our listings - you don't need to register to do that.
      If you find an item that you would like to bid on, or if you would like
      to sell something, we will ask you to register with us.
    </p>
    <hr>
    <table width="100%">
      <tr>
        <td Width="33%" align="middle">
          <a href="BrowseListing.aspx">Browse the Listings</a>
        </td>
        <td Width="33%" align="middle">
          <a href="Login.aspx">Login</a>
        </td>
        <td Width="34%" align="middle">
          <a href="Register.aspx">I'm a new user</a>
        </td>
      </tr>
    </table>
  </body>
</html>
```

The output of the code will look like this:

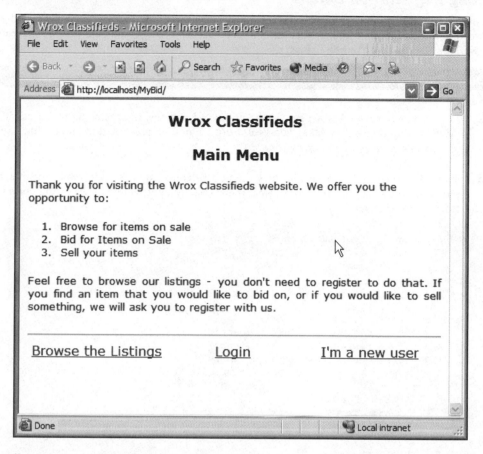

This is all created using HTML, and it's quite straightforward, so let's quickly move on.

User Registration and Login

So, our user has arrived at the site and been presented with `Default.aspx`, which offers three options:

- ❑ They can choose to browse the items-for-sale list (by choosing the **Browse the Listings** link).
- ❑ If they're a first-time user, they can register with the system (by selecting the **I'm a new user** link).
- ❑ If they've visited the site before, they can use their e-mail/password combination to login to the system (by selecting the **Login** link).

We'll cover the browsing option later in the chapter; in this section, we'll focus on registration and login.

Collecting Registration Details

In order to allow a new user to register for the first time, we'll need to collect their details, check their password, and enter all that information into the database. In order to manage this, we'll create a new ASP.NET page called `Register.aspx`.

Try It Out – Collecting Registration Details with Register.aspx

1. Let's create our new ASPX page. In the Solution Explorer, right click on the application name (MyBid), and then select **Add I Add Web Form**. You'll be prompted to enter a file name, which you should give as `Register.aspx`.

2. The `Register.aspx` page will show the user's details, such as their name, address, and password information. As before, select the **HTML** tab, and enter the following code for `Register.aspx`:

```
<%@ Page Language="vb" AutoEventWireup="false"
        Codebehind="Register.aspx.vb" Inherits="Bid.Register"%>
<html>
  <head>
    <title>Registration</title>
  </head>
  <body style="FONT: 10pt verdana">
    <form id="Form1" method="post" runat="server">
      <h3 align="center">Wrox Classifieds</h3>
      <h3 align="center">Registration Info</h3>
      <table Width="50%" Align="center" CellPadding="0" CellSpacing="0">
        <tr>
          <td>E-Mail Address</td>
          <td><asp:TextBox ID="txtEmail" Runat="server" /></td>
        </tr>
        <tr>
          <td>Given Name</td>
          <td><asp:TextBox ID="txtGivenName" Runat="server" /></td>
        </tr>
        <tr>
          <td>Family Name</td>
          <td><asp:TextBox ID="txtFamilyName" Runat="server" /></td>
        </tr>
        <tr>
          <td>Address</td>
          <td><asp:TextBox ID="txtAdd1" Runat="server" /></td>
        </tr>
        <tr>
          <td> </td>
          <td><asp:TextBox ID="txtAdd2" Runat="server" /></td>
        </tr>
        <tr>
          <td>City</td>
          <td><asp:TextBox ID="txtCity" Runat="server" /></td>
        </tr>
```

```
    <tr>
      <td>State</td>
      <td><asp:TextBox ID="txtState" Runat="server" /></td>
    </tr>
    <tr>
      <td>Postal Code</td>
      <td>
        <asp:TextBox ID="txtZip" Runat="server" />
      </td>
    </tr>
    <tr>
      <td>Country</td>
      <td><asp:TextBox ID="txtCountry" Runat="server" /></td>
    </tr>
    <tr>
      <td>Password</td>
      <td><asp:TextBox ID="txtPwd" TextMode="Password" Runat="server" />
      </td>
    </tr>
    <tr>
      <td>Confirm Password</td>
      <td>
        <asp:TextBox ID="txtPwdConfirm" TextMode="Password"
                   Runat="server" />
      </td>
    </tr>
    <tr>
      <td><asp:Button ID="btnSubmit" Text="Submit" Runat="server" /></td>
      <td><input id="btnReset" type="reset" Runat="server" value="Reset">
      </td>
    </tr>
    <tr>
      <td colspan="2"><asp:Label ID="lblMsg" Runat="server" /></td>
    </tr>
</table>
<hr>
<asp:Panel ID="GuestMenu" Runat="server">
  <table width="100%" align="center">
    <tr>
      <td align="middle" width="33%">
        <a href="default.aspx">Home</a>
      </td>
      <td align="middle" width="33%">
        <a href="BrowseListing.aspx">Browse the Listings</a>
      </td>
      <td align="middle">
        <a href="Login.aspx">Login</a>
      </td>
    </tr>
  </table>
</asp:Panel>
```

```
          <asp:Panel ID="RegisteredMenu" Runat="server">
            <table width="100%" align="center">
              <tr>
                <td align="middle" width="25%">
                  <a href="MenuForRegisteredUsers.aspx">Home</a>
                </td>
                <td align="middle" width="25%">
                  <a href="BrowseListing.aspx">Browse the Listings</a>
                </td>
                <td align="middle" width="25%">
                  <a href="ViewMySaleItems.aspx">List/Edit Sale Items</a>
                </td>
                <td align="middle" width="25%"><A href="Logout.aspx">Logout</a>
                </td>
              </tr>
            </table>
          </asp:Panel>
        </form>
      </body>
</html>
```

3. Select the **Design** view; this adds the ASP.NET controls to the code file. Save your changes.

4. That's the interface, so now it's time to write our first code. In the Solution Explorer, right click on `Register.aspx`, and choose **View Code**. As you can see in the following screenshot, you'll open up `Register.aspx.vb`, which is the code-behind file for `Register.aspx`:

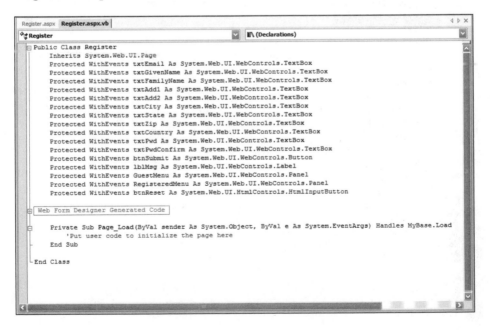

5. Replace the definition of the `Page_Load()` event handler with the following:

```
Private Process As String

Public Sub Page_Load(ByVal sender As System.Object, _
                        ByVal e As System.EventArgs) Handles MyBase.Load

    If Tools.IsLoggedIn() Then

        Process = "MODIFY"

        Dim myPersonDetails As Bid.PersonDetails = New Bid.PersonDetails()
        Dim obj As Bid.Person = New Bid.Person()

        myPersonDetails = obj.GetPersonDetails(Request.Cookies("email").Value)
        txtFamilyName.Text = myPersonDetails.FamilyName
        txtGivenName.Text = myPersonDetails.GivenName
        txtEmail.Text = Request.Cookies("email").Value
        txtPwd.Text = myPersonDetails.Password
        txtAdd1.Text = myPersonDetails.StreetAddress1
        txtAdd2.Text = myPersonDetails.StreetAddress2
        txtCity.Text = myPersonDetails.City
        txtState.Text = myPersonDetails.State
        txtZip.Text = myPersonDetails.PostalCode
        txtCountry.Text = myPersonDetails.Country
        txtEmail.Enabled = False
        obj = Nothing

        GuestMenu.Visible = False
        RegisteredMenu.Visible = True
    Else
        Process = "ADD"

        GuestMenu.Visible = True
        RegisteredMenu.Visible = False
    End If
End Sub
```

6. Now add a new procedure, to be run when the user presses the **Submit** button:

```
Private Sub btnSubmit_Click(ByVal sender As System.Object, _
                        ByVal e As System.EventArgs) Handles btnSubmit.Click

    If Page.IsValid Then
        Dim obj As Bid.Person = New Bid.Person()
        Dim strStatus As String
        If Process = "ADD" Then
            strStatus = obj.AddCustomer(txtFamilyName.Text, _
                            txtGivenName.Text, _
                            txtEmail.Text, _
                            txtPwd.Text, _
```

```
                                    txtAdd1.Text, _
                                    txtAdd2.Text, _
                                    txtCity.Text, _
                                    txtState.Text, _
                                    txtZip.Text, _
                                    txtCountry.Text)

        If IsNumeric(strStatus) Then
          Response.Cookies("GivenName").Value = txtGivenName.Text
          Response.Cookies("EMail").Value = txtEmail.Text
          Response.Cookies("PersonID").Value = strStatus
          Response.Redirect("MenuForRegisteredUsers.aspx")
        ElseIf Len(strStatus) > 1 Then
          lblMsg.Text = strStatus
        End If
      Else

        ' Code for Update goes here
        strStatus = obj.ModifyCustomer(txtFamilyName.Text, _
                                    txtGivenName.Text, _
                                    txtEmail.Text, _
                                    txtPwd.Text, _
                                    txtAdd1.Text, _
                                    txtAdd2.Text, _
                                    txtCity.Text, _
                                    txtState.Text, _
                                    txtZip.Text, _
                                    txtCountry.Text)

        If strStatus = "1" Then
          Response.Cookies("GivenName").Value = Request.Form("txtGivenName")
          Response.Cookies("EMail").Value = txtEmail.Text
          Response.Redirect("MenuForRegisteredUsers.Aspx")
        ElseIf Len(strStatus) > 1 Then
          lblMsg.Text = "Update Failed! " & strStatus
        End If
      End If
    End If
End Sub
```

The output of `Register.aspx` will look like this:

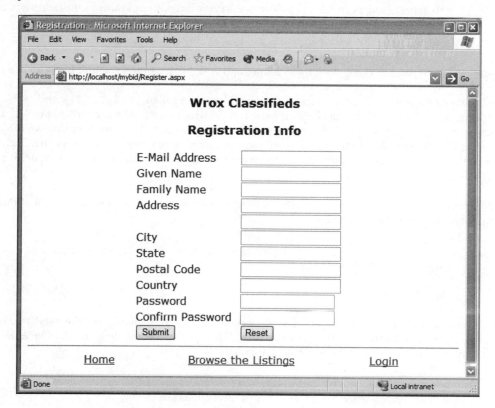

How It Works

There seems to be quite a lot of code here, but it's not too difficult. The main task of `Register.aspx` is to present the user with a form that they'll use to submit their registration information. When the user has completed the form, they press the Submit button.

The first line in `Register.aspx` is the `Page` directive, which (among other things) specifies the code-behind file that we'll be using:

```
<%@ Page Language="vb" AutoEventWireup="false"
        Codebehind="Register.aspx.vb" Inherits="MyBid.Register"%>
```

If you look at the `Register.aspx` file, you can see that we're using a considerable number of web server controls, such as text boxes and labels. (The plain HTML elements are just used to lay out the controls in a pleasing fashion.) Among these, we have a text box called `txtFamilyName`:

```
<td><asp:TextBox ID="txtFamilyName" Runat="server" /></td>
```

Because VS.NET uses the code-behind model, we have to provide a link between the two files. For each ASP.NET web server control in the `.aspx` file, we have a line similar to this in the `.aspx.vb` file:

```
Protected WithEvents txtFamilyName As System.Web.UI.WebControls.TextBox
```

This allows us to refer to the control by its name, and ASP.NET handles the link between the two files.

Moving on to `Register.aspx.vb`, we have event handlers called `Page_Load()` and `btnSubmit_Click()`. When the page is loaded, the `Page_Load()` event handler is called, and we check to see if the user is logged in by using the `Tools.IsLoggedIn()` method that we discussed earlier in the chapter. We do this because the page not only allows entry of new user details, but also allows editing of existing user details. This saves us from having to write two pages that do exactly the same thing.

If the user *is* logged in, then we are modifying their details, so we use the features of one of our components to fetch the existing data:

```
Dim myPersonDetails As Bid.PersonDetails = New Bid.PersonDetails()
Dim obj As Bid.Person = New Bid.Person()

myPersonDetails = obj.GetPersonDetails(Request.Cookies("email").Value)
```

These calls in our code ultimately call stored procedures to fetch the data from the database. We know which user to fetch details for, because we've stored their e-mail address in a cookie. Once the data has been fetched, we display it in the text boxes, like so:

```
txtFamilyName.Text = myPersonDetails.FamilyName
txtGivenName.Text = myPersonDetails.GivenName
```

When the data has been displayed, we hide the menu that's used for new users, and show the menu for registered users:

```
GuestMenu.Visible = False
RegisteredMenu.Visible = True
```

Each of these menus is really just a set of plain HTML controls (tables for layout, and hyperlinks for the menu items), but we've wrapped them in an `asp:Panel`. The `Panel` is just a container control that allows us to hide or show whole sections of the interface with ease.

If the user isn't logged in, then we simply do the opposite with the menus: we show the one for guests, and hide the one for registered users:

```
GuestMenu.Visible = True
RegisteredMenu.Visible = False
```

That's all for the `Page_Load()` event handler, so let's look now at what happens when the **Submit** button is pressed. The first thing we do is check to see if the page content is valid:

```
Private Sub btnSubmit_Click(ByVal sender As System.Object, _
                        ByVal e As System.EventArgs) Handles btnSubmit.Click
    If Page.IsValid Then
```

In fact, since there's no validation, this isn't *actually* necessary on this page – but it does protect the code in case we add validation later on. We'll talk about this at the end of the chapter.

Next, we create an instance of the `Person` object. This will be used to create or update the user details:

```
Dim obj As Bid.Person = New Bid.Person()
Dim strStatus As String
```

If we're adding a new record, we call the `AddCustomer()` method, and pass in the details:

```
If Process = "ADD" Then
  strStatus = obj.AddCustomer(txtFamilyName.Text, _
                              txtGivenName.Text, _
                              txtEmail.Text, _
                              txtPwd.Text, _
                              txtAdd1.Text, _
                              txtAdd2.Text, _
                              txtCity.Text, _
                              txtState.Text, _
                              txtZip.Text, _
                              txtCountry.Text)
```

This method places one of two things in `strStatus`: the ID number of the newly added user, or an error message. If the value returned is numeric, we know that adding the customer succeeded, so we can store their details in cookies and send them to the menu for registered users. If the return value *isn't* numeric, then we display an error message:

```
If IsNumeric(strStatus) Then
  Response.Cookies("GivenName").Value = txtGivenName.Text
  Response.Cookies("EMail").Value = txtEmail.Text
  Response.Cookies("PersonID").Value = strStatus
  Response.Redirect("MenuForRegisteredUsers.aspx")
ElseIf Len(strStatus) > 1 Then
  lblMsg.Text = strStatus
End If
```

For existing users, the process is much the same, but this time calling the `ModifyCustomer()` method:

```
strStatus = obj.ModifyCustomer(txtFamilyName.Text, _
                               txtGivenName.Text, _
                               txtEmail.Text, _
                               txtPwd.Text, _
```

```
                                 txtAdd1.Text, _
                                 txtAdd2.Text, _
                                 txtCity.Text, _
                                 txtState.Text, _
                                 txtZip.Text, _
                                 txtCountry.Text)
```

Checking for errors is also similar, but this time we already have a user ID, so we use 1 as the return value for success:

```
If strStatus = "1" Then
  Response.Cookies("GivenName").Value = Request.Form("txtGivenName")
  Response.Cookies("EMail").Value = txtEmail.Text
  Response.Redirect("MenuForRegisteredUsers.aspx")
ElseIf Len(strStatus) > 1 Then
  lblMsg.Text = "Update Failed! " & strStatus
End If
```

OK, that's the user registered – let's look at the login page.

Managing User Login

If the user has registered on a previous occasion and is now revisiting the site, they wouldn't expect to be asked to go through the registration process again. To allow previously registered users to identify themselves, we present a login page: Login.aspx.

Try It Out – The Login Screen and Login Checker

1. Create a new ASP.NET page using the same method as before. Call it Login.aspx, and add the following in the HTML view:

```
<%@ Page Language="vb" AutoEventWireup="false"
        Codebehind="Login.aspx.vb" Inherits="MyBid.Login"%>
<html>
  <head>
    <title>Login</title>
  </head>
  <body style="FONT: 10pt verdana">
    <form id="Form1" method="post" runat="server">
      <h3 align="center">Wrox Classifieds</h3>
      <h3 align="center">Login Page</h3>
      <asp:Label ID="lblMsg" Font-Bold="True" ForeColor="#ff0000"
                Runat="server" />
      <table>
        <tr>
          <td>E-mail Address</td>
          <td><asp:TextBox ID="txtEmail" Runat="server" /></td>
        </tr>
        <tr>
          <td>Password</td>
```

```
        <td><asp:TextBox ID="txtPwd" TextMode="Password"
                        Runat="server" /></td>
     </tr>
     <tr>
        <td><asp:Button ID="btnSubmit" Text="Submit" Runat="server" /></td>
        <td><input id="btnReset" type="reset" NAME="btnReset"
                Runat="server" /></td>
     </tr>
   </table>
   <table Width="50%">
     <tr>
        <td Width="50%">
          <a href="MenuForRegisteredUsers.aspx">Home</a>
        </td>
        <td Width="50%">
          <a href="Register.aspx">I'm a new user</a>
        </td>
     </tr>
   </table>
 </form>
 </body>
</html>
```

2. Switch to the Design view, and save your changes.

3. View the code for this file, and add the following:

```
Private Sub btnSubmit_Click(ByVal sender As System.Object, _
                    ByVal e As System.EventArgs) Handles btnSubmit.Click

  If Page.IsValid = True Then
    Dim obj As Bid.Person = New Bid.Person()
    Dim myPersonDetails As Bid.PersonDetails = New Bid.PersonDetails()

    myPersonDetails = obj.Login(txtEmail.Text, txtPwd.Text)

    If myPersonDetails.PersonID <> 0 Then
      Response.Cookies("EMail").Value = txtEmail.Text
      Response.Cookies("GivenName").Value = myPersonDetails.GivenName
      Response.Cookies("PersonID").Value = myPersonDetails.PersonID
      Response.Redirect("MenuForRegisteredUsers.Aspx")
    Else
      lblMsg.Text = "Login failed. Please try again."
    End If
  End If
End Sub
```

4. The output of `Login.aspx` will look like this:

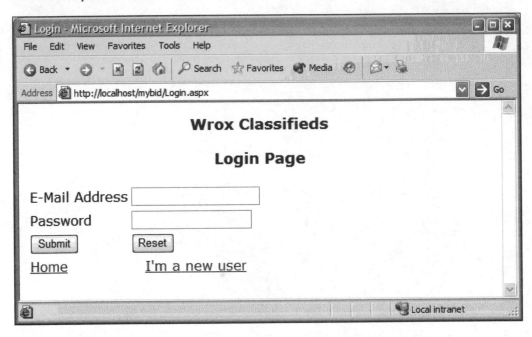

5. After entering the e-mail address and password, click on the Submit button. This will check your login information against the information contained in the database, and then take you to the registered users' home page, `MenuForRegisteredUsers.aspx` (we haven't created this yet, so expect an error if you try it!).

How It Works

Compared to some of the code we've been looking at, this page is extremely simple. As in the registration page, we first check to see if the page content is valid:

```
If Page.IsValid = True Then
```

We then create an instance of the `Person` object and call its `Login()` method, passing in the e-mail address and password. This calls a stored procedure that compares these details with those held in the database:

```
Dim obj As Bid.Person = New Bid.Person()
Dim myPersonDetails As Bid.PersonDetails = New Bid.PersonDetails()

myPersonDetails = obj.Login(txtEmail.Text, txtPwd.Text)
```

A valid user will have an ID that's greater than 0; if they *are* valid, we set the cookie details and send them to the menu for registered users:

```
If myPersonDetails.PersonID <> 0 Then
  Response.Cookies("EMail").Value = txtEmail.Text
  Response.Cookies("GivenName").Value = myPersonDetails.GivenName
  Response.Cookies("PersonID").Value = myPersonDetails.PersonID
  Response.Redirect("MenuForRegisteredUsers.aspx")
Else
  lblMsg.Text = "Login failed. Please try again."
End If
End If
```

That's it for registration and logging in. Let's now see how the menu for registered users differs from the one for guests.

Menu for Registered Users

In this menu, we want to show not only a list of things a registered user can do (add items, browse, and so on), but also a grid of items that the user has placed winning bids on. This is where we start to see data binding getting into the action.

Try It Out – Registered Users' Home Page

1. Create a new ASPX page as before, and enter the following code for
`MenuForRegisteredUsers.aspx`:

```
<%@ Page Language="vb" AutoEventWireup="false"
        Codebehind="MenuForRegisteredUsers.aspx.vb"
        Inherits="MyBid.MenuForRegisteredUsers"%>
<html>
  <head>
    <title>Wrox Classifieds</title>
  </head>
<body style="FONT-SIZE: 13px; FONT-FAMILY: Verdana">
    <form id="default" method="post" runat="server">
      <h3 align="center">Wrox Classifieds</h3>
      <h3 align="center">Registered Users Menu</h3>
      <p><asp:Label id="lblUserName" Runat="server" Font-Size="13px"
                  Font-Name="verdana" /></p>
      <p>Thank you for visiting the Wrox Classifieds website.
        We offer you the opportunity to:
      </p>
      <ol>
        <li>Browse for items on sale</li>
        <li>Bid for Items on Sale</li>
        <li>Sell your items</li>
      </ol>
      <p align="justify">
        <b>You have placed the winning bid on these items.</b>
      </p>
```

409

```
        <asp:Label id="lblStatus" Runat="server"
              ForeColor="#ff0000" Font-Bold="True" />
      <asp:DataGrid id="myWinningBids" AutoGenerateColumns="False" Width="50%"
                 HeaderStyle-BackColor="#ff0000" HeaderStyle-Font-Bold="True"
                 HeaderStyle-Font-Name="Verdana" HeaderStyle-Font-Size="13px"
                 HeaderStyle-ForeColor="#ffffff" ItemStyle-BackColor="Beige"
                 ItemStyle-Font-Name="verdana" ItemStyle-Font-Size="13px"
                 BorderColor="#000000" Runat="server"
                 OnItemCreated="myWinningBids_ItemCreated">
    <Columns>
      <asp:TemplateColumn
          HeaderText="Item Name - Click to Complete purchase.">
        <ItemTemplate>
          <asp:hyperlink id="hypItemName"
             NavigateUrl=
        '<%# FormatUrl(DataBinder.Eval(Container.DataItem, "ItemID"),
            DataBinder.Eval(Container.DataItem, "Highestbid")) %>'
            Text='<%# DataBinder.Eval(Container.DataItem, "ItemName") %>'
            Runat="server" />
        </ItemTemplate>
      </asp:TemplateColumn>
      <asp:BoundColumn DataField="HighestBid" HeaderText="Winning Bid"
                    runat="server" id="Boundcolumn1" />
    </Columns>
  </asp:DataGrid>
  <hr/>
  <table width="100%">
    <tr>
      <td Width="10%" align="middle">
        Home
      </td>
      <td Width="20%" align="middle">
        <a href="BrowseListing.aspx">Browse the Listings</a>
      </td>
      <td Width="20%" align="middle">
        <a href="ViewMySaleItems.aspx">List/Edit Sale Items</a>
      </td>
      <td Width="20%" align="middle">
        <a href="Register.aspx">Registration Info</a>
      </td>
      <td Width="10%" align="middle">
        <a href="Logout.aspx">Logout</a>
      </td>
    </tr>
  </table>
  </form>
  </body>
</html>
```

2. Switch to the Design view, and then save the page.

3. View the code for this page, and add the following to the `Page_Load()` event handler:

```
Private Sub Page_Load(ByVal sender As System.Object, _
                      ByVal e As System.EventArgs) Handles MyBase.Load

    ' If they haven't logged in, send them to the default menu
    If Tools.IsLoggedIn() Then
      lblUserName.Text = "Welcome <b>" & _
                          Request.Cookies("EMail").Value & "</b><br/>"
    Else
      Response.Redirect("Default.aspx")
    End If


    If Not Page.IsPostBack Then
      BindGrid()
    End If


    lblStatus.Text = Request.QueryString("msg")
End Sub
```

4. Next, add the `BindGrid()` method, which shows the grid of winning bids:

```
Private Sub BindGrid()
    Dim intPersonID As Int32 = CInt(Request.Cookies("PersonID").Value)
    Dim objItemList As Bid.Item = New Bid.Item()

    myWinningBids.DataSource = objItemList.GetMyWinningBids(intPersonID)
    myWinningBids.DataBind()
End Sub
```

5. The next method is an event handler that will run when each item in the grid is created (we'll explain why we need this a little later on):

```
Sub myWinningBids_ItemCreated(ByVal Sender As Object, _
                              ByVal e As DataGridItemEventArgs)


    If e.Item.ItemType = ListItemType.Item Or _
       e.Item.ItemType = ListItemType.AlternatingItem Then
      Dim temphypAcceptBid As HyperLink
      temphypAcceptBid = e.Item.FindControl("hypItemName")
      temphypAcceptBid.Attributes.Add("onclick", _
                    "return confirm('You are about to buy this product?');")
    End If


End Sub
```

Finally, add the `FormatUrl()` function that does some formatting for us:

```
Public Function FormatURL(ByVal intItemID As Int32, _
                          ByVal dblWinningBid As Double) As String
  Return "AcceptBid.aspx?itemid=" & intItemID & "&bid=" & dblWinningBid
End Function
```

6. The output of the page will look like this:

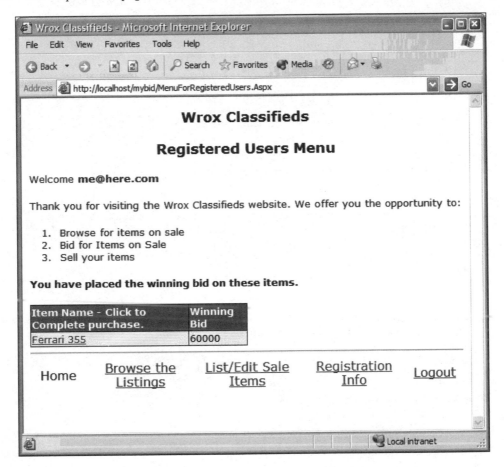

If the user doesn't have any winning bids, then the grid will be empty.

How It Works

The first thing we do in this page (in the `Page_Load()` event handler) is to decide whether the user is logged in or not:

```
If Tools.IsLoggedIn Then
  lblUserName.Text = "Welcome <b>" & _
                      Request.Cookies("EMail").Value & "</b><br/>"
```

```
Else
   Response.Redirect("Default.aspx")
End If
```

If the user is logged in, we show them a welcome message. If not, we redirect them to the default menu page. Now, since this page should only ever be seen by a user who is already logged in, you might wonder why we do this. But that's exactly the point: it *shouldn't* be seen by a user who isn't logged in, but there's nothing to stop someone from typing in this page as part of a URL and jumping to it directly. This means that in theory at least, we should check the login for each and every page.

> *We can actually avoid the need for this by using some of ASP.NET's security features, which do all of the checking for us. We're not going to cover that here, but it's worth reading about for your future projects.*

So, having verified that the user is logged in, we need to load the data. We only do this on the first load of the page, and not when any buttons have been pressed. This saves a call to the database when it's not required:

```
If Not Page.IsPostBack Then
   BindGrid()
End If

lblStatus.Text = Request.QueryString("msg")
```

Loading the data is then extremely simple:

```
Private Sub BindGrid()
   Dim intPersonID As Int32 = CInt(Request.Cookies("PersonID").Value)
   Dim objItemList As Bid.Item = New Bid.Item()

   myWinningBids.DataSource = objItemList.GetMyWinningBids(intPersonID)
   myWinningBids.DataBind()
End Sub
```

Here, we extract the ID of the user from the cookie, and then pass this into the GetMyWinningBids() method of the Item class. This will fetch those bids that this user has won from the database. The data is returned in the form of a SqlDataReader object, which is set to the DataSource of the grid. Calling BindGrid() reads this data and constructs the grid for us.

We now need to look at what happens as each item in the grid is created. Of course, the DataGrid control does most of the footwork for us, but we want to do a little more with our data: we want to show the winning bids together with hyperlinks that will let the user confirm that they wish to buy the items in question. These links will take us to the AcceptBid.aspx page (which we'll describe later).

However, we've decided that rather than jump directly to this page, we'd like the user to confirm that they really do wish to buy the item. We could do this in AcceptBid.aspx, but that would mean that if they said no, we'd have to jump back here. Instead, we'll use a JavaScript popup dialog – the user then gets the chance to confirm the purchase, but the underlying page remains the same. What we're doing is adding this popup to the hyperlink, so that it shows before the link takes effect.

To get a procedure to run as each item is created in the grid, we've added the following attribute to the grid definition:

```
OnItemCreated="myWinningBids_ItemCreated"
```

This identifies the procedure to run:

```
Sub myWinningBids_ItemCreated(ByVal Sender As Object, _
                     ByVal e As DataGridItemEventArgs)
```

Notice that the arguments for this handler are slightly different from the ones in many of the other procedures we've dealt with. In many of those, the second argument (e) is of type EventArgs. Here, it is DataGridItemEventArgs. For every row in the grid, this procedure is called, and e will contain details of the row. One of those details is Item, which contains the row contents. At this point, we can use another property, ItemType, to determine what type of item we are creating – a Header, an Item, an AlternatingItem, and so on. We are only interested in Item and AlternatingItem, since this is where our data will be shown:

```
If e.Item.ItemType = ListItemType.Item Or _
    e.Item.ItemType = ListItemType.AlternatingItem Then
```

When we know that we're dealing with the correct item type, we need access to the hyperlink. To do this, we use the FindControl() method of the item to find the control by name:

```
Dim temphypAcceptBid As HyperLink
temphypAcceptBid = e.Item.FindControl("hypItemName")
```

Finally, we add an attribute to this hyperlink control. It's this attribute that will provide the JavaScript popup:

```
temphypAcceptBid.Attributes.Add("onclick", _
            "return confirm('You are about to buy this product?');")
```

There are two arguments to the Add() method. The first is the attribute name, and the second is the value of this attribute. In our case, the attribute is named onclick, which is a client-side event handler. The value for this type of attribute is either the name of a client-side function, or the actual JavaScript code itself. We've chosen the latter, since the code is extremely small. In fact, all it does is to call the confirm() function – which pops up the dialog:

This gives us two choices: to confirm our purchase (and return a value of `true`), or to cancel our purchase (and return a value of `false`). The really clever thing about this, though, is that we now have a server-side hyperlink control, but we can intercept the user action when they click the link. Our custom code is run before the link takes effect, and the link is only followed if the return value from the popup is `true`.

This may seem like a slightly complex mechanism, but there are two really important lessons to learn here:

- ❑ You can intercept actions on the client.

- ❑ You can manipulate the items in the grid as they are created. This means you can do things like changing the formatting depending upon the grid contents (showing negative values in red, perhaps).

It's well worth getting used to these techniques, which can prove extremely useful, especially as the complexity of your applications grows.

The final function we added in this section, `FormatUrl()`, performs some formatting of the URL for us. Often, this isn't necessary, because we can simply bind to data. With this hyperlink, however, we want to pass in two pieces of information: the ID of the item, and the bid value. This means we have to construct the URL manually. Here's a reminder of the binding syntax for this control:

```
NavigateUrl='<%# FormatURL(DataBinder.Eval(Container.DataItem, "ItemID"),
                   DataBinder.Eval(Container.DataItem, "Highestbid")) %>'
```

The `NavigateUrl` property is the URL to jump to, but instead of binding it directly to a data item, we are binding to the result of a function, and passing into that function the two items we need:

```
Public Function FormatURL(ByVal intItemID As Int32, _
                          ByVal dblWinningBid As Double) As String
    Return "AcceptBid.aspx?itemid=" & intItemID & "&bid=" & dblWinningBid
End Function
```

The function simply takes these two items and constructs a string that represents the URL we need. It's this string that becomes the result of the binding.

Managing Items for Sale

Once a user is registered, they can start posting items for sale. Naturally, when posting an item for sale, the user must provide some information about it. The information involved for each sale item is:

- ❑ A name for the item

- ❑ A long description of the item

- ❑ The desired price for the item (this is the price that the seller would like to achieve)

- ❑ The price at which the system should notify the seller (this is the price the seller would accept)

- ❑ The date after which the item will no longer be for sale

Some of this information will be displayed to potential buyers, and some is used internally in the system. And clearly, there's more to managing the 'for sale' items than just adding them to a list – we need a mechanism that allows the seller to edit the details, or to remove an item from listings. We'll cover these interfaces in the following *Try It Out* sections.

Viewing One's Own Sale Items

Let's first look at how we view the items that we've put up for sale. You might argue that we should add some items before we start to view them, but the menu structure we have means that the option to add new items is accessed from the view page.

Try It Out – Displaying the Items that a User Has for Sale

1. Create a new ASPX page called `ViewMySaleItems.aspx`, and type in the following code:

```
<%@ Page Language="vb" AutoEventWireup="false"
         Codebehind="ViewMySaleItems.aspx.vb"
         Inherits="Bid.ViewMySaleItems"%>
<html>
  <head>
    <title>ViewMySaleItems</title>
  </head>
  <body style="FONT: 10pt verdana">
    <form id="Form1" method="post" runat="server">
      <h3 align="center">Wrox Classifieds</h3>
      <h3 align="center">Selling Items</h3>
      <asp:Label ID="lblUserName" Font-Name="verdana" Font-Size="13px"
           Runat="server" />
      <asp:Label ID="lblMsg" Font-Name="verdana" Font-Size="14px"
          ForeColor="#000099" Font-Bold="True"
          Text="You currently have the following items for sale."
          Runat="server" /><br>
      <br>
      <asp:Label ID="lblStatus" ForeColor="#ff0000" Font-Name="verdana"
          Font-Size="11px" Runat="server" />

      <asp:DataGrid ID="myItems" AutoGenerateColumns="False" Width="99%"
          HeaderStyle-BackColor="#ff0000" HeaderStyle-Font-Bold="True"
          HeaderStyle-Font-Name="Verdana" HeaderStyle-Font-Size="13px"
          HeaderStyle-ForeColor="#ffffff" ItemStyle-BackColor="Beige"
          ItemStyle-Font-Name="verdana" ItemStyle-Font-Size="13px"
          BorderColor="#000000" OnCancelCommand="myItems_Cancel"
          OnEditCommand="myItems_Edit" OnUpdateCommand="myItems_Update"
          OnDeleteCommand="myItems_Delete" OnItemCreated="myItems_ItemCreated"
          DataKeyField="ItemID" Runat="server">
        <Columns>
          <asp:EditCommandColumn EditText="Edit" CancelText="Cancel"
              UpdateText="Update" />
          <asp:ButtonColumn text="Delete" CommandName="Delete"
              ItemStyle-Width="50px" />
          <asp:TemplateColumn HeaderText="Name">
```

```
    <ItemTemplate>
      <asp:Label ID="lblItemName"
      Text='<%# DataBinder.Eval(Container.DataItem, "ItemName") %>'
      Runat="server" />
    </ItemTemplate>
    <EditItemTemplate>
      <asp:TextBox ID="txtitemName" Width="100"
      Text='<%# DataBinder.Eval(Container.DataItem, "ItemName") %>'
      Runat="server" />
    </EditItemTemplate>
  </asp:TemplateColumn>
  <asp:TemplateColumn HeaderText="Description">
    <ItemTemplate>
      <asp:Label ID="lblDescription"
      Text='<%# DataBinder.Eval(Container.DataItem, "Description") %>'
      Runat="server" />
    </ItemTemplate>
    <EditItemTemplate>
      <asp:TextBox ID="txtDescription" TextMode="MultiLine" Rows="3"
      Columns="20"
      Text='<%# DataBinder.Eval(Container.DataItem, "Description") %>'
      Runat="server" />
    </EditItemTemplate>
  </asp:TemplateColumn>
  <asp:TemplateColumn HeaderText="Asking Price">
    <ItemTemplate>
      <asp:Label ID="lblAskPrice"
        Text='<%# DataBinder.Eval(Container.DataItem, "AskingPrice") %>'
        Runat="server" />
    </ItemTemplate>
    <EditItemTemplate>
      <asp:TextBox ID="txtAskPrice" Width="65"
      Text='<%# DataBinder.Eval(Container.DataItem, "AskingPrice") %>'
      Runat="server" />
    </EditItemTemplate>
  </asp:TemplateColumn>
  <asp:TemplateColumn HeaderText="Notify Price">
    <ItemTemplate>
      <asp:Label ID="lblNotifyPrice"
      Text='<%# DataBinder.Eval(Container.DataItem, "NotifyPrice") %>'
      Runat="server" />
    </ItemTemplate>
    <EditItemTemplate>
      <asp:TextBox ID="txtNotifyPrice" Width="65"
      Text='<%# DataBinder.Eval(Container.DataItem, "NotifyPrice") %>'
      Runat="server" />
    </EditItemTemplate>
  </asp:TemplateColumn>
  <asp:TemplateColumn HeaderText="Listing Date">
    <ItemTemplate>
      <asp:Label ID="lblListingDate"
      Text='<%# DataBinder.Eval(Container.DataItem, "ListingDate") %>'
```

```
                              Runat="server" />
                    </ItemTemplate>
                </asp:TemplateColumn>
                <asp:TemplateColumn HeaderText="Highest Bid">
                    <ItemTemplate>
                        <asp:Label ID="lblCurrentBid"
                                   Text=
        '<%# FormatHighBid(DataBinder.Eval(Container.DataItem, "HighestBid")) %>'
                                   Runat="server" />
                    </ItemTemplate>
                </asp:TemplateColumn>
                <asp:TemplateColumn HeaderText="Bidder ID">
                    <ItemTemplate>
                        <asp:Label ID="lblBidderID" Text=
        '<%# FormatBidderID(DataBinder.Eval(Container.DataItem, "HighestBidNumber")) %>'
                                   Runat="server" />
                    </ItemTemplate>
                </asp:TemplateColumn>
                <asp:TemplateColumn HeaderText="Accept Bid">
                    <ItemTemplate>
                        <asp:HyperLink ID="hypAcceptBID"
                                       Text=
        '<%# ShowText(DataBinder.Eval(Container.DataItem, "HighestBid")) %>'
                                       NavigateUrl=
        '<%# FormatURL(DataBinder.Eval(Container.DataItem, "HighestBid"),
                    DataBinder.Eval(Container.DataItem, "ItemID"),
                    DataBinder.Eval(Container.DataItem, "HighestBidNumber"))%>'
                                       Runat="server" />
                        <asp:Label ID="lblMark" Text=
         '<%# IsPending(DataBinder.Eval(Container.DataItem, "itemstatus")) %>'
                                   Font-Bold="True" ForeColor="#000099"
                                   Font-Size="14px"
                                   ToolTip="Item Pending for Buyers Acceptance"
                                   Runat="server" />
                    </ItemTemplate>
                </asp:TemplateColumn>
            </Columns>
        </asp:DataGrid><br>
        <asp:Label ID="lblNote1" Text="*" Font-Bold="True" ForeColor="#000099"
                   Font-Size="14px" Visible="False" Runat="server" />
        <asp:Label ID="lblNote2" Text=" Item Pending for Buyers Acceptance."
                   ForeColor="#ff0000" Font-Size="12px" Visible="False"
                   Runat="server" />
        <hr>
        <table Width="100%">
          <tr>
            <td Width="25%">
              <a href="MenuForRegisteredUsers.Aspx">Home</a>
            </td>
            <td Width="25%">
              <a href="BrowseListing.aspx">Browse the Listings</a>
            </td>
```

```
            <td Width="25%">
              <a href="Items.aspx?action=addnew">Add Sale Items</a>
            </td>
            <td Width="25%">
              <a href="Register.aspx">Edit Registration Info</a>
            </td>
          </tr>
        </table>
      </form>
    </body>
</html>
```

2. As usual, switch to the Design view and save the file.

3. And as we've also done before, let's start adding the code with the `Page_Load()` event handler.

```
Private Sub Page_Load(ByVal sender As System.Object, _
                      ByVal e As System.EventArgs) Handles MyBase.Load
```

```
    If Not Page.IsPostBack Then
      BindGrid()
      lblUserName.Text = "Welcome <b>" & _
                      Request.Cookies("email").Value & "</b><br/><br/>"

      If Request.QueryString("msg") = "1" Then
        lblStatus.Text = "You have accepted the bid successfully"
      End If

      If Request.QueryString("msg") = "0" Then
        lblStatus.Text = "Bid acceptance Failed."
      End If
    End If
  End Sub
```

4. Next, enter the code to bind the `DataGrid`, and to format items as they are created:

```
Private Sub BindGrid()
  Dim intSellerID As Int32 = CInt(Request.Cookies("PersonID").Value)
  Dim objItemList As Bid.Item = New Bid.Item()

  myItems.DataSource = objItemList.ViewItems(intSellerID)
  myItems.DataBind()
End Sub
```

```
  Sub myItems_ItemCreated(ByVal Sender As Object, _
                      ByVal e As DataGridItemEventArgs)

    If e.Item.ItemType = ListItemType.Item Or _
      e.Item.ItemType = ListItemType.AlternatingItem Then
```

```
        Dim temphypAcceptBid As HyperLink
        temphypAcceptBid = e.Item.FindControl("hypAcceptBid")
        temphypAcceptBid.Attributes.Add("onclick", _
                "return confirm('Are you Sure you want to accept this bid?');")
    End If
End Sub
```

5. Next comes the code that allows editing in the grid:

```
Sub myItems_Edit(ByVal Sender As Object, ByVal E As DataGridCommandEventArgs)
    myItems.EditItemIndex = CInt(E.Item.ItemIndex)
    BindGrid()
End Sub
```

```
Sub myItems_Cancel(ByVal Sender As Object, _
                    ByVal E As DataGridCommandEventArgs)
    myItems.EditItemIndex = -1
    BindGrid()
End Sub
```

```
Sub myItems_Update(ByVal Sender As Object, _
                    ByVal E As DataGridCommandEventArgs)
    Dim strItemID As String = myItems.DataKeys(CInt(E.Item.ItemIndex))
    Dim strItemName As String = _
                    CType(E.Item.FindControl("txtItemName"), TextBox).Text
    Dim strItemDesc As String = _
                    CType(E.Item.FindControl("txtDescription"), TextBox).Text
    Dim strAskingPrice As String = _
                    CType(E.Item.FindControl("txtAskPrice"), TextBox).Text
    Dim strNotifyPrice As String = _
                    CType(E.Item.FindControl("txtNotifyPrice"), TextBox).Text

    Dim myItem As Bid.Item = New Bid.Item()
    Dim strResult As String

    strResult = myItem.UpdateItem(strItemID, strItemName, strItemDesc, _
                                strAskingPrice, strNotifyPrice)

    If strResult = "1" Then
        lblStatus.Text = "Update Success!"
    ElseIf Len(strResult) > 1 Then
        lblStatus.Text = "Update Failed! " & strResult
    End If

    myItems.EditItemIndex = -1
    BindGrid()
End Sub
```

```
Sub myItems_Delete(ByVal sender As Object, _
                   ByVal e As DataGridCommandEventArgs)
  Dim strItemID As String = myItems.DataKeys(CInt(e.Item.ItemIndex))
  Dim myItem As Bid.Item = New Bid.Item()
  Dim strResult As String

  strResult = myItem.DeleteItem(strItemID)

  If strResult = "1" Then
    lblStatus.Text = "Update Success!"
  ElseIf Len(strResult) > 1 Then
    lblStatus.Text = "Update Failed! " & strResult
  End If

  myItems.EditItemIndex = -1
  BindGrid()
End Sub
```

6. And finally, we'll need some code to provide formatting:

```
Public Function FormatUrl(ByVal dblHighestBid As Double, _
                          ByVal intItemID As Int32, _
                          ByVal intBidID As Int32) As String
  If dblHighestBid = 0 Then
    Return ""
  Else
    Return "AcceptBid.aspx?itemid=" & intItemID & "&bidid=" & intBidID
  End If
End Function
```

```
Public Function ShowText(ByVal dblHighestBid As Double) As String
  If dblHighestBid = 0 Then
    Return ""
  Else
    Return "Accept Bid"
  End If
End Function
```

```
Public Function FormatHighBid(ByVal dblHighBidAmount As Double) As String
  If dblHighBidAmount > 0 Then
    Return CStr(dblHighBidAmount)
  Else
    Return "Yet to be bid on"
  End If
End Function
```

```
Public Function FormatBidderID(ByVal intBidderID As Int32) As String
  If intBidderID > 0 Then
    Return "<a href=ShowPersonDetails.aspx?bidid=" & _
           intBidderID & ">" & intBidderID & "</a>"
```

```
      Else
        Return "Yet to be bid on"
      End If
    End Function
```

```
    Public Function IsPending(ByVal strItemStatus As String) As String
      If UCase(Trim(strItemStatus)) = "PENDING" Then
        lblNote1.Visible = True
        lblNote2.Visible = True
        Return "*"
      Else
        Return ""
      End If
    End Function
```

7. The output of this page will look something like this:

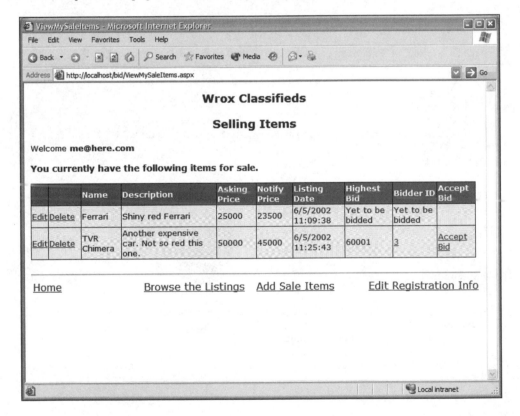

How It Works

There really is quite a lot of code here, but once again it's actually not too difficult. Let's start our analysis when the page loads for the first time, when we want to bind the grid to the data and display a welcome message:

```
If Not Page.IsPostBack Then
  BindGrid()
  lblUserName.Text = "Welcome <b>" & _
                     Request.Cookies("email").Value & "</b><br/><br/>"
```

After that, we check for any message that's been passed into this page. This will be 1 for successful acceptance of a bid and 0 for an unsuccessful acceptance.

```
If Request.QueryString("msg") = "1" Then
  lblStatus.Text = "You have accepted the bid successfully"
End If

If Request.QueryString("msg") = "0" Then
  lblStatus.Text = "Bid acceptance Failed."
End If
End If
```

The method for loading the data and binding it to the grid is similar to the code we've seen before. It first creates an instance of the `Item` object, and then calls `ViewItems()`, passing in the ID of the seller. This returns the data that's shown in the grid.

```
Private Sub BindGrid()
  Dim intSellerID As Int32 = CInt(Request.Cookies("PersonID").Value)
  Dim objItemList As Bid.Item = New Bid.Item()

  myItems.DataSource = objItemList.ViewItems(intSellerID)
  myItems.DataBind()
End Sub
```

We also have an `ItemCreated()` event handler for the grid, which is similar to the one you saw earlier. This simply finds the hyperlink used to accept a bid, and adds the JavaScript popup confirmation:

```
Sub myItems_ItemCreated(ByVal Sender As Object, _
                        ByVal e As DataGridItemEventArgs)

  If e.Item.ItemType = ListItemType.Item Or _
     e.Item.ItemType = ListItemType.AlternatingItem Then
    Dim temphypAcceptBid As HyperLink
    temphypAcceptBid = e.Item.FindControl("hypAcceptBid")
    temphypAcceptBid.Attributes.Add("onclick", _
              "return confirm('Are you Sure you want to accept this bid?');")
  End If
End Sub
```

Let's now look at the editing features of the grid. When we defined the grid, we gave it these attributes:

```
OnEditCommand="myItems_Edit"
OnUpdateCommand="myItems_Update"
OnCancelCommand="myItems_Cancel"
OnDeleteCommand="myItems_Delete"
```

These identify the event handlers that run in order to edit, update, and delete items from the grid. How does ASP.NET know which procedures to run? The answer lies in the first set of controls added to the grid:

```
<asp:EditCommandColumn EditText="Edit" CancelText="Cancel"
    UpdateText="Update" />
<asp:ButtonColumn text="Delete" CommandName="Delete"
    ItemStyle-Width="50px" />
```

As we first saw in Chapter 7, the first of these shows a single column with the buttons shown as links. Initially, the column will show **Edit**, and when **Edit** is clicked, we are put into edit mode. This then changes the **Edit** button to show **Cancel** and **Update**; selecting either of these takes us out of edit mode, and the **Edit** button is once again shown. The **Delete** button is always shown.

The `EditCommandColumn` is a special column that handles all of this button and label changing for us. Moreover, ASP.NET knows that there are three commands (edit, update, and cancel), and automatically maps these to the appropriate `On...Command` attributes. The **Delete** button is shown as a separate column, so we use a `ButtonColumn` for this. Because we want it to participate in the editing, we set the `CommandName` to `Delete` – this tells ASP.NET to run `OnDeleteCommand` when it's pressed. Let's now look at these event handlers.

When the **Edit** button is pressed, the event handler specified by the `OnEditCommand` attribute is run. In it, we set the `EditItemIndex` of the grid to the current `ItemIndex`; that identifies the current row. We then re-bind the grid:

```
Sub myItems_Edit(ByVal Sender As Object, ByVal E As DataGridCommandEventArgs)
   myItems.EditItemIndex = CInt(E.Item.ItemIndex)
   BindGrid()
End Sub
```

When we re-bind the grid, and the `EditItemIndex` is set to a value other than -1, the grid is put into edit mode. This has the following effects:

❑ For a `BoundColumn`, text boxes replace the label.

❑ For a `TemplateColumn`, the `EditItemTemplate` replaces the `ItemTemplate`.

The great thing about this is that we just have to define what the templates look like (or use bound columns), and ASP.NET takes care of displaying the correct controls.

Once in edit mode, the user has the option of canceling any changes they make. For this, we simply set the `EditItemIndex` to `-1` (which takes the grid out of edit mode), and then re-bind the grid to show the original data:

```
Sub myItems_Cancel(ByVal Sender As Object, _
                   ByVal E As DataGridCommandEventArgs)
  myItems.EditItemIndex = -1
  BindGrid()
End Sub
```

There's a little more work required for updating the data, but it's still fairly straightforward. The event handler takes two parameters, and you've already seen that the `E` parameter identifies the current row.

```
Sub myItems_Update(ByVal Sender As Object, _
                   ByVal E As DataGridCommandEventArgs)
```

First, we need to get the key from the grid. This is the unique `ItemID`, and it's stored in the grid's `DataKeys` collection. This like a special hidden column, and it's used to store ID values that we need for editing, but we don't want to show on the screen. When we defined the grid, we used the following attribute to identify which column in the data represented the this key:

```
DataKeyField="ItemID"
```

When the grid was loaded, ASP.NET automatically filled the `DataKeys` collection with the values from the `ItemID` column. We can then index into this column (using the current `ItemIndex` to identify the row) to find the `ItemID` for this row:

```
Dim strItemID As String = myItems.DataKeys(CInt(E.Item.ItemIndex))
```

Next, we need to extract the other editable details from the grid. We use the `FindControl()` method to find each text box, and extract the value from the `Text` property:

```
Dim strItemName As String = _
                  CType(E.Item.FindControl("txtItemName"), TextBox).Text
Dim strItemDesc As String = _
                  CType(E.Item.FindControl("txtDescription"), TextBox).Text
Dim strAskingPrice As String = _
                  CType(E.Item.FindControl("txtAskPrice"), TextBox).Text
Dim strNotifyPrice As String = _
                  CType(E.Item.FindControl("txtNotifyPrice"), TextBox).Text
```

Once the data is safely stored in some local variables, we create an instance of the `Item` object, and call its `UpdateItem()` method, passing in those values.

```
Dim myItem As Bid.Item = New Bid.Item()
Dim strResult As String

strResult = myItem.UpdateItem(strItemID, strItemName, strItemDesc, _
                  strAskingPrice, strNotifyPrice)
```

Like our other update routines, a return value of 1 indicates success, so we show either a successful update message, or an error message:

```
If strResult = "1" Then
   lblStatus.Text = "Update Success!"
ElseIf Len(strResult) > 1 Then
   lblStatus.Text = "Update Failed! " & strResult
End If
```

Finally, we set the EditItemIndex to -1 to take the grid out of edit mode, and we re-bind the data:

```
   myItems.EditItemIndex = -1
   BindGrid()
End Sub
```

Deleting an item is simpler, since we don't have to extract any data. First, we extract the ItemID from the DataKeys collection:

```
Sub myItems_Delete(ByVal sender As Object, _
                   ByVal e As DataGridCommandEventArgs)
   Dim strItemID As String = myItems.DataKeys(CInt(e.Item.ItemIndex))
   Dim myItem As Bid.Item = New Bid.Item()
   Dim strResult As String
```

Then we pass this value to the DeleteItem() method of the Item object. This calls the stored procedure that deletes this item from the database.

```
   strResult = myItem.DeleteItem(strItemID)
```

Finally, we have the check for success, and take the grid out of edit mode.

```
   If strResult = "1" Then
      lblStatus.Text = "Update Success!"
   ElseIf Len(strResult) > 1 Then
      lblStatus.Text = "Update Failed! " & strResult
   End If

   myItems.EditItemIndex = -1
   BindGrid()
End Sub
```

Continuing the story, let's now look at the formatting functions. First, we have the FormatUrl() function, which differs slightly from the one we saw in the last section. It examines the value of the highest bid, and uses this to decide which URL to use:

```
Public Function FormatUrl(ByVal dblHighestBid As Double, _
                          ByVal intItemID As Int32, _
                          ByVal intBidID As Int32) As String
```

```
      If dblHighestBid = 0 Then
         Return ""
      Else
         Return "AcceptBid.aspx?itemid=" & intItemID & "&bidid=" & intBidID
      End If
   End Function
```

This formatting is used on the URLs in the **Accept Bid** column. You can see that the first row has an empty cell, whereas the second has a URL. This is because the first row didn't have any bids.

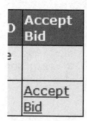

A similar technique is used for the display text of this URL:

```
   Public Function ShowText(ByVal dblHighestBid As Double) As String
      If dblHighestBid = 0 Then
         Return ""
      Else
         Return "Accept Bid"
      End If
   End Function
```

The remaining functions perform a similar task for the **Highest Bid** and **Bidder ID** columns, as shown below:

Highest Bid	Bidder ID
Yet to be bidded	Yet to be bidded
60001	3

The code for these functions examines the data passed in, and decides what URL and text is to be used;

```
   Public Function FormatHighBid(ByVal dblHighBidAmount As Double) As String
      If dblHighBidAmount > 0 Then
         Return CStr(dblHighBidAmount)
      Else
```

427

```
        Return "Yet to be bidded"
      End If
   End Function


   Public Function FormatBidderID(ByVal intBidderID As Int32) As String
      If intBidderID > 0 Then
         Return "<a href=ShowPersonDetails.aspx?bidid=" & _
               intBidderID & ">" & intBidderID & "</a>"
      Else
         Return "Yet to be bidded"
      End If
   End Function


   Public Function IsPending(ByVal strItemStatus As String) As String
      If UCase(Trim(strItemStatus)) = "PENDING" Then
         lblNote1.Visible = True
         lblNote2.Visible = True
         Return "*"
      Else
         Return ""
      End If
   End Function
```

The really important point about all of this formatting is that it shows another way of changing the content of bound data. You could use long and complex calculations, or combine strings, or do just about anything else you fancy. Functions like these give you great flexibility.

Adding an Item for Sale

To add an item for sale, we have an ASP.NET page called Items.aspx. Let's see what that one looks like.

Try It Out – Adding an Item

1. We can begin by creating the Items.aspx page in a similar manner to the pages we've already created. Create another new web form, name it Items.aspx, and add the following code.

```
<%@ Page Language="vb" AutoEventWireup="false"
        Codebehind="Items.aspx.vb" Inherits="Bid.Items"%>
<html>
  <head>
    <title>Items</title>
  </head>
  <body style="FONT:13px verdana">
    <form id="Form1" method="post" runat="server">
      <h3 align="center">Wrox Classifieds</h3>
      <h3 align="center">Add New Sale Item</h3>
      <asp:Label ID="lblUserName" Font-Name="verdana" Font-Size="13px"
```

```
                          Runat="server" />
 <asp:Label ID="lblHeader"
Text="Please add the following information for the item you have for sale."
Runat="server" /><br>
 <br>
 <table>
   <tr>
     <td>Item Name</td>
     <td>
       <asp:TextBox ID="txtItemName" Runat="server" />
     </td>
   </tr>
   <tr>
     <td>Description</td>
     <td>
       <asp:TextBox ID="txtItemDesc" TextMode="MultiLine" Rows="5"
                    Columns="50" Runat="server" />
     </td>
   </tr>
   <tr>
     <td>Asking Price</td>
     <td>
       <asp:TextBox ID="txtAskPrice" Runat="server" />
     </td>
   </tr>
   <tr>
     <td>Notify Price</td>
     <td>
       <asp:TextBox ID="txtNotifyPrice" Runat="server" />
     </td>
   </tr>
   <tr>
     <td>Sale Expiration Date</td>
     <td>
       <asp:TextBox ID="txtExpDate" Runat="server" />
     </td>
   </tr>
   <tr>
     <td>
       <asp:Button ID="btnSubmit" Text="Add New Item" Runat="server" />
     </td>
     <td>
       <input id="btnReset" type="reset" Runat="server" value="Reset">
     </td>
   </tr>
 </table>
 <asp:Label ID="lblMsg" Runat="server" />
 <hr>
 <table>
   <tr>
     <td Width="25%" align="middle">
       <a href="MenuForRegisteredUsers.aspx">Home</a>
     </td>
```

```
      <td Width="25%" align="middle">
        <a href="BrowseListing.aspx">Browse the Listings</a>
      </td>
      <td Width="25%" align="middle">
        Add Sale Items
      </td>
      <td Width="25%" align="middle">
        <a href="Register.aspx">Edit Registration Info</a>
      </td>
    </tr>
  </table>
</form>
</body>
</html>
```

2. Switch to the Design view, save the page, and we can begin to add the code, starting as ever with the `Page_Load()` event handler:

```
Private Sub Page_Load(ByVal sender As System.Object, _
                      ByVal e As System.EventArgs) Handles MyBase.Load

    lblUserName.Text = "Welcome <b>" & _
                      Request.Cookies("email").Value & "</b><br><br>"
End Sub
```

3. Next, we have the code for the **Add New Item** button:

```
Private Sub btnSubmit_Click(ByVal sender As System.Object, _
                           ByVal e As System.EventArgs) Handles btnSubmit.Click
  Dim obj As Bid.Item = New Bid.Item()
  Dim strStatus As String

  strStatus = obj.AddItem(txtItemName.Text, _
                         txtItemDesc.Text, _
                         txtAskPrice.Text, _
                         txtNotifyPrice.Text, _
                         Request.Cookies("PersonID").Value, _
                         txtExpDate.Text)

  If IsNumeric(strStatus) Then
    Response.Redirect("MenuForRegisteredUsers.aspx")
  ElseIf Len(strStatus) > 1 Then
    lblMsg.Text = "Error while adding the item. Please try again." & strStatus
  End If
End Sub
```

4. The output of `Items.aspx` will look like this:

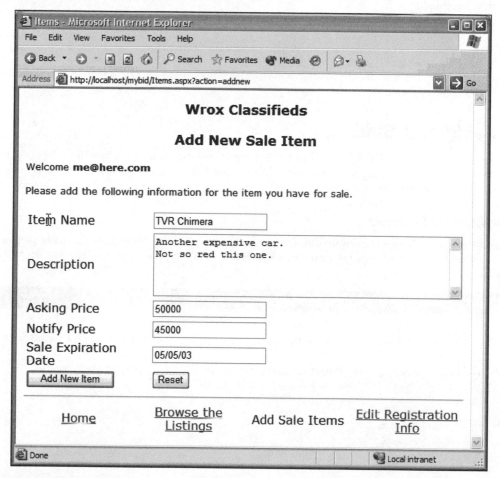

How It Works

The code that executes on loading the page we've seen before – it just displays a welcome message. For the Add New Item button, we first create a new instance of the `Item` object:

```
Dim obj As Bid.Item = New Bid.Item()
Dim strStatus As String
```

Next, we call the `AddItem()` method, passing all of the information for the item.

```
strStatus = obj.AddItem(txtItemName.Text, _
                        txtItemDesc.Text, _
                        txtAskPrice.Text, _
                        txtNotifyPrice.Text, _
                        Request.Cookies("PersonID").Value, _
                        txtExpDate.Text)
```

Finally, we check the status – if it's numeric, we send the user back to the menu. Otherwise, we display an error message:

```
If IsNumeric(strStatus) Then
  Response.Redirect("MenuForRegisteredUsers.aspx")
ElseIf Len(strStatus) > 1 Then
  lblMsg.Text = "Error while adding the item. Please try again." & strStatus
End If
```

Browsing and Bidding

Where have we reached? Well, at this point, any registered user can now place items in the sale listings. The next step is to allow users to browse the listings and bid for the items that are on sale there. For these tasks, we'll write two more new pages: BrowseListings.aspx and BidItem.aspx.

Browsing the Listings

Our system provides a very simple interface for browsing all of the items our users have placed for sale – all of the items are just presented in a list. This leaves the door open for later enhancements to be made.

Try It Out – Browsing the Items for Sale

1. Create a new web form called BrowseListing.aspx, and key in the following code:

```
<%@ Page Language="vb" AutoEventWireup="false"
        Codebehind="BrowseListing.aspx.vb" Inherits="Bid.BrowseListing"%>
<html>
  <head>
    <title>BrowseListing</title>
  </head>
  <body style="FONT: 10pt verdana">
    <form id="Form1" method="post" runat="server">
      <h3 align="center">Wrox Classifieds</h3>
      <h3 align="center">Selling Items</h3>
      <asp:Label ID="lblUserName" Font-Name="verdana" Font-Size="13px"
                Runat="server" />
      <asp:Label ID="lblMsg" Font-Name="verdana" Font-Size="14px"
                ForeColor="#000099" Font-Bold="True"
                Text=
    "Here's a list of all items that our users have made available for purchase:"
                Runat="server" /><br>
      <br>
      <asp:Label ID="lblStatus" ForeColor="#ff0000" Font-Name="verdana"
                Font-Size="11px" Runat="server" />
      <asp:DataGrid ID="myItems" AutoGenerateColumns="False" Width="99%"
            HeaderStyle-BackColor="#ff0000" HeaderStyle-Font-Bold="True"
            HeaderStyle-Font-Name="Verdana" HeaderStyle-Font-Size="13px"
            HeaderStyle-ForeColor="#ffffff" ItemStyle-BackColor="Beige"
```

```
        ItemStyle-Font-Name="verdana" ItemStyle-Font-Size="13px"
        BorderColor="#000000" Runat="server">
  <Columns>
    <asp:TemplateColumn HeaderText="Name">
      <ItemTemplate>
        <asp:HyperLink
           text='<%# DataBinder.Eval(Container.DataItem, "ItemName") %>'
           NavigateUrl=
         '<%# FormatURL(DataBinder.Eval(Container.DataItem, "ItemID"),
                    DataBinder.Eval(Container.DataItem, "ItemName"),
                    DataBinder.Eval(Container.DataItem, "Description")) %>'
           Runat="server" />
      </ItemTemplate>
    </asp:TemplateColumn>
    <asp:BoundColumn DataField="Description" HeaderText="Description" />
    <asp:BoundColumn DataField="AskingPrice" HeaderText="Asking Price" />
    <asp:BoundColumn DataField="ListingDate" HeaderText="Listing Date" />
    <asp:BoundColumn DataField="HighestBid" HeaderText="Highest Bid" />
  </Columns>
</asp:DataGrid>
<hr>
<asp:Panel ID="GuestMenu" Runat="server">
  <table width="100%">
    <tr>
      <td align="middle" width="25%"><a href="default.aspx">Home</a>
      </td>
      <td align="middle" width="25%">Browse the Listings</td>
      <td align="middle" width="25%"><a href="Login.aspx">Login</a>
      </td>
      <td align="middle" width="25%">
        <a href="Register.aspx">I'm a new user</a>
      </td>
    </tr>
  </table>
</asp:Panel>
<asp:Panel ID="RegisteredMenu" Runat="server">
  <table width="100%">
    <tr>
      <td align="middle" width="10%">
        <a href="MenuForRegisteredUsers.aspx">Home</a>
      </td>
      <td align="middle" width="20%">Browse the Listings
      </td>
      <td align="middle" width="20%">
        <a href="ViewMySaleItems.aspx">List/Edit Sale Items</a>
      </td>
      <td align="middle" width="20%">
        <a href="Register.aspx">Registration Info</a>
      </td>
      <td align="middle" width="10%">
        <a href="Logout.aspx">Logout</a>
      </td>
    </tr>
```

433

```
          </table>
        </asp:Panel>
      </form>
    </body>
</html>
```

2. You know the routine by now: switch to the Design view, save the page, and start the next phase by adding the code for the `Page_Load()` event handler:

```
Private Sub Page_Load(ByVal sender As System.Object, _
                    ByVal e As System.EventArgs) Handles MyBase.Load
```

```
    If Not Page.IsPostBack Then

      BindGrid()

      ' Show the appropriate menu
      If Tools.IsLoggedIn() Then
        lblUserName.Text = "Welcome <b>" & Request.Cookies("EMail").Value & _
                        "</b><br/><br/>"
        GuestMenu.Visible = False
        RegisteredMenu.Visible = True
      Else
        lblUserName.Text = "Welcome guest<br/><br/>"
        GuestMenu.Visible = True
        RegisteredMenu.Visible = False
      End If
    End If
  End Sub
```

3. Next come the data binding and the formatting:

```
Private Sub BindGrid()
  Dim objItemList As Bid.Item = New Bid.Item()

  myItems.DataSource = objItemList.ViewItemsForSale()
  myItems.DataBind()
End Sub
```

```
Public Function FormatUrl(ByVal intID As Integer, _
                        ByVal strName As String, ByVal strDesc As String)
  If Tools.IsLoggedIn() Then
    Return "BidItem.aspx?itemid=" & CStr(intID) & "&itemname=" & _
            Server.UrlEncode(strName) & "&itemdesc=" & _
            Server.UrlEncode(strDesc)
  Else
    Return ""
  End If
End Function
```

4. The output of `BrowseListing.aspx` will look like this:

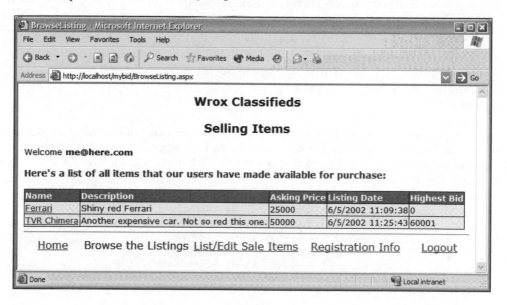

How It Works

The code for this page is comparatively simple, and you should now be getting quite familiar with the kind of code we're writing. First, we have the code in the `Page_Load()` event handler that calls a procedure to load the data, and then checks to see if the user is logged in. This page allows both registered and unregistered users, so we display a different message and menu bar depending on which they are:

```
If Not Page.IsPostBack Then

    BindGrid()

    ' Show the appropriate menu
    If Tools.IsLoggedIn() Then
        lblUserName.Text = "Welcome <b>" & Request.Cookies("EMail").Value & _
                           "</b><br/><br/>"
        GuestMenu.Visible = False
        RegisteredMenu.Visible = True
    Else
        lblUserName.Text = "Welcome guest<br/><br/>"
        GuestMenu.Visible = True
        RegisteredMenu.Visible = False
    End If
End If
```

Loading and binding the data to the grid is simple: we just call the `ViewItemsForSale()` method of an `Item` object, which fetches all items for sale from the database:

```
Private Sub BindGrid()
   Dim objItemList As Bid.Item = New Bid.Item()

   myItems.DataSource = objItemList.ViewItemsForSale()
   myItems.DataBind()
End Sub
```

We've seen `FormatUrl()` functions before, but this one shows that you can use other functions as part of the dynamic formatting process. Here, we're checking for a logged in user, and changing the contents of the string returned. For logged in users, this will be a URL to point to the item for sale; for guests, there is no URL. This means that the item becomes read-only for guests:

```
Public Function FormatURL(ByVal intID As Integer, _
                          ByVal strName As String, ByVal strDesc As String)
   If Tools.IsLoggedIn() Then
      Return "BidItem.aspx?itemid=" & CStr(intID) & "&itemname=" & _
             Server.UrlEncode(strName) & "&itemdesc=" & _
             Server.UrlEncode(strDesc)
   Else
      Return ""
   End If
End Function
```

Bidding for an Item

The `FormatUrl()` function shown above allows a logged-in user to click on the name of an item. This takes them to the page where they can bid for that item.

Try It Out – Bidding for an Item

1. Create a new web form called `BidItem.aspx`, and enter the following. Make sure that you type the `confirmbid()` function exactly as it is – JavaScript is case sensitive!

```
<%@ Page Language="vb" AutoEventWireup="false"
         Codebehind="BidItem.aspx.vb" Inherits="Bid.BidItem"%>
<html>
  <head>
    <title>Bid</title>
    <script language="javascript">
      function confirmbid()
      {
        var highbid;
        var currbid;

        highbid = parseFloat(document.Form1.txtHighBid.value);
        currbid = parseFloat(document.Form1.txtBidAmount.value);
        if (currbid <= highbid)
```

```
        {
          alert("You should bid higher than " + highbid + ".");
          return false;
        }
        else
          return true;
      }
    </script>
</head>

<body style="FONT: 8pt verdana">
  <form id="Form1" method="post" runat="server">
    <h3 align="center">Wrox Classifieds</h3>
    <h3 align="center">Selling Items</h3>
    <asp:Label ID="lblUserName" Font-Name="verdana" Font-Size="13px"
        Runat="server" />
    <asp:Label ID="lblMsg" Font-Name="verdana" Font-Size="15px"
        ForeColor="#000099" Runat="server" /><br>
    <br>
    <asp:Label ID="lblStatus" ForeColor="#ff0000" Font-Name="verdana"
        Font-Size="11px" Runat="server" />
    <input type="hidden" ID="txtHighBid" runat="server">
    <asp:DataGrid ID="myItems" AutoGenerateColumns="False" Width="99%"
        HeaderStyle-BackColor="#ff0000" HeaderStyle-Font-Bold="True"
        HeaderStyle-Font-Name="Verdana" HeaderStyle-Font-Size="13px"
        HeaderStyle-ForeColor="#ffffff" ItemStyle-BackColor="Beige"
        ItemStyle-Font-Name="verdana" ItemStyle-Font-Size="13px"
        BorderColor="#000000" Runat="server">
      <Columns>
        <asp:BoundColumn HeaderText="Bidder ID" DataField="BidderID" />
        <asp:BoundColumn HeaderText="Time" DataField="Timestamp" />
        <asp:BoundColumn HeaderText="Bid Amount" DataField="BidAmount" />
        <asp:BoundColumn HeaderText="Last Change" DataField="BidChange" />
      </Columns>
    </asp:DataGrid>
    <asp:Label ID="lblNoBid" Runat="server" />
    <table Width="99%">
      <tr>
        <td Width="15%">Item:</td>
        <td Width="85%">
          <asp:Label ID="lblItemName" Runat="server" />
        </td>
      </tr>
      <tr>
        <td Width="15%">Description:</td>
        <td Width="85%">
          <asp:Label ID="lblItemDesc" Runat="server" />
        </td>
      </tr>
      <tr>
        <td Width="15%">Bid Amount:</td>
        <td Width="85%">
```

```
            <asp:Textbox ID="txtBidAmount" Runat="server" />
          </td>
        </tr>
        <tr>
          <td align="Left" Width="100%" ColSpan="2">
            <asp:Button ID="btnSubmit" Text="Bid for this item"
                   Font-Bold="True" BackColor="Beige" Width="30%"
                   Runat="server" />
          </td>
        </tr>
      </table>
      <hr />
      <table Width="100%">
        <tr>
          <td Width="25%">
            <a href="MenuForRegisteredUsers.Aspx">Home</a>
          </td>
          <td Width="25%">
            <a href="BrowseListing.aspx">Browse the Listings</a>
          </td>
          <td Width="25%">
            <a href="Items.aspx?action=addnew">Add Sale Items</a>
          </td>
          <td Width="25%">
            <a href="Register.aspx">Edit Registration Info</a>
          </td>
        </tr>
      </table>
    </form>
  </body>
</html>
```

2. Switch to the Design view; save the page; this is what the `Page_Load()` event handler looks like:

```
Private Sub Page_Load(ByVal sender As System.Object, _
                    ByVal e As System.EventArgs) Handles MyBase.Load
    If Not Page.IsPostBack() Then
      lblUserName.Text = "Welcome <b>" & _
                         Request.Cookies("EMail").Value & "</b><br/><br/>"
      lblMsg.Text = "Bidding for <b>" & _
                    Request.QueryString("ItemName") & "</b>"
      lblStatus.Text = "Bid history (Highest bid first)"
      lblItemName.Text = "<b>" & Request.QueryString("itemname") & "</b>"
      lblItemDesc.Text = "<b>" & Request.QueryString("itemdesc") & "</b>"
      Response.Cookies("ItemID").Value = Request.QueryString("ItemID")
      btnSubmit.Attributes.Add("onclick", "return confirmbid();")
      BindGrid()
      GetHighBid()
    End If
End Sub
```

3. Next, add the `BindGrid()` subroutine:

```
Private Sub BindGrid()
  Dim intItemID As Int32 = CInt(Request.QueryString("ItemID"))
  Dim objItemList As Bid.Item = New Bid.Item()

  myItems.DataSource = objItemList.GetBidDetails(intItemID)
  myItems.DataBind()
End Sub
```

4. And then the routine that finds the highest bid:

```
Private Sub GetHighBid()
  Dim obj As Bid.Item = New Bid.Item()
  txtHighBid.Value = obj.GetHighestBid(CInt(Request.Cookies("itemid").Value))
End Sub
```

5. Finally, add the code for submitting the bid:

```
Private Sub btnSubmit_Click(ByVal sender As System.Object, _
                            ByVal e As System.EventArgs) Handles btnSubmit.Click
  Dim obj As Bid.Item = New Bid.Item()
  Dim strStatus As String = obj.AddBid(CInt(Request.Cookies("ItemID").Value), _
                            CInt(Request.Cookies("PersonID").Value), _
                            CDbl(txtBidAmount.Text))

  If strStatus = "1" Then
    lblMsg.Text = "Your bid has been accepted."
    BindGrid()
  Else
    lblMsg.Text = "Bid Failed." & strStatus
  End If
End Sub
```

6. The output of the above file will look something like this:

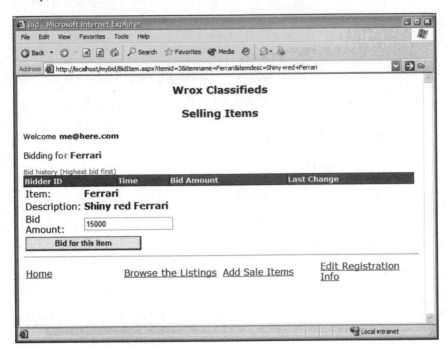

How It Works

Once again, the code here is fairly simple. When the page loads, we extract the details of the item from the QueryString, as these are passed in from the calling page:

```
If Not Page.IsPostBack() Then
  lblUserName.Text = "Welcome <b>" & _
                     Request.Cookies("email").Value & "</b><br/><br/>"
  lblMsg.Text = "Bidding for <b>" & _
                Request.QueryString("itemname") & "</b>"
  lblStatus.Text = "Bid history (Highest bid first)"
  lblItemName.Text = "<b>" & Request.QueryString("itemname") & "</b>"
  lblItemDesc.Text = "<b>" & Request.QueryString("itemdesc") & "</b>"
  Response.Cookies("ItemID").Value = Request.QueryString("ItemID")
  btnSubmit.Attributes.Add("onclick", "return confirmbid();")
  BindGrid()
  GetHighBid()
End If
```

You'll also notice that we use the trick of adding attributes for client-side code. This time, however, we're not just displaying a popup. What we're doing is running the following client-side JavaScript routine:

```
function confirmbid()
{
  var highbid;
  var currbid;

  highbid = parseFloat(document.Form1.txtHighBid.value);
  currbid = parseFloat(document.Form1.txtBidAmount.value);
  if (currbid <= highbid)
  {
    alert("You should bid higher than " + highbid + ".");
    return false;
  }
  else
    return true;
}
```

This extracts the current highest bid, compares it to the current bid, and ensures that the current bid is higher. At the end of the chapter, we'll mention another way in which this could be accomplished.

The last thing that happens when the page is loaded is that the data is fetched into the grid, and the highest bid is placed into a hidden field (we'll explain why in a moment). Binding the grid is simply a matter of fetching the data using the GetBidDetails() method from our data access layer.

```
Private Sub BindGrid()
    Dim intItemID As Int32 = CInt(Request.QueryString("ItemID"))
    Dim objItemList As Bid.Item = New Bid.Item()

    myItems.DataSource = objItemList.GetBidDetails(intItemID)
    myItems.DataBind()
End Sub
```

To get the highest bid, we call another method in our data access layer. This just searches through the bids for this item and extracts the highest. We put this into a hidden field on the page, so that the user can't see it. It is actually extracted in the JavaScript function:

```
Private Sub GetHighBid()
    Dim obj As Bid.Item = New Bid.Item()
    txtHighBid.Value = obj.GetHighestBid(CInt(Request.Cookies("itemid").Value))
End Sub
```

When the user submits their bid, the AddBid() method of an Item object is called, which adds the bid to the database. As usual, this returns 1 for a successful operation.

```
Private Sub btnSubmit_Click(ByVal sender As System.Object, _
                            ByVal e As System.EventArgs) Handles btnSubmit.Click
    Dim obj As Bid.Item = New Bid.Item()
    Dim strStatus As String = obj.AddBid(CInt(Request.Cookies("itemid").Value), _
                                CInt(Request.Cookies("personid").Value), _
                                CDbl(txtBidAmount.Text))
```

```
    If strStatus = "1" Then
      lblMsg.Text = "Your bid has been accepted."
      BindGrid()
    Else
      lblMsg.Text = "Bid Failed." & strStatus
    End If
End Sub
```

Completing a Sale

The final section of this chapter explains how we'll tie up a sale. We'll do it by having the seller accept a bid, and then having the successful bidder acknowledge the acceptance and thus complete the sale.

Accepting a Bid

First, we'll look at how we can allow the seller to accept a bid. When this happens, the buyer is notified, and can accept (or reject) the deal at that point. When both parties accept the deal, the information is logged to the database.

Try It Out – Accepting a Bid

1. Create a new web form called `AcceptBid.aspx`. There's no interface for this page, so just view the code. Add the following to the `Page_Load()` event:

```
Private Sub Page_Load(ByVal sender As System.Object, _
                      ByVal e As System.EventArgs) Handles MyBase.Load
```

```
    ' Put user code to initialize the page here
    Dim strFrom As String = LCase(Request.ServerVariables("HTTP_REFERER"))

    ' When the Seller accepts the Bid
    If InStr(strFrom, "ViewMySaleItems.aspx") > 0 Then
      Dim intItemID As Int32 = CInt(Request.QueryString("itemid"))
      Dim intBidID As Int32 = CInt(Request.QueryString("bidid"))

      Dim obj As Bid.Item = New Bid.Item()
      Dim strStatus As String

      strStatus = obj.AddSale(intItemID, intBidID)

      If Trim(strStatus) = "1" Then
        Response.Redirect("ViewMySaleItems.aspx?msg=1")
      Else
        Response.Redirect("ViewMySaleItems.aspx?msg=Bid-Acceptance-Failed")
      End If
    End If

    ' When Buyer accepts the Sale
    If InStr(strFrom, "MenuForRegisteredUsers.aspx") > 0 Then
      Dim intItemID As Int32 = CInt(Request.QueryString("itemid"))
```

```
            Dim intBidID As Int32 = CInt(Request.QueryString("bid"))

            Dim obj As Bid.Item = New Bid.Item()
            Dim strStatus As String

            strStatus = obj.CompleteSale(intItemID, intBidID)

            If Trim(strStatus) = "1" Then
              Response.Redirect( _
                 "MenuForRegisteredUsers.aspx?msg=Purchase Succesfully Completed!")
            Else
              Response.Redirect( _
                 "MenuForRegisteredUsers.aspx?msg=Sale-Completion-Failed.")
            End If
          End If
        End If
        Response.Write(strFrom)
      End Sub
```

How It Works

This code simply confirms the bid and redirects us back to the page we came from. First, we use one of the ServerVariables of the Request to find out which page we came from:

```
        Dim strFrom As String = LCase(Request.ServerVariables("HTTP_REFERER"))
```

If we've come from the ViewMySaleItems page, then we're accepting a bid on one of our items. So, we extract the details from the QueryString, and add this as a sale using the AddSale() method of an Item() object.

```
        If InStr(strFrom, "ViewMySaleItems.aspx") > 0 Then
          Dim intItemID As Int32 = CInt(Request.QueryString("itemid"))
          Dim intBidID As Int32 = CInt(Request.QueryString("bidid"))

          Dim obj As Bid.Item = New Bid.Item()
          Dim strStatus As String

          strStatus = obj.AddSale(intItemID, intBidID)
```

We then redirect back to the original page, passing back a message indicating whether the process succeeded.

```
        If Trim(strStatus) = "1" Then
          Response.Redirect("ViewMySaleItems.aspx?msg=1")
        Else
          Response.Redirect("ViewMySaleItems.aspx?msg=Bid-Acceptance-Failed")
        End If
      End If
```

If, on the other hand, we've come from the `MenuForRegisteredUsers` page, then we're a buyer confirming the sale. In this case, we call the `CompleteSale()` method of an `Item` object to complete the sale.

```
' When Buyer accepts the Sale
If InStr(strFrom, "MenuForRegisteredUsers.aspx") > 0 Then
   Dim intItemID As Int32 = CInt(Request.QueryString("itemid"))
   Dim intBidID As Int32 = CInt(Request.QueryString("bid"))

   Dim obj As Bid.Item = New Bid.Item()
   Dim strStatus As String

   strStatus = obj.CompleteSale(intItemID, intBidID)
```

And finally we redirect, giving an appropriate message.

```
   If Trim(strStatus) = "1" Then
     Response.Redirect( _
        "MenuForRegisteredUsers.aspx?msg=Purchase Succesfully Completed!")
   Else
     Response.Redirect( _
        "MenuForRegisteredUsers.aspx?msg=Sale-Completion-Failed.")
   End If
End If
Response.Write(strFrom)
```

Try It Out – Accepting Bids

Let's take a look at how this code works in practice. When you click to accept a bid, you get the notification:

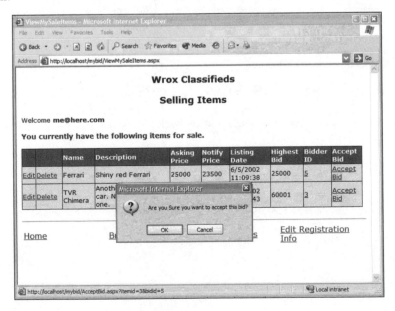

If you accept this bid, then you are passed to the `AcceptBid.aspx` page, which logs the details and passes us back again:

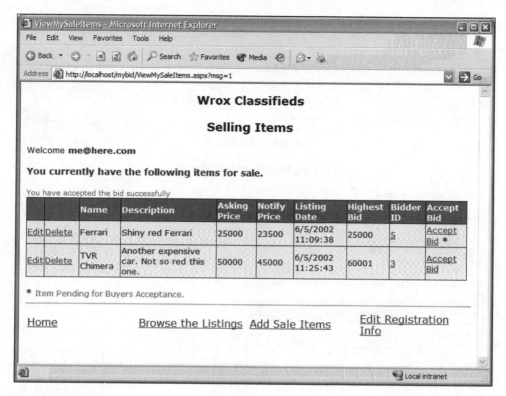

Here you can clearly see the message that `AcceptBid.aspx` sent us.

Notifying the Bidder

Now that all of the database tables have been updated, there's just one last step: notifying the buyer that their bid has been accepted.

Try It Out – Notifying the Buyer

The code for accepting a bid by the buyer is in the `MenuForRegisteredUsers.aspx` page. When the buyer logs in to this application, he will see the list of winning bids in this page.

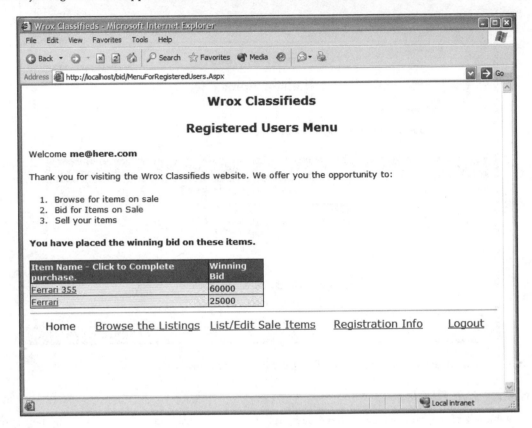

At this stage, you have the option to confirm the purchase by clicking on the item name – this gives you the popup confirmation. If you accept, `AcceptBid.aspx` is loaded, and you are returned to the menu.

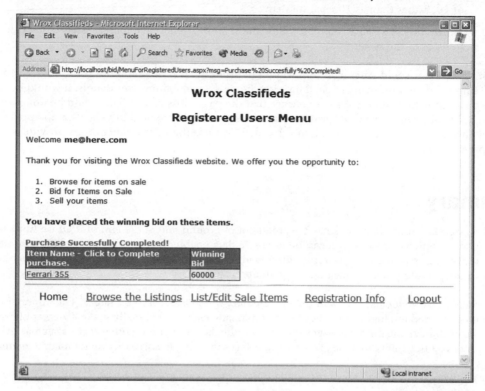

Here, you can see that I eventually plumped for the cheaper Ferrari. If only this were for real!

Adding to this Application

Although this is an application of significant size, we've only scratched the surface of what it could be possible to achieve in an online classified ad system. There are lots of ways in which you could extend and enhance the application, to provide better functionality. For example, you could:

❑ Add a `Category` field to the `Item` table. This would allow the seller to categorize their items better, and also opens up possibilities for different ways of browsing, instead of presenting a one-dimensional list of items.

❑ Create a "bid status" window, which the seller could leave open on their desktop. Ideally, this would automatically refresh itself periodically, showing the current highest bids on items they have for sale.

❑ Add support for richer information about the items, such as pictures, links to other sites, and reviews from buyers.

❏   Extend the database to support multiple quantities of the same item being sold. If, for example, you had 10 computers to sell, you could enter them as a single item with a quantity of 10, rather than as 10 separate items.

❏   Utilize the `SmtpMail` object to allow the server to generate e-mail messages that can be sent to users of the system.

Additionally, you could amend the application in order to make it a bit more robust. For example, there's no validation on many of the data entry fields – when editing user details, it would be sensible to force passwords to be entered, and to ensure that the passwords match. This could be done with the use of the validation controls, which provide an extremely simple way to add validation to applications. We could also use this method for the highest bid details, since the validation controls provide a way to compare two values.

Summary

Well, congratulations! This book has covered a lot of ground, but at the end of it all we hope that we've managed to show you how easy it can be to create data-enabled web applications. This case study has been a distillation of many of the topics discussed in earlier chapters, and we've showed you how to put those concepts into practice when building an application.

In particular, we've looked at how to manipulate data within the ASP.NET pages. The importance of this cannot be stressed too highly – it's these sort of dynamic features that really make a web application shine. You can customize the output of pages not only on the data, but also on other factors such as user details. This gives you the ability to build great user interfaces in a simple and easily maintainable manner.

After all, what it's really all about is making it easier to create great sites – and ASP.NET does that.

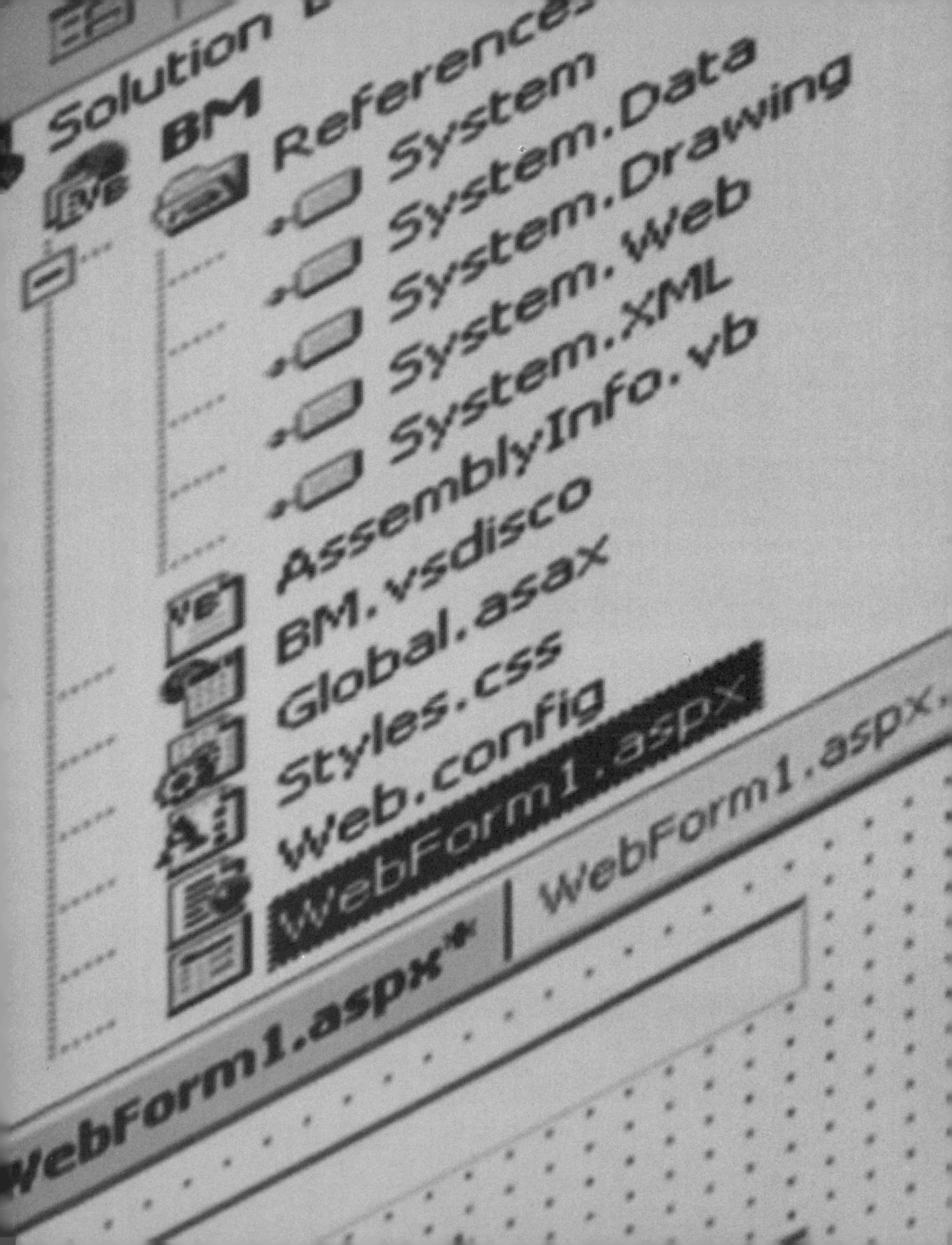

Solution
BM References System
System.Data
System.Drawing
System.Web
System.XML
AssemblyInfo.vb
BM.vsdisco
Global.asax
Styles.css
Web.config
WebForm1.aspx

WebForm1.aspx* | WebForm1.aspx

Index

Symbol

.NET data providers, 20-21, 61
  ODBC, 21, 61-62
  OLE DB, 21, 61-62, **70-79**, **210-11**
  SQL Server, 21, 61-62, **63-70**
.NET Framework
  errors, **294-98**
  SDK, 27
@@ERROR variable, SQL Sever, 286-91

Number

1NF (first normal form), 52-53
2NF (second normal form), 53-54
3NF (third normal form), 54-55
3-tier model, 22-23

A

`AcceptChanges` method, ADO.NET `DataRow` class, 238
`AcceptChanges` method, ADO.NET `DataSet` class, 212
`AcceptChanges` method, ADO.NET `DataTable` class, 238
Access (Microsoft), 55-56, 70-73
  JET data engine, 70
ACID acronym, transactions, 299
Active Directory, 14
`Add` method, ADO.NET `DataRelationCollection` class, 156
`Add` method, ADO.NET `DataRowCollection` class, 212
`Add` method, ADO.NET `DataTableCollection` class, 141
`Add` method, `AttributeCollection` class, 414
Add Reference dialog, Visual Studio .NET, 332
`AddRange` method, `ArrayList` class, 329
ADO, 18
  connections, **61**
  `Recordset` objects, 61, 374, 377

ADO.NET, 16-21, 96-99, 339
  columns (*see also* `DataColumn` class), **142**
  command builder objects, **213**, **238**
  command objects, **19**, **69**, **96-98**, **203-5**, **231-35**
  connection objects, **19**, 60-61, 62, 72, **79-81**, 92, 212
  connections, **59-86**
  data adapter objects, **20**, **137-38**, 212
  data reader objects, 61, **98-99**, **134-35**, 377, **379**
  `DataColumn` class, 136, 145, 154-55, 159
  `DataRelation` class, 155-56
  `DataRow` class, 136, 142, 145, 156, 160, 195, 350
  `DataSet` class, 61, 81, 87, 90-91, **133-96**, **211-26**, **235-46**, **248-52**, 376-79, **381**
    typed `DataSet` objects, **377-79**
  datasets (*see also* `DataSet` class), **20**
  `DataTable` class, 87, 90-91, **135-36**, 138-39, 141-42, 148-50, **154-62**, 166, 187, 195, 350
  `DataView` class, **162-67**, 174, 177-79, 194
  rows (*see also* DataRow class), **142**
  `SqlException` class, 294-97
  tables (*see also* `DataTable` class), **138-39**, **141-42**
  transaction objects, 305, 307-8
  transactions, **304-9**
aliasing, SQL, 128
`AllowPaging` attribute, `DataGrid` controls, 179
`AllowSorting` attribute, `DataGrid` controls, 174
ALTER PROCEDURE statements, SQL, 269
`AlternatingItemStyle` subelements, `DataGrid` controls
  `BackColor` attribute, 192
application architecture, 22-26
`appSettings` element, `web.config` file, 92
`AppSettings` property, `ConfigurationSettings` class, 92
architecture (*see* application architecture)
arguments, stored procedures (*see* parameters)
`ArrayList` class, 328
  `AddRange` method, 329
  `Sort` method, 329
AS keyword, SQL, 128-29
ASC keyword, SQL, 163
atomic data, 53
atomicity, SQL stored procedures, 260

ASP Today

The daily knowledge site for professional ASP programmers

ASPToday brings the essence of the Wrox Programmer to Programmer philosophy to you through the web. Every working day, www.asptoday.com delivers a new, original article by ASP programmers for ASP programmers.

Want to know about Classic ASP, ASP.NET, Performance, Data Access, Site Design, SQL Server, and more? Then visit us. You can make sure that you don't miss a thing by subscribing to our free daily e-mail updates featuring ASPToday highlights and tips.

By bringing you daily articles written by real programmers, ASPToday is an indispensable resource for quickly finding out exactly what you need. ASPToday is THE daily knowledge site for professional ASP programmers.

In addition to our free weekly and monthly articles, ASPToday also includes a premier subscription service. You can now join the growing number of ASPToday subscribers who benefit from access to:

- Daily in-depth articles
- Code-heavy demonstrations of real applications
- Access to the ASPToday Living Book, our collection of past articles
- ASP reference material
- Fully searchable index and advanced search engine
- Tips and tricks for professionals

Visit ASPToday at: www.asptoday.com

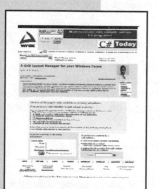

p2p.wrox.com
The programmer's resource centre

A unique free service from Wrox Press
With the aim of helping programmers to help each other

Wrox Press aims to provide timely and practical information to today's programmer. P2P is a list server offering a host of targeted mailing lists where you can share knowledge with four fellow programmers and find solutions to your problems. Whatever the level of your programming knowledge, and whatever technology you use P2P can provide you with the information you need.

ASP
Support for beginners and professionals, including a resource page with hundreds of links, and a popular ASP.NET mailing list.

DATABASES
For database programmers, offering support on SQL Server, mySQL, and Oracle.

MOBILE
Software development for the mobile market is growing rapidly. We provide lists for the several current standards, including WAP, Windows CE, and Symbian.

JAVA
A complete set of Java lists, covering beginners, professionals, and server-side programmers (including JSP, servlets and EJBs)

.NET
Microsoft's new OS platform, covering topics such as ASP.NET, C#, and general .NET discussion.

VISUAL BASIC
Covers all aspects of VB programming, from programming Office macros to creating components for the .NET platform.

WEB DESIGN
As web page requirements become more complex, programmer's are taking a more important role in creating web sites. For these programmers, we offer lists covering technologies such as Flash, Coldfusion, and JavaScript.

XML
Covering all aspects of XML, including XSLT and schemas.

OPEN SOURCE
Many Open Source topics covered including PHP, Apache, Perl, Linux, Python and more.

FOREIGN LANGUAGE
Several lists dedicated to Spanish and German speaking programmers, categories include. NET, Java, XML, PHP and XML

How to subscribe:
Simply visit the P2P site, at http://p2p.wrox.com/